beyond brecht

Über Brecht hinaus

Über Brecht hinaus

Brecht Jahrbuch, Jahrgang 11, 1982
Herausgeber John Fuegi, Gisela Bahr,
und John Willett
Mitherausgeber: Uwe Hartung

Wayne State University Press   Detroit
edition text + kritik GmbH   München

beyond brecht

The Brecht Yearbook, Volume 11, 1982
edited by John Fuegi, Gisela Bahr,
and John Willett
associate editor: Uwe Hartung

Wayne State University Press   *Detroit*
edition text + kritik GmbH   *München*

Produced in the United States of America.

ISSN 0734-8665

ISBN 0-8143-1735-9

Special acknowledgement to Uwe Hartung for providing the German synopses and to Françoise Taylor for providing the French synopses.

The International Brecht Society

The International Brecht Society has been formed as a corresponding society on the model of Brecht's own unrealized plan for the Diderot Gesellschaft. Through its publications and regular international symposia, the Society encourages the free and open discussion of any and all views on the relationship of the arts to the contemporary world. The Society is open, of course, to new members in any field and in any country and welcomes suggestions and/or contributions (in German, English or French) for future symposia and for the published volumes of its deliberations.

Die Internationale Brecht-Gesellschaft

Die Internationale Brecht-Gesellschaft ist nach dem Modell von Brechts nicht verwirklichten Plänen für die Diderot Gesellschaft als korrespondierende Gesellschaft gegründet worden. Durch Veröffentlichungen und regelmäßige internationale Tagungen fördert die Gesellschaft freie und öffentliche Diskussionen von jeglichen Blickpunkten, die Beziehungen aller Künste zur heutigen Welt betreffend.

Die Gesellschaft steht selbstverständlich neuen Mitgliedern in jedem Fachgebiet und Land offen und begrüßt Vorschläge und Aufsätze in deutscher, englischer oder französicher Sprache für zukünftige Tagungen und für die veröffentlichten Bände ihrer Protokolle.

La Société Internationale Brecht

La Société Internationale Brecht a été formée pour correspondre à la société rêvée par Brecht, "Diderot Gesellschaft". Par ses publications et congrès internationaux à intervalles réguliers, la S. I. B. encourage la discussion libre de toutes les idées sur les rapports entre les artes et le monde contemporain. Bien entendu, les nouveaux membres dans toutes les disciplines et tous les pays sont accueillis avec plaisir, et la Société sera heureuse d'accepter des suggestions et des contributions (en français, allemand, ou anglais) pour des congrès futurs et les volumes de communications qui en résulteront.

Addresses

Gisela Bahr, Department of German, Russian and East Asian Languages, Miami University, 44 Irvin Hall, Oxford, Ohio 45056, U.S.A.

John Fuegi, Comparative Literature Program, University of Maryland, Jimenez Hall, College Park, Md. 20742, U.S.A.

John Willett, Volta House, Windmill Hill, London NW 3 65J, England

Antony Tatlow, President International Brecht Society, 3 Felix Villas, 61 Mt. Davis Road, Hong Kong

Karl-Heinz Schoeps, Secretary/Treasurer, Department of German, University of Illinois, Urbana, Illinois 61801, U.S.A.

Marc Silberman, Editor *Communications,* Department of German, University of Texas, San Antonio, Tx 78285

IBS dues are $10.00 Student Member (up to three years)
$15.00 Regular Member, annual income under $20.000
$20.00 Regular Member, annual income $20.000 and over
$25.00 Sustaining Member
$25.00 Institutional Member
Send dues to Karl-Heinz Schoeps, Secretary/Treasurer, Department of German, University of Illinois, Urbana, Illinois 61801, U.S.A.

Brecht's works are quoted from the twenty volume *Gesamelte Werke* (*GW*) (Frankfurt: Suhrkamp, 1967), from his *Arbeitsjournal* (*AJ*) (Frankfurt: Suhrkamp, 1973) or from *Briefe* (Frankfurt: Suhrkamp, 1981).

Introduction

It is now eleven years since the International Brecht Society first began the publication of the *Brecht Yearbook*. At its inception the *Yearbook* was planned as a tri-lingual publication that would make available the best and liveliest work on Brecht to an international audience. We are delighted to be able to continue this work with our new publisher, the Wayne State University Press in conjunction with edition text + kritik of Munich. As a functional help to our readers, each text in this volume is accompanied by a tri-lingual synopsis of that text.

The editors encourage submissions of essays on any aspect of Brecht studies. The next two volumes of the Yearbook will be organized around the subjects: Brecht and Women (1984), and Brecht and Socialism (1985). To be considered for inclusion in any given volume, essays must reach the editors by January 1 of the year of proposed publication.

John Fuegi
College Park, Maryland
April 1983

Contents

John Willett. "Brecht for the media, 1981."

John Willett tells about his summer spent on various Brecht projects. Three items were scheduled: a volume of the short stories; a record (with Brecht songs translated by Willett) of the Australian singer Robyn Archer; and a BBC production of *Baal*. Willett wrote the screenplay for this production, which he based on the 1926 version, *Life Story of a Man Called Baal*. He describes the genesis of the film, directed by Alan Clarke and produced by Louis Marks, from the first draft of the screenplay up to the ambiguous reaction of the audience and his own disappointment after "David Bowie in *Baal*" was finally broadcast on March 2, 1982. It becomes clear, how the production of the film was influenced by the competition between the BBC and the commercial TV channel in Great Britain and by the conditions of production within the BBC's apparatus. Willett concludes with remarks about how to most effectively present Brecht in the mass media: special emphasis should be given to the songs, that is to say to records, such as Robyn Archer's or David Bowie's with the film music to *Baal*.

John Willett. "Brecht für die Medien, 1981."

John Willett erzählt von seinem Sommer mit Bertolt Brecht. Drei Projekte standen an: ein Band mit Kurzgeschichten, die Antony Tatlow und Hugh Rorrison ins Englische übersetzt hatten; eine Langspielplatte der australischen Sängerin Robyn Archer mit Brecht-Liedern, übersetzt von John Willett; und eine BBC-Produktion von *Baal*. Willett lieferte für diese Produktion das Drehbuch, das auf der Fassung von 1926, *Lebenslauf des Mannes Baal,* basiert. Er beschreibt den gesamten Entstehungsprozeß des Films unter der Regie von Alan Clarke, produziert von Louis Marks, vom ersten Drehbuchentwurf bis zur gespaltenen Publikumsreaktion und der eigenen Ernüchterung nach der Sendung von "David Bowie in *Baal*" am 2. März 1982. Es wird deutlich, wie die Herstellung des Films von der Wettbewerbssituation, in der die BBC steht, und den Produktionsbedingungen innerhalb der Anstalt beeinflußt wird. Willett schließt seinen Bericht mit Gedanken über Wege, Brecht in Massenmedien zu vermitteln, wobei er die Rolle von Schallplatten wie der Robyn Archers oder David Bowies mit der Filmmusik zu *Baal* hervorhebt.

John Willett. "Brecht dans les médias, 1981."

John Willett nous parle de ses projets brechtiens de l'été 1981 ; il y en avait trois : un volume de contes; un disque (des chansons de Brecht traduites par Willett) du chanteur australien Robyn Archer ; et la mise en scène de *Baal* pour la BBC. Willett en a écrit le scénario basé sur la version de 1926, *Histoire de la vie d'un homme nommé Baal*. M. Willett nous décrit la genèse du film (mise en scène d'Alan Clarke et produit par Louis Marks), du premier jet du scénario jusqu'à la réaction ambiguë de l'audience et sa propre déception quand "David Bowie dans Baal" fut finalement diffusé le 2 mars 1982. Il apparait comme évident que la mise en scène du film fut influencée par la concurrence entre la BBC et la chaine commerciale en Grande-Bretagne et par les conditions de production imposées par l'organisation de la BBC.

Enfin Willett conclut par des suggestions pour une présentation plus efficace de Brecht dans les médias, l'accent doit être mis sur les chansons, c'est à dire sur les disques, comme ceux de Robyn Archer ou de David Bowie dans la musique du film "Baal".

Brecht for the Media, 1981–82

John Willett

Early in 1981 my Brecht agenda for the rest of the year looked interesting but manageable. For the Eyre Methuen edition I had to complete the preparation of a volume of the short stories, which Antony Tatlow and Hugh Rorrison had translated; this would entail a visit to Berlin to gather material for the notes. Otherwise the main job would be the long-delayed rehearsal and recording of a first album of Brecht songs in English by the Australian singer Robyn Archer, who had arrived just before Christmas to spend a year in Europe. I had first worked with her in 1975 when she sang Jenny in Wal Cherry's Adelaide production of *The Threepenny Opera* with New Opera, South Australia (the enterprising nucleus of the present state opera company). Two years later we were both involved, with Dominic Muldowney as musical director, in a National Theatre programme called *To Those Born Later,* since when she had added to her Brecht repertoire on various occasions in both Australia and England under the guidance of Michael Morley and Muldowney respectively. The plan for a full-scale recording supported by the Australian Music Board had been in the air some time, and now it was settled that it would be made in England by EMI. Muldowney would conduct and accompany, and the band would be the excellent London Sinfonietta.

In the spring Archer and her manager Diana Manson went off to the European mainland on a trip that was to take in visits to the Berliner Ensemble and to Georg Eisler in Vienna as well as one of the Goethe-Institut language courses at Prien. I went on a short visit to Philadelphia to see the graduate acting students of Temple University perform my version of Lenz's *The Tutor* under Carl Weber's direction. While I was away my wife was quite unexpectedly telephoned by the

11

English film director Alan Clarke to say that he had been asked to direct *Baal* for BBC television and would be interested to talk to me about the 1926 *Lebenslauf des Mannes Baal* of which I had given a brief account in the notes to the Manheim/Willett edition. What had drawn him to this shortened and somewhat deromanticised version of Brecht's first play, so it turned out, was the notion that it might have a more technological, mid-20s, slightly *Neue Sachlichkeit* flavour in keeping with the austere toughness of some of his own productions. We talked in the office given him at the BBC Television Centre, where I gathered that he was intending to record the play in the biggest studio making use of gauzes for the outdoor scenes and a split-screen technique for the inter-scene titles. I wasn't instantly clear what these ideas might mean, but Clarke himself was refreshingly straightforward and free from bullshit, and I decided that the best thing I could do would be to take what I'd put in my notes and turn it into a full translation of the 1926 text. He and the BBC producer and script editor (Louis Marks and Stuart Griffiths) could then decide if it was suitable or not.

On going back to the German (in Dieter Schmidt's *Baal. Drei Fassungen. Materialienband,* edition suhrkamp 170) I found of course that the *Lebenslauf* version wasn't as technological as all that. So on sending in the complete translation—which was a slightly inelegant collage of extracts from the published notes and some handwritten pages—I added a separate commentary, starting with a discussion of where and when the *Life Story of a Man called Baal* should be set. Thus, I wrote:

> I see it isn't the mid-20s after all, since BB sets it very specifically between 1904 (at the start) and 1912 (Baal's death). And it is half urban, half countryside.
>
> If we stick to 'Baal the abnormality trying to come to terms with the twentieth century world' then this is ok, I think. It is a meeting between pre-1914 Bavaria and the new technology. . . .
>
> I'm for setting it visibly in Germany, and south Germany at that. But with 'Mr' and 'Mrs' rather than 'Herr' and 'Frau'. . . .
>
> From halfway through the play the countryside dominates: woods, trees and those marvellous great German landscapes. And right through, from start to finish, a great variety of skies.

The Baal Hymn (or *Choral*), I then pointed out quite unoriginally, could be used for the opening and closing titles and also to link the different scenes:

> With it one should sometimes see Baal's face, but always at some point the sky. Skies of all sorts and colours: sunny, stormy, windy, starry, pre-dawn, sunset etc. Perhaps with the odd technological hint: telephone wires, an airship. Or a flight of birds, suddenly shot.

Unlike anyone else involved at that stage, I had seen the West German
TV version of 1969, which Volker Schlöndorff had filmed in natural
Bavarian settings, always with a hint of modern industrial life in the
background—cooling towers on the horizon, or a distant autobahn with
great articulated lorries trundling by. Though Wolfgang Gersch has criti-
cised this for 'de-historicising' Brecht and failing to show the 'asocial'
nature of the social framework I have never understood why the Berliners
so objected both to the film itself and to Fassbinder's powerful performance in the title part. I thought we'd be lucky if we could do as well.

The 1926 text was instantly accepted as a basis, photocopied and
retyped with some additional material. Clarke wanted to include the
discarded episodes with two more women, first Ekart's red-haired girl-
friend among the young hazel bushes (and the scene leading up to this),
then the peasant girl whom Baal meets after Ekart's murder and who,
alone among the five of them, is impervious to his charisma because she
sees that he has grey hairs. Meanwhile I for my part wanted to bring back
'Death in the Forest' as a chain of verbal imagery dragging across Baal's
mind while Ekart observes him sleeping immediately before the murder
scene. Together, too, we agreed to add the two *Landjäger* who go over
Baal's criminal (and other) record as they trudge uneasily after him in the
last scene but one of the final version. All this was duplicated as the first
draft script on May 22nd. I then went through it making amendments
and adding suggestions for the action, many of which Clarke took over
into the stage directions of the second draft a week later; this then had to
be amended and corrected once more. Such a process was highly instructive for anyone who, like me, now and again has to compare different
scripts and stages of a play in order to try and reconstruct a dramatist's
thoughts. For not only is one apt to overlook the most obvious infelicities
and inconsistencies, but absurd mistakes keep insinuating themselves into
the work of the expert copyists, sometimes at quite a late stage. Thus 'a
vast waitress in costume' in one of my stage directions became 'vast
waiters in costumes'; 'the man in question is about to clear out' became
'the man in question is to clear out'; while Baal's historicising statement
in the first scene was half turned into a stage-direction, to wit: '*Baal*: In
the year 1904. *Joseph Mech offers Baal a light for his cigar.*' In fact almost
anything may happen at any stage, and the writer has to keep very wide
awake if ineradicable misunderstandings are not to arise.

From the second draft we hammered out what was in effect the final
version of our text. The two extra women, having added little to the story,
were now dropped again, though we kept the *Landjäger* since their summary of Baal's career just before his death seemed useful. 'Death in the
Forest' too was included after Ekart's monologue over the sleeping Baal

13

(scene 9 of the 1926 version). Otherwise the structure was almost entirely that of the *Lebenslauf des Mannes Baal* which Brecht and Homolka had directed for the Junge Bühne—the only version of the play ever to have been directed by Brecht himself. Its great advantage from a television point of view was that it was both shorter and clearer than Brecht's 'definitive' (but unperformed) version of 1953 which Manheim and I had had to use for our edition. Its only lapse in clarity—the failure to spell out Johanna's suicide before the oblique allusion in the 'Drowned Girl' song—could be remedied by a shot of her walking by the river to the accompaniment of some chords from the song or maybe a glimpse of Millais's *Ophelia*. To set against that it had a number of passages which we greatly liked: the Ichthyosaurus monologue, Baal's comments on our planet, his concern with 'the devising of an evil deed', his ignorance of (and indifference to) Sophie's pregnancy, his dialogue with Ekart about the vanishing country-side and Ekart's subsequent remarks about the human potentialities implied in the tall buildings of Manhattan—these and others like them would, we thought, more than make up for the loss of some of the stranger sub-episodes in the pre-Berlin versions, such as the selling of the bulls and the theft of Teddy's schnapps. For we thought we saw a well-defined line running through the *Lebenslauf* which the prodigal inventions of the earlier texts would have confused rather than strengthened.

The pattern as I set it out in some notes at the end of May was one of steady decline from the social and domestic high point represented by the opening scene. This, I wrote:

> shows the bourgeois world of early Wilhelmine Germany, which (like the Federal Republic after 1948) was outstripping England economically and seemed headed for the leadership of a brave new technologically advanced Europe. What mattered was industry, inventiveness, enterprise; but along with these things went good design—so that people like Mech were far more design-conscious than their English or French opposite numbers—and also, by tradition, increased patronage for the arts. Paintings and poetry became a visible justification of the money-making process, and parasites like Piller acted as a useful means of access to them. This still holds good (and not only in Germany), so that the scene offers a chance to underline certain incompatibilities between moneyed good taste and real creativeness. It also sets things up for the nemesis that comes after the second pub scene.

The 'small swinish café' scene was a climax: noisy, dirty-minded and jovial-sadistic in the worst Bavarian tradition, with the drunk customers ready to lynch the Soubrette when she sings the Marseillaise (all wrong, starting 'Allons, enfants de la batterie'). Either side of this, and eight years apart in time, the two scenes in the pub were lesser peaks, with the crowd in the second all raring to tear Baal limb from limb only a few moments after his singing. I was thinking, I'm afraid, of Munich 'die Hauptstadt der Bewegung' a decade or two later, and accordingly wanted the woodcutters in the last scene to be

> akin to the rustic element of the crowd in the pub and swinish café scenes. Only now they are relaxed, mocking, indifferent rather than actively brutal. They are the types whom the Nazis put forward as models of rural blood-and-soil Nordic authenticity, and who at the same time happen to be very much the pious Christian peasantry approved by many decent, high-principled and normally tolerant traditionalists.

Before the 'swinish café' scene the element of contrast lies in Baal's three episodes in the garage: those with Johannes, with Johanna and with Sophie (the uprooted descendant of the actress in the 1918 version). Afterwards it comes with the break out into the countryside and 'a succession of more even and reflective (if windblown and morally shabby) episodes follows'.

> These should be suffused with one kind or another of south German rural beauty, so that all the time the (at most) three figures are secondary to the vastness of the landscape and the elements. In these episodes—which cover three years at least—Baal and Ekart must get browner and more weatherbeaten, their clothes tattier but also more practical. . . . They are never in a hurry, though the swift recitation of the 'Death in the Forest' poem as Baal lies motionless shows how quickly time is really passing and how fast the images flicker across Baal's apparently inert mind.

Interspersed throughout the play were the songs. Using Brecht's own tunes wherever I could, I had radically reworked the words for singability from the earlier translations which I had (unattributedly) grafted on to Peter Tegel's and William Smith's versions of the dialogue in our edition. Such was the case with the 'Ballad of the Adventurers' (in the second café scene), 'The Drowned Girl' (for which we would use Weill's beautiful setting) and the 'Baal Hymn' (where we envisaged using three verses for the opening titles, one or possibly two at the end, and the rest individually between the scenes). For the 'ballad' sung by Baal in the first café scene, where the standard version has 'Orge's Song', I suggested we should use 'Remembering Marie A.', which Oskar Homolka had once told me was sung in the 1926 production, along with its sentimental fin-de-siècle tune. For the dirty song in the swinish café, where the 1926 text specifies nothing and the definitive version is useless, we went back to the 1918 version's 'If a woman's hips are ample' which had been translated by me for the notes in our edition and sung in the Papp/Foreman New York production of *The Threepenny Opera*. Even this was hardly shocking enough by modern standards to justify the ensuing hullaballoo, so I later added the two obscene epigrams which Ekkehard Schall performs in his one-man shows (and which are now published in *Gedichte aus dem Nachlass*, pp. 33 and 46). Finally we felt that Savettka, the soubrette in the swinish café scene should be seen and heard doing her act, so I gave her three verses of 'Song of the ruined innocent folding linen' in Lesley Lendrum's translation and proposed that she also do a dramatic dance to that epitome of 'die ewige Kunst', according to *Mahagonny*, the nineteenth-century piano piece called 'The Maiden's Prayer'.

By this point, which was reached in early June, a number of important steps had been taken towards the actual production. To start with, Clarke and the BBC's designer Tony Abbott had worked out the basic settings and use of studio space. Up against Studio 1's four walls would be four naturalistic sets showing early twentieth-century German interiors: Mech's nouveau-riche apartment, the doctor's garage with Baal's squalid quarters leading off it, the pub of scenes 3 and 10 in the 1926 text (suitably refurbished in the intervening eight years), and finally the swinish café with its small stage and dressing-room and toilet at the back (subsequently replaced by the woodcutters' hut). There would be four cameras for each scene, but not much camera movement, so that the prevailing view would be of the set seen square-on right across the whole length or width of the studio. Gauzes would be used to cover these sets for all the exterior shots, which would generally show the actors—Baal and Ekart, and at first Sophie, then in the penultimate scene the two country policemen again and again—walking the whole length of the studio towards the camera. Right from the start, it seems, there had been no question of filming in South Germany, not even to get views and skies for projection. The only chance then to show the sky at all would be in the split-screen interludes when the verses of the Hymn would be sung and the next scene title shown ('Baal on the run. 10° East of Greenwich' and so on, as in Brecht's text). I argued as strongly as I could that we should in that case show details of paintings, preferably by Hans Thoma, who would have been most apt on various counts, or at a pinch some of Constable's sky studies. But this would have meant additional work and expense and it was felt that the BBC graphics department could run up adequate substitutes.

Clarke and Louis Marks the producer were already in touch with various actors and their agents; recondite pieces of equipment like a nickelodeon for the pub, a mechanical organ for Mech's drawing room and an early motorcycle on which Baal was originally to make his entrance were all being hired. Catalogues of these specialist hire firms lay around Clarke's office along with fascinating but potentially misleading casting directories. For the more frightful-looking Bavarians—Barbarians, one of our typing errors had called them—he had turned to an agency named Ugly, which sets out to provide peculiar-looking people; but too often the peculiarity was merely one of height or age and the photos provided were disappointing. There remained the problem of Baal himself, the central figure who has to carry the whole improbable and ultimately quite juvenile play on his shoulders. Clarke clearly felt strongly inclined towards Steven Berkoff, a powerful if slimly built East End London actor with an obsessive dislike of the peculiar English class system—something that I felt might be a distraction in Brecht's play. I suggested the great Australian comic Barry Humphries, who can produce a certain chilling demonic quality even in his classic female impersonations and would make a convincing genius, though one rather older than envisaged by Brecht. This intrigued Marks, who evidently hadn't thought of looking outside the straight theatre and cinema, and he jumped at my next suggestion, which was David Bowie. Bowie I knew of course as a charismatic singer, but he had just been acting in New York as *The Elephant Man* (which suggested that he was seeking to extend his range even to the point of looking hideous), and I inferred more or less by guesswork that he might be interested in pre-1933 Germany and even in Brecht. As it turned out this was indeed so. Marks and Clarke looked at whatever they could find of Bowie on film or in the BBC's archives, approached his agents and in mid-July arranged to spend a day with him in Switzerland to discuss details. When they came back we had our Baal.

Meantime I was spending four days closeted in the EMI Abbey Road Studios, where Robyn Archer was now recording her album; a fifty-minute selection of Brecht songs of all kinds and periods, all of them in English and for the most part translated by me. She had returned from her travels not long before in excellent heart and voice, and the clarity of her words was stunning. We only had the orchestra for two of those days however, so that it was a quite remarkable achievement on the part of Muldowney (who is normally thought of as a composer rather than a conductor) not only to fit in the rehearsal and recording of some ten songs largely unfamiliar to the players, but to get performances of such vitality. There were a number of Eisler's songs to piano accompaniment, which Muldowney played on EMI's very beautiful best Steinway, while the remainder were for small combinations, notably involving our saxophonist friend John Harle who acted as a valuable adviser and helper throughout the whole recording. At the end of each session we had a replay with Diana Manson and John Mordler, the record's producer, at which it was quickly and amiably decided what needed re-recording and how the final version of each song should best be put together. It was up to Mordler and his colleagues to complete the editing before we got down to the difficult problem of the exact composition and running order of the two 33 rpm sides, which would in due course be pressed in Australia. Muldowney then was more or less free, so far as his National Theatre job allowed, and I persuaded Marks and Clarke to engage him as our musical director for *Baal*. This would entail a good deal of work with Bowie— who was to play the banjo, having never previously done anything of the sort—, setting the 'Ruined Innocent' song for Savettka, finding music for Emilie's mechanical organ performance and for background noise in the pub scenes, and equipping the swinish café scenes with a small but typical Bavarian band. We called the latter 'Lohengrin und seine Leder-hosen' and painted the title in gothic letters on their drum, though I am not sure how many of the eventual audience were able to read it.

A much thicker script now came off the duplicators, headed impressively 'THE SENDING OF THIS SCRIPT DOES NOT CONSTITUTE AN OFFER OF A CONTRACT FOR ANY PART IN IT'. Tacitly (and I think now wrongly) the 'Life Story' title had been dropped in favour of the single word *Baal*. This was the Rehearsal Script, and on July 13th we began working on it with the first members of the cast at the BBC's rehearsal rooms in North Acton, an area of West London which is mainly given over to industrial buildings. The actors, thank goodness, saw nothing all that alarming in the thought of performing Brecht, nor was there any of that discussion of alienation or other special techniques which can bedevil over-ambitious productions. Clarke was friendly and matter-of-fact, Bowie serious and unassuming. At the opening session I tried to suggest that the key to this play, even more than to others by Brecht, lay in his poetry, and persuaded Marks to give copies of the paperback *Poems 1913– 1956* to any of the actors who were interested. There were to be four weeks of rehearsal altogether before moving into Studio 1 on August 9th, i.e. around the middle of the school holidays. We also learned, more or less indirectly, that Bowie's involvement was not to be made publicly known until he and the BBC wished it. Even the title of the play was not to be put up on the board in the entrance hall (which simply announced us as 'Classic Play'); no outsiders were to be allowed in; what's more, one of Bowie's two aides was always on guard inside the rehearsal room door. At the same time morale seemed high all through, and this was due surely to Bowie's professionalism and to Clarke's equable firmness. Muldowney, who had attended many more temperamental opening rehearsals at the National Theatre, was slightly amazed.

How far the other actors were worried by Bowie's rather unusual approach to the job I never knew, though I must have attended about half the rehearsals and could talk easily enough to them except where their performances were concerned (which I could discuss only with Clarke). The rest of us were pretty impressed. Right from the start he knew virtually the whole part, except for 'Death in the Forest' which he never securely mastered, so that in the end this poem had to be cut. He understood the play and had thought about it, and it was my impression that he knew more about Germany as a whole and Brecht's ambience in particular than anyone except possibly Marks and myself. As a collector of Expressionist graphics, he at once grasped the relevance of Masereel's intensely poetic *Mon Livre d'Heures* whose final pages I had thought might help shape Baal's end: the skull-headed protagonist strolling nonchalantly through the stars and planets. He was also marvellously equipped for the songs, imposing the sense and rhythms of the words on Brecht's recitative-like tunes, which he rightly compared to plainchant. But where he was so unlike an actor was in his inability to build up a performance from the most tentative beginnings, adding a little at each rehearsal till it begins to take shape. With him each rehearsal was like a performance, often a very interesting one but not necessarily a direct development from what he had done the time before. His speech was sometimes less clear than his singing voice, and once background noise was added it wasn't always easy to follow. But at any rehearsal whatever he said had meaning—the meaning of the part and of the play: nothing he said was routine. I remember in particular one discussion about Baal's attitude to the Mechs and their guests in the opening scene: he was trying to score off them and show his contempt for them, and was this a class attitude or what? I argued that it was trivialising the poet to make him *mind* so much about people: he would be secure enough in his own genius to remain detached from them. 'Detached?' said Bowie. 'Don't tell me to be detached, or I'll be so detached you won't know I'm there'.

Another image: Bowie on the last day of recording in Studio 1. This was to be devoted to the recording of the Baal Hymn, the 'Drowned Girl' and 'Death in the Forest' and the accompanying split-screen images with no one on the floor but Bowie, Muldowney, a guitarist and the cameramen and managers. It was 11 a.m. on a Thursday. Bowie was right at the end of nearly five weeks of highly concentrated and disciplined work during which he had had to carry a pretty difficult play on his shoulders. He began singing the first three verses of the Hymn, which would be crucial for the start of the play and for that matter for his own commitment to it, when suddenly there was a tremendous banging through the studio wall. Everything stopped while someone was sent round to Studio 2 to tell them to be quiet. Studio 2 turned out to be locked. Telephoning produced no answer. Clearly this was some quite different part of the BBC machine at work, so Marks got on to some superior administration and the noise suddenly stopped. Bowie began singing again, but the noise restarted. Marks again telephoned up through the hierarchy. Noise stopped. Bowie sang a few lines. Noise began again, this time from somewhere up in the roof. Marks back to the telephone. Clarke all the time amazingly unruffled, as indeed he was throughout the whole five weeks; I take my hat off to him. Then silence, Bowie once more started to sing. Noise. Telephone. And so on—I forget how many times. Finally Bowie strode out into the centre of the studio floor saying 'I know how to stop it'. He then put his hands to his mouth, looked up at the roof and shouted 'Lunch!'. It didn't work, I fear, but as a one-man demonstration of how to keep one's cool it really wasn't bad.

This whole process of rehearsal and recording was otherwise very smoothly managed, and my own role became increasingly that of a privileged onlooker. The actors didn't seem to have much trouble with their dialogue, not even with Baal's long and deliberately stilted sentences to Emilie just before he sings 'The Ballad of the Adventurers', which were easily and intelligently managed by Bowie. Now and again an actress would mildly hanker after the longer and more familiar version of the play, but in the event very little had to be reworked, or even argued over. Johanna's *Leibchen* in her seduction scene was a bit of a problem; I had inexpertly translated it first as 'vest', then 'tummy-band' (a childhood memory), then after consultation 'liberty bodice'. Nobody was satisfied, so we settled for 'corset', which at least didn't jar on the ear and looked interesting when Tracy Childs as Johanna got out of her bed to fetch it. Sophie too had difficulties in her scene on the road, when she tells Baal 'Es ist sicherlich ein schöner Abend, der dir gefällt. Aber es wird dir nicht gefallen, daß du einmal ohne einen Menschen verrecken sollst'. I had made this 'I know it's a beautiful evening and you like it. But you won't like it one day . . . ' etc. Zoe Wanamaker found this artificial verbal transition rather awkward, but in the end she delivered it as written and I don't think it jarred more than Brecht meant it to. Another passage which gave me trouble myself was the whole story arising out of Baal's remark in the second pub scene that he felt 'noch immer gesund'— the one about the man who went off into the woods. I tried various expressions for this: 'perfectly well', 'perfectly all right', then (in the final Camera Script—a massive document on multi-colored paper with many technical details and the scenes rearranged in order of shooting—) 'perfectly healthy'. This last didn't work—whether for Bowie or for Jonathan Kent as Ekart I don't remember—so we changed it back to 'perfectly all right'. Where I did feel I had slipped up was in not attending the first rehearsal of the final scene with the woodcutters, where one or two minor changes had crept in during my absence and became too deeply engrained to be corrected. These were in the direction of 'normalising' the men's language and were in my view a mistake, though I don't suppose that anybody else noticed them.

Most of the time, however, I was able to watch fascinatedly as the various elements of the show began to come together. Numbers of additional extras (or 'Supporting Artists' as the script termed them) would appear to thicken up the crowd scenes in pub and swinish café which Clarke had rehearsed first with the leading actors only, then with a select group of ringleaders from the crowd and finally with the whole noisy mob. Polly James as the Soubrette sang the song which Muldowney had composed for her, finishing on a kind of coloratura flourish that had the ringleaders blocking their ears and groaning, then went on to interpret 'The Maiden's Prayer' in a solemnly Isadora-like dance involving a rather stiff dummy baby. I had to write a few words with which Mjurk could introduce this tear-jerking number, also a complete verse of the Marseillaise for her to sing in the mangled French suggested by Brecht ('Allons, enfants de la batterie' etc.); these were not really to be heard. After the initial rehearsals the whole swinish café scene was taken apart, so that eventually it was shot twice over: once to show whatever was going on onstage and among the clientèle, then again so as to concentrate on events backstage—each time with the noises from the other part of the set ensuring synchronisation. Here and in the country walking scenes it was a matter of recording the raw material for subsequent editing; likewise the shots for the split-screen interludes left a variety of options open. This 'video fx', as the script cryptically termed it, was in the hands of a technician with a special gadget which could record on one part of the screen in such a way as to combine with other pictures or graphics on the rest of it. With these exceptions however it was possible to get a fairly good idea of the eventual result from watching the recording in Studio 1's central room, since Clarke had specified the camera angles to be used and any unforeseen changes could be carried out then and there. Most of us, I think, were enthusiastic about what we saw, though some of the more hardened BBC technicians preferred to spend their time in the neighboring cabin where one screen was given up to cricket.

For the moment that was that, and we went off on our various occasions. For me this meant (among other, sadder things) thinking about the final composition of Robyn Archer's album, whose tapes had now been very skilfully edited by John Mordler to make what was clearly going to emerge as a most impressive performance. Australian EMI were insistent that the selection should open with the 'Alabama Song', on the grounds that this would already be familiar to the customers from a forthcoming Australian Opera production of *Mahagonny*. There were also commercial reasons for not starting with the voice and piano songs: the

Sinfonietta's presence must, as it were, be felt from the outset. So we hammered out an order giving roughly 25 minutes on each side, and in due course the edited tape went off to Australia, leaving it still unsettled whether the record was going to be issued anywhere else. There were at this time a number of contractual loose ends, not least because EMI wanted Muldowney to commit himself to an undertaking not to make Brecht recordings for anyone else. Bowie however (who records for RCA, not EMI) was keen to make an EP (or 45 rpm) record of the Baal songs, partly, I think, because he genuinely loved them and sang them so well and partly to stop his fans taping them from their TV sets. And he had asked Muldowney to work with him on this. Accordingly there was a recording session in West Berlin under the supervision of Bowie's highly gifted record producer, Tony Visconti, where some fifteen musicians (as against the nineteen used by the Sinfonietta) were conducted by Muldowney in new arrangements of the five songs. I greatly welcomed this, since only 'The Drowned Girl' would overlap with Archer's album and otherwise the two recordings would complement one another; and shortly drove off to the Brecht-Archiv to complete my work on the short stories. While there I was taken to a cafe in the Dimitroffstraße (of all inappropriate names) which convinced me that our café customers and woodcutters in *Baal* had not been nearly nasty enough. As I wrote to Marks, I had been told that this was an old Nazi *Lokal* from which (before 1933) brawls had been mounted against the SPD across the way and the *Roter Frontkämpfer-Bund* further down the street. On certain evenings, it was said, the old believers gathered there and the band played the old songs. Sure enough they were there that night, along with a crowd of younger followers, and we were turned away with no pretence of amiability—something that has never happened to me before. Not so inappropriately this time, the place is called 'Hackepeter'.

In September the publicity and public relations machine started rolling: a factor that I suspect critics of the arts will increasingly have to take into account. 'The new Bowie—warts and all', said the headline to a centrepage spread in the *Daily Express;* 'Pop goes Bowie's image' said the *Daily Mail*. 'ROCK star David Bowie', began the story in Rupert Murdoch's *The Sun,* 'gets a grubby new look for his TV acting debut . . . as a hell-raising singer, poet and womaniser'. And the *Daily Mirror,* clearly working from the same PR handout, 'He plays a singing poet with a huge appetite for sex and wine called Baal by German' (*sic:* at this point words evidently failed). The BBC's competition with commercial television is thus a two-edged process: on the one hand it has made that old body a good deal more enterprising, on the other it has reduced it to playing the personality game. So eventually the date for the showing of

Baal was decided by the availability of the front cover of the corporation's programme magazine *Radio Times,* which was to bear an excellent colour photograph of an unshaven, gap-toothed Bowie caressing the beautiful art-deco banjo which an admirer had perceptively given him; this also appears on the sleeve of his record. The original idea was that the play would be shown during the first available week in January 1982, but the editing took longer than expected, and the rival demands on the relevant BBC facilities—another hierarchical limitation—meant in the end that the date would have to be postponed to March 2nd, some six months after the actual recording. I was asked along to see the first consecutive edit, which I found effective and quick-moving: this normally rambling play actually took only five minutes over the hour, though I was unexpectedly worried by the dingy uniformity of the colour. The trouble with such massive and highly professional organisations is that they tend to have a routine answer for everything, so that our early twentieth-century *Baal,* from the look of it, could equally well have been Gorky's *The Lower Depths.* Next the remaining sound effects were added, including the mechanical organ, the fragment of Ekart's fugue and the music in the pub. Finally there was a kind of trade show for critics and others in a projection theatre in Wardour Street. Here again I came and answered questions and thought, I must say, that the play seemed quite good.

Yet sitting a week later and watching the actual transmission like any other viewer I was disappointed. Partly this may have been because I knew there was an important new play on the commercial channel—John Mortimer's play about his father, acted by Laurence Olivier, which had been cunningly timed to start half an hour earlier than ours. Partly it was the titling of the play *David Bowie in Baal,* which I think was a bad mistake by the BBC whether or not it was their idea: it got the priorities wrong from the start. Partly it could have been the fact that neither play nor production stood up to repeated viewing, and my appreciation of it was by then wearing a bit thin. But there was also another factor which I have noticed before in other contexts, and this was the curious contagion which occurs as soon as one becomes part of an audience, even if there is no communication whatever between its individual members. Willy-nilly some kind of *Verfremdung* sets in, and one suddenly sees the work through other eyes. As a result I went to bed that night none too cheerfully, despite one or two approving telephone calls, and was not surprised by the very mixed verdicts which I read or heard over the next few days. Some, like the BBC's own team of critics, were truly enthusiastic about Bowie's performance, and there were reviews of his songs which welcomed them as something new and strong. Generally, however, the TV critics devoted themselves to Mortimer's play instead, and there was a certain tendency to dismiss *Baal* as scarcely justifying its production. Discussing it with a group of 'A' level drama students not long after, I found that they too felt the lack of a 'story' and were baffled by the protagonist's apparent freedom from any kind of emotion. Right up to the end, said one girl, he 'showed little vulnerability—which he should have had'.

In the subsequent calculation of audience figures, so Marks told me, we were reckoned to have had 3½ million viewers; the Mortimer play had done better. All the same it would have been taken about sixteen years of full houses at the *Theater am Schiffbauerdamm* six nights a week to achieve even this total, and a lot of people must have seen *Baal* who would not normally think of looking at a play by Brecht. This fact has to be set against all my gloomier afterthoughts, which were concerned in particular with the hybrid style of our production. Clarke, I felt, had originally envisaged something much starker and simpler, and this would perhaps have appealed better to the critics, who doubtless expected something recognisably 'Brechtian', reflecting the *Neue Sachlichkeit* of the mid-20s Berlin or even the angularities and exaggerations of *Dr. Caligari*. However, I had helped influence the naturalistic setting of the main scenes, while all the exteriors had been shot in the non-naturalistic, recognisably theatrical mode of the initial conception. My thinking here had been that TV audiences are used to naturalism, and that by placing the events firmly in pre-1914 Bavaria we could explain Baal's urge to break out of that society, while at the same time showing the latent nastiness of the peasants and pub habitués who would be hunting down Communists and Jews two or three decades later. As it turned out we failed to do this for various reasons; so maybe the whole approach had been wrong. This didn't apply to the casting of Bowie, whose performance was always interesting and sometimes inspired, nor (with the exception of the failure to convey Johanna's death) to the 'alienating' division of the episodes by the split-screen presentation of titles and the singing of verses of the Hymn which seemed to achieve Brecht's intended effects without affectation. The square-on, longshot emphasis in the shooting also worked, giving the audience a slightly formal, remote view of the naturalistic scenes, though it was a pity that the predominantly brownish colours made the effect quite so old-masterly. But despite the tightness of the editing we never achieved anything like the edge and power that the play needs if its immaturity is not to jar.

The most interesting of the press reactions, to my mind, came in an article in the *New Musical Express* (p. 27, 27 March 1982) where a contributor by the evocative name of Biba Kopf wrote about the relevance of Brecht as playwright and song writer to the avant-garde pop music world served by that magazine. The writer's thesis, already outlined in a more general article several months earlier, was that the allegiance of that world had been shifting from the Nazi and SS nostalgias evident in the work of certain pop groups to the more forward-looking Weimar culture symbolised by the Bauhaus (now the title of one British group) and even the *AIZ* (whose logo is used by another). Bowie's EP record had made the charts—it then stood at number 26 in the United Kingdom—even though, as the article put it with eighty per cent accuracy, 'Baal has no Kurt Weill tune to disguise its vibrant dirtiness or whiff of Weimar decadence to perfume its filthy smells'.

> Bowie might be responsible for introducing Baal into your home, but having done so he leaves him standing there alone in all his threatening nakedness.

Certainly for me the most successful aspect of the whole operation was this short record, which had been exceptionally well presented by RCA and showed Bowie as one of the most gripping Brecht singers of all time, sounding even more committed to the material than in the play, and helped now by Muldowney's very clever and compelling arrangements. The Baal Hymn in particular comes brilliantly together as a long ballad given shape and variety by occasional stanzas in an Eislerish marching rhythm with semitone shifts of key. Perhaps the 'Drowned Girl', with its oddly staccato delivery, comes over less well than in the play (and, I'd say, less well than on Archer's record) but there is at least one unforgettable moment in the 'Ballad of the Adventurers' such as no other singer could have given us, and after the BBC's over-selling of Bowie it was cheering to find that the pop magazine had got the order right. For the familiar quizzical face of Brecht looks out at us across three columns of the *NME* from Gerda Goedhart's old photograph, towering over the smaller faces of Bowie, Bobby Darin and Jim Morrison of The Doors, the three singers who have got works by Brecht into the charts. Of all his possible candidates for this honourable and commercially useful position *Baal,* as Kopf rightly says, 'is his unlikeliest and therefore the one he'd probably love best'.

If I'm pleased about this I'm even more so by the Archer album which, unlike our BBC production, stands up to repeated replaying. What is so special here, aside from the quality of performance, is first of all the range of material covered—from the very early 'Ballad of the Pirates' through familiar and unfamiliar settings by Weill, 1930s songs by Eisler and Dessau's very tricky 'Ballad of the Girl and the Soldier' right up to Eisler's Hollywood and post-Hollywood songs. Not only has no other singer, to my knowledge, attempted such a catholic selection even in German, but the whole thing makes up a Brecht anthology of

25

exceptional richness which is bound together by what can only be identified as the poet's genius. This will, I hope, emerge all the more clearly
because, secondly, the meaning of his texts (and therefore of the songs
themselves) comes across intelligibly to the non-German listener, something that is largely due to the singer's commitment and ability to make
each word and each phrase comprehensible. Archer has of course been
involved with this material—and for that matter with Muldowney for the
music and myself for the English words—a great deal longer than Bowie,
but she too owes her ability to perform it to her experience as a popular
entertainer (starting at the age of six in the family pub in Adelaide, and
working up via football club dinners and young businessmen's outings)
and also to her initial lack of conventional voice training. One only has to
listen to Teresa Stratos's beautiful but quite unintelligible singing of the
Kurt Weill songs to realise what an advantage this supposed handicap can
be. Trained singers, as Muldowney told an audience at the National
Theatre in the course of our work, only sing the vowels: consonants are
somehow regarded as unmusical. At worst this makes it impossible for
the listener even to identify the language used, let alone to pick out what
is being said. And this is ultimately due to the traditional concept of the
composer's role. As Brecht so perceptively suggested, the words are usually seen as a disposable inspiration to the composer, who transfers their
emotional meaning to the music, using the vowels as sound, and then
throws the empty consonantal husks away. If anything still needs to be
communicated it can be done in that lowest form of musico-literary life,
the programme note.

At the end of a year spent thus dabbling in the media I remain
fascinated (and of course hopeful about the financial rewards, though
without any very solid reason). What seems to me clearer than ever is that
the songs are the most immediately convincing way into Brecht, and not
only into his other writings and ideas but into the whole future relationship between music and words. Accordingly Muldowney and I hope to
plan some kind of practical inquiry which will suggest some of the new
possibilities implicit in what we have learned, and help perhaps to extend
the horizon of the popular entertainer and his or her audience even
further. Already this has begun to encompass some of the more interesting experimental video work—an important new area—nor can anybody
now believe that easily accessible words and music must always be banal,
because Brecht has shown otherwise. Whether a comparable post-mortem
on the televising of *Baal* would be as potentially constructive I don't
know, for what is at issue there is the manner of working in large,
well-greased and smoothly functioning machines, where the crucial decisions may have been taken in advance and much can hinge on apparently

non-artistic issues such as budgeting and publicity. Much then has to be left to people with clearly defined jobs where unsolicited advice is not welcomed; when everyone is treated as a specialist a system of 'divide and rule' grows up almost unthinkingly. Does this mean that the lesson in such cases is that one should steer clear of the machine altogether unless one is prepared to stick within the limits of one's own immediate task? Brecht, I'm sure, wouldn't have said so, though his own experience was of course with less tightly and efficiently organised, unionised and compartmentalised apparatuses. But he never got very far in Hollywood, did he?, and all his most telling critiques were of the kind of apparatus he knew in Berlin. What we need to know more about in this context is the true history—administrative and financial as well as artistic—of those occasional original masterpieces which despite everything are still to be seen on TV. The problem still is how to present Brecht to the viewers so convincingly—not that he is seen as a television playwright, which he wasn't—but that his basic socio-artistic approach can be absorbed.

Erwin Leiser. "Truth Is Concrete: A Film-Maker's Remarks on Brecht and Film."

Brecht's attempts to master the film medium were blocked by his inadequate understanding of the differences between the two media: film and theatre. This is as clear from his unsuccessful film exposés as it is from his participation in various film projects. It is for this reason that Brecht's influence on contemporary film-makers is not through his work as a film author but rather through his work as a playwright. Erwin Leiser describes Brecht's influence on Leiser's own work as a documentary film-maker. In *Mein Kampf, Eichmann and the Third Reich* and *Germany Awake!* Leiser used contrastive picture montage and *Verfremdung* (distancing) through contrast between sound and picture in order to document real events. Film-makers influenced by Brecht do not so much copy Brecht's theatre work as actually translate these perceptions drawn from his work into their own medium, the film.

Erwin Leiser. "Die Wahrheit ist konkret: Notizen eines Filmemachers über Brecht und Film."

Brechts Versuche, das Medium Film zu meistern, scheitern an seinem mangelnden Verständnis für die Unterschiede zwischen Film und Theater, was sowohl an seinen mißglückten Filmentwürfen als auch an seiner Beteiligung an einigen Filmprojekten deutlich wird. Deshalb beeinflußt Brecht nicht als Filmautor sondern als Stückeschreiber einige zeitgenössische Filmregisseure. Erwin Leiser beschreibt diesen Einfluß Brechts auf seine eigene Arbeit als Dokumentarfilmer. In *Mein Kampf, Eichmann und das Dritte Reich* und *Deutschland, erwache!* benutzte Leiser kontrastive Bildmontage und Verfremdung durch Kontrastierung von Bild und Ton, um Realität zu dokumentieren. Filmemacher im Einfluß Brechts kopieren nicht dessen Theaterarbeit, sondern übersetzen die Erkentnisse, die aus dieser Arbeit gewonnen wurden, in ihr eigenes Medium.

Erwin Leiser. "Remarques d'un cinéaste sur Brecht et le cinéma."

Les tentatives de Brecht pour maîtriser le moyen cinématographique se sont heurtées à son manque de compréhension des différences entre les deux médias: cinéma et théâtre. C'est ce dont témoigne l'échec de ses films, ainsi que sa participation dans divers projets cinématographiques. C'est la raison pour laquelle l'influence de Brecht sur les metteurs en scène de cinéma contemporains ne s'exerce pas à travers son travail de cinéaste, mais bien plutôt par son oeuvre de dramaturge. Erwin Leiser décrit l'influence de Brecht sur sa propre activité de réalisateur de documentaires. Dans *Mein Kampf, Eichmann and the Third Reich* et *Allemagne, réveille-toi!* Leiser a utilisé un montage très contrasté et obtenu un effet de distanciation (Verfremdung) par le contraste entre son et image pour filmer des événements réels.

Les cinéastes influencés par Brecht copient moins ses oeuvres théâtrales qu'ils n'en traduisent leur perception dans le médium qui leur est propre, le film.

"Die Wahrheit ist konkret"
Notizen eines Filmemachers
über Brecht und Film

Erwin Leiser

1

Am 30. Oktober 1947 erklärte der Emigrant Bertolt Brecht in den USA vor einem Ausschuß, der seine "unamerikanische Tätigkeit" untersuchen wollte: "Ich bin mir keines Einflusses bewußt, den ich auf die Filmindustrie ausgeübt haben könnte, weder eines politischen noch eines künstlerischen." (*GW*, XX, 305.)

Brecht spricht ausdrücklich über die Film*industrie*. Als Zusammenfassung seiner Einstellung zum kommerziellen Film kann man eine Eintragung in seinem *Arbeitsjournal* vom 12. Oktober 1943 betrachten: "rezept für erfolg im filmschreiben: man muß so gut schreiben, als man kann, und das muß eben schlecht genug sein." (*AJ*, 633.) Brechts Verhältnis zum Film war zwiespältig. Einerseits wollte er, wie sein Herr Keuner, andere Filme als die Produkte der Traumfabriken, andererseits war er, wie es in seinem Gedicht "Hollywood" heißt, bereit, sich auf dem "Markt, wo Lügen gekauft werden", um des Broterwerbs willen "zwischen die Verkäufer" einzureihen (*GW*, X, 848). Das Honorar für seine Mitarbeit an dem Film *Hangmen Also Die* verschaffte ihm "luft für drei stücke" (*AJ*, 24. 6. 1943, 576). Schreiben für den Film diente nur dem Zweck, Schreiben für die Bühne zu ermöglichen.

Als Filmautor war Brecht jedoch nicht "schlecht genug", er vermochte der Industrie nicht zu liefern, was sie verlangte. Seine zahlreichen Texte für Filme waren mißglückte Spekulationen auf kommerziellen Erfolg und blieben im Rahmen des Konventionellen. Sie drücken Brechts Spaß am Trivialfilm aus. Manchmal interessieren Brecht Filmentwürfe als Parodien oder als Variationen dramatischer Vorlagen, aber die künstlerische Qualität seiner Gedichte, Stücke und Prosatexte lassen sie vermissen. Nicht als Filmautor sondern als Stückeschreiber übte Brecht Einfluß auf einige Filmregisseure aus, die nicht seiner Generation angehören. In der Filmindustrie hinterließ er keine Spuren. Während er genau wußte, was bühnenwirksam ist, hatte er haarsträubende Vorstellungen von den Möglichkeiten des Spielfilms, wofür ich später Beispiele geben werde. Seine theoretischen Äußerungen über Film sind dagegen wichtig, wo sie sich mit den Möglichkeiten der Montage und des Dokumentarfilms auseinandersetzen, die er früh erkannte.

Vielleicht hätte Brecht ganz andere *Texte für Filme* geschrieben als die erst 1970 unter diesem Titel in Buchform veröffentlichten Spielfilm-Manuskripte, wenn er noch erlebt hätte, wie sich der Film von Regeln befreite, die Brecht auf der Bühne außer Kraft gesetzt hatte, im Film aber nicht aufzuheben vermochte. Man darf nicht vergessen, daß auf der Bühne das Zentrale für Brecht eine praktische Theaterarbeit war, für die der Stückeschreiber Brecht dem Regisseur Brecht eine Partitur lieferte, die nie als endgültig aufgefaßt wurde. Der Filmautor Brecht war, von *Kuhle Wampe* abgesehen, immer Regisseuren und Produzenten mit anderen Interessen ausgeliefert. Wenn es überhaupt zu einer filmischen Umsetzung eines Brechttextes kam, war ein Konflikt unvermeidlich.

2

Brecht bewunderte Chaplin. Aber diese Bewunderung galt vor allem der Leistung des Mimen Chaplin und der Einfachheit seiner Fabel, und bekanntlich bestand die Funktion des Filmischen bei Chaplin darin, so direkt wie möglich zu vermitteln, was der Solist Chaplin zu bieten hatte. In einem Gespräch mit mir wies Brecht auf thematische Berührungspunkte mit Chaplin hin. Ich wollte seinen Mackie Messer, den Räuber als Bürger, neben Chaplins Monsieur Verdoux stellen, den Bürger als Räuber, und den geänderten Schlußchor der *Dreigroschenoper* ("Verfolgt das kleine Unrecht nicht so sehr") neben die Schlußszene des Chaplinfilms. Brecht erwiderte: "Chaplin sagte mir einmal, das Thema seines *Monsieur Verdoux* sei ganz einfach folgendes Problem: Es ist für einen kleinen Mann ohne besondere Gaben nicht so einfach, in diesen Zeiten eine Familie zu versorgen."

Bezeichnend für die Haltung Brechts gegenüber filmischen Leistungen ist eine Eintragung in seinem *Arbeitsjournal* vom 28. Dezember 1941. Brecht notiert, daß er den Film *Citizen Kane* von Orson Welles gegen den Vorwurf verteidigt habe, er sei eklektisch und stilistisch zu uneinheitlich:

> ich finde den begriff eklektisch auf techniken angewendet unfair und eine vielfalt von stilen für eine vielfalt von funktionen modern. sie wenden sich gegen orson welles' showmanship. aber er zeigt sozial interessantes. und als schauspieler hat er vielleicht nur die showmanship noch nicht zu einem stilelement ausgestaltet. (*AJ*, 347.)

Brecht sah das filmisch Wesentliche in *Citizen Kane* nicht, und als er später eine Zusammenarbeit mit Welles diskutierte, galt sein Interesse Welles als Theaterregisseur—für die Aufführung von *Leben des Galilei*, die schließlich von Joseph Losey inszeniert wurde.

In den Jahren 1953 bis 1955 besuchte ich Brecht regelmäßig in der Chausseestraße in Berlin und ging manchmal mit ihm ins Kino. Ich nahm auch an einigen Diskussionen über die damals bevorstehende Filmfassung von Brechts *Herr Puntila und sein Knecht Matti* teil. Brecht konsumierte Filme wie englische Kriminalromane, als reine Unterhaltung. Er schätzte die italienischen Neorealisten, vor allem Vittorio de Sica, und war von der optischen Phantasie und der effektiven Montagetechnik Eisensteins fasziniert. Spezifisch filmische Ausdrucksmittel interessierten ihn nur, wenn sie sich auch auf der Bühne verwenden ließen. Die im Stummfilm üblichen Zwischentitel setzte er als episches Theaterelement ein. Zur Zeit der Entstehung des *Puntila*-Films hatte er mit der Inszenierung seines Stückes *Der kaukasische Kreidekreis* den Höhepunkt seiner Theaterarbeit erreicht. Wenn er sich über Fragen des künstlerischen Films äußerte, ging er von seiner Bühnenerfahrung aus.

Nur in *Kuhle Wampe* (1932) hatte Brecht Gelegenheit, als Mitglied eines Kollektivs an allen Phasen der Vorbereitung und Durchführung einer Filmproduktion teilzunehmen. Die von Brecht auf der Bühne entwickelte gleichzeitige Gestaltung des Geschehens auf verschiedenen Ebenen wurde hier erfolgreich auf den Film übertragen. Außer *Kuhle Wampe* und *Herr Puntila und sein Knecht Matti* sind noch drei Filme mit dem Namen Brechts verknüpft. Zwei von ihnen waren in ihrer Art Meisterwerke, *Die Dreigroschenoper* (1931) von G. W. Pabst und *Hangmen Also Die* (1942) von Fritz Lang, entsprachen aber nicht den Vorstellungen Brechts und wichen von seinen Drehbüchern ab. Eine mit Brecht zusammen erarbeitete Filmfassung von *Mutter Courage und ihre Kinder* wurde aufgrund eines Konfliktes zwischen Brecht und dem Regisseur Wolfgang Staudte nicht fertiggestellt. Erst nach dem Tode Brechts wurde die Inszenierung des Stücks auf der Bühne des Berliner Ensembles mit Hilfe des Films konserviert. Es läßt sich heute nicht mehr feststellen, welche Wirkung die Erfüllung der Forderung Brechts, auch im Film *Mutter Courage und ihre Kinder* eine verfremdende Spielweise zu verwenden, auf das damalige Publikum gehabt hätte. Sicher überschätzte Brecht die Möglichkeiten, einerseits die Situationen im Film auf die Gegenwart zu beziehen und andererseits gleichzeitig dem Film den optischen Charakter eines vergoldeten illustrierten Volksbuches aus dem Mittelalter oder braun eingefärbter Daguerreotypien zu geben.

Der schweizer Regisseur Ettore Cella, mit dem Brecht in Zürich verkehrte, als er 1948 am Schauspielhaus *Herr Puntila und sein Knecht Matti* inszenierte, hat mir erzählt, daß man während der Proben diskutierte, ob man die Szenen streichen solle, in denen der betrunkene Puntila "auf dem Aquavit wandelt". Cella fand, daß diese Szenen wichtig seien, "da liegt doch die Poesie des Stückes". Brecht antwortete ihm: "Ja, damit fange ich das Publikum, sodaß es bereit ist, aufzunehmen, was ich zu sagen habe." In einer Notiz im *Arbeitsjournal* vom 2. September 1940 nennt Brecht als seine Aufgabe bei der Arbeit an diesem Stück unter anderem "den gegensatz 'herr' und 'knecht' szenisch zu gestalten und dem thema seine poesie und komik zurückzugeben" (*AJ*, 164). Zunächst ist der nüchterne Puntila nur der Betrunkene, der wegen seines Katzenjammers schlechter Laune ist. Daß der Reiche erst im Rausch menschlich wird, ist ein Motiv, das aus dem Chaplinfilm *City Lights* übernommen ist. Aber der Held Chaplins glaubt an die Freundschaft des berauschten Millionärs, während sich der klassenbewußte Matti nicht durch den Charme des vom Alkohol beeinflußten Puntila einlullen läßt. Der Film, den Alberto Cavalcanti nach dem Stück schuf, enthält weder die Poesie noch die politische Aussage des Brechtschen Volksstückes. Curt Bois, Puntila auf der Bühne des Berliner Ensembles und in der Filmfassung, hatte Recht mit seinem Wortspiel über den Film: "Herr Puntila und kein Brecht."

Hier wird so ausführlich über diesen mißglückten Film gesprochen, weil das Fiasko so bezeichnend für das Verhältnis Brechts zum Film ist. Alberto Cavalcanti schien für die Regie geeignet zu sein. Er hatte bereits ein Jahr vor Ruttmanns Film *Berlin—Symphonie einer Großstadt* einen ähnlichen Film über Paris gestaltet, *Rien que les heures* (1926); sein Name gehörte in die Reihe der Größen des klassischen englischen Dokumentarfilms. Er hatte sowohl einen berühmten Montagefilm über Mussolini signiert, *Yellow Caesar* (1941), als auch eine Reihe von Spielfilmen in England und Brasilien, die von seiner Vielseitigkeit und seinem politischen Engagement zeugten. Den Drehbuchautor Vladimir Pozner hatte Brecht selbst vorgeschlagen, über die Arbeit am Manuskript erzählte mir Pozner in einem Interview, das ich am 21. November 1964 mit ihm während der Dokumentarfilmwoche in Leipzig für Radio Zürich machte:

"Erst diskutierten wir, wie es aussehen sollte, dann schrieb ich es allein, dann schrieb es der Regisseur um, und Brecht wurde diese endültige Fassung vorgelegt." Er war nicht einverstanden, und es begann eine Reihe von Diskussionen, zu denen auch Außenstehende hinzugezogen wurden. Ich nahm an einer dieser Debatten teil und erinnere mich vor allem an die Irritation Brechts darüber, daß so vieles von dem, was ihm wichtig war, mit der Begründung gestrichen wurde, daß es vielleicht auf der Bühne gut sei, für den Film aber nicht in Frage kommen könne.

Ein Beispiel, das Pozner in dem Interview mit mir anführte, zeigt jedoch, daß Brecht manchmal bizarre Vorstellungen von filmischer Erzählungsweise hatte. Zu den schönsten Szenen des Stückes gehört Puntilas Verlobung mit den Frühaufsteherinnen. Apothekerfräulein, Kuhmädchen und Telefonistin geben hier eine knappe und prägnante Beschreibung ihres Lebens. Diese Selbstportraits wurden von Pozner gestrichen, und auf Brechts Frage nach der Ursache sagte er, hier werde zu viel gesprochen. Brecht erwiderte, daß das Gesagte aber doch sehr schön sei. Pozner pflichtete ihm bei, meinte aber, was hier so großartig auf der Bühne wirke, sei filmisch unmöglich. Darauf schlug Brecht vor, daß Hanns Eisler eine besondere Musik für die Untermalung der Erzählung des Kuhmädchens schreiben solle, und daß das Mädchen von einer besonders häßlichen Schauspielerin verkörpert werden müsse, damit die Schönheit von Text und Musik durch die Häßlichkeit des Mädchens gesteigert werde. Pozner lehnte mit dem Argument ab, daß diese Szene dann vier Minuten dauern würde, und bereits zwei Minuten seien zu viel.

Wenn man heute von diesem Dialog hört, zwischen einem Dichter, der soviel wie möglich von seinem Text retten möchte, und einem Vertreter der damaligen Filmroutine, hat man den Eindruck, daß die für die Herstellung des Filmes Verantwortlichen die Möglichkeit nicht ausnützten, die Diktion Brechts und die Poesie seines Stückes zu retten. Die Szene, um die es hier geht, ist auch ohne die Musik Eislers und die von Brecht vorgeschlagene Besetzung filmisch umsetzbar. Man kann die Erzählung des Kuhmädchens mit einer filmischen Beschreibung ihres Arbeitstages illustrieren und an einigen Stellen Großaufnahmen der Schauspielerin einsetzen. Weder Brecht noch Cavalcanti oder Pozner dachten an diese Lösung, die nicht einmal besonders originell ist. Solche Szenen kommen bereits in den sowjetischen Dokumentarfilmen der dreißiger Jahre vor. Dziga Vertov verließ sich auf die filmische Ausdruckskraft des Gesichtes und die Wirkung eines schlichten Textes.

Der Film hat eine Rahmenhandlung. Die Mägde des Herrn Puntila kommentieren die Handlung "von der Küche aus". Diese Szenen sind charakteristisch sowohl für Brecht als auch für Cavalcanti. Brecht sah in der Rahmenhandlung einen Weg, die Optik des Films zu verändern; das Publikum sollte die Handlung von außen und von unten sehen. Er überschätzte jedoch die Möglichkeit, solche kurzen Einlagen gegen die Handlung selbst auszuspielen. Cavalcanti inszenierte die Rahmenhandlung aus Rücksicht auf Brecht, aber ohne Verständnis für ihre Funktion und ohne sie deutlich genug vom Naturalismus der Spielhandlung abzuheben.

3

Es ist müßig, darüber zu mutmaßen, wie sich Brecht zu filmischen Versuchen gestellt hätte, die sich nach seinem Tod auf ihn berufen. Godard hat in mehreren Filmen formale Elemente des epischen Theaters übernommen und in *La Chinoise* linke Studenten alle Namen bis auf den Brechts von der Tafel im Hörsaal wegwischen lassen. Das Theater Brechts ist jedoch nur eine von vielen zitierten Inspirationsquellen Godards, und der Einfluß Brechts ist in den Arbeiten Alexander Kluges oder René Allios eindeutiger und tiefer. Allio hat jedoch im Gespräch mit P. M. Ladiges (*Film*, No. 1 [1965]) darauf hingewiesen, daß der beste Weg, "einen Film im Sinne Brechts zu machen, ist, nicht allzuviel über Brecht zu sprechen." Aus den Entdeckungen Brechts für das Theater ziehen Allio (in der Verfilmung der Brecht-Novelle *Die unwürdige Greisin*) und Kluge (vor allem in *Die Artisten in der Zirkuskuppel: ratlos*) Lehren für den Film. Alain Tanner wertet in *Jonas—qui aura 25 ans en l'an 2000* Erkenntnisse sowohl von Brecht als auch von Godard aus.

Wer bei Filmregisseuren, die sich auf Brecht berufen, und ihrem Vorbild gemeinsame Ausdrucksformen feststellt, darf die oft sehr wesentlichen Unterschiede nicht vergessen. Für Brecht war das künstlerische Experiment nie Selbstzweck, bei ihm bilden Ausdruck und Aussage eine Einheit. Brecht wandte sich nie an eine kleine Elite, sondern wollte ein großes Publikum gewinnen, durch "das Einfache, das so schwer zu machen ist". Ein Film in seinem Sinn ist Theodor Kotullas *Aus einem deutschen Leben,* der den Werdegang des Kommandanten von Auschwitz mit epischen Mitteln nachvollzieht und um des politischen Schwerpunktes willen auf die äußere Spannung verzichtet. Brecht hätte wohl auch einen Film wie *Hair* begrüßt, in dem der in die USA ausgewanderte Tscheche Milos Forman die Vorlage vertieft und dem Musical durch die Verknüpfung mit dem Krieg in Vietnam Züge von *Mann ist Mann* verleiht.

Wie René Allio zähle auch ich mich "zu jenen Leuten, für die die Lektüre und das Theater Brechts von ausschlaggebender Bedeutung waren". Für Allio drückt sich der Einfluß Brechts eher in seiner Denkweise als in einer äußeren Form aus. Im Gegensatz zu jenen Brecht-

Jüngern, die aus Brecht einen toten Klassiker und aus seinem Theater ein Museum gemacht haben, sind "Brechtianer" wie Allio, oder Losey, oder ich, nicht dogmatisch und nicht nur Brecht verpflichtet. In dem, was wir wollen und tun, unterscheiden wir uns mehr als wir einander gleichen.

Zur Zeit meiner Gespräche mit Brecht war ich Journalist und Theaterkritiker. Erst zwei Jahre nach seinem Tod begann ich, für Fernsehen und Film zu arbeiten. Ich saß zum ersten Mal an einem Schneidetisch, als ich für meine erste Sendung im Schwedischen Fernsehen über Brecht und die *Dreigroschenoper* eine Montage aus Ereignissen des Jahres 1928 zusammenstellte, in dem die *Dreigroschenoper* uraufgeführt wurde. Sonst habe ich mich in meiner Filmarbeit nicht direkt mit Brecht befaßt, abgesehen von dem Film *Wähle das Leben* über die Geschichte der Atombombe und die Situation der überlebenden Atomopfer in Hiroshima. Die einzigen literarischen Texte, die sich in der Wirklichkeit von Hiroshima behaupten konnten, wie ich sie im Frühling 1962 erlebte, waren Gedichte von Brecht, und ich zitierte sie in dem Sprechertext, der in meinem Film Aufnahmen von Demonstrationen japanischer Atomopfer gegen die Bombe untermalte.

Von Brecht habe ich einen Satz übernommen, den er im Exil, "unter dem dänischen Strohdach", immer vor Augen hatte: "Die Wahrheit ist konkret." Was Brecht 1935 über "Fünf Schwierigkeiten beim Schreiben der Wahrheit" (*GW*, XVIII, 222–238) sagte, gilt für meine Filmarbeit 1979 wie 1959:

> Wer heute die Lüge und Unwissenheit bekämpfen und die Wahrheit schreiben will, hat zumindest fünf Schwierigkeiten zu überwinden. Er muß den *Mut* haben, die Wahrheit zu schreiben, obwohl sie allenthalben unterdrückt wird; die *Klugheit,* sie zu erkennen, obwohl sie allenthalben verhüllt wird; die *Kunst,* sie handhabbar zu machen als eine Waffe; das *Urteil,* jene auszuwählen, in deren Händen sie wirksam wird; die *List,* sie unter diesen zu verbreiten.

Mit Brecht glaube ich an die Notwendigkeit einer "Propaganda für das Denken" (S. 235) und einer genauen Wortwahl, die den Ton der Wahrheit trifft. Mit Brecht glaube ich: "Wer den Faschismus und den Krieg, die großen Katastrophen, die keine Naturkatastrophen sind, beschreiben will, muß eine praktikable Wahrheit herstellen." (S. 229)

Als ich in dem Montagefilm *Mein Kampf* über das Dritte Reich die beiden Fragen stellte, was damals geschah, und wie es möglich war, ging es mir bei der Beantwortung zunächst darum, die Authentizität meines Beweismaterials zu demonstrieren. Ich wußte aber auch: "Wenn man erfolgreich die Wahrheit über schlimme Zustände schreiben will, muß man sie so schreiben, daß ihre vermeidbaren Ursachen erkannt werden können." (*GW*, XVIII, 229.) Immer wieder zeigte ich, wann es möglich gewesen wäre, den Aufstieg Hitlers noch aufzuhalten. Meine Überzeugung, daß man dem Publikum Material für einen selbständigen Denkprozeß vorlegen muß, damit es zu einer eigenen Stellungnahme gelangt, statt nur die des Filmemachers zu übernehmen, mein Glaube an die Kraft eines anscheinend einfachen aber dichten Sprechertextes mit leiser Eindringlichkeit, meine Bereitschaft, einen Text und eine Montage immer wieder zu überprüfen und abzuändern, und dabei auch die Auffassung von Außenstehenden zu berücksichtigen, die zufällig im Schneideraum mit einem *work in progress* konfrontiert werden, gehen auf Erfahrungen zurück, die ich bei Proben von Brecht im Berliner Ensemble gesammelt habe.

In meinen kontrapunktischen Filmmontagen erreiche ich auch Verfremdungseffekte. Als ich im ersten Teil von *Mein Kampf* die Faszination darstelle, die von der Propaganda Hitlers ausging, damit einem heutigen Publikum die Versuchung verständlich wird, der soviele Deutsche damals erlagen, zitiere ich eine Szene aus *Triumph des Willens,* in der die Vertreter der deutschen Jugend beim Nürnberger Parteitag vor ihrem "Führer" aufmarschiert sind. Der Ton des Originals soll zeigen, daß sie aus allen deutschen Gauen stammen. Immer wieder wird die Frage gestellt: "Von wo kommst du, Kamerad?" Jedesmal wird ein anderer Ort genannt. Schließlich ruft einer der Jungen begeistert aus: "Wir standen nicht im Trommelfeuer der Granaten, und sind dennoch Soldaten!" In einem späteren Abschnitt meines Films wird verdeutlicht, wohin der Marsch für Hitler die jungen deutschen Soldaten führte. Nach Aufnahmen von der Niederlage von Stalingrad hört man zu den Bildern frierender und verschmutzter deutscher Gefangener in der russischen Winterlandschaft die Rede des "Reichsmarschalls" Göring, der zu diesem Zeitpunkt von den herrlichen Zeiten sprach, denen Hitler das deutsche Volk entgegengeführt hatte. Dann sieht man deutsche Kriegsgefangene durch Moskau marschieren und hört zum zweiten Mal das Band "Von wo kommst du, Kamerad?". Die Wiederholung des Tondokumentes, das jeder Zuschauer wiedererkennt, stellt die grausame Wirklichkeit des Krieges gegen die vielversprechende Propagandakundgebung aus der Glanzzeit des Dritten Reiches.

Das Tonband mit der Rede des Propagandaministers Dr. Goebbels im Sportpalast, wo auf die Frage "Wollt ihr den totalen Krieg?" immer wieder jubelnde Ja-Rufe antworten, wird in *Mein Kampf* unter eine Sequenz gelegt, die Ruinen im zerschossenen Deutschland zeigt. Der Kommentar fügt hinzu: "Die, die damals nicht mitschrien, hatten ihn auch" (den totalen Krieg). Die Schilderung des Todes im Warschauer Ghetto ist mit einem Gebet aus dem jüdischen Gottesdienst unterlegt, in dem ein Wort ständig widerholt wird: Chajim—Leben. Hitlers Ankündigung bei

Kriegausbruch, er kenne das Wort "Kapitulation" nicht, und einen November 1918 werde es nie wieder in der deutschen Geschichte geben, wird wiederholt, während die Bilder zeigen, wie Generalfeldmarschall Keitel die Kapitulationsurkunde unterschreibt und wie die Berliner Bevölkerung bei Kriegsende leidet.

In dem Film *Eichmann und das Dritte Reich* habe ich die Hitler-Rede über die "jüdische Gefahr" unter eine Sequenz gelegt, die im Warschauer Ghetto aufgenommen wurde und ein geschwächtes krankes Mädchen zeigt, das sich mühsam in seinem Bett aufrichtet. Die Feststellung Eichmanns, daß er kein Blut sehen könne, von ihm selbst gesprochen, wird mit Aufnahmen weinender Frauen vor Blutlachen mit den Körpern ermordeter KZ-Insassen verbunden. Auf die Zeugenaussage eines der wenigen Überlebenden von Treblinka folgt die Mitteilung Eichmanns: "Und dann fuhren wir von Lublin—ich weiß nicht mehr, wie diese Stelle heißt—verwechsle ich—ich kann nicht mehr sagen, ob es Treblinka hieß oder ob das anders hieß—ich habe wirklich keine Ahnung mehr, wo ich damals hingefahren wurde." Drei Kontrastmontagen zeigen, wie zur Zeit des Massenmordes an den Juden die "jüdische Gefahr" wirklich aussah, welches Leid der Schreibtischmörder verursachte, der den Anblick seiner Opfer nicht ertrug, und wie sich die Sicht des früheren Treblinka-Insassen von der des inspizierenden SS-Offiziers unterschied.

In dem Film *Deutschland, erwache!* habe ich versucht, Spielfilmszenen zu einem Dokumentarfilm zusammenzusetzen und dadurch die Rolle des Spielfilms als Propagandawaffe des Nationalsozialismus zu demonstrieren. Die Spielszenen werden in meinem Film durch einen bewußt knappen Kommentar zusammengehalten. Die vor jedem Zitat eingesetzte Orientierung über das folgende Stück lenkt die Aufmerksamkeit des Publikums auf bestimmt Elemente in den ausgewählten Szenen. Durch das Fehlen jedes weiteren Kommentars ist der Zuschauer gezwungen, sich selbst, individuell, mit dem Stoff auseinanderzusetzen. Es ist ihm nicht möglich, unreflektiert die Propaganda der Spielszenen oder meine (indirekte) Aussage zu übernehmen.

Wer genau hinhört, entdeckt bereits in den Namen meiner Filme Verfremdungseffekte. Ein Mann sagt großspurig "*Mein* Kampf" und läßt die Millionen von Menschen unerwähnt, die diesen Kampf mit ihm kämpften. Hinter der Parole *Deutschland, erwache!* verbarg sich das entgegengesetzte Ziel: Einschläfern des Gewissens und selbständigen Denkens. Der Rausch, in den Hitler die Massen versetzte, widersprach dem Wortlaut des Rufes "Deutschland, erwache!".

An ein paar Stellen von *Deutschland, erwache!* schien es notwendig zu sein, eine direkte Beziehung zwischen der Lüge des Spielfilms und der historischen Wirklichkeit herzustellen. Vor dem Zitat aus *Jud Süß* wird zwar darauf hingewiesen, daß es sich hier um Karrikaturen handelt, und daß man den Mitwirkenden bescheinigt hatte, daß sie Nichtjuden waren, die nur ihre Rolle spielten; dennoch war es meiner Ansicht nach notwendig, dem Zuschauer einen Vergleich zwischen wirklichen jüdischen Gesichtern und der verzerrten Darstellung zu ermöglichen. Deshalb zeigt der Film Portraits von authentischen Kennkarten, die mit einem "J" und dem Vermerk über das Schicksal der Abgebildeten versehen sind ("Deportiert am . . . "). Auf das Zitat aus *Jud Süß* folgt im Faksimile der Befehl Himmlers, daß die gesamte SS und Polizei den Film *Jud Süß* zu sehen habe. Damit wird die Herstellung dieses Films in Zusammenhang mit der "Endlösung der Judenfrage" gebracht.

In der letzten Sequenz meines Films macht ein deutlich in allen seinen Bestandteilen erkennbares Arrangement die wahren Proportionen zwischen *fact* und *feature,* Wahrheit und Propaganda, sichtbar. Auf eine Szene aus dem Film *Kolberg,* dem Gespräch zwischen Horst Caspar als Gneisenau und Heinrich George als Nettelbeck über einen gemeinsamen Tod für das Vaterland Preußen im Jahre 1807, folgen authentische Filmszenen aus dem brennenden Berlin während der letzten Kriegsphase; der Text stellt lakonisch fest, daß solche Appelle die Katastrophe nicht aufhalten konnten. Die Kampfgeräusche sind plötzlich realistisch und steigern sich—dann hört und sieht man Zarah Leander, die in einem Ausschnitt aus dem Film *Die große Liebe* vor deutschen Soldaten im besetzten Paris ihr Lied "Davon geht die Welt nicht unter" vorträgt. Die Zuhörer im Film singen begeistert mit. Ein etwas verschlafener Soldat wird von den Bewegungen seiner schunkelnden Kameraden mitgerissen, dann verklingt die Musik, und auf einer stummen Wochenschau-Aufnahme sieht man einen verstörten jungen deutschen Soldaten allein vor einem Tank in der wirklichen Kriegslandschaft sitzen und wortlos den Kopf schütteln. In dieser kurzen Szene, der letzten des Films *Deutschland, erwache!,* dringt die Wahrheit in die Traumfabrik des NS-Filmes ein.

4

Montagen dieser Art kopieren nicht die Methoden, die Brecht auf der Bühne entwickelt hat, sondern knüpfen an Erkenntnisse an, die durch das epische Theater gewonnen wurden, und übersetzen sie in die Sprache des Films. Nirgends werden hier theatralische Elemente übernommen, vielmehr werden filmische Mittel wiederentdeckt. Es sei an das Manifest erinnert, das die sowjetischen Filmregisseure Eisenstein, Pudovkin und Alexandrov bereits 1928 in Moskau unterzeichneten. Dort wird unter anderem der Ton als Kontrast zum sichtbaren Teil der Montage aufgefaßt und gefordert, daß Experimente mit dem Tonfilm nicht Bild und Ton synchronisieren sollten. Brecht selbst stellte in seinem amerikanischen Exil fest:

> Die besondere Natur der Experimente, welche das deutsche Theater der Vorhitlerzeit veranstaltet hat, macht es möglich, einige seiner Erfahrungen auch für den Film zu verwerten—vorausgesetzt dies sehr vorsichtig. Dieses Theater verdankte dem Film nicht wenig. Es machte Gebrauch von epischen, gestischen und Montageelementen, die im Film aufraten. Es machte sogar Gebrauch vom Film selber, indem es dokumentarisches Material verwertete. (*GW*, XV, 487.)

Der Dokumentarist kann von Brecht lernen, "daß weniger denn je eine einfache Widergabe der Realität etwas über die Realität aussagt. Eine Photographie der Kruppwerke oder der AEG ergibt beinahe nichts über diese Institute. Die eigentliche Realität ist in die Funktionale gerutscht." (*GW*, XVIII, 161.) Der politisch engagierte Dokumentarist kann sich Brechts Definition zueigen machen, "daß ein kunstwerk desto realistischer ist, je erkennbarer in ihm die realität gemeistert wird. das pure wiedererkennen der realität wird oft durch eine solche darstellung erschwert, die sie meistern lehrt." (*AJ*, 142.) In unseren Bemühungen, das Beispielhafte einer Geschichte herauszuschälen, ohne ihren Unterhaltungswert zu beeinträchtigen, in unseren Versuchen, mehrere Schichten der Wirklichkeit gleichzeitig zu durchdringen und unser komplexes Sehen auf den Zuschauer zu übertragen, bewegen wir uns oft in den Spuren Brechts, ohne sie immer wahrzunehmen. Das ist jedoch in seinem Sinne, denn er hatte "kein Bedürfnis danach, daß ein Gedanke von mir bleibt. Ich möchte aber, daß alles aufgegessen wird, umgesetzt, aufgebraucht."

Joel Schechter. "Beyond Brecht. New Authors, New Audience."

Brecht's theatre changed our traditional notions of "author" and "spectator" in the theatre. His habit of involving co-workers in his projects and of adapting classical texts and his attempts to free spectators of passivity in the theatre have all had effects on a number of contemporary playwrights. The British playwrights, Edward Bond and Howard Brenton, for instance, adapt classical texts and use elements of "epic theatre" in order to describe contemporary realities. In addition, Bond takes a critical stance vis à vis the classics themselves. The Brazilian director/playwright, Augusto Boal, has developed techniques and concepts in his theatre workshops that draw the public deeper into the theatrical event itself than was possible for Brecht to do with his audiences. Above all Boal's work is distinguished by the use of "invisible theatre" and openness to spectator participation. Other attempts to move "beyond Brecht" include the well-known play *Offending the Audience* of the Austrian Peter Handke and the less well-known experiments of Armand Gatti in France in which whole communities seek to analyze community problems through theatrical means. Finally, mention is made of the way Brecht's influence has shown up in the work of the Italian Dario Fo who, like Brecht, has resuscitated older forms of popular theatre and has reshaped them for modern usage.

Joel Schechter. "Über Brecht hinaus: Neue Autoren, neue Zuschauer."

Brechts Theater veränderte die traditionellen Begriffe des Autors und des Zuschauers im Theater. Seine Praxis, Mitarbeiter an Projekten zu beteiligen, seine Bearbeitungen klassischer Vorlagen und seine Versuche, das Publikum aus seiner Passivität zu befreien, wirken in einigen zeitgenössischen Dramatikern nach. Die britischen Stückeschreiber Edward Bond und Howard Brenton adaptieren klassische Stücke, um zeitgenössische Realität zu beschreiben und benutzen Elemente des epischen Theaters. Bond beschäftigt sich zudem in seinen Stücken kritisch mit Klassikern des Theaters. Der Brasilianer Augusto Boal hat Konzepte und Techniken entwickelt, die das Publikum weiter in das Theatergeschehen einbeziehen, als es Brecht je möglich war, was er vor allem durch Theaterwerkstätten, "unsichtbares Theater" und Offenheit für Zuschauerbeiträge erreicht. Ähnliches gilt für das Stück *Publikumsbeschimpfung* des Österreichers Peter Handke, das Brechts didaktische Distanz zum Publikum überwindet, und für die "Spektakel ohne Zuschauer" des Franzosen Armand Gatti, in denen ganze Gemeinden ihre Probleme zu Theater umformen. Brechts Einfluß wird darüberhinaus deutlich, wo Theater heute auf ältere Formen populären Theaters zurückgreift, wie es der Italiener Dario Fo erfolgreich praktiziert.

Joel Schechter. "Au-delà de Brecht : nouveaux auteurs, nouveaux publics."

Le théâtre de Brecht a changé nos notions traditionelles "d'auteur" et de "spectateur". L'habitude de Brecht d'associer ses collaborateurs à ses plans, d'adapter des textes classiques et ses tentatives pour faire sortir le spectateur de sa passivité ; tout ceci a considérablement influencé nombres d'écrivains contemporains. Les anglais Edward Bond et Howard Brenton, par exemple, adaptent des textes classiques en même temps qu'ils se servent des éléments du "théâtre épique" pour décrire la réalité contemporaine. De plus, Bond prend une position critique vis-à-vis des classiques eux-mêmes. Augusto Boal a dévelopé dans ses ateliers théâtraux des techniques et des concepts qui plongent le public dans l'évènement théâtral plus profondément que ne l'a fait Brecht. Surtout, la nouveauté du travail de Boal est l'utilisation du "théâtre invisible" et l'ouverture à la participation du spectateur. Les autres tentatives d'aller au-delà de Brecht comprennent la pièce célèbre *Insulte au public* de l'auteur autrichien Peter Handke et les expérimentations moins connues d'Armand Gatti en France par lesquelles une communauté entière cherche à analyser ses problèmes au moyen du théâtre. Enfin, M. Schechter indique l'influence de Brecht dans les oeuvres de l'écrivain/acteur italien Dario Fo, qui, comme Brecht a ressucité de vieilles formes du théâtre populaire et les a adaptées à la sensibilité contemporaine.

Beyond Brecht: New Authors, New Spectators

Joel Schechter

The debt owed to Brecht by his successors is so extensive that it is tempting to divide the century's political theatre into two categories, "Before Brecht" and "After." At the same time, the most prominent creators of contemporary political theatre have not slavishly imitated Brecht. His innovations have been rethought and extended by writers such as Augusto Boal, Edward Bond, Howard Brenton, Dario Fo, Armand Gatti and Peter Handke. Their plays could be called post-Brechtian insofar as the new work advances beyond Brecht's, but the plays are also Brechtian in that they employ conventions of Brecht's epic theatre and *Lehrstücke*.

Of course, a complete catalogue of the plays influenced by Brecht would fill a book. In this essay I will limit myself to discuss only two related aspects of contemporary political theatre in which Brecht's influence continues: namely, the concepts of authorship and spectatorship, both of which Brecht called into question through his processes of play creation.

Brecht and some of his successors have collectively written and staged their texts. The concept of the playwright as a single individual who writes in isolation is not applicable to their situation. While Brecht did not write everything collectively, he did so often enough to develop an aesthetic based on the activity. His play *Man Is Man*, which asks whether one can speak of less than two hundred men at once in an age of mass movements, was written by several men and one woman known

43

as "The Brecht Collective." When the group completed *Man Is Man* in 1925, Brecht told Elisabeth Hauptmann that "piecing together the manuscript from twenty pounds of paper was heavy work; it took me two days, a half bottle of brandy, four bottles of soda water, eight to ten cigars, and a lot of patience, and it was the only part I did on my own."[1]

By 1927 Brecht was writing in another collective at the Piscator Stage in Berlin. Brecht did not necessarily regard himself as the equal of other collective members. In *The Political Theatre*, Erwin Piscator recounts that Brecht "strutted up and down the stage shouting, 'My name is my trademark, and anybody who uses it must pay for it.' " Rather than pay for it, Piscator cancelled a production of Brecht's new play, *Wheat* (also later known as *Joe Meat-Chopper* and *St. Joan of the Stockyards*), which had been announced for the 1927–28 season. Still, Brecht continued to write throughout his career, as he had at the Piscator Stage, in collaboration with directors, other playwrights and dramaturgs. After he founded the Berliner Ensemble, his "collaboration" with other artists extended to Shakespeare, Molière and Lenz, as he adapted their plays. (Earlier, of course, he had adapted other classics, including Gay's *The Beggar's Opera*.) At the Berliner Ensemble this approach to classics was institutionalized, as young writers and dramaturgs were trained to collectively adapt great plays.

If he had simply adapted classics or written plays with co-authors, Brecht's creative process might not have had so much influence on later playwriting. However, he engaged in these activities out of political and aesthetic convictions that can be seen in the structure and contents of the plays, as well as in the process of their creation. The structures, themes and aims of the *Lehrstücke* in particular have counteracted a tendency among playwrights to portray individuals of heroic stature. While admirable or sympathetic tragic heroes had their counterparts off-stage in Romantic, secluded and suffering authors, Brecht's interest in collectivity (as well as agitation) led him to explore collective behavior in plays such as *The Measures Taken*—whose central characters, a cadre of four interchangable agitators, are not particularly heroic or sympathetic and who are, least of all, "isolated individuals." Brecht also sought to end the spectator's isolation from actors behind an imaginary fourth wall. Instead of fostering the passivity of voyeurism, an actor's "performance becomes a discussion (about social conditions) with the audience he is addressing."[2] The roles of those in Brecht's audience, those on his stage, and those who wrote the plays were linked in new ways that have been clarified and further developed by his successors.

Authors Against Authors

Edward Bond, a socialist playwright in England has furthered Brecht's alteration of the nature of authorship both by rewriting the classics and by writing epic plays critical of famous authors. When Brecht wrote *Baal* to debunk myths about Romantic poets, he invented the title character. Bond has written three plays demystifying actual poets: Basho, John Clare and Shakespeare. His plays explore the relationships of these poets to English society. (Even in *Narrow Road to the Deep North*, set in Japan, the poet Basho encounters some violently imperialistic British soldiers.) Basho sets out on a quest for enlightenment by passing an abandoned, starving child and ignoring it; ignoring such reality seems to be the poet's vocation in Bond's plays.[3] In *Bingo: Scenes of Money and Death*, Bond shows William Shakespeare in Stratford with landowners against landless peasants. Bond's Shakespeare is probably the same man Brecht's Jeremiah Peachum admired for retiring to a little country house after successful business enterprises. Of the poet John Clare, whom he portrays in *The Fool*, Bond has said: "Clare was driven into madness by the ruling class, who made it impossible for him to produce culture in direct relationship with his society."[4] The poets in Bond's plays are unable or unwilling to speak out against social injustice and cruelty, despite—or even because of—their ability to write eloquent poetry. When Clare visits a prison in *The Fool* and an inmate asks him to "write 'bout this place. What goo on," he replies: "Who'd read that?"

For Bond himself, writing about injustice and indifference to injustice has almost become a form of insurrection: a revolt against ruling class reverence for authors who do not face the prisons and poverty around them. Bond the iconoclast sees Shakespeare as icon in a church where fine imagery and language are offered to people instead of bread and employment. His plays about poets may be more aggressive toward traditional veneration of authors than anything Brecht wrote.

Bond has also rewritten Shakespeare's *King Lear*. He said his version, titled *Lear*, does not "get its life merely from being a commentary on [Shakespeare's] *Lear*, or an attack on it or correction of it."[5] Bond's king learns from his errors, and after surviving a guerrilla war and extremely cruel, modern technological violence, Lear attempts to tear down the wall he built earlier to protect his land.

At the same time Bond was writing *Lear* in 1970, we know that he was collaborating on a translation of *Round Heads and Pointed Heads*, Brecht's version of another Shakespeare play. Bond has often explicitly acknowledged his debt to Brecht, which began when the Berliner En-

semble visited London in 1956. He says he has "worked consciously—
starting with Brecht but not ending there. Brecht's contribution to the
creation of a Marxist theatre is enormous and lasting, but the work is not
yet finished."[6] One difference between them is Bond's decision to write
overtly about England's past and present; his plays are rarely set in distant
lands, as Brecht's were. His concern with England's past and present
continues in Bond's two latest plays. *The Worlds* (1979) portrays a terrorist kidnapping of a British industrialist. Another new play, *Restoration*
(1981), refashions the conventions and language of Restoration drama
(adding rock music and songs) to portray the genre's underside, as a Black
servant in London resists exploitation and the false arrest of her husband.

Howard Brenton, another British socialist playwright, has said that
"the search for something other than what Brecht was doing goes on
endlessly amongst the writers of my generation."[7] One result of the
search is that Brenton, like Bond, writes plays in a variety of styles and
settings, although his plays, too, are almost all set in England. Brenton's
texts frequently employ epic structures, and they share Brecht's commitment to socialism even when they explicitly critique socialist extremism.

These plays often portray unsuccessful revolutions. In *Thirteenth
Night* (1981), Brenton has rewritten *Macbeth* as a warning to the Left. Set
in the near future, this dream play starts with socialists winning control
of parliament. A new national leader, who resembles labourite Tony
Benn, unilaterally disarms the nation of its nuclear weapons, and inspires
a riot against the American embassy. Later the Macbeth-like Prime Minister adapts Stalinist tactics, eliminating his opponents through secret
police arrests. As his life comes to an end in a bunker, he asks the ghosts
of victims parading before him:

> But what do you expect? Someone must take it up. Authority, the banner, the
> will. You want universal justice, the common good? Well, the unjust, you
> know, aren't going to say 'Fine. Great. Here's our money and our houses and
> our banks, oilfields, all our revenues and power and very lives.' Oh no. You're
> going to have blood on your hands. You're going to have your dead. Eh,
> comrades?[8]

Brenton's special achievement as a post-Brechtian writer may be
more apparent in another recent play, *The Romans in Britain* (1980),
which is currently on trial for "sexual offences" in London. The play, first
staged at the National Theatre of Great Britain, opens with Roman
soldiers brutally invading and raping ancient Celts; the action then
switches to modern day Ireland, to depict British troops policing the
North as violently as the ancient, imperialistic Romans did in their
marauding. One suspects that the court case against Brenton and the

National Theatre represents conservative distress at the political implications of his epic history, as well as its sexual violence. Brenton sees ancient and recent British history in far less flattering terms than many historians; but then the others were not usually writing from an anti-imperialistic perspective. In a sense Brenton is *changing* history by writing it anew, and this too may have provoked the outcry against his play.

In his modest way Brenton is a provocateur disguised as an epic playwright. He has said that "theatre's a real bear pit . . . not the place for reasoned discussion." Prior to the *success de scandal* of *The Romans in Britain,* he confessed to dreaming of "a play acting like a brushfire, smouldering into public consciousness. . . . No playwright of my generation has actually got into public, actually touched life outside the theatre. But it can be done."[9] Now he has managed to intervene in history, or at least in public discourse with one of his plays, and the British court system has practically become Brenton's co-producer. (At one point early in the legal proceedings against *The Romans in Britain,* after the play closed, rumor had it that the entire production would have to be restaged for the court.) In May 1982, the British courts were still examining the case. Meanwhile, as it went forward, Brenton himself was translating another play about the failures of revolution, Büchner's *Danton's Death,* for the National Theatre.

Authors Against Spectators

At times Brecht himself compared theatre to a courtroom, but his reasons for the analogy had more to do with the audience than with lawsuits. He wanted spectators to judge his plays as experts and reach their own verdicts. In another analogy he compared the theatre audience to a legislative body and noted that:

> Once illusion is sacrificed to free discussion, and once the spectator, instead of being enabled to have an experience, is forced as it were to cast his vote; then a change has been launched which goes far beyond formal matters and begins for the first time to affect the theatre's social function.[10]

Brecht experimentally implemented this theory by asking spectators at *The Measures Taken* to perform the role of the Control Chorus and by incorporating their suggestions for changes in the text. Experiments toward such democratization of theatre have been considerably extended by some of Brecht's successors, who have virtually abolished the audience, turning spectators into actors and co-authors. The concepts of authorship, spectatorship, and the function of theatre change radically in the work of Augusto Boal, Armand Gatti and Dario Fo, as performer, author and spectators become almost interchangeable.

Brecht's friend, Walter Benjamin, anticipated the aesthetics of recent collective creation in several of his essays on epic theatre. He noted that the didactic play "facilitates and encourages the interchangeability of actors and audience, audience and actors. Every spectator can become one of the actors."[11] He cited Brecht's epic theatre as an example of a production apparatus that "will be the better the more consumers it brings in contact with the production process—in short, the more readers or spectators it turns into collaborators."[12] Brecht pursued this collaboration primarily by encouraging a decision-making, critical attitude in spectators. He knew that as long as they were "plunged in self-identification with the protagonist's feelings, virtually the whole audience failed to take part in the moral decisions of which the plot is made up."[13]

When Brecht encouraged audience participation in his play's moral decisions, it was generally to take the form of silent critical consciousness during the performance, and discussion or action afterwards. Augusto Boal, a Brazilian playwright and director now living in exile in Paris, has developed techniques that allow the audience to express its decisions verbally and physically *during* a performance. It may be misleading to speak of an "audience" at all when referring to Boal's theatre. While he has written and staged conventional plays for seated spectators, he generally conducts workshops in which everyone participates as actor or author. In his book, *The Theatre of the Oppressed,* Boal distinguishes between his theatre and Brecht's:

> Brecht proposes a poetics in which the spectator delegates power to the character who thus acts in his place but the spectator reserves the right to think for himself, often in opposition to the character. [The result is] an awakening of critical consciousness. But the poetics of the oppressed focuses on the action itself: the spectator delegates no power to the character (or actor) either to act or to think in his place; on the contrary, he himself assumes the protagonic role, changes the dramatic action, tries out solutions, discusses plans for change—in short, trains himself for real action. In this case, perhaps the theatre is not revolutionary in itself, but it is surely a rehearsal for the revolution. The liberated spectator, as a whole person, launches into action.[14]

Boal offers an example of a Peruvian theatre workshop in which fish meal factory workers devised scenarios for protesting exploitive working conditions. One solution they acted out in private was a speedup of their fish grinding, a legal protest which would break overloaded machinery and offer the workers much-needed rest. After rehearsing scenarios for several other solutions in the workshop, they decided that formation of a union would be the best long-term response.

Boal also developed a form he calls "invisible theatre," which is slightly different from "guerilla theatre" practiced elsewhere. In one performance of "invisible theatre," actors dine in an expensive Brazilian restaurant. When given the bill, one actor claims he cannot afford to pay it, and loudly discusses the high cost of food. Actors planted elsewhere in the restaurant take up the discussion, and collect money to help pay the exorbitant bill. Most of the other diners would have no idea that they are witnessing a staged drama, and functioning as spectators, as they overhear discussion of the cost of living and national economic policies. Boal developed this form of participatory theatre when he feared police repression would close any stage that was not "invisible." Unlike some forms of "guerrilla theatre," this performance in no way assaults its audience or invades a territory foreign to its concerns. Where is it more fitting to discuss the cost of food than in an expensive restaurant? Other diners are able to overhear the discussion, but not forced into it.

Following his arrest and torture in Brazil, Boal transferred his experimental workshops to Europe. There he found that problems raised by participants from industrially developed countries are not always as obvious or pressing as those in the Third World. "Sometimes the work may approach the boundaries of psychodrama," he says of the European workshops in which romance and family problems are discussed more often than factory strikes or government repression.[15] But Boal adds that in Europe "there is a strong psychological oppression, there are lots of cops in the minds of the people . . . and there are many concrete problems too: unemployment, lack of security for the workers. . . . Repression there is more sophisticated."

In Brazil Boal developed a series of techniques for public intervention in, and co-authorship of more traditional drama, too, so that even *Hamlet* could become a collective creation. A master of ceremonies called the Joker prefaces and interrupts the play. He invites spectators to question aloud action on stage or offer new endings. Spectators and the Joker interview actors about their roles during a performance, the way a television sports announcer might interview an athlete at halftime during a game; those on stage should be prepared to improvise accordingly to explain why their character is behaving as he or she does. The procedure here is slightly reminiscent of Brecht's unrealized plan (noted in his published diaries) to have two clowns "perform in the interval and pretend to be spectators. They will bandy opinions about the play and about the members of the audience. Make bets on the outcome. . . . The idea would be to bring reality back to the things on stage."[16]

Another playwright who has brought the audience into his work is the Austrian, Peter Handke. Continuing Brecht's reliance on direct address to spectators in his well-known play, *Offending the Audience,* Handke

49

has actors inform the audience that they will not witness a conventional play: no characters, no plot, no scenery tonight. Instead, they will be insulted. The four speakers on stage then proceed to hurl a lengthy series of insulting names and epithets at their audience. The accusations contained in the epithets are so contradictory that it would be difficult to take them seriously. There is a parodying and self-negating aspect to the invective. In any case, the assault ends any possible identification between the audience and the actors. Quite the contrary, it turns the audience into the central protagonist of the evening. As one of the speakers in Handke's play says to his witnesses: "You are the subject. . . . You are the event." The audience, deprived of its role as voyeur, and any other single, private identity its members may have had, is turned into a collective body of names.

There is in this play a hostility toward the received ideas and illusions of theatre which require passive spectators to pretend they sit invisibly behind an imaginary fourth wall; but hostility is also shown toward the receivers of these illusions—the audience. Handke's hostility is an extension of Brechtian attitudes beyond those Brecht himself discussed. In a recent critique of Brecht's didacticism, British playwright John McGrath notes its "hostility to the audience": "Pedagogics, after all, is the art of passing *down* information and judgements, the art of the superior to the inferior. Distance, in place of solidarity."[17] A critique of Brecht's "distance" has been composed by Handke for different reasons; he once objected that, much as the players in soccer games act out all possible shots at the goal, Brecht's theatre parables "acted out" alternatives merely as a game, "infinitely removed from the reality which he wished to change."[18] Insofar as Handke sets out to change or restore the reality of theatre in *Offending the Audience*, he does it quite directly, with almost no distance or artifice (aside from the pre-written text) between audience and actors.

In other, later plays Handke launches a Wittgensteinian attack on language and consciousness by parodying their processes, and his characters play games with language as much as Brecht played them (in Handke's view) with social behavior. But at least in this one early play (1966), Peter Handke abolished the spectator's role as a voyeur, and gave the audience a new collective identity.

Another successor of Brecht who has altered the role of spectators is French playwright, Armand Gatti. Gatti stages what he calls "spectacles without spectators." He and his assistants known as "The Tribe" have lived in French provinces for months at a time, working with local residents to create huge pageants that are written and performed by the community. One such pageant in the Brabant Wallon region of France

involved 3000 local people for eight months in preparation for a performance and parade that traversed 25 miles of countryside. Such productions not only help non-theatre people articulate issues that affect their
lives, but give them a sense of their own creativity, their own potential to
express themselves collectively and as individuals in a collaboration.[19]

Last year, Gatti and his tribe worked with residents of London-
derry, Northern Ireland, to create a film about the troubles there. His
decision to employ video in the process of collective creation may eventually remove Gatti from the theatre, but if so he will have arrived at his
new position slowly, after many years of work as a playwright and pageant director. Brecht's ideal of the audience as legislative body has given
way, in Gatti's projects, to an even more democratized form of involvement, where every man and woman is a potential creator. Roland Barthes'
praise of Brecht's theatre for its innovation also applies to Gatti's work;
both produce theatre in which:

> Participation is altogether reconceived. . . . Our traditional dramaturgies are
> radically false; they congeal the spectator, they are dramaturgies of abdication.
> This theatre is a theatre of solidarity.[20]

Clowns Before Brecht and After

Gatti's collective creation, and the plays of Italian satirist Dario Fo
(discussed elsewhere in this volume), may owe more to the popular the-
atre forms in carnivals and circus parades than to epic playwriting. But
Brecht himself, as is widely known, took great interest in popular theatre, beginning with his admiration for the Munich beer hall clown, Karl
Valentin, continuing with his adaption of cabaret and jazz styles in *The
Threepenny Opera*, culminating though hardly ending in the folk comedy of
Puntila and the Saturnalian mockery of justice in *The Caucasian Chalk
Circle*. One need only look at the 1920 photograph of Brecht playing
clarinet beside a white-faced clown and a tuba player in Karl Valentin's
band, or read his 1920 diary entry describing a clown who has more "wit
and style" than "the entire contemporary theatre,"[21] to sense his affinity
with these popular forms. At the Augsburg fair Brecht was able to study
the crowds, carnival gatherings in which, according to Bakhtin, "the
individual feels that he is an indissoluble part of this collectivity, a
member of the people's mass body."[22] In the center of such crowds one
might find Dario Fo performing today, as a modern, post-Brechtian
Valentin.

The crowds that have collected around Fo have often done so inside
occupied factories or union halls and stadiums, where he frequently per-

forms. Fo is a political satirist who has acted and written in several collectives, most recently *La Comune* in Milan. He has acknowledged sharing Brecht's interest in popular theatre, particularly cabaret.

Asked by *Theater heute* in 1978 to explain his own popularity throughout Europe, especially in Germany, Fo replied that the demand for his plays may be great because there is no Brecht, no Toller, no Piscator competing with him today. Fo's assumption that he is their heir is not presumptuous, given his achievements. When he performs his own work, as many as 5000 spectators may watch him in a stadium, which becomes a continuing political carnival as Fo allows activists to read appeals and manifestos in between his comic monologues.

Like Boal and Gatti, Fo also involves the audience in the creation of his plays. He too creates plays collectively, improvising scenes with actors in his company, and then asking the audience for comments on works in progress. Suggestions from spectators are incorporated into, or effect changes in, the work. Some Fo plays, such as *The Boss's Funeral*, contain an "unwritten" last act; instead of finishing the story, Fo and his cast discuss the play and its political issues with the audience. In this way he allows spectators to "enter" (his word) the performance and modify it; they too become agents of change.

This survey of Brecht's successors is far from complete, but even the small sampling here should suggest that in the 1980's political theatre is still alive and experimenting in Brecht's tradition, further developing the radical forms of authorship and spectatorship advocated by Brecht, especially in his pedagogical theatre phase. It would·be wrong to attribute the origin of these contemporary practices solely to Brecht—they extend back to medieval carnivals and minstrels, and forward to other twentieth century innovators such as Meyerhold and Piscator. To name any single artist as the primary model for recent collective creation contradicts the unifying function of collectivity. Ultimately, if these artists succeed as a collective, they will be joined by yet more collaborators, the type that Louis Althusser once described as "a new spectator, an actor who starts where the performance ends, who only starts so as to complete it, but in life."[23]

Notes

1. Brecht quoted in *Collected Plays*, edited by John Willett and Ralph Manheim, II (New York: Random House, 1977), p.xiv.
2. *Brecht on Theatre*, edited by John Willett (New York: Hill and Wang, 1964), p.139.
3. See Malcolm May and Philip Roberts, *Bond: A Study of His Plays* (London: Eyre Methuen, 1980), p. 92.
4. Bond quoted in Catherine Itzin, *Stages of Revolution* (London: Eyre Methuen, 1980), p. 78.

5. Bond quoted by Hay and Roberts, pp. 107–108.
6. Ibid., p. 64.
7. Brenton quoted in *New Theatre Voices of the Seventies*, edited by Simon Trussler (London: Eyre Methuen, 1981), p. 90.
8. *Methuen New Theatre Scripts* (London: Eyre Methuen, 1981), p. 39.
9. *New Theatre Voices of the Seventies*, p. 97.
10. *Brecht on Theatre*, p. 39.
11. Walter Benjamin, "What Is Epic Theatre?" in *Understanding Brecht* (London: New Left Books, 1977), p. 20.
12. Walter Benjamin, "The Author as Producer," in *Understanding Brecht*, p. 98.
13. *Brecht on Theatre*, p. 28.
14. Augusto Boal, *The Theatre of the Oppressed* (New York: Urizen, 1979), p. 122.
15. Boal quoted in an interview by Yan Michalski, *Theater* Magazine (Yale School of Drama, Fall 1980), p. 16.
16. Bertolt Brecht, *Diaries 1920–1922*, edited by Hertha Ramthun (New York: St. Martin's Press, 1979), pp. 32–33.
17. John McGrath, *A Good Night Out: Popular Theatre: Audience, Class and Form* (London: Eyre Methuen, 1981), p. 40.
18. Peter Handke, "Brecht, Play, Theatre, Agitation," *Theatre Quarterly*, 1, No.4 (1971), 89.
19. See Lenora Champagne, "Armand Gatti: Toward Spectacle without Spectators," *Theater* Magazine (Yale, Fall/Winter 1981), pp. 26 and following for more on this.
20. Roland Barthes, "Mother Courage Blind," in *Critical Essays* (Evanston, Il.: Northwestern University Press, 1972), p. 35.
21. Brecht, *Diaries 1920–1922*, p. 32.
22. Mikhail Bakhtin, *Rabelais and His World* (Cambridge, Mass.: MIT Press, 1968), p. 255.
23. Louis Althusser, "The Piccolo Teatro: Bertolazzi and Brecht—Notes on a Materialist Theatre," in *For Marx* (New York: Vintage, 1970), p. 151.

Vittorio Felaco. "New Teeth for an Old Shark."

Vittorio Felaco introduces the theatre of Dario Fo and Franca Rame, which is very successful in Italy, though largely rejected by critics and the authorities. Among the reasons for the popularity of Fo/Rame are: the usage of traditional forms of popular entertainment usually excluded from the regular circuits of the theatre, Fo's talent as an actor, and, finally, his ideologic position to consciously make theatre from the perspective of ordinary, everyday people. This effort to make the theatre significant for those who have been excluded up to now shows both Brecht's influence and a progress beyond Brecht's conception of the theatre. Fo's and Rame's theatre is most frequently criticized for being political, and therefore inferior; an attack which is contradictory in itself, because a theatre which consciously avoids direct political statements is necessarily a political theatre in that it propagates political escapism.

Four types of plays can be distinguished in the theatre of Fo/Rame: abstract metaphoric dramas, such as *The Story of the Tiger*; spectacular comedies, based on real events, especially *Accidental Death of an Anarchist*; plays standing within the Italian folk tradition, such as *Mistero buffo*; and updated versions of classical plays, most recently Brecht's *Threepenny Opera,* which Fo radically transformed into the reality of the eighties, thus giving new teeth to Brecht's old shark.

Vittorio Felaco. "Neue Zähne für einen alten Haifisch."

Vittorio Felaco stellt das Theater Dario Fos und Franca Rames vor, das beim italienischen Publikum großen Erfolg hat, von Kritikern und Behörden aber weitgehend abgelehnt wird. Für die Popularität von Fo/Rame gibt es zahlreiche Gründe, wie etwa das Zurückgreifen auf traditionelle Formen der Volkskunst, die vom regulären Theaterbetrieb ausgeschlossen sind, aber ebenso das schauspielerische Talent Fos und vor allem die ideologische Position seines Theaters, ganz bewußt Kunst aus der Sicht des Volkes zu produzieren. Dieses Bestreben, Theater für diejenigen bedeutsam zu machen, die bislang ausgeschlossen waren, zeigt sowohl den Einfluß Brechts als auch eine Fortentwicklung seiner Theaterkonzeption durch Fo/Rame. Der häufigste Vorwurf, dieses Theater sei politisch und daher minderwertig, ist in sich widersprüchlich, da jedes Theater, das politische Aussagen bewußt vermeidet, einen politischen Eskapismus propagiert und somit gar nicht "unpolitisch" sein kann.

Vier Typen von Stücken lassen sich im Theater von Fo/Rame unterscheiden: abstrakte metaphorische Dramen, wie z. B. *Die Geschichte des Tigers*; spektakuläre Komödien, die auf tatsächlichen Ereignissen basieren, vor allem *Der zufällige Tod eines Anarchisten*; Stücke, die auf die italienische Volkskunst zurückgreifen, wie *Mistero buffo* und Bearbeitungen von klassischen Vorlagen, zuletzt Brechts *Dreigroschenoper,* die Fo radikal an die Verhältnisse der achtziger Jahre angepaßt hat: der alte Haifisch bekam ein neues Gebiß.

Vittorio Felaco. "De nouvelles dents pour un vieus requin."

Dans son introduction au théâtre de Dario Fo et Franca Rame, Vittorio Felaco essaie de démontrer que le refus des critiques et des autorités (soit le "pouvoir", au dire de Fo) est le premier indice d'une popularité inquiétante. Parmi les raisons de sa popularité, on trouve l'utilisation de formes traditionelles du spectacle, normalement écartées des sentiers battus du théâtre traditionnel, le talent du Fo acteur et mime, et enfin sa position idéologique consciente en faveur d'un théâtre accessible aux gens du peuple. Cette tentative de faire du théâtre destiné à ceux qui en ont été écartés jusqu' à maintenant démontre l'influence de Brecht et un progrès qui va au-delà des concepts dramatiques de Brecht lui-même. On reproche souvent au théâtre de Fo et de Rame d'être politique et pour cela inférieur ; c'est pourtant une contradiction, parce qu'un théâtre qui essaie consciemment d'éviter d'aborder directement les réalités politiques ne peut être qu'un théâtre politique parce que, en effet, il propose l'évasion de la politique.

On peut distinguer quatre types de mises-en-scène dans le théâtre de la "Compagnia Dario Fo Franca Rame" : la métaphore abstraite de l'*Histoire de la tigresse* ; la comédie spectaculaire des événements réels contemporains, particulièrement *Mort accidentalle d'un anarchiste* ; mises-en-scène du folklore italien, comme *Mistero buffo* ; et de nouvelles versions de pièces classiques dernièrement l'*Opéra de quatre sous* de John Gay et de Brecht, une oeuvre que Fo a complètement transposèe dans la rèalitè des années quatre-vingt donnant ainsi "de nouvelles dents au vieux requin" de Brecht.

New Teeth for an Old Shark

Vittorio Felaco

In the history of any art form certain events and persons take on such importance as to mark a watershed separating a before and after that can never be ignored by subsequent practitioners and observers. Brecht has played this role in the history of the Western stage; for the last fifty years, every serious theatre person has had to acknowledge his presence and contribution.

This truism, however, is followed by an equally compelling and valid one: Eventually, no substantial progress beyond Brecht can be made until his presence is thoroughly assimilated into the historical tradition and allowed to bring forth new developments. "After Brecht" must therefore be followed by "Beyond Brecht," a necessity that goes beyond the development of the poetics of theatre.

One theatre group that has posed itself the task of discovering what "Beyond Brecht" entails is the Compagnia Dario Fo-Franca Rame. Their theatre has sought not only to apply the lesson of Brecht to their activities, but also to explore where "Beyond Brecht" may lead us.

Our purpose, therefore, in attempting to define their work as an uncompromising dedication to the truest and most effective tenets of theatre, aims also at demonstrating the range and the parameters of their solution to the program that "Beyond Brecht" proposes.

On the theatre of Dario Fo and Franca Rame, there is a wide range of contrasting and often contradictory opinions and evaluations. But in general, in Italy, their theatre attracts far more spectators than all the combined resident theatres. Some of the shows have been viewed by an estimated twenty-five million spectators on Italian television. Dario Fo's works are presented by a number of different theatre groups and directors

57

with a great deal of success. This phenomenon is rather uncommon for a living Italian playwright. Not even the great Eduardo De Fillippo can boast such widespread appeal.[1]

In Europe, in the United States and in Canada, Dario Fo and Franca Rame are the most frequently represented authors of the contemporary Italian stage. In the West End of London *Accidental Death of an Anarchist* (1970) and *Can't Pay, Won't Pay* (1978) have been playing to packed audiences for over two years. The French are also avid importers of the theatre of the Italian couple, and major French critics, such as Bernard Dort, have been supporting their efforts to develop a new form of theatre more responsive to the needs and aspirations of people outside the regular circuit of the established theatre. Their works are translated into a number of languages and included in various journals and anthologies.[2]

However, neither the authorities nor the critics have been kind towards the theatre couple from Milan. Dario and Franca have faced prison, physical violence from rightist, neo-fascist groups, alienation from the regular circuits of the theatre, have been dragged through the courts and lost a major suit. The problem is that Italian authorities have historically been too intolerant, when they have not altogether acted within fascist parameters and guidelines, and the critics have not learned to differentiate between the actors/authors and the political activists. Overall, Dario and Franca have won incredible victories, as they embody the concentration of too much talent to be neglected or disregarded by affixing to them the label of "political theatre."[3]

In "Una testimonianza di Franca Rame," now prefaced to one of the many volumes of *Le commedie di Dario Fo* (Torino: Einaudi, 1975), and available in English in the volume *We Can't Pay, We Won't Pay* (London: Pluto Plays, 1980), Franca tells the story of her company's debut at the Community Center of Sant'Egidio, in the suburbs of Cesena. The company was called Nuova Scena at the time, and was still affiliated with ARCI, the Communist Entertainment and Recreational Organization. It was 1967 and the spirit of that now distant and mythical 1968, year of revolts and reforms almost everywhere in the west, was certainly in the air. Having abandoned the regular circuits of the Ente Teatrale Italiano, the group sought to bring the theatre to those segments of the population that hardly ever went to the theatre and to those who had never seen a live performance before.

The group—Franca Rame recalls—moved into the community center amidst the skepticism of the members of the center who continued with their card games, their billiards and their unending discussions and pastimes. The actors and actresses, aided by a small team of workers and students, all volunteers at ARCI, began to set up their stage. The distrust of the bystanders was obvious. After all, they were in the eyes of these proletarians another group of intellectuals afflicted of populism, once again advocating a move toward the people, out to gain another little meritorious medal, and then move on again to bigger and better things. But as both actors and actresses began the hard work of installing the heavy pipes that sustain the frame and the reflectors, etc., the community center members began to look on with surprise; could it be that these men and women were different?

After a while the group ran into a very difficult problem. Despite all the work they had already done, the acoustics of the hall were still inadequate. It was decided that Franca and another actress should make panels by sewing together a whole bunch of egg cartons to a wooden frame. They went to their task with eagerness but, alas, with a naive lack of preparation. They were using small upholstery needles. Before long they were surrounded by a group of club members who had stopped whatever they were doing to watch intently. As if to himself one man suggested that longer needles would certainly be much better. Another, still thinking out loud, said he could make some out of bicycle tire wires. Another told him to go quickly and get some. Before long the whole community group was involved in the activities of the theatre company, and not just in setting the stage, but also in helping the actors decide what would make the play work better. Later they followed the company to other community centers helping in a number of ways.

In that first year Dario Fo and Franca Rame played in more than eighty community centers, in covered make-shift structures, in factories, in community cinemas, and even some theatres. They recited before more than 200,000 spectators, 70% of whom had never seen a performance before. In the discussion that followed most of the shows, they learned not only the themes and the stories that were important to the people, but, above all, the language, more direct, devoid of any false glitter and sophistry. They were able to verify the great truth expressed by Brecht when he said, as Franca Rame recalls it, "The people can say deep and complex things with simplicity; the populists, who come down from their height to write for the people, say with great simplicity things that are empty and banal."

Perhaps it is the popularity of Dario Fo's and Franca Rame's theatre that disturbs some critics, the authorities, and, more recently, even the very heirs of Bertolt Brecht at the Berliner Ensemble.[4] How much popularity will the established theatre of the left or the right withstand? What level of informality (or even vulgarity) and improvisation will it permit? These are no idle questions when it comes to Dario Fo and Franca Rame. In an age that has largely banned from the formal theatre experience of western people Commedia dell'arte crudity, slapstick and improvisation, and thus the whole tradition of low-brow forms of entertainment, it is most difficult even to appreciate the significance of the problem. Having delegated such "trade entertainment" to the music hall, it is much too easy for us to dismiss the whole problem in the name of a concept of "poetry" that is bound to fail to set the issue right.

Yet the issue is not one that lacks significant input. The inexcusable and undemocratic differentiations that society continues to make between low-brow and high-brow forms of entertainment recall the interventions of such diverse critical and artistic personalities as T. S. Eliot and Antonio Gramsci, the brilliant Italian thinker, whose expertise on theatre is still little known outside of Italy. For T. S. Eliot the opportunity presented itself when discussing in *The Sacred Wood* (1920) the changing appreciation of poetic drama. For Gramsci it was a more direct intervention on a type of theatre that had, potentially at least, more popular appeal. In so doing they both reached a similar conclusion that when it comes to truly "poetic" dramatic art, the pendulum would do better to swing toward the popular music hall comedian. T. S. Eliot puts it thus:

> Possibly the majority of attempts to confect a poetic drama have begun at the wrong end; they have aimed at the small public which wants poetry. . . . The Elizabethan drama was aimed at the public which wanted entertainment of a crude sort, but would stand a good deal of poetry. Our problem should be to take a form of entertainment, and subject it to the process which would leave it a form of art. Perhaps the music hall comedian is the best material.[5]

From his part Antonio Gramsci took such a polemical position against the worst kind of pseudointellectual, morally rigid and insincere theatre, that he ended up signifying his disapproval by giving a real panegyric to a form of theatre which he considered pure mechanical device, the *pochade*. Writing on January 22, 1916, Gramsci, like T. S. Eliot, sees the renewal of theatre coming from the popular forms of communications where spontaneity and sincerity rule, and where pretense and deceit are done away with:

> Thus I must make this confession: I love the pochade and I enjoy myself immensely listening to it. I know its defects, I know its tricks and its machinations, I can foresee almost from the first act where it will lead, but I feel, precisely for that, safe from the deceits, the nasty tricks of serious art. The big names that make the big, fancy public run to the great, expensive theatres, scare me and fill me with apprehension. . . . That's why I prefer the pochade. I consider it more hygienic for my nerves. Between the *Falena* of Bataille, or *The Strong Woman* of Sardou and *La Dame de chez Maxim* I prefer

the latter, which has no pretensions, and does not hide its superficiality and impudence.[6]

But what is popularity? How have Dario Fo and Franca Rame achieved it within the confines of contemporary taste for dramatic art? For them popularity cannot be divorced from the correct ideological posture of each theatre piece. They are not Hollywood stars whose popularity comes out of a public relations can, and must be constantly fed with another "scandal." It is not just the cleverness of the actors that can account for the popularity of the theatre. Dario and Franca insist that can tire the public. It is rather the overall ideological message in which the public identifies its own condition, and recognizes the relevance of the theatre to life, without seeing the level of entertainment diminish.[7]

From the earliest radio monologues of the Poer Nano, Dario Fo has always displayed a talent for the polemic and the derisive. In those distant monologues of the late fifties he was always offering the "other side of the story." This dedication to counterculture and information combine in his theatre with one of the greatest mimic talents of our century. Not everything, of course, can be explained this way, for Franca Rame and Dario Fo have a vision of post-Brechtian theatre that affirms the absolute necessity of theatre, a situational concept of entertainment totally integrated with all other aspects of society and life. Such a vision of theatre resists, at least initially, any stylistic analysis, such as the study of irony and satire may suggest; for in true Brechtian tradition, Fo's *spectacles* reject the easy classifications of its techniques.

Today after more than forty highly successful shows, the work of Dario Fo and Franca Rame can be seen as conceived, written and staged according to a manual of true post-Brechtian theatre. However, they are no mere epigones of the great German master, but are an unusually inventive, imaginative and resourceful team, a theatre couple that embodies not only the very spirit of the epic theatre but one that has expanded and broadened the concepts of Brecht. What Brecht began to envision as a new theatre—non-aristotelian, anti-naturalistic, different from the normal tenets of conventional dramaturgy—Dario Fo and Franca Rame have developed not only to its most logical conclusion, but—and this is much more important—to the conclusions that the theatre and the community themselves wished and achieved by themselves.

For nearly thirty years Dario Fo and Franca Rame have constantly sought to make theatre relevant to the people for whom it is meant, and to give it the political and social structures that it needs to reach the millions of people who are left outside of the established theatre for whatever reasons. This goal of the theatre is not just another expedient, but a "necessity" that looms gigantically at the root of any democracy. After a number of years of participation in the regular circuits of the established Italian theatre, during which they considered themselves the "giullari della borghesia," the couple chose to become the "giullari del popolo." But this was no sudden conversion. The switch was totally consistent with their original tendency of giving to the theatre a sense of cultural independence separate from the traditional and conventional tenets of contemporary dramaturgy.

The decision, of course, coincides with the late arrival in Italy of a new sensibility in theatre poetics. This new sensibility was generated by the decision of the then recently founded Piccolo Teatro di Milano to embark on a rejuvenation of Italian (prose) theatre culture through the works of Brecht. Dario Fo had worked and collaborated with the internationally known director Giorgio Strehler. It was at the time of Strehler's representation of Brecht's *Galileo,* that Fo put together his own, similarly structured and conceived play *Isabella, tre caravelle e un cacciaballe.* The story of the intellectual in the presence of the authorities, political or ecclesiastical, focuses, in the play by Fo, on Christopher Columbus, rather than Galileo. The play exploits Columbus's condemnation after being forced to recite a forbidden text by Rojas, the black beast of the power structure, and author of the *Celestina,* Dario tells us.[8]

At another time, writing against a classical background in a Brechtian manner, Dario Fo and Franca Rame sought to refute the popular perception of Aristophanes as a feminist playwright *ante-litteram.* By staging in *Lysistrata* a near take over of leadership by Greek women, Aristophanes is not trying to bring about more equitable and just rapport between the sexes—Dario Fo insists—on the contrary, his aim is to bring about, through the technique of catharsis, the total reversal of the movement and the return of the status quo, which the incipient feminist movement of communism risked to destroy.[9]

New as this is, a significant tradition of theatre based on the tenet of representation of a particular situation and staged without manipulative intentions has always existed. Here one of Fo's favorite examples is Ruzante. In an attempt to recapture the essence and the spirit of his popular Italian predecessors Dario Fo relies enormously on the personal gift that he has of being the greatest mime of the century, whose skills and achievements have been compared to those of Chaplin.[10]

In this "situational" theatre to achieve an opening on reality and preparation to action, there should be no manipulation of the spectator. The situation must be truly a metaphor of the reality surrounding the viewer, but the representation cannot be "rigged" to arouse the spectator to this or that particular action, but to action as the outcome of knowledge and rationalization. Thus when Dario Fo and Franca Rame speak of revolt, they are not calling for violence in the streets, or bloodshed, but for the systematic and orderly evolution of society and the state in which free institutions become more sensitive to the needs of all, and quite apart from the conventional tenets of the politics of the right or the left.

The ties which connect the theatre of Franca Rame and Dario Fo to Bertolt Brecht are by now obvious. It was Brecht who first and systematically defined the differences between traditional theatre as he encountered it and the new epic theatre as he came to formulate it. In his well known notes on *Mahagonny*, Brecht sought to differentiate between dramatic theatre and epic theatre. Not by accident his first distinction is between the concept of plot and narrative and the last differentiation concerns reason and feeling.[11]

At the very center of the distinction is the concept of man and his perception. In traditional theatre the spectator is totally implicated, as the capacity for action is worn down, preserves his own instincts, is himself unalterable. The story totally manipulates the spectator with a plot that emphasizes the continuity of all its frames, scenes, acts. The dramatic play has a linear and evolutionary development. The eyes of the spectator are fixed on the finish as they share the entire experience.

The most significant difference here is that in epic theatre theory people are viewed as being in flux, as creatures capable of altering the reality around them, and themselves subject to change. This change is brought about by reason. In Franca Rame's and Dario Fo's theatre all representations have two acts, some three, very few more, and some are one long performance, but all end by giving the audience an opportunity for reactions, rebuttals and clarifications. At times these encounters become themselves a sort of theatrical activity.

One favorite criticism of this sort of theatre is, of course, to call it "political," as though this were a negative factor in the theatre. Dario Fo and Franca Rame object to this label and correctly point out that theatre is always political, even when it claims no direct *engagement*, for in that case it tends to make the spectator forget the civic aspect of the stage and the play in which he is participating. Soliciting detachment from the problems of every day existence is one way in which conventional theatre tries to make the spectator dwell only on the superficial and innocuous vices of society.[12] The state and the regular theatre circuits have been guilty of precisely this kind of political game in relationship to the Milanese couple.

For Franca and Dario, true theatre is an ideological comedy. Diderot, Fo insists, is the best example of a writer who develops his own comical discourse by poking fun at the state and its instruments of repression. (Should we call Diderot's work political theatre?) The correct form of theatre for our generation, Fo says, starts from the tragedy of our present situation. Echoing Brecht, he insists that the use of allegory marks the end of any "involvement with reality" because allegory begins by breaking down things, the real, in order to reach the "paradox." Thus allegory can only offer us a kind of "sub-reality."

How can one test the validity of this sort of theatre? The ultimate test is with the public and with oneself. A series of appropriate questions are sufficient to assure the meaning of such theatre. Does it offer an alternative form of entertainment? Is it done with originality, with enjoyment, with the kind of value that we continue to expect from "play" and—above all—does it hold to something positive, rather than flee, escape, hide from reality? For we must refuse—Fo says—to succumb to terror which the power structure wishes to instill in us, and in all those who wish to "fly" like Icarus, that is to say to place oneself outside of the rules of the game.[13]

In this it is easy to see a reference to the sort of cultural revolution that has swept Italy for years. The Italians may have understood the concept of the necessity of the theatre far better than many other people. Elsewhere I have insisted that Dario Fo and Giuliano Scabia, though in very distinct styles, have understood and remained faithful to the concept of a necessary theatre. Giuliano Scabia, reviewing a congress on Brecht held in Florence in April of 1971, reminds us of Alfredo Giuliani's most pertinent question: "A cosa serve la poesia?" (What use does poetry have?), and most appropriate answer: Of poetry one must know how to make use. Similarly Giuliano Scabia says, "one must know how to make use of theatre.[14]

While allegory is out and cannot be considered a valuable mode of translating reality on the stage, the metaphor is, instead, a most useful tool of theatre communication, along with the parable and the farce. Many plays of Franca Rame and Dario Fo revolve around a central metaphor: power, struggle, survival, hope, delegation of power, counterinformation. The message is always positive and directed to the audience for which it is meant. At the most abstract metaphorical level are plays such as *The Story of the Tiger* and *Daedalus and Icarus,* which deal with the central theme of delegation of power and with "flying" outside of the labyrinth (even if it is one created and constructed by ourselves) as a visual metaphor for getting out of the rules of the game.

The Tiger is a Chinese soldier story that Dario, supposedly, brought back from his visit in China in the early seventies. A guerrilla soldier fatally wounded by Chiang Kai-shek's army asks his friends to leave him behind, so as not to slow down their retreat. The arrival of a tiger and her cub makes him faint from fear; but when he awakens he finds himself in a cave where the tiger has begun to nurse him back to health.

The story may sound Chinese, but it is nothing but a modern version of the She-wolf story, and of course it invites the spectator to reconsider the very foundation of Western history with its orientation on direct confrontation and personal involvement. The story of Daedalus and Icarus would appear to stage counterinformation plots similar to the ones of the early days of the Poer Nano radio monologues. The intellectual (Daedalus, architect and inventor) with the help of his son realizes how he has been terribly used to make a labyrinth that the state is now using to imprison and torture. Fortunately the intellectual has one more weapon: the art to make his wings and fly away to place himself outside the rules of the game. Dario Fo narrates the whole text in both of these plays as he had done in *Mistero buffo.*

The majority of the plays are still in the category of those complex, carefully constructed and researched works that aim at combining the tragedies of contemporary life with a totally uninhibited and most entertaining *vis comica.* The best example of this type of work is still *Accidental Death of an Anarchist,* but others are: *Pum! Pum! Who Is It? . . . The Police,* and *They Have Kidnapped Fanfani.* The *Fanfani rapito* is a take off on the Aldo Moro kidnapping, and it tries to show who benefits the most from the uses of terrorism and violence.[15]

Accidental Death of an Anarchist, by far the most important and entertaining play by Dario Fo, revolves around the successful blending of historical data and the most hilarious and imaginative farce of a definite Italian stamp.

In early summer 1970, the editor Samona-Savelli published an extraordinary document called *La strage di stato* (*Slaughtered by the State*). The documents verified the innumerable suspicions that behind the alleged bank bombings in Milan, and the assassination of Pinelli (an anarchist unjustly accused of the crimes) there were incredible right wing plots aimed at destabilizing the Italian political and economic situation. In the fall of that year, Pio Bandelli and his organization "Lotta Continua" (Unending Struggle) were denounced by the Police chief Calabresi. La Comune saw this as an abuse of power and as one more factor in a pattern of continued repression and censorship by the State. La Comune began to initiate some research of their own into the illegal activities of the neo-fascist authorities.

A group of lawyers and journalists friendly to La Commune were eventually able to obtain some unpublished documents. Among these documents was the official decree by which the authorities had placed on file and eventually closed forever the whole Pinelli trial when the defendant was declared dead by accident. The ruling was finally proved incorrect, but the case has never been officially reopened and remains "unsolved."

Dario Fo's play, *Accidental Death of an Anarchist,* sets up a number of situations very close to the actual facts and assigns the task of unraveling them to a sort of mad inspector general capable of disguising himself as a number of characters, while the story unfolds as linear as a plumb line. The link to the United States is carefully indicated by tracing another historical event, the "accidental" death in 1921 of the Italian immigrant Salsedo, who allegedly "flew" from the window of a fourteenth floor police office. Eventually after a great deal of public pressure it was ascertained that the police had, not so gingerly, pushed Salsedo out of the window. This historical event disguises the central theme of the play. Dario Fo and Franca Rame were forced to stage it that December 1970 at La Comune headquarters on a subscription basis and as an event of a private club, and not as a public theatre performance in one of the many theatres of Milan. It would have been censored any other way.

Panorama's theatre critic, and one of Italy's most respected, Franco Quadri, says of *Death of an Anarchist:*

> It does not happen too often that we relive on one of our stages such disturbing current events, or indeed an Italian scandal still to be resolved. But to stage the Pinelli case, Dario Fo has had to use some extraterritorial rights of his private club, and to disguise the events as the transposition of a fact that really happened in New York in 1921. And that is not all, but the leading character, who imagines himself conducting the investigation, and to whom all the funniest and most violently provocative lines are given, is a mad mythomaniac, who has the craziest tendencies to disguise himself, and is monstrously impersonated by Fo himself. . . . With the help of this external character (a mad man dressed as a judge), Fo succeeds in doing and undoing over and over the mountain of accusations/investigations, destroying them with the powerful force of laughter. . . . [16]

In the end nothing is resolved and we are certainly far from the ideological clarity that one would expect. But, as is well known by now, Dario Fo and Franca Rame do not seek to manipulate the audience through catharsis, but rather wish to allow the impact of the message to sink in and enable the public to do what it must to change the reality it does not like.

Between these two kinds of theatre reduced to pure metaphorical, didactic device and the most hilarious *exposé,* there is a middle genre, that of *Mistero buffo* which seeks to find in the very roots of the rich Italian dialect tradition the energies and the will to bring people to a greater appreciation of what theatre means in the life of the individual and in the life of the nation. However, an analysis of this kind of intervention by the Milanese actor/playwright on the life of the Italian stage would require a separate chapter and goes well beyond the scope of our task.

On yet other occasions the energies and talents of the Compagnia Dario Fo Franca Rame have been challenged by existing texts for the theatre. Even then the intervention has aimed at the ideological and dramatic revamping of the text as a means of reaching the desired entertainment value. The first work of this category was Igor Stravinskij's *L'Histoire du Soldat* done by Fo for the famous Opera House La Scala in Milan.[17]

Similarly last December Dario Fo and Franca Rame staged *L'Opera dello sghignazzo* in which they blend together the *Beggar's Opera* of John Gay and Bertolt Brecht's *Threepenny Opera*. The Compagnia was invited by the Berliner Ensemble to stage *The Threepenny Opera* in East Berlin. The couple accepted and went to work on their project. Soon, however, their work came to odds with the Brecht heirs, namely Barbara Schall-Brecht, staunch guardian of her father's intellectual property. She objected to the changes the theatre couple wanted to make to the text by Brecht, while Fo insisted that he was doing no more to the Brechtian treasure than Brecht had done to the original John Gay opera. Rame and Fo then returned to Italy to stage their version there. In the words of *Der Spiegel* on the production:

> Dario Fo brushed off the nostalgic wickedness of the *Threepenny Opera* and made the shark, who had lost his teeth, bite again. His up-to-date Mack the Knife acts in a world of mass media and business crime; he is no longer the noble villain in his best suit, but a young, dynamic criminal, sitting behind a desk, whose face looks just like the faces of all these multinational salespersons. The Mack, who in the grand style production of the Turin "Teatro Stabile" was finally allowed to present himself, is a big business gigolo made in Italy, a cynic, but somehow likeable.
>
> He is the hero of a spectacle which has not very much to do with the Puritan theatre of Brecht, but a lot with a parody of a Broadway supershow: see-saws, sex-machines, revolving and suspended stages, acrobats as in a circus. Sure, the beggars are still begging, thieves are stealing, whores whoring, but their faces already show the death of irony and the boredom of an advanced industrial society: instead of a pub-like atmosphere there is bright neon light, instead of Weill-sound, there is a mixture of rock and cocktail bar music.[18]

The latest report from Italy indicates that, despite some losses on this the last venture of the Compagnia Dario Fo Franca Rame upon its return to the regular circuits of the Italian theatre, the play is a success and is slated to travel to Germany and Denmark sometime soon. Dario

Fo's and Franca Rame's career and this last staging demonstrate that the spirit of the Brechtian lesson has been thoroughly assimilated and continues to bring forth fruits. In the process the Milanese couple may just have succeeded in giving contemporary theatre, that old toothless shark, a new set of teeth.

Notes

1. A complete bibliography of the works of Dario Fo and Franca Rame is not available as of this date. A fair amount of bibliographic information is available in the following volumes: Chiara Valentini, *La storia di Fo* (Milano: Feltrinelli, 1977), pp. 181–196; Bent Holm, *Dem Omvendte Verden: Dario Fo og den folkelige fantasi* (n.p.: Drama, 1980), pp. 148–160; Helga Jungblut, *Das politische Theater Dario Fos* (Frankfurt/M.: Peter Lang, 1978), pp. 334–355. There are literally thousands of reviews of the performances of their theatre. The municipal Library in Milan has the most extensive file anywhere. For information on the staging of Dario Fo's work by other directors and theatre groups in Italy consult: Franco Quadri, *La politica del regista* (Milano Edizioni II Formichiere, 1980).

2. An old farce by Dario Fo appears also in a very recent reader, *Tempi moderni*, edited by Anna Chelotti Burney (New York: Holt, Rinehart and Winston, 1982). The Spring 1979 issue of *Theater* (the former *Yale Theater*) carries Suzanne Cowan's translation of *Accidental Death of an Anarchist*.

3. The relationship of the Italian couple with the U.S. consular authorities is in great need of clarification. I wish to take this opportunity to shed some light on it.

   In May 1980, Dario Fo and Franca Rame, together with their son Jacopo, and another member of their theatre group, were found ineligible for visas under Section 212(a) (28) of the Immigration and Nationality Act. According to a letter from the State Department, signed by J. Brian Atwood, Assistant Secretary for Congressional Relations, sent to Rhode Island Senator John H. Chafee and forwarded to me, "the ineligibility is based upon their membership in and activities with Soccorso Rosso (Red Aid), an organization which provides support for Italian terrorist groups."

   Dario Fo, Franca Rame and their theatre group had been invited to participate in the 5th Annual Italian Theatre Festival to be staged in May in New York and Baltimore. Members of the theatre community in this country and in other parts of the world, besides Italy, reacted quickly and emphatically to the denial by the American Consulate in Milan. The denial accentuated and exacerbated a long running antagonistic relationship between authorities and Italy's most loved and respected satirist and actor. "An Evening with Dario Fo," in which participated Arthur Miller, Richard Foreman, Lee Breuer, Martin Scorsese, Ellen Stewart, Joseph Chaikin, Bernard Malamud, Tom O'Horgan, Sol Yurick, and Eve Merriam among others, was sponsored by New York University. Richard Foreman seems to have spoken for the entire group when he stressed that the American theatre will not be able to learn to be more responsive to social needs and popular trends without the opportunity to see the very clever Italian actor-playwright and his talented actress wife.

   The protests of these and many other people aimed also at clarifying the nature of Soccorso Rosso and the kind of involvement that the theatre group La Comune, an independent Collettivo (Cooperative) directed by Dario Fo and Franca Rame, had exercised with it. According to Franca Rame, whom I interviewed in the summer of 1981 in Milan, Soccorso Rosso is barely an organization of any kind. It was a label given by some to the efforts of herself and a few other individuals who were filling a terrible void by lending assistance to prisoners in Italian jails. The group, like any other international assistance organization, does not and cannot discriminate on the basis of the political affiliation of the needy it seeks tó assist. Political, religious, moral and ethical orientations are not part of the philanthropic scope of the group of which Franca Rame is a primary figure. Franca Rame, who no longer has any party affiliation, belonged for many years to the Italian Communist Party, one may add, like the majority of Italian intellectuals and artists did at least till the early sixties. Since then the broadly leftist orientation of an outstanding poet like Montale who was otherwise reluctant to join any organization, is by far more common in Italy among intellectuals.

Dario Fo, on the contrary, despite his early affiliation with ARCI, the Communist entertainment and recreational organization, was never a card carrying member of the Communist Party, and broke away even from ARCI because of the overall revisionism of the Italian leftist parties and labor unions. Dario Fo, however, has not worked for Soccorso Rosso. Franca's activities revolve around hospital and prison visitation and letter writing to a number of prisoners.

In a country which, despite its excellent constitution, still holds on to a number of fascist laws and thus still makes no provision for bail, individuals can rot in jail for years, victims of overcrowded court calendars (something which is not peculiar to Italy). Soccorso Rosso simply seeks to help these people so that they may not altogether disappear, drowned in a sea of bureaucracy. But none of these things, one can be sure, was ever brought to the attention of the American authorities involved in making the visa decision for the theatre group.

Despite the immense progress made in Italy in the last few years (more changes are in the works right now), social assistance organizations are still terribly antiquated and too often overly dominated by the prevailing outreach of the Catholic Church, a sort of monopoly delegated to it by the Fascist government of Benito Mussolini in the Concordat of 1929 with the implicit promise, naturally, that such assistance would be handed out with careful pro-government orientation. Therefore there is a great need for such "secular" and "unofficial" sorts of outreach by concerned, but disinterested citizen groups. Things, of course, have changed from the time when Vittorio De Sica made the film *Bicycle Thief,* but the grotesque image that he gave of a rich, well-educated upper middle-class aiding the poor and the disinherited is still an all too vivid one.

4. For some background on the rapport Dario Fo/the Berliner Ensemble see the following: the interview with Enrico Pugnaletto in the November 1981 issue of the Italian monthly *Oggi,* pp. 124–127; *Der Spiegel,* December 7, 1981, p. 232; *L'Espresso,* January 10, 1982; *Panorama,* 20, No. 821, 12; *La Nazione,* December 8, 1981; *La Stampa,* December 8, 1981.

5. T. S. Eliot, *The Sacred Wood* (London: Methuen, 1960), p. 70.

6. Antonio Gramsci, *Sotto la mole,* quoted in Guido Davico Bonio, *Gramsci e il teatro* (Torino: Einaudi, 1971), pp. 71–72.

7. Interview with Dario Fo in *Playboy,* December 1974, reprinted in Lanfranco Binni, *Attento te . . . ! Il teatro politico di Dario Fo* (Verona: Bertani, 1975), pp. 383–399. A number of other similar texts appear in various volumes, too many to list here. Many interviews have been collected by Erminia Artese, in the volume *Dario Fo parla di Dario Fo* (Cosenza: Lerici, 1977).

8. The statement appears, among other places, in the interview with Luigi Ballerini in *Drama Review,* 22, No. 1 (1978). The whole issue is on Italian theatre; Fo's statement appears expanded in the *Playboy* interview, mentioned above, and in the volume edited by Erminia Artese.

9. *Drama Review,* op. cit.; and Dario's preface to *Il teatro politico di Dario Fo* (Milano: Mazzotta, 1977).

10. The earliest reference to Dario Fo, heir of Chaplin, belongs to Bruno Argenziano, *Sipario,* January 1963, pp. 20–21.

11. John Willett (ed.), *Brecht on Theatre* (New York: Hill and Wang, 1978), p. 37.

12. For many of these ideas I have sought to summarize and synthesize a wealth of materials that would require too much space to cite here. The reader can trace the various discussions on popular theatre in the following texts: *Ci ragiono e canto,* I

(Verona: Bartani, 1966), II (1972) and III (1973); Lanfranco Binni, *Attento te . . . !*, op. cit.; *Il teatro politico di Dario Fo*, op. cit.; "Teatro di situazione uguale teatro popolare," *Sipario*, No. 300 (1971), p. 43; Cesare Molinari, "Sul teatro popolare italiano," *Biblioteca teatrale*, No. 12 (1975) and No. 17 (1976); and Erminia Artese (ed.), op. cit.; as well as a number of other interviews too numerous to list. Dario Fo caused quite an uproar in Italy when he published his interpretation of "Rosa fresca aulentissima," a well known *Contrasto* by the thirteenth century poet Cielo (Ciullo) D'Alcamo. A great number of scholars intervened both in defense of and against Fo's interpretation. Fo's arguments can be read in the volume *Mistero buffo* (Verona: Bertani, 1974), now also available in the Einaudi series *Gli Struzzi* in which most of Fo's works have appeared, and in a number of other editions and collections. The discussion centered on whether the *contrasto* (a sort of theatrical dialogue made up of satirical and pungent retorts) was indeed of popular or aristocratic origin. Without attempting to settle the issue, what is truly important, and often overlooked by the critics, is this, that if a comic actor, a mime of the caliber of Dario Fo, whose popular roots are well-known, and whose artistic orientation is, likewise, deeply rooted in the popular tradition, recognizes the text as one of his, and makes it do on the stage what the text may have done in the 1300's, then perhaps we must give credence to what he says. That Dario Fo is not abusing the text in any way, we can be sure. Elsewhere I have discussed Fo's kind of intervention on the theatrical texts and cited the authoritative social anthropologist, Alberto Cirese, who affirms the validity of the comedian's contribution to the theatre.

13. The text of *Dedalo e Icaro* is available in the volume *Storia della tigre e altre storie*, a cura di Franca Rame e Arturo Corso, (Milano: Edizione La Comune, 1980).

14. For these and other pertinent remarks I recommend the Spring 1971 issue of *Biblioteca teatrale*.

15. Dario Fo, "Due note sulla rappresentazione," in *Morte accidentale di un anarchico* (Torino: Einaudi, 1974), pp. 111–118; the English translation by Suzanne Cowan appeared in *Theater*, op. cit.; *Pum! Pum! Chi e? La polizia!* (Verona: Bertani, 1974); and *Il Fanfani rapito* (Verona: Bertani, 1976).

    On the subject of violence and terrorism let us consider a text published by Dario Fo before the visa incident and translated in *Semiotext (e)*, 3, No. 3 (1980), 214–216; the whole issue is entitled "Italy: Autonomia." In this article Dario Fo, after "reciting" Clytemnestra's invective against power (the Italian word *potere* also translates *authority*, the *state*), affirms unequivocally his opposition against violence and terrorism because they are the very tools of the power structure of the state:

> Terrorism never destabilizes the established rule; rather it strengthens it, since it destabilizes the opposition (even when the opposition is most moderate) which is thus forced, in order to avoid being suspiciously drawn in as a cover to terrorism, to accept, support and allow those laws and those uncontrollable, violent acts which will in fact be used against citizens and workers (and their class struggle), not to mention the spontaneous movement of those who have been deceived.

> Terrorism works to "disguise" the real issues and reduces any discourse to the formula "there is need to establish order, no matter what the cost." The cost is always the sacrifice of democracy and the rights of the people.

> Those in power have no interest in seriously fighting terrorism with any determination, by coinvolving, on the democratic plane, the responsible presence of the citizens; this would mean taking away the basic motivations that constitute it, that give a space for action and a consensus, especially among the "emarginated" and the hopeless, those who have no real prospects. . . . [Just as] power has no real interest in reorganizing (in a controlled, more efficient and democratic form) the police, but prefers to delegate everything to a super-cop (in Italy Gen. Dalla Chiesa) giving him *carte blanche* so that the big shots may be brought to justice,

similarly, Fo charges that the party in power—that is to say the state—prefers the "sandstorm" method to real solutions:

> What interests those in power is the spectacle and the emotional participation of the spectator citizen in a continuous merry-go-round of bombastic facts, much like a television mystery where everyone is suspect, everyone is the murderer—the accomplice—the investigator—the terrorist—the right-hand man; even if it cannot be proved that he or she is guilty, anymore, nobody is ever left innocent.

This way the state sets itself up as the only righteous force, the only organization endowed with a sense of fairness and self discipline, while it "has the free rein in this pot-shot scene: leaking news, making inferences." Finally Fo notes that this is a very old game, one that Machiavelli unmasked in 1589 in his *Discourses.*

16. Franco Quadri, *La politica del regista,* op. cit., p.216. This book in two volumes brings together a number of short reviews by the prolific critic of *Panorama.* The title is noteworthy in that it validates, in a way, what we have been implying, that the adjective *politico* (. . . *ci,* . . . *ca,* . . . *che,* as the various gender and number spellings require) and the noun *politica,* besides being overused presently in Italian, have come to have a number of other meanings. Here the word *politica* would have to be translated as the "work," "activity," "trade" of the director. Its use approximates the English usage of the "politics" of writing, of medicine, of the university, etc. One would hope that perhaps this way we will have learned not to be scared by words, but to try to understand them.

17. *La storia di un soldato* di Dario Fo, photography by Silvia Lelli Masotti, with an introductory essay by Ugo Volli, (Milano: Electa Editrice, 1979).

18. *Der Spiegel,* op. cit.; for the translation of this text I am very grateful to Uwe Hartung for his excellent and valuable collaboration.

Fo's *L'opera dello sghignazzio* demonstrates the kind of *aggiornamento* of the text of which we spoke earlier. *Sghignazzio* means making fun of situations and people, as a way of dealing with a most unpleasant situation. Thus even the title shows the significant attempt to update the masterpiece by Gay and Brecht. It denotes a theatre piece dynamically irreverent and funny (according to most critics) and capable of placing the spectator truly in a position similar to the one in which the audience must have been when Gay and Brecht originally staged their works.

For this timely return to the regular circuits of the Italian theatre, Dario Fo and Franca Rame have also brought back the collaboration of the musician with whom they have always had great success, Fiorenzo Carpi, even if his best genre is not rock.

Rustom Bharucha. "Beyond Brecht: Political Theatre in Calcutta."

The lively political theatre of Calcutta is rooted deep in the cultural life of the city. Rustom Bharucha presents the work of the two leading theatre practitioners of Calcutta: Utpal Dutt with his spectacular and entertaining and massively popular theatre actively dedicated to the revolutionary change of political relationships and the theatre of Badal Sircar, whose avant-garde theatre appeals to the individual conscience of the members of his usually small middle-class audiences. The general problem of the political theatre in Calcutta is the question of understandability. This shows itself not only with certain plays of Dutt which politicize the traditional *jatra* play form, but also shows up in attempts to win over Bengali audiences to Brecht's plays. The distance between the realities of Calcutta and the world depicted even in those plays of Brecht that have been adapted for Calcutta is so great that it destroys the original political content of Brecht's plays and damns the plays to become trivial. The political theatre of Bengal must find its own relevant form. It must produce its own plays and, finally, must integrate the population, particularly the rural population, in its political theatrical work.

Rustom Bharucha. "Jenseits von Brecht: Politisches Theater in Kalkutta."

Kalkuttas lebendiges politisches Theater ist tief in der Kultur dieser Stadt verwurzelt. Rustom Bharucha stellt die beiden bedeutendsten Theatermacher Kalkuttas vor: Utpal Dutt mit seinem spektakulären, unterhaltsamen Massentheater, das aktiv zur revolutionären Veränderung der politischen Verhältnisse beitragen will, und Badal Sircar, dessen Avantgarde-Theater sich an das Schuldbewußtsein jedes Einzelnen im gewöhnlich kleinen Publikum wendet. Das gemeinsame Problem des politischen Theaters in Kalkutta ist seine Verständlichkeit. Das zeigte sich sowohl bei einigen Stücken Dutts, die das traditionelle Genre *jatra* politisierten, wobei handlungsverfremdende Elemente nicht erhalten werden konnten, als auch bei Versuchen, Brecht für ein bengalisches Publikum zu gewinnen. Die Distanz zwischen der Realität Kalkuttas und den adaptierten Brecht-Stücken zerstört deren politischen Gehalt und verurteilt sie zur Bedeutungslosigkeit. Das politische Theater Bengalens muß seine eigene Form finden, eigene Stücke hervorbringen und schließlich das Volk, vor allem auch auf dem Lande, wirklich ins Theater integrieren.

Rustom Bharucha. "Après Brecht : le théâtre politique à Calcutta."

Le théâtre politique est profondément établi dans la vie culturelle de Calcutta. Rustom Bharucha présente le travail de deux metteurs-en-scène : Utpal Dutt, avec son théâtre spectaculaire, amusant et populaire, toujours consacré au changement révolutionnaire des rapports politiques, et Badal Sircar, dont le théâtre d'avant-garde est bien reçu des spectateurs bourgeois qui, quoique peu nombreux, suivent régulièrement son travail.

Le problème général du théâtre politique de Calcutta est une question de compréhensibilité. C'est évident, non seulement dans certaines pièces de Dutt où il essaie de politiser la dramaturgie traditionnelle du *jatra*, mais aussi dans ses tentatives de gagner les spectateurs bengalis au théâtre de Brecht. La distance entre la réalité sociale de Calcutta et celle du monde décrit dans les pièces de Brecht (adaptées pour Calcutta) est si grande qu'elle détruit le contenu politique original de l'oeuvre de Brecht et condamne ses pièces à la banalité.

Le théâtre politique du Bengale doit trouver sa propre forme. Il doit produire ses propres pièces et, enfin, il doit intégrer sa population, particulièrement la population rurale, dans se oeuvres politiques.

72

Beyond Brecht: Political Theatre in Calcutta

Rustom Bharucha

Ever since Rudyard Kipling envisioned Calcutta as the "City of Dreadful Night," there has been a tendency in the West to sensationalize the extremities of life in Calcutta. No one can deny that millions of people in this tortured city are denied the basic necessities of life. Children scavenging for food in garbage heaps, beggars lying on the streets, people hanging out of buses and trams . . . these are just some of the everyday "sights" of Calcutta. And yet, this city with eight and a half million people survives its chaos despite twenty thousand telephones perpetually out of order, an acute water shortage, and daily power cuts lasting six to eight hours. Its precarious equilibrium is sustained by an energy that can be felt not merely in the streets but in the theatres. In no part of the world is the connection between the life in the streets and the activity in the theatres more immediate. Theatre is not a mere recreation in Calcutta: it is integral to the life of the city.

After watching a play by Utpal Dutt or Badal Sircar—two of the most prominent theatre practitioners in Calcutta—one realizes that their theatres are strong enough to sustain the pressure of life in Calcutta: they *belong* to Calcutta. Though they relate to this city and its innumerable problems in radically different ways, they are both committed to Calcutta and its people with an intensity that transcends their differences. By examining the threatres of Dutt and Sircar, I hope to demonstrate that the political theatre in Calcutta is rooted in a particular milieu. In order to address the needs of a specific community, it has to use conventions, techniques and strategies that illuminate the contradictions and problems of this community. In addition, it has to use a language that stimulates this community to think and raise questions. Both Dutt and Sircar feel the necessity to create their own models of theatre based on their under-standing of the people. While they have been inspired by foreign models—Dutt has acknowledged his debt to Brecht, Piscator, and Okh-lopkov while Sircar has learned much from the American avant-garde theatre, notably *The Living Theatre* and *The Performance Group*—both men have incorporated these influences in their theatres which are fundamen-tally original in their modes of utterance and structure of performance.

There could not be two more fundamentally opposed practitioners of the Bengali theatre than Dutt and Sircar. Unlike Dutt who believes that the political theatre should be "epic" and reach thousands of workers, Sircar works on a much smaller scale for a predominantly middle-class audience. While Dutt strategically uses the conventions of the commercial theatre to preach "the revolutionary struggle of the people," Sircar deliberately works outside the commercial theatre frame-work in order to maintain his integrity as an artist. While Dutt ha-rangues his audience and hypnotizes them with slogans, songs, proletar-ian rhetoric, and spectacular stage devices, Sircar works with the barest minimum of effects and questions his audience quietly, urgently, and with total simplicity.

Perhaps the crucial difference between the two men concerns their understanding of "politics." Even though he may not always adhere to the party line, Dutt interprets his function as an artist according to Marxist-Leninist precepts. As an advocate of "revolutionary theatre," he believes that his theatre has to do more than *expose* the system that is responsible for the exploitation of the masses: it has to preach revolution in such a way that the *overthrow* of the system is an imminent possibility. While Dutt sees his theatre as a weapon in the struggle of the people, Sircar views his theatre in less militant terms. Without adhering to the rigors of the party line or to any specific political ideology, he makes his audience confront its indifference to the suffering of the oppressed people living in Calcutta and the rural areas of Bengal. By playing at once on the guilt and humanity of his spectators, Sircar advocates neither revolution nor the overthrow of the system, but a heightened awareness of the injustices in this world. All he demands from his audience is some responsibility for these injustices.

These significant differences between Dutt and Sircar indicate that there is no fixed model for the political theatre in Calcutta. It is somewhat merciful that the Bengali theatre has no figure like Zhdanov instituting rules and legislating interpretations about the "content" of political plays. Despite censorship difficulties, particularly during the Emergency Rule of Indira Gandhi, the Bengali theatre has been relatively free to comment on the political situation in India and the repressive policies of the Central Government in New Delhi. Compared to the rigors and sheer violence of the censorship in certain Latin American countries, the state of censorship in India, bothersome and occasionally asinine as it is, can be strategically circumvented by wily directors like Dutt. Sometimes the audiences come to the rescue of the political theatre in Calcutta. During the Emergency, for instance, they supported many underground plays that played to packed houses with no publicity whatsoever. And, on three occasions, they literally "protected" Dutt's actors when they performed *Duswapner Nagari* (Nightmare City) by barricading the theatre and preventing the police from stopping the performances.

The political theatre in Calcutta was not always free to say what it wanted to say. Early in the growth of the political theatre movement in Bengal, the Communist Party exerted considerable authority in matters concerning the ideology and subject matter of plays. But this authority lasted only so long as the Party existed as a unified body. Once it splintered into various factions, there were disagreements among the Marxists themselves about the integration of politics with the culture of the people. Despite this factionalism, however, one cannot deny the historical role of the I.P.T.A., the Indian People's Theatre Association supported by the Communist Party. Organized in the early 1940s, it co-ordinated the first national theatre movement in India that performed anti-fascist and anti-imperialist plays for the masses. Coinciding with the freedom movement in India the various branches of the I.P.T.A. improvised agit-prop plays on subjects such as police repression, colonialism, strikes, the food crisis, and most memorably, the Bengal Famine of 1943 which killed 5,000,000 people.[1] For the first time in the history of the Indian theatre, actors, directors, and audiences collectively discovered the inflammatory power of the theatre, which ceased to be a mere entertainment with some social and political significance: it became the very forum of the people.

When Dutt joined the Bengal unit of the I.P.T.A. in 1950, he discovered for the first time in his career the intensity and tumultuous excitement of the "people's theatre" in India. After performing in traditional Shakespearean productions for an English-speaking audience, it was an intoxicating experience for him to face 20,000 workers in a field or a street. The open space, the mobility of the performances, the exchanges with the audience, the rough immediacy of the acting, the singing of the Internationale, the possibility of police intervention, the tension in the

75

air—all these elements contributed to a theatrical experience that was unlike anything Dutt had imagined.

Pathnatika

It was at the I.P.T.A. that Dutt first explored the form of the *pathnatika* (street corner play) that was used to dramatize immediate issues such as the imprisonment of Communist leaders. Dutt discovered that this most naive and rough form of political theatre was also the most effective medium of propaganda. He also realized that a *pathnatika* is not simply an illustration of a political message: it is a theatrical activity that incorporates particular strategies and modes of communication. It is potentially effective only insofar as it is theatrically immediate.[2]

Though Dutt's association with the I.P.T.A. was enlightening, it was not without problems. He was a member for only ten months before he was blacklisted by the more doctrinaire members of the Party. Dutt left the I.P.T.A. dismissing plays that religiously follow the party line where the hero is inevitably presented as a "superhuman Captain Marvel." Not only does the perfect proletarian hero falsely evoke a utopian world where everything works with clockwork efficiency, he etherealizes communism by mouthing pious platitudes and projecting "oversimplified, anemic, spiritless symbols of revolution."[3] Such a hero succeeds only in numbing an audience into a kind of blind, self-righteous submission.

Dutt's opposition to the doctrinaire policies of the I.P.T.A. shaped one of his fundamental beliefs about political theatre, namely, its reliance on *entertainment,* the noblest of functions in the theatre, once described by Brecht as that "business which always gives (theatre) its particular dignity." Dutt realized that lectures on dialectical materialism and sermons on illustrious comrades merely isolated a working-class audience who were prepared to see their imperfections reflected on stage. At the same time, this audience wanted to see its enemies—the sacrosanct figures of the ruling class—humiliated, lampooned, and ultimately, crushed on stage. Even in the most abstract plays of the I.P.T.A., Dutt was amazed to see how spontaneously the audiences responded when an oppressor came on stage—the money lender, the landlord, or the police officer. A villain, Dutt realized, was indispensable for a political play not only because he had to be crushed (thereby providing the play with a thrilling climax), but because he provoked the audience to jeer at him.

The audience is central to Dutt's conception of "revolutionary theatre." They loudly cheer the actions of his revolutionary heroes not unlike spectators at a football match or a commercial Hindi film (the most appealing form of mass entertainment in India). Dutt seriously believes that any theatre for a mass audience has to be magical in its presentation. It has to invigorate the workers with tempestuous action, violent deaths, and rousing songs. The action of the drama has to be played for all its worth with loud voices, extravagant gestures, bold expressions, assertive entrances, and thunderous exits. This theatre has no patience with nuances and subleties of characterization. It ignores rationales and motivations. It relies extensively on massive visual structures—iron girders, bridges, wagons, trains, factories, battleships—and stunning scenic effects such as workers drowning in a mine flooded with water, characters positioned behind cardboard cutouts, newspaper backdrops, immense shadows of Hitler gesticulating like a madman, and inevitably, the red flags and the hammer and sickle. In order to preach revolution, Dutt never fails to reiterate how necessary it is "to heighten the visual properties of the theatre to a point where the theatre itself casts a spell on the audience."[4]

The more fastidious among Dutt's critics complain that his theatre is too crude and simplistic to be taken seriously. The more enlightened assert that Dutt does not present his spectator with choices. By immersing them in a panorama of action, so compelling and sensational that it is impossible to resist, he seduces them into a blind acceptance of the spectacle. He does not permit them to *choose* how they can change their lives. He *dictates* their way of life. This criticism indicates the limitations of empathy in a theatre that claims to be "revolutionary." Whenever Dutt is questioned about the efficacy of his plays, he invariably stresses how loudly the audiences cheer the actions of his heroes. What needs to be stressed, however, is that there is a difference between merely striking a rapport with a dynamic hero and learning about revolution from him. Though one does not exclude the other, all too often one feels that Dutt's spectators cheer his heroes not because they validate any particular principle or ideology but because they stimulate the emotions of the audience on a visceral level.

Jatra

A very apt analogy to this empathetic relationship between Dutt's heroes and spectators can be found in the *jatra*—the quintessential folk opera of Bengal which originated in the religious processions of the Krishna movement inspired by Shri Chaitanya (A.D. 1485–1533).[5] What is riveting about a *jatra* performance is precisely the evocation of its atmosphere, so hectic and intoxicating, that it is impossible to resist. You are carried along in a *jatra* production by its endless murders and love scenes and machiavellian soliloquies and anguished scenes of repentance. According to Dutt, these actions move in a series of "convulsions." The very structure of *jatra* compels a spectator to submit to its violent momentum.

Dutt's contribution to the politicization of *jatra* is immense. He has a canny understanding of its mechanics and conventions. The rough trestle stage surrounded by an audience on all sides, the prominence of the musicians and the chorus, the absence of unnecessary props and technical devices, the flamboyant costumes: these are conditions of the theatre that stimulate an actor to *display* his histrionic talent. While these conditions are congenial to Dutt's sense of the theatre, he has compromised on certain conventions of *jatra,* yielding to his audience's demand for certain changes.

A *jatra* audience is notoriously assertive. There could be at least 20,000 workers from tea gardens, mines, and steel plants at a single performance. Since many of the workers have a workshift next morning, they do not have time (as their ancestors did in the nineteenth century) to watch twelve-hour *jatra* performances with over twenty-five songs. Apart from minimizing the number of songs, Dutt has to restrict the entrances of the *Vivek*—a Morality-like character, the conscience of *jatra,* who interrupts the narrative to comment on the action, externalize the emotions of the characters, and raise appropriate questions. By functioning in his own time-zone that clashes with the action of *jatra,* the *Vivek* operates like an alienation device in much the same way as the *juri*—another convention of the *jatra* that Dutt has attempted to revive.

It appears that in the second half of the nineteenth century, when *jatra* became increasingly dramatic, many actors were not employed because they could not sing. So the convention of the *juri* was introduced where musicians sang *on behalf of* the actors. Musicians became the "doubles" of actors. A character tossed the first line of a song to one of the singers and the chorus completed the song for him. This convention is intrinsically Brechtian in its interruption of stage action. The *juri* invariably functions as a jury. The musicians, dressed in long black coats and turbans, sit on stage through the performance and observe the action. At climactic moments, they stop the action and proceed to distance it by singing about it. After watching a murder, for instance, they can confront the villain and remind him, in no uncertain terms, that he will not be able to escape the consequences. At such moments, the *jatra* is transformed into a mock-trial where the *juri* function as judges and the spectators in the audience serve as witnesses.

It is interesting to speculate why the conventions of the *juri* and the *Vivek* no longer appeal to mass audiences in Bengal. Apart from the fact that they both rely on a surfeit of songs (which can be tedious), they blatantly impede the momentum of the action. They break the spell of the *jatra*. In this sense, they function as primitive Brechtian devices which direct an audience to view the action of a play more critically. This is intolerable for most Bengali spectators who demand *sustained* dramatic action with frequent climaxes. Reflecting on how fundamentally alien Brecht is to the people's theatre in Bengal, Dutt remarks that

> The Brechtian style interferes with our people's responses because they are used to another kind of theatre, and all forms must come from the people's understanding . . . As I understand it, epic structure advances the action to a certain point and then halts, cuts it entirely and proceeds with another episode, or with the same episode in a different light. This directly contradicts our people's expectations. They're accustomed to the dramatic atmosphere getting thicker and thicker, until it becomes almost unbearable.[6]

The Bengali Brecht

It is to Dutt's credit that he has consciously avoided staging Brecht's plays which are among the most popular and misconceived productions in the Bengali theatre. The problem with most Bengali adaptions of Brecht is their blatant commercialism, their synthetic creation of a theatre where the spectacle dominates the commentary, the co-ordination of the entire production resists the idea of interruption, and the music proves to be more appealing than the argument. This conversion of Brecht's parables into musical entertainments results in a politically reactionary theatre—a theatre totally unrelated to the contradictions that permeate the socioeconomic situation in Bengal. Instead of unsettling the bourgeois assumptions of life shared by a predominantly middle-class audience, the Bengali Brecht caters to these assumptions by providing a reassuring view of the world.

In a spirited adaptation of *The Threepenny Opera* entitled *Tin Poyshar Pala*, produced by a prominent Bengali theatre group *Nandikar* in 1969, there were many laughs, countless burlesque situations, hilarious songs with innuendos, and a consistently festive atmosphere. But, as Samik Bandyopadhyay, Calcutta's most astute theatre critic, impatiently points out, there was no connection between this production and the political situation in Bengal. Speaking to A. J. Gunawardana who interviewed him for *The Drama Review*, Bandyopadhyay says:

> When we in the Bengali theatre have a production of *The Threepenny Opera* which simply goes in for wild fun, we regard it as a compromise, a betrayal. This production has no point when there is serious political violence in Calcutta. When Macheath says, "This is your bourgeois society," people laugh.

They take it as a joke for that is the spirit of the entire production. And when I come out of the theatre, the life I live, the connections and associations to which I respond are very different from what I get in *Tin Poyshar Pala*. This is status quo theatre, which means nothing to a generation that thinks in political terms. This production makes us very angry, not merely unhappy.[7]

Bandyopadhyay's anger is justified. There is no reason to stage *The Threepenny Opera* as a farce since Brecht's examination of the bourgeois view of the world can be strategically adapted to highlight the corruption of traders and profiteers in Bengal. This adaptation is only possible if the Bengali actors are in a position to examine the attitudes towards money and property of Brecht's characters which determine their functions in the play. Unfortunately, *Nandikar's* actors romanticize Brecht's characters and transform their bourgeois vices into endearing characteristics. Macheath is played like a matinee idol whose manner is so engaging that one cannot believe that he is capable of opportunism and exploitation. Likewise, the Bengali Peachum unlike his German counterpart does not seem to regard human misery as a commodity: he is simply a patriarchal figure with a caustic sense of humor. His wife is a shrew, his daughter an ingenue, his employees a wretched lot of buffoons and innocuous villains. At no point in the production do the actors seem to criticize the attitudes and choices of their characters. They are too busy enjoying themselves in the roles of their characters and empathizing with their emotions.[8]

In a seminar on Brecht organized by the Max Muller Bhavan in Calcutta, Ajitesh Banerjee defended his production of *Tin Poyshar Pala* as an attempt to situate Brecht in a "Bengali experience." "Adaptation," he said, "is possible only when one knows one's own country. I would like to know Brecht through my own tradition. I am not interested in a German presentation of Brecht."[9] This is a legitimate point of view, but what does the Indianization of Brecht really signify? Does it simply imply an alteration of certain facts and a transformation of German characters into corresponding Bengali types? Or does it involve something more integral—an interpretation of the socio-political conditions in India in accordance with (or in contradiction to) the view of the world offered in Brecht's plays? At the moment, the Indianization of Brecht does not seem to go beyond an indiscriminate alteration of details and characters. It has yet to extend to that process of analysis by which Brecht can be reinterpreted according to the contradictions of the political situation in Bengal.

The remoteness of Brecht from the conditions of life in Bengal was most conspicuous in another Bengali production—the *Theatre Unit's* adaptation of *Arturo Ui* directed by Shekhar Chatterjee. Unanimously praised by the critics in Calcutta for his "authentic" productions of Brecht,

Chatterjee refuses to Indianize Brecht if he feels that the play does not lend itself to "local color." While he felt that the ironies of *Puntila* could be sustained in a Bengali adaptation (with a predominantly Bengali milieu and ambience), he was less sure that the study of fascism in *Arturo Ui* could be presented without the allegorical framework created by Brecht. His decision to retain the milieu of "Chicago" in his production was attacked by Utpal Dutt in a violently polemical article *Kabarkhana* (Cemetery) where Japenda, Dutt's alter ego and spokesperson for the political theatre in Bengal, criticizes the *Theatre Unit* production in no uncertain terms.

> Some dense illiterate intellectuals say that they are doing Brecht to introduce him to the local people. Such posturings do not convince anybody . . . *Arturo Ui's* symbolism will not be understood by the Bengali audiences. To show Indian fascism, why not choose an Indian background? Like Indira Gandhi as a Chambal dacoit? . . . What is the point of turning to Chicago, my friend, when you see everything at home? If you want to produce a Hitler-story for the Bengali audience, it must be more intelligible than the story in *Arturo Ui*.[10]

There is something to be learned from this pragmatic criticism of Japenda. Why should a Bengali production imitate the minutiae of gestures and movements of the actors in a Berliner Ensemble production of *Arturo Ui* when they relate so intrinsically to the conditions of life in Germany? It is true that Brecht himself advised his followers to "copy" models of his productions before proceeding to create their own. In an interview with E. A. Winds, he once remarked, "We must realize that copying is not so despicable as people think. It isn't the easy way out. It is no disgrace, but an art."[11] On a certain level, Shekhar Chatterjee is to be praised for "copying" Brecht with such artistry, but at the same time, he needs to question whether the Bengali theatre needs such perfect replicas of Brecht particularly at a time when the political situation in Bengal demands a more specific concentration on its problems, dissentions, and areas of corruption. It is ironic that Chatterjee claims that, "The value of Brecht lies in his concern for the exploited . . . He is relevant in a situation of hunger and starvation. He must be taken to the villages, to the masses."[12] This statement rings very hollow when one considers the sophistication of Chatterjee's Brecht productions which have never, to my mind, been performed for a rural audience. Villagers would not be able to grasp the significance of the Westernized techniques used in his plays. Perhaps, Chatterjee needs to acknowledge that "authentic" Brecht is something of a luxury in the Bengali theatre.

Though Dutt asserts that "the only *raison d'être* for doing Brecht is

81

to spread the revolutionary message in Bengal," it is significant that he has refrained from producing Brecht. He is aware that the political theatre in Bengal needs to create its own plays that relate directly to the political turmoil in the city. Not only has Dutt written plays for his group, the *People's Little Theatre,* on a number of topical issues such as elections, police brutality, terrorism, guerrilla warfare, the Naxalite movement, Party politics, strikes, he never fails to confront the political exigencies of Bengal even when he dramatizes seemingly "foreign" subject matter such as the Scottsborough Trial of 1931, the war in Vietnam, the Communist movement in Cuba, and the personal histories of Lenin and Stalin. For instance, when he dramatized the rise of the Nazi Party in Berlin, 1933, in his spectacular production *Barricade,* he ingeniously related the German political scene to immediate political events in Bengal, notably the rigging of the 1972 West Bengal State Elections by the Congress Party. Reacting to the discomfiture of the Congressmen, Dutt says:

> Somehow the Congressmen in Calcutta think that *Barricade* is a terrible insult to them. They even tried to break up a show of ours. I asked them, "Do you admit then that you rigged the election?" They said, "Certainly not." I said, "Why are you so furious then? We are only showing how the Nazis rigged the elections."[13]

Badal Sircar

This strategic use of political allegory is not to be found in the theatre of Badal Sircar. His group *Satabdi* asserts its political independence by resisting Party politics. Though its plays frequently deal with the false promises, hypocrisies, and the corruption of politicians, there are no specific references to the misdeeds of the Congress Party or the CPI(M) Party. Nor does Sircar contend that the problems of the people can be solved by the removal of "reactionary" elements within any particular party or, more extravagantly, by the overthrow of the "repressive forces" in the Central Government. His theatre does not attempt to be militant. Instead of advocating strikes, lock-outs, and the destruction of government property, it is content to disturb the consciousness of its spectators. One leaves a play by *Satabdi* acutely aware of the exploitation and injustices that pervade life in Calcutta and rural Bengal. Instead of exaggerating the threat of the exploiters and the callousness of the political leaders (which is what Dutt tends to do), Sircar focuses on the callousness of the middle class and their capacity to watch the suffering of the people without doing anything about it.

Despite his attack on the bourgeois values of his spectators and their innate selfishness, Sircar never fails to appeal to their humanity. Instead of advocating revolution with red flags and Marxist jargon, he urges them to feel more compassionately about the underprivileged people who have been denied the basic necessities of life. In this respect, Sircar represents a kind of radical humanism one associates with William Blake who believed that no revolution was possible in the social and political structure until men were prepared to break "the mind-forged manacles." If there is anything Sircar preaches to his spectators—he is the least dogmatic of thinkers in the Bengali theatre—it is the necessity of changing their lives before endeavouring to change the world.

When Sircar's actors confront the spectators, look them in the eyes, and tell them that in such and such village a man is dying because he has no means of subsistence and there is no one to help him, it is difficult to be indifferent to this fact. There is nothing to interfere with it—no spectacle, no obtrusive acting style, no melodrama. The spareness of Sircar's theatre is what makes it so effective: it compels the audience to concentrate on what the actors are saying. In this respect, the plays of *Satabdi* are more instructive than the "revolutionary" spectacles of the *People's Little Theatre* where the message is generally sensationalized, if not overwhelmed, by the proliferation of scenic effects, bursts of deafening music, and loud rhetorical passages.

Spartan in its simplicity, Sircar's theatre dispenses with almost all the accessories one associates with the commercial theatre—sets, lights, costumes, sound, and make-up. Most significantly, it takes place in a room that seats barely a hundred people. The eye-contact between *Satabdi's* audiences and actors facilitates a most immediate form of communication. Questions are directly addressed to individual spectators who are made to confront their indifference to particular issues. Unlike Dutt's "epic" productions where one tends to react with the crowd, Sircar's theatre is intimate enough to confront the spectators as individuals. Countering Dutt's proud assertions that he has performed for twenty thousand spectators at a time, one can legitimately ask: What does that prove? Is a political theatre more effective because it addresses thousands of people rather than a hundred? Are the loud cheers of a crowd more reliable indications that a play is making them think than the attentive silence of a few people? What is more important—the size of an audience or the impact of a play on the lives of people?

Apart from emphasizing the sheer size of his audiences, Dutt claims that his theatre reaches the working class while Sircar's theatre is too intellectual for the people. Such statements convey Dutt's assurance, even arrogance, that *he* knows what the people want. He needs to acknowledge, however, that there is more than one way of doing political theatre in Calcutta, and that the working class can respond to more "intellectual" theatre than *jatra* or the productions of the *People's Little Theatre*. It is true that Sircar's plays disregard commercial conventions of the Bengali theatre such as an episodic plot, consistent characters, farcical interludes, melodramatic gestures, and ornate diction. His plays can best be described as scenarios of gestures and images utilizing a fragmented script, a chorus of voices, doublings of "characters," stylized movement, and nonverbal acting techniques. While these conventions are undeniably innovative in the Bengali theatre, it is significant that they do not bewilder audiences in the working-class districts of Bengal and the villages of the Sunderbans where *Satabdi* has performed some of its plays. Recalling the enthusiastic reception to his somewhat abstract production of *Spartacus,* Sircar emphasizes that, "The people often understood the main points and spirit of the play more than the so-called urban intelligentsia."[14]

Significantly, the Spartacus in Sircar's production is neither a Roman warrior nor does he allude to any particular political leader in Bengal. He is represented as a *group* of slaves. All of Sircar's actors playing slaves in the production consititute the reality of Spartacus. There are no stars in *Satabdi.* Though Sircar is unquestionably the playwright and director of the group, he believes that theatre is essentially a communal creation, a process of learning that emerges from workshops, improvisations, and group discussions. In this respect, he is very different from Dutt who directs his plays like an impresario of the nineteenth-century theatre. His presence can be felt in the smallest detail of his *mise-en-scène.* Every grouping, every climax, every sound-cue is orchestrated by him. As for the acting style of the *People's Little Theatre,* it is well known that Dutt directs the gestures, movements, and voice-patterns of his actors with utmost rigor. Sircar gives his actors more freedom to question and shape their roles in his theatre. Even when he dominates the action of a particular play, he never exhibits any virtuosity as an artist. Nor does he, at any point, indulge in the kind of self-congratulatory righteousness one associates with advocates of the Poor Theatre.

It would have been very easy for Sircar to display his martyrdom as an artist in his one-man show called *Prastab* (Proposition). In this play, which voices the essential credo of *Satabdi,* the audience enters the room and sees Sircar spread-eagled on platforms that are shaped to form a "T." Ropes tied to his wrists and ankles are stretched to the four corners of the room. Three "sentries" holding a knife, a whip, and a gun respectively loom behind the still, corpse-like figure of Sircar. The "play" begins with Sircar asking the audience to look at an "obscene" picture that is concealed behind a screen in the room. Somewhat embarrassed, the audience moves to one end of the room to "peep" at the picture—a collage of bank notes and coins. When the spectators return to their seats, Sircar makes his *prastab* to abolish the "obscene" picture and the materialism that it represents. It all sounds somewhat trite. The "sentries" and three actors planted in the audience break out into raucous laughter. Once it subsides, Sircar begins his diatribe on the enslavement of human beings to money. His reasoning is very simple, very uncompromising, but one is compelled to respond to his words. They are spoken with a belief that demands attention. At the end of the speech, which is improvized from performance to performance, Sircar asks the audience to "release" him. Some of the spectators invariably untie the ropes from his wrists and ankles. At this moment, Sircar does not stand apart from his spectators like an enlightened guru. He is one with them.

Though Sircar maintains the distinction between spectators and actors, he orchestrates the actions of his plays in such a way that the audience becomes part of the *mise-en-scène*. His actors move around, between, and in front of the audience: they are juxtaposed against the bodies, backs, faces, and profiles of the spectators. In *Michil* (Procession), the proximity of the spectators and actors is palpable, particularly towards the end of the play when the actors enter the room singing about "the true procession—the procession that will show the way. The way home . . . the procession of men." As they sing with increasing resonance and volume, the actors move closer to the spectators who become part of the procession. The spectators and actors intermingle and the entire space of the room becomes a swirling mass of humanity. It is a moment that transcends the immediate issues of the play—police interference in everyday life, political hypocrisy, and middle-class ennui. It lingers long after the play ceases, compelling an audience to re-examine its relationship to men in their society and to problems in their everyday lives.

Sircar never fails to remind his spectators that they are responsible for the world they live in. Unlike most political playwrights who concentrate on familiar villains (the Super Powers, the C.I.A., neofascist organizations), Sircar is more concerned with the villains that exist *within* us, the repressive forces of our consciousness. Though he acknowledges the existence of an anonymous system of bureaucratic power that monitors calamities in the world, he also emphasizes the innate destructiveness of man and his indifference to other men. "The system alone is not responsible for the calamities in the world," Sircar seems to say, "*we* have to acknowledge our guilt for allowing such calamities to happen."

This is the thrust of his argument in *Tringsha Satabdi* (The Thirtieth Century), a play that dramatizes the calamity of Hiroshima—its organization and execution, its effect on the lives of the Japanese, and its significance in a world where nuclear threats and atomic pollution are becoming increasingly severe realities. In the form of a court-room drama interspersed with tableaux and documentary narratives, the play dramatizes the most devastating facts with utter candor and simplicity. Sircar speaks a language that illuminates the most problematic issues in life concerning human guilt and responsibility. As Samik Bandyopadhyay observes so astutely about *Tringsha Satabdi*, "Sircar manages to suggest the sheer size of the crisis and its aftermath and yet keep it within human dimensions, within individualized modes of suffering."[15]

The "human dimensions" in Sircar's plays are frequently created through juxtapositions of events that embody the contradictions and disparities of the socio-economic situations examined in the plays. For instance, in *Bhoma*, Sircar's most vigorous indictment of the urban bourgeoisie in Calcutta, the innate selfishness and insularity of middle-class residents of Calcutta are sharply juxtaposed with the destitute conditions of life in rural areas of Bengal like the Sunderbans. At one point in the play, an actor representing Bhoma, a villager from the Sunderbans, dies slowly and despairingly at one end of the room while a group of four actors watch an imaginary Hindi film with avid interest in the center of the room. When the cries of Bhoma become increasingly anguished, the "audience" watching the film begins to start shouting, "Stop interrupting the film." A moment later, a matinee idol appears on the screen and they begin to whistle. Bhoma continues to die at the other end of the room.

After watching this grotesque juxtaposition of events, Sircar's statement—*Manusher rakta thanda* (The blood of man is cold)—which has been repeated like a leitmotif through the play, acquires a terrifying significance. More powerfully than any production I have experienced in the Bengali theatre, *Bhoma* makes an audience confront its indifference to poverty. "Sights" like Bhoma are everyday presences in Calcutta. One cannot avoid seeing them. They are to be found everywhere like the garbage in the streets. One walks past them without feeling a twinge of guilt. Occasionally, when their clamor becomes obtrusive, one drops a few coins beside them on the pavement. But more often than not, one is more anxious to keep an appointment or reach the bus-stop on time. It is precisely this absorption in the minutiae of everyday life that Sircar attacks in *Bhoma*. Without lecturing us, he urges us, even demands from us, a recognition of our callousness.

Bhoma is so deeply affecting as a human experience that a play like *Gondi* (Circle)—Sircar's austere, yet lyrical, adaptation of *The Caucasian Chalk Circle*—seems almost inconsequential in comparison. Though the script is admirably spare and the transformation of Brecht's songs into choral recitatives is skillful, the production fails to raise questions, however subtle and tentative, that have some bearing on the lives of a Bengali middle-class audience. *Gondi* is curiously removed from the turbulence of life in Calcutta; it is apolitical and somewhat pointless. It proves that Sircar needs to continue creating his own plays if he wishes to confront his primary concern as an artist—the dichotomy between urban and rural life in Bengal. As much as there is to be learned from Brecht, one has to acknowledge that his plays do not ultimately address the contradictions and extremities of life in Calcutta and rural Bengal.

Towards a People's Theatre

The political theatre in Calcutta can only grow if it develops its own models and structures of performance. Though many theatre groups in Bengal function outside the commercial theatre framework in the tradition of Sircar, it is disheartening to realize that in a state where the vast majority of people live in rural areas, there is no theatre that involves the active participation of the people. Instead of merely performing plays *for* the people, it is time for *Satabdi,* the *People's Little Theatre,* and other theatre groups in Bengal to work actively *with* the people. No one stressed this fact more vehemently than Bijon Bhattacharya, one of the staunchest supporters of a people's theatre movement in Bengal. Towards the end of his life, he attended a seminar on political theatre in Calcutta where he expressed his despair about the limitations of an "urban" political theatre.

> I feel frustrated and insecure when I realize that we have not been able to take our work to the masses in the rural areas and that we have not been able to involve them in our work . . . I can only dream of a group of laborers playing themselves and destroying in the process all the familiar gestures and forms of our urban theatre. As long as we do not realize that dream, we can only play with faint shadows of life and reality. It is a shame to be estranged from the people and the truth that they embody.[16]

The Bengali theatre will continue to be essentially "estranged" from the people so long as it continues to perform for a predominantly urban audience, so long as it is reconciled to bourgeois actors from the city playing the suffering and oppression of the masses. It is true that the political theatre in Calcutta has produced innumerable plays where the people have been symbolized, deified, evoked, cheered, and warmly supported. The significance of the work of Dutt and Sircar has to be acknowledged. But what needs to be explored are forms of theatre where the people can confront their own oppression and speak freely of their grievances.[17] A true rapport with the people can only be achieved if the political theatre in Calcutta is willing to open itself to the immediate influence and participation of the people. Only then, perhaps, will Bijon Bhattacharya's "dream" of a people's theatre be realized.

Notes

1. The most significant play on the Bengal Famine was Bijon Bhattacharya's *Nabanna* (New Harvest) co-directed by the playwright and Sombhu Mitra for the Bengal unit of the I.P.T.A. in October 1944. Radical in form and content, terrifyingly honest in its depiction of suffering, and daringly innovative in its use of colloquial language and spare scenery, *Nabanna* is a landmark in the history of the Bengali theatre. It was the first Bengali play that succeeded in representing the destitution of villagers with realism and authentic feeling.

2. Dutt has continued to write and perform *pathnatikas* often extending them to full three-hour performances. For instance, in *Din Badaler Pala* (Play of Changing Times), a propagandist play written specifically in support of the 1967 Communist election campaign in West Bengal, the action is elaborate. Structured in the form of courtroom drama, it features a young Party worker who is accused of murdering a police officer during the food riots. Almost till the end of the play which lasts three hours, the audience is absolutely convinced of the worker's innocence when he proudly admits his "crime" during the cross-examination. Reversing the evidence against the worker had, in Dutt's words, a "double effect" on the audiences: "shock at the realization that the worker had been legally guilty all along, and thrill at the challenge thrown at the state machinery."

3. Interview with A. J. Gunawardana entitled "Theatre as Weapon" published in *The Drama Review*. 15, No. 3 (1971), 242.

4. Quoted by Kironmoy Raha in *Bengali Theatre*. (New Delhi: National Book Trust, India, 1978), pp. 133–34.

5. It appears that this illustrious Vaishnava saint and religious reformer used the medium of *jatra* to propagate his teachings on *bhakti* (devotion) and love. Apart from celebrating the glory of Lord Krishna, the archetypal hero of *jatra*. the early *jatras* dramatized Puranic legends, folk tales, and episodes from the *Ramayana* and the *Mahabharata*. By the nineteenth century, the tradition of *jatra* had lost much of its religious significance even though it retained a sacrosanct aura. It was Mukunda Das, a fiery poet and lyricist in Bengal, who first recognized the political possibilities of *jatra*. He used its songs and conventions to preach nationalism to the villagers in Bengal during the early years of the Freedom Movement in India. With his pioneering work, topical political figures and situations crept into the mythological framework of *jatra*. The gods and goddesses became freedom fighters and patriots. The devils and villains were transformed into members of the ruling class. This politicization of *jatra* continues to thrive in rural areas where villagers are now quite accustomed to seeing Lenin and Mao Tse Tung appear in the coveted roles of the *jatra* heroes.

6. Interview with A. J. Gunawardana (cited above), p. 236.

7. "Problems and Directions: Calcutta's New Theatre," *The Drama Review*. 15, No. 3 (1971), 242.

8. The limitations of *Tin Poyshar Pala* are more blatantly displayed in two later productions by *Nandikar—Bhalomanush* and *Khair Ghondi* (adaptations of *The Good Person of Setzuan* and *The Caucasian Chalk Circle* respectively). These productions are hopelessly cluttered with a surfeit of emotional effects and distracting technical devices, notably strobe lights and mood music. The acting is, for the most part, melodramatic; the crowd scenes evoke nineteenth-century "historical" productions; and the stage business invariably distracts by its sheer excess. Though there is some attempt to imitate the

formal aspects of the "epic theatre," the posters, placards, and projections in *Nandikar's* productions are not sufficiently related to the unfolding of action in the plays. They are primarily decorative in effect.

9. Quoted by Samik Bandyopadhyay in his article entitled "Bertolt Brecht," published in *Quarterly Journal of the National Centre for Performing Arts.* 8, No. 3 (1979), 41; a New Delhi publication.

10. Utpal Dutt, *Kabarkhana* (Cemetery), trans. Dilip Kumar Chakravarty, published in *Epic Theatre,* December 1978–January 1979. (Calcutta: Ganashakti Printers), p. 26.

11. Bertolt Brecht, "Does Use of the Model Restrict the Artist's Freedom?" included by John Willett in his edition of *Brecht on Theatre.* (New York: Hill & Wang, 1964), p. 224.

12. Quoted by Samik Bandyopadhyay in "Bertolt Brecht" (cited above), p. 41.

13. "In West Bengal: A Political Theatre," an interview with Dutt conducted by Kumud Mehta and Vijay Tendulkar. *International Theatre Information.* Summer 1974.

14. Badal Sircar, *The Third Theatre.* Calcutta: (Sri Aurobindo Press, 1978) p. 77. The "Third Theatre" is the rubric that categorizes groups like *Satabdi* in the Bengali theatre that function outside the commercial theatre framework in Calcutta. These groups are committed to the principles of the "Poor Theatre."

15. Quoted by Samik Bandyopadhyay in "Badal Sircar: Middle-Class Responsibilities," *Sangeet Natak,* No. 22, a journal of the Sangeet Natak Akademi in India.

16. Unpublished manuscript dated August 1977 recorded by Samik Bandyopadhyay. I am grateful to Mr. Bandyopadhyay for providing me with a copy of the manuscript.

17. I am thinking in particular of recent forms of theatre practised by Augusto Boal in the villages of Peru, Argentina, and Brazil where the people enacted their own problems in collective situations. Boal's model of the "forum theatre," in particular, needs to be examined by theatre practitioners in Bengal. It is admirably explained and documented in Boal's *Theatre of the Oppressed* (New York: Urizen Books, 1979)

A Letter From Cyprus

Christakis Georghiou

Of all the arts which have survived in Cyprus after the debacle of 1974, it has been the theatre which soonest recovered. In fact, the getting together of creative people, even under stress, produced a synergetic experience resulting in plays which were of considerably higher quality than those presented in earlier years. It was as if the search for identity and security created a near perfect environment for new creative work. As native playwrights were thin on the ground, it was inevitable that classics were chosen and it is understandable that they often related to the contemporary situation and practically always caught the spirit or mood and even more, the need, of the audience at the time.

The Cyprus Theatrical Organization, under the direction of Evis Gabrielides, is subsidized by the government. At a time when the population was unsettled, many citizens having to leave the country for work, many living in tents, it was fortuitous that some money was set aside for the performing arts. Cinemas at that time hardly suited audiences' tastes, as the average film of violence was nauseating to them and escapist movies, if such films were available, did not seem appropriate either. The country does not have a strong theatrical tradition, but talents abound in both acting and directing. However, there were, and are, many diverse elements in the structure of the Cypriot theatre which could possibly not have welded into a dynamic force if, at a time of real creative awareness, an outside director, Heinz-Uwe Haus, had not come to the country.

Many foreign visitors come to Cyprus through cultural contracts with their governments and the Cultural Service of the Cypriot Ministery of Education. Mr. Haus came on an agreement between Cyprus and the German Democratic Republic. As well as his fine talents as a director, he proved to be the perfect choice, being at once extremely popular as a person, giving confidence all around, and by brilliant intuition soon got to the nub of what was needed. What was needed was a bringing together of all the best available talent in a play which was a classic in its own right, but with which performers and audience could feel they belonged.

He chose Brecht's *Caucasian Chalk Circle,* a play which had enough fantasy or fairy tale plot to make palatable a theme to which people could relate. It was as if harsh realities were turned into a work of art especially for them. It was a huge success, with a fine central performance by Despina Bembidelli as Grusche—an actress already established, but who was to reach new heights under Haus's direction. The play toured the island and was later directed for television by Mr. Haus. So popular was the play that for the first time a national theatre seemed to have been born. There was a formidable reviving of energies. Cypriot directors worked with greater confidence and actors played with more purpose. Inevitably, standards were raised all around.

The following year Mr. Haus came back to direct Shakespeare's *Measure for Measure.* This was a fresh interpretation of the play: brisk, brutal, reflecting a power corroding within its own corruption and a population scrambling for survival. Set in front of a large painting in which the complex reality of chaos and torture created a wall of seething energies, and with a gentle, "washed with time" front curtain of medieval London showing the Thames, St. Paul's and the Globe Theatre, the actors were placed on a sloping ramp and the characters, while full of vigor, were at the same time mere cogs in the world's mechanism. The production—in which the director used the Duke as the narrator—ricocheted from harsh realism to abstraction. When this play was later (1977) shown at the Weimar Shakespeare Festival, the Cypriot actors, appearing vulnerable against the massive backdrop, gave performances of great pathos.

The G. D. R. director made us realize how contemporary both these plays are. In addition it can be said that the public lectures and discussions he gave in the last years at the different clubs and cultural societies helped enormously in clarifying questions on the social and political functions of the theatre in general.

The third production by Mr. Haus for Cyprus was Brecht's *Mother Courage.* The cast was now ready for Brecht's masterpiece and with Despina Bembidelli as Mother Courage, the play was a huge success and when the production went to the National Theatre of Greece in Athens in 1978, it took that city by storm. A typical blue-painted Cypriot cart was used as Mother Courage's vehicle and the costumes, though having a firm base in early 17th century costume design, related in color and texture to the folk culture of Cyprus.

Cyprus in 1977 was an ideal place for *Mother Courage*. Everybody had first hand experiences of war in 1974. But in a culture where rhetoric is a main strand in the fabric of everyday life, the question was, is there a demand for it in theatre? Drama is already present on the streets. If there is this demand, then modern theatre in a European tradition is not likely to satisfy it, and the Cypriots will have to make their own kind of drama. Satire is one possible answer. There is a role for the theatre that complicates. There is no better place than the theatre for slapping the public in the face, and despite the hardships which many people in Cyprus have suffered in the last few years it could be argued that Cyprus society is ripe for a few slaps. The conformism of the intellectuals, the consumerist obsessions of the middle classes, the political delusions of the whole nation are fertile fields for the satirist; which brings us back to Brecht, the man who irritated—before he became a fossilized classic.

Not many producers find themselves realizing two completely different interpretations of the same play in the space of a few months. It is worth noting of Mr. Haus's production that it is not just his Weimar production scaled down and hotted up. he did not try to repeat his means and solutions but instead sought new critical solutions in the way in which Brecht so often did. I believe it would be a most "un-Brechtian" attitude not to adopt a critical attitude with regard to Brecht himself, for the Brechtian method is endangered wherever it is made into a style which is reserved for specific plays and times and which like every style is then outmoded by time. Haus's concentration on the "story" as that medium through which the social contradictions implicit in the theme are revealed in a sensually perceptible form, and the effort to develop such groupings and attitudes of characters on their stage which demonstrate this dialectic of the social struggle, corresponds exactly to the situation in Cyprus. In a country which suffered a brief but traumatic bout of war it also made sense to naturalize the play, to give it a Cypriot flavor. Thus the wagon was one of the traditional bright blue painted farm carts from the central plain, a local focus for the play. The chaplain appeared as a suave, bearded Orthodox cleric, and the Swedish general, played with conscious self-parody, looked more the UN officer from Ledra palace. Eilif, too, was very much the EOKA man from the hills. The music, too, supported this orientation: George Kotsonis's tactile, suggestive and versatile music bridges the Brechtian lyrics to the Nicosia audience with a definite Cypriot style which succeeds on every dramatic level. This combination lays bare contradictions which are dramatically calculated. Music as commentary meant that the music had to avail itself of such means, which, without abandoning their emotional content, allowed mental processes to take place, and even stimulated them.

Brecht has always been obsessed with the interaction between society and man, has focussed attention to the destructive effects a rotten system may have on man. But in an indirect way he has also pointed out the potentialities of man to change society, to shape it in a manner which will transform it from a scene of exploitation and corruption to a world where man's basically good qualities will flourish. The basic question Brecht asks in *The Good Person of Setzuan* is "Can a human being live with goodness and remain good in this world that is full of wickedness and where the prevailing axiom is 'homo homini lupus'?" Unlike Shakespeare, Brecht does not believe in the "attractiveness" of evil: there is nothing good about evil. "Evil is a kind of awkwardness. Evil men are inexperienced. When you sing a song or build a machine or plant rice shoots . . . this is, in the last analysis, goodness."

In Haus's fourth production with THOK—originally produced in 1979 in Cyprus and also presented in Athens in the frame of "Ekfrasis" in 1980—society comes under the scorching examination of Brecht's dialectical mind. Man is born essentially good but he is transformed by the system he grows under into an animal that is essentially antisocial. Poverty, wealth, necessity are concrete products of any social system that is based on man's exploitation, corrupt man. He is conditioned to accepting evil as a means of survival and no matter what his motives are in the beginning, he will end up practicing evil. Is Brecht's view, therefore, essentially pessimistic? I think not. By accepting man's basic goodness Brecht points out indirectly the way by which this vicious circle can break. Change society, place relations and real equality and you have the solution. Only then can man break the endless conditioning that forces him to accept evil as a means of survival.

Brecht's dialectical way of thinking is combined in *The Good Person of Setzuan* with feeling, the vision of a poet. We have in this play the main characteristics of Brechtian writing. Lyricism—a powerful expression of sorrow and love for man who is endlessly trapped by society, satire so that certain social aspects would be fully revealed, and the way to salvation may be fully grasped by the mind. The characters come alive in front of us, the one after the other. There is no tone of cruelty in Brecht's attitude to man. His evil men are victims trapped by society—their responsibility lies indirectly in the fact that they don't do enough to free themselves from the shackles of social convention. In *The Good Person of Setzuan* there is a marvellous balance between alienation and identification. The environmental setting is China, the mask that tends to bevel human characters enables the characters to grow independent of time and place and to keep the audience at a "safe distance"—they are not emotionally trapped, therefore their brains can function relatively free from emotion. But at the same time the poet's vision is too powerful not to be felt, as the audience's sympathy is needed for a deeper understanding of the workings of a system that traps man into accepting evil as a way of life. And this delicate balance is achieved marvellously by the dramatist and the poet, but it is a challenge for every director because a false step may bring the whole edifice down.

Heinz-Uwe Haus preserved this balance in an admirable manner. The characters were at the same time distant and near—distant in the sense that you were led to believe that you were watching an event outside your immediate cycle of experiences and near in the sense that you felt how human they were both in their weaknesses and strong points, in their small vices and their great virtues. You felt they were part of you, you were part of them. Haus had at his disposal a varied series of actors all trained in different ways—many had studied in Greece, some in the United Kingdom, others in the U. S. S. R. Each one had his own "theatrical philosophy," yet these differences in approach and acting were ironed out and the director got out from each individual what he wanted. He turned them into a team. Personally I was astonished at the transformation. Each one was part of a bigger unit and the end result was the perfect functioning of the ensemble from the first line to the very last. The messages came down to the audience in a strikingly original way and the audience left the theatre carrying with it a rare experience which will keep its individual members intellectually busy for a long time. The direction aimed at giving the story at a point somewhere beyond a specific place and a specific time. Glyn Hughes and Costas Kafkarides with their setting and costumes underlined this "beyond place and time" side of the Brechtian play. Probably the only "Chinese" elements were to be found in the music of George Kotsonis but these elements passed through an assimilation process that in the end became something familiar, something that belongs to our world. The evolution of the play, oriental and rather slow at the beginning, gains such momentum as it unfolds itself, that is develops in a gripping spectacle which mercilessly occupies your mind, taxes your emotions. You, as a spectator, are forced to participate in this theatrical experience with both your reasoning powers and your emotional involvement.

It would be meaningless if I made a reference to each actor separately. Any reference should correspondingly mean something to the reader. However I think that an exception can be made. The young actress Lenia Sorokou (the unforgettable dumb girl of *Mother Courage*) gave the difficult double role of Shen Te and her cousin Shui Ta with an astonishing freshness. She had no difficulty in switching from the role of the kind-hearted young prostitute to that of her tough cousin. All the other actors gave their best self and no doubt this is one of the best, if not the best, performance THOK has ever given. The presence of Mr. Haus among the theatre people of Cyprus, something that is possible because of the existing cultural agreement between the G. D. R. and Cyprus, has enabled the theatre of Cyprus to establish very strong links with the European theatre at its best. We can't but feel grateful both to his country and himself.

Theaterspiel als Vorgriff und Aneignung von Lebenspraxis

Heinz-Uwe Haus

Regieführen hat mit Vermittlungsformen und Kommunikation im Theater und mit den Bedingungen, die diese Kommunikation ermöglichen, zu tun. Ausgangs- und Endpunkt ist die gesellschaftliche Produktivität des Theaters.

Stellen wir die Behauptung auf, daß ein Regisseur das Theater umso besser handhaben kann, je genauer er dessen Wirkungen kennt, das heißt je bewußter er die Vermittlungsformen des Theaterspiels einsetzt. Wekwerth spricht von vier Formen: Historie, Parabel, Clownerie, Modellspiel. Sie bestimmen nicht nur das Wie, sondern zugleich das Was: Die Struktur erst enthüllt alle Möglichkeiten des Inhalts.

Kommunikation im Theater ist in erster Linie vom Inhalt des Theaterspiels abhängig, vom Anspruch, mit dem das Theater auftritt, in der Gesellschaft als Kommunikationszentrum zu wirken, und erst in zweiter Linie von den dabei entwickelten Formen.

Von Jessner stammt die folgende Maßgabe, die die küntlerische Verantwortung ebenso wie die Rechte und Pflichten des Regisseurs erfaßt:

Um die künstlerischen Forderungen seiner Zeit zu verstehen, darf sich der Regisseur nicht der Welt verschließen, im Gegenteil, wenn er den Wert des Theaters im Sinne der Schillerschen Schaubühne erfassen will, so muß er in der Welt stehen und seine Zeit politisch verstehen. So wird er dem Theater das sein, was er soll: das Programm.

Dieses Bekenntnis vom Oktober 1913 hat über die Jahre nichts von seiner Aktualität verloren.

Theater als gesellschaftlich bestimmte Einrichtung schließt die Suche nach dem gesellschaftsgemäßen Publikum als Kommunikationspartner ein. Aktivitäten des Publikums zu erzeugen, bedeutet zu fragen, inwieweit das Publikum qualifiziert wurde, mit dem Theater in Kommunikation zu treten, denn die Krisis des Theaters ist immer auch eine Krisis des Publikums. Da hilft nicht werbende Aufklärung oder elitäre Bescheidung, sondern nur konsequente Nutzung, also auch Selbstverständigung, der dem Inszenieren immanenten Prozesse und adäquaten Methoden. Drei Schwerpunkte lassen sich folgendermaßen umreißen: 1. das Beobachten und Beschreiben, 2. das Fabulieren als Grundvorgang in der Regiearbeit, 3. das Vermitteln und Wirken durch Theater. Ihre systematische Betrachtung, ja ein Training dieser Arbeitsstufen, sollte zur kunstvollen Handhabung führen.

Das Entdecken von Wirklichkeit

Was man abbildend verändern will, muß man kennen. Die Entdeckerfunktion der Kunst beginnt mit der Fähigkeit, Wirklichkeit erfassen und analysieren zu können. Die Beobachtung von Wirklichkeit verlangt aber bereits Wissen, nicht nur Wissen um die Gesetze gesellschaftlichen Zusammenlebens, sondern auch Wissen um die Möglichkeiten des Theaters, Wirklichkeit darzustellen. Bevor man bewußt den Alltag beobachten kann, muß man wissen, was man suchen und entdecken will. Es ist festzuhalten, daß Theater von der Wirklichkeit auszugehen hat, um auf diese dann einwirken zu können, und die Regisseure müssen dabei zugleich ihren Sinn für gestisches Erzählen und schauspielerisches Handeln entwickeln. Der Vorgang des Entdeckens sollte also nicht auseinandergerissen werden. Wirklichkeit suchend, lernen wir, Wirklichkeit grundsätzlich im Hinblick auf die Kommunikation im Theater zu suchen.

Im Prinzip ist das Zustandekommen von Kommunikation nicht primär von bestimmten Formen abhängig. Sowohl die traditionelle Guckkastenbühne als auch alle anderen Arten der Aufführung existieren heute und ermöglichen Kommunikation in dem Maße, wie Form und Inhalt künstlerisch in Übereinstimmung gebracht werden.

Dabei soll die Beobachtung bereits mehr und Wesentlicheres aufdecken als das, was ein Erscheinungsbild nur äußerlich im Sinne platten Augenscheins hergibt: Sinnfälligmachen verborgener Gegensätze, Hervorkehren unerwarteter Entwicklungssprünge, Überraschung durch ungewohntes Verhalten, kurz—wie es Brecht ausgedrückt hat—die Dialektik aufdecken und zum Genuß machen:

Die Überraschungen der logisch fortschreitenden oder springenden Entwicklung, der Unstabilität aller Zustände, der Witz der Widersprüchlichkeiten und so weiter.

Das Darstellen von Wirklichkeit

"Es ist ein Vergnügen des Menschen," sagt Brecht, "sich zu verändern durch die Kunst wie durch das sonstige Leben und durch die Kunst für dieses. So muß er sich und die Gesellschaft als veränderlich spüren und sehen können."

Damit Theaterleute und Zuschauer in ein gegenseitiges, aktives Verhältnis kommen, müssen Tatbestände der Wirklichkeit spielerisch strukturiert, verändert, umgebildet werden, sodaß mit der Darstellung von Vorgängen zwischen Menschen auf der Bühne zu bestimmten Zwecken etwas erzählt werden kann. Hierbei stellt die Fabel (nicht im Sinne eines Gattungsbegriffes) und die Tätigkeit des Fabulierens (Erzählens) die Organisation des Spiels dar. Diese Fähigkeit zum Fabulieren gilt es zu entwickeln, denn sie lebt von den Strömungen des Zeitgeistes. Sie macht frei für Ideen der Darstellung. Und hier kann ich nur an jenen Vers Goethes erinnern, der lautet:

> Und umzuschaffen das Geschaffne,
> Damit sich's nicht zum Starren waffne,
> Wirkt ewiges lebendiges Tun.

Das Spielen mit Wirklichkeit

Die Beziehung zum Zuschauer ist die wichtigste Beziehung im Theater. Sie muß genauso gehandhabt werden wie das Entdecken und das Darstellen von Wirklichkeit.

Es ist ein Anliegen der Theaterarbeit, die Spielweise und die Spielformen zu finden, die einer ganz bestimmten historischen Situation, bestimmten konkreten Erfahrungen und Erwartungen entsprechen.

Die Entwicklung von Bedürfnissen, Interessen, Fähigkeiten und Genüssen der Persönlichkeit vollzieht sich in drei Arten menschlicher Tätigkeit: in der Arbeit, im Lernen und im Spiel. Alle drei Arten zusammen machen den Komplex der Lebenstätigkeit des Menschen aus. In den verschiedensten Unterhaltungsformen durchdringen sich diese drei Formen menschlicher Tätigkeit; wirft man aber die Frage nach der Spezifik der theatralischen Unterhaltung auf, dann muß man der Funktion des Spiels bei der Persönlichkeitsformung besondere Bedeutung beimessen.

Während die Ziele der Arbeit und des Lernens zweckgebunden sind, ist das Spiel zweckfrei, das heißt, im Spiel wird an Stelle des gegenständlich—dinglichen Bezuges der Handlung der gegenständlich-menschliche Bezug hergestellt. Das Spiel hat seinen Zweck in sich, in der Produktivität und Harmonie der Fähigkeiten der Persönlichkeit.

Im Theater bleibt die Spieltätigkeit ein Teil der Arbeit, die damit von ihrer strengen Zweckgebundenheit gelöst wird, um aus Tatbeständen der Wirklichkeit Späße zu machen. Diese Späße stellen Unwirkliches dar, real Folgenloses, nämlich erdachte Menschen, mögliche Situationen, vorgestellte Entscheidungen, die Vorspieler wie Mitspieler jedoch in genußvolle Aktivität versetzen und individuell oder kollektiv zu bewältigender Lebenspraxis vorgreifen.

Dieses Zusammenhangs zwischen Spiel und Unterhaltung wegen spricht Schiller davon, daß die "Schönheit das Produkt zwischen dem Geist und den Sinnen" sei, "es spricht zu allen Vermögen des Menschen zugleich und kann daher nur unter der Voraussetzung eines vollständigen und freien Gebrauchs aller seiner Kräfte empfunden und gewürdigt werden."

Wir werden unsere Zuschauer am Entdecken von Problembereichen beteiligen müssen, wobei historisch gewachsene Spielstrukturen (Vermittlungsformen) neu zu ordnen und zu handhaben sind.

Die Last der Lehre

Fünf Thesen zu den
späten Stücken Bertolt Brechts

Hans-Dieter Zimmermann

Wie kaum ein anderer Autor der jüngsten deutschen Literaturgeschichte hat Brecht sich mit Theorie beschäftigt und sich theoretisch geäußert: zur Gesellschaft, zur Kunst, zu seinen eigenen Arbeiten, zu dem, was seine Arbeiten zeigen und was sie bewirken sollen. Brecht hat festgelegt, in welchem Zusammenhang er gesehen werden will, auf welche Weise er rezipiert werden will. Was die Regisseure zu tun haben, wie sich die Schauspieler in seinen Stücken zu verhalten haben, hat er festgelegt, und wie die Zuschauer sich zu diesen Stücken zu verhalten haben. Der Weg der Interpretation und der Rezeption wurde weitgehend festgeschrieben.

Wenn wir uns heute fragen, warum die großen Stücke des späten Brecht so rasch an Faszination verloren haben, müssen wir an diesem Punkt mit unseren Überlegungen einsetzen. Wir müssen das bis ins Detail festgelegte Werk Brechts auseinandernehmen und nicht nur die Phasen seiner historischen Entwicklung berücksichtigen, wie es bisher geschah. So wandte sich die literaturwissenschaftliche Diskussion in der letzten Zeit vielfach vom alten Brecht ab und den Lehrstücken des mittleren Brecht zu. Die jüngeren Regisseure inszenieren lieber die impulsiven Stücke des jungen Brecht als die des alten.

Auseinandernehmen müssen wir Brechts Theorie und Praxis nicht nur nach ihrer historischen Entwicklung. Wir müssen anfangen zu unterscheiden zwischen den Intentionen Brechts und den Aussagen seiner Stücke: Wurde in seinen Stücken denn tatsächlich realisiert, was er beabsichtigte? Und wir müssen weiterhin unterscheiden zwischen der Aussage seiner Stücke und der Wirkung dieser Stücke: Erreichen sie denn tatsächlich die Wirkung, die sie erreichen sollen?

Dazu fünf Thesen, die nicht als das letzte Wort zum späten Brecht, zu dem Autor des "epischen Theaters", verstanden werden wollen. Es sind vielmehr Antithesen zu der üblichen orthodoxen Brecht-Auslegung: die Synthese steht noch aus. Sie wollen auch nicht verwechselt werden mit einer antimarxistischen Ignoranz, die nur ihre Vorurteile bestätigt haben will. Die Thesen kommen aus der Auseinandersetzung mit Brecht und wollen zu weiterer Auseinandersetzung mit ihm auffordern.

Wenn man die germanistische Sekundärliteratur zu Brecht liest, etwa Jan Knopf's Überblick über die Situation der Brecht-Forschung, hat man oft den Eindruck, Brecht sei Theoretiker einer marxistischen Ästhetik gewesen und kein Stückeschreiber. Inwieweit es ihm gelungen ist, seine—im übrigen widersprüchliche—marxistische Position in seinen Stücken umzusetzen, bleibt dann unerörtert. Andererseits gehen die meisten Interpretationen seiner Stücke wie selbstverständlich davon aus, daß die theoretische Leitlinie, die Brecht selbst gegeben hat, das Ergebnis der Interpretation liefere, daß also die Absicht des Autors und die Aussage der Stücke übereingehen.

Die 1. These: Das hohe Reflexionsniveau, das Brecht in seinen theoretischen Äußerungen erreicht hat, hat er in seinen späten Stücken nicht einlösen können.

Der kaukasische Kreidekreis zum Beispiel ist von erschreckender Simplizität. Der Widerspruch, den Brecht selbst nennt, daß die Magd Grusche ihr eigenes Leben gefährdet, um das des Kindes zu retten, wird in die Länge gezogen, bis endlich der Azdak sein Urteil fällt. Der zweite, erheblichere Widerspruch, daß Gerechtigkeit nur in kurzen Zeiten des Umbruchs durch einen glücklichen Zufall zu erreichen ist, gibt nicht mehr her als eine Novelle oder einige Szenen wie hier, in denen der Azdak Recht spricht. Die Figur des Azdak ist die einzige, die ein wenig komplexer ist als die anderen, die ein wenig mehr ist als das, was sie in der Parabel demonstrieren soll; sie hat noch einen Abglanz vom frühen *Baal.*

Im Vorspiel des *kaukasischen Kreidekreises* wird ein Widerspruch, wiewohl angelegt, nicht ausgeführt; es wird vielmehr künstlich eingeebnet, was im darauf folgenden Stück künstlich in die Länge gezogen wird. Im Nachspiel der ersten Fassung, das in die zweite Fassung nicht übernommen wurde, wird das ausgesprochen von der "Bäuerin rechts", die allerdings schnell übergangen wird: der schroffe Gegensatz zwischen der überaus bösen richtigen Mutter und der überaus guten falschen Mutter im *Kreidekreis* hat keine Entsprechung im Vorspiel, das—in der letzten Fassung—in der Sowjetunion im Jahre 1944 spielt. Da gibt es keine überaus Bösen mehr, nur noch Gute, so daß die einen guten Kolchosbauern den anderen guten Kolchosbauern leichthin ihr Tal für einen Staudamm überlassen.

Wir müssen annehmen, daß Brecht hier ernstlich behaupten wollte, in der stalinistischen Sowjetunion seien die alten Widersprüche überwunden, obwohl er es besser wußte. Hier fällt der Dialektiker Brecht auf eine präreflexive Stufe zurück, in die verlogene Idylle. Vor den Widersprüchen im eigenen Lager verschließt hier Brecht die Augen. Daß auch eine andere Position möglich ist, sehen wir heute etwa an Wolf Biermann, der von der Grundlage seines Marxismus aus nicht nur die Widersprüche im Westen, sondern auch die im Osten kritisiert. Kritik am Stalinismus hat Brecht—in seinem veröffentlichten Werk—nicht ausdrücklich geübt: da gibt es immer nur kompromißbereites Taktieren und Paktieren. Brecht stand sicher in einer anderen historischen Situation als Biermann; aber gerade wer das sieht, kann Brecht schwerlich als Vorbild für heutiges Denken und Handeln betrachten.

Die 2. These: Der Abfall von der ästhetischen Theorie zur literarischen Praxis beim marxistischen Stückeschreiber Brecht hat seinen Grund darin, daß Brecht die Kunst zur Magd der Wissenschaft macht.

Die Wissenschaft bietet Brecht die Grundlage zur Kritik, seine Kritik benutzt die Kunst als Instrument. Brechts Ziel, eine neue Vereinigung von Kunst und Wissenschaft zu leisten, wurde nicht erreicht; was er bringt, ist meist eine literarische Illustration wissenschaftlicher Erkenntnisse. Brecht sah in der Wissenschaft die dominierende Erkenntnismöglichkeit. Die Literatur kann nicht Wissenschaft sein. Eine Parabel beweist gar nichts. Eine "wissenschaftliche" Literatur kann eine sein, die sich an der Wissenschaft orientiert, also deren Erkenntnisse umsetzt und leicht faßlich darstellt. Dadurch wird die Literatur zur Didaktik der Wissenschaft. Die Didaktik muß vereinfachen, um verständlich zu sein.

So kommt es bei Brecht zu einer doppelten Vereinfachung. Die Wissenschaft, an der er sich orientiert, ist bereits eine vereinfachte: die Gesellschaftswissenschaften in Gestalt des Marxismus, der—in der Tradition der Philosophie des deutschen Idealismus stehend—ein relativ einfaches Erklärungsmodell der Welt bietet. Dieses relativ einfache Modell wird bei der Übertragung in literarische Szenarien noch einmal vereinfacht.

Die Stücke des Marxisten Brecht stehen und fallen mit dem Marxismus, den sie vertreten, als die Vereinfachung einer Vereinfachung. Wenn der Marxismus voranschreitet—wie in den letzten Jahrzehnten—, bleiben diese Stücke zurück. Wenn die Wissenschaft voranschreitet—und das entspricht unserer Konzeption von Wissenschaft—, verlieren sie ihre Aktualität. Brechts Optimismus, die Wissenschaft habe die Erde schon fast bewohnbar gemacht, können wir heute schon nicht mehr teilen. Wir fürchten, die Wissenschaft könne die Erde unbewohnbar machen.

Ob eine andere Konzeption von Kunst als die von Brecht entworfene innerhalb des Marxismus möglich ist? Ernst Bloch hat sie vorgeschlagen. Seine antizipatorische Kunst bringt gerade das noch nicht Bekannte, das noch nicht wissenschaftlich oder sonstwie Erfaßte, sie bringt also nicht das Alte, sondern das Neue.

Wenn bei Brecht Hegel als Vorbild zu nennen wäre—die Philosophie hat die Kunst eingeholt—, so bei Bloch Hegels Antipode Schelling, der zeitweise die Kunst über die Philosophie stellte, weil sie zur ästhetischen Anschauung bringen könne, was die Philosophie nicht auf den Begriff bringen kann.

Dieses "in der poetischen Sprache zur Anschauung bringen", was auf keine andere Weise zum Ausdruck gebracht werden kann, könnte man als die beherrschende Tradition der Moderne bezeichnen, in der Brecht nicht steht, wohl auch nicht stehen wollte.

Die 3. These: Brecht steht in einer vorklassischen und vormodernen Tradition, nämlich in der der Aufklärung des 18. Jahrhunderts.

Daher sein Glaube an die völlige rationale Durchschaubarkeit der Welt, an die didaktische Aufgabe der Literatur—ganz im Sinne der Popularaufklärung—, daher auch seine philosophischen Dialoge wie *Flüchtlingsgespräche* oder *Messingkauf*. Mit der Wirkungsästhetik der Aufklärung hat auch Brechts Ästhetik Ähnlichkeit, wenn sie auch eine Neuformulierung ist. In der alten rhetorischen Tradition stehend, lehrte auch die Aufklärung noch das *delectare* (Unterhalten), das *movere* (Bewegen) und das *docere* (Belehren), dem die Literatur zu entsprechen habe.

Bei Brecht steht das Belehren im Vordergrund, doch soll es nicht ohne Genuß (delectare) geschehen; das Rühren und Bewegen ist dagegen ganz in den Hintergrund getreten. Brecht steht damit in der Tradition der aristotelischen Poetik, auch wenn er behauptete, eine nichtaristotelische Dramaturgie entworfen zu haben. Eine nichtaristotelische Position hat dagegen die moderne Literatur eingenommen, in deren Tradition Brecht nicht steht.

Eine nichtaristotelische Poetik beginnt in dem Moment, in dem die alte Wirkungsästhetik—die Wirkungen bei Lesern und Zuschauern erzielen will—durch die Darstellungsästhetik abgelöst wird—die vom Leser zunächst einmal absieht und nach Vollkommenheit des Werkes in sich selbst strebt. Mit den theoretischen Arbeiten von Karl Philipp Moritz beginnt diese nichtaristotelische Poetik vor ziemlich genau 200 Jahren.[1] Goethes Symbolbegriff könnte dafür ein Beispiel sein. Das Symbol—kurz gesagt—offenbart und verrätselt zugleich. Es bringt zur Sprache, was vorher sprachlos war, ohne es bereits einer wissenschaftlichen Erklärung zuzuführen.

Verrätseln war Brechts Sache nicht. Er wollte offenlegen, einsichtig machen. Ob seine Wirkungsästhetik freilich ihr Ziel erreicht, nämlich die Belehrung des Zuschauers, ist sehr fraglich.

Über die Wirkungen eines literarischen Textes auf Leser oder Zuschauer wissen wir wenig. Auf die Kluft zwischen Absicht und Wirkung bei Brecht hat Hans Mayer hingewiesen: die jungen Arbeiter Ost-Berlins gingen lieber ins Metropol-Theater, wo es die alte Wiener Operette gäbe, als in Brechts Theater.

Die 4. These: Es gibt keine Anhaltspunkte dafür, daß Brechts "episches Theater" die vom Autor beabsichtigten Wirkungen tatsächlich erreicht.

Empirische Untersuchungen über die Wirkungen seiner Stücke liegen nicht vor, sie sind auch nur schwer möglich. So bleibt die Spekulation. Es ließe sich die Behauptung aufstellen, daß Ibsens Stücke die gleiche gesellschaftsdurchschauende, zur Veränderung antreibende Wirkung haben wie die Brechts. Es ließe sich auch behaupten, daß die Stücke Ödön von Horvaths viel eher die von Brecht beabsichtigte Wirkung auslösten als Brechts eigene Stücke. Zumindest hätten diese Behauptungen so viel Plausibilität für sich wie die Brechts und seiner Anhänger.

In den Stücken Brechts ist sicherlich eine bestimmte Zuschauerrolle festgeschrieben; diese vom Stück dem Zuschauer zugewiesene Rolle darf aber nicht verwechselt werden mit dem tatsächlichen Verhalten des Zuschauers. Allerdings lassen die Zuschauerrollen in Brechts späten Stücken, also seit der *Heiligen Johanna der Schlachthöfe,* dem Zuschauer nicht viel Freiheit des Mitdenkens oder gar des Selberdenkens.

Zum Beispiel *Der kaukasische Kreidekreis.* Hat der Zuschauer die Möglichkeit, sich auf die Seite der Gouvernerin zu stellen oder auf die Seite der Gegenspieler des Azdak, ohne für einen Idioten gehalten zu werden? Er hat sie nicht. Die Welt ist überschaubar und einfach wie die eines Märchens, wo der Böse von vornherein böse ist und das gute Ende absehbar. Der Zuschauer wird konfrontiert mit einem Spiel, das ihm keine Wahl läßt. Offene Schlüsse—wie im *Guten Menschen von Sezuan*—sind nur vermeintlich offen. Der Zuschauer wird konfrontiert mit einer Lösung, die er akzeptieren muß. Ob er sie tatsächlich akzeptiert und auch noch als eine, die auf andere Probleme übertragbar ist, ist sehr fraglich. Ob er gar seine politische Einstellung verändert, ist höchst unwahrscheinlich.

Die 5. These: Die den Stücken des "epischen Theaters" implizierte Zuschauerrolle ist so festgelegt, daß sie dem tatsächlichen Zuschauer, über dessen Reaktion wir nichts wissen, keine Wahl läßt.

Wenn der Zuschauer sich die Freiheit der Wahl nimmt, tut er dies gegen die Aussage der Stücke. Und es wäre wünschenswert, wenn einmal diese späten Stücke so gegen ihre Aussage und gegen die ihres Autors inszeniert würden, wie heute von respektlosen Regisseuren Goethe und Kleist inszeniert werden. Dann sähen wir etwa die Magd Grusche mit menschlichen Bedürfnissen, z. B. sexuellen. Das wäre sicher erfrischend nach so viel protestantischer Ethik.

Wenn heute Goethe inszeniert wird, wird auch nicht lange gefragt, welche Anweisungen der Theaterleiter seinen Weimarer Schauspielern gab oder was seine Welt- oder Naturanschauung war. Man stellt eines seiner Stücke auf die Bühne und untersucht es gemäß unserem Interesse. Eine Haltung, die wir u.a. bei Brecht gelernt haben. Warum soll diese Haltung, die Brecht Villon, Shakespeare, Lenz gegenüber einnahm, ihm selbst gegenüber verboten sein? Es wäre Zeit, ihm mit der gleichen kaltschnäuzigen Respektlosigkeit zu begegnen, mit der er allen anderen begegnet ist. Nehmen wir uns etwas heraus, wie er sich etwas herausgenommen hat. Erst dann werden wir sehen, ob er für uns noch brauchbar ist.

Nehmen wir uns die Freiheit, die er uns nicht gibt. Andere Autoren, die nicht wie Brecht von vornherein meinen, sie wüßten alles besser als die Leser—das ist die Unart der Pädagogen—, lassen dem Leser die Möglichkeit, sich als Partner zu sehen, der ernst genommen wird, und nicht als jemanden, dem dekretiert wird und der im übrigen das Maul zu halten hat.

Günter Kunert hat den hier skizzierten Sachverhalt auf seine Weise in einer Rede vor dem Stockholmer PEN-Kongreß ausgedrückt. Er steht hier stellvertretend für DDR-Autoren wie Heiner Müller oder Peter Hacks, die ihre Vorbehalte gegen Brecht formuliert haben, und für westdeutsche Autoren. Günter Kunert:

> Ich rede nicht der Parabel Brechtscher Machart das Wort, deren Erfolg aus dem Umstand resultiert, daß sie Gewußtes bestätigt, aber nicht das bis dato Ungesagte, Unsagbare, Unsägliche durch sprachliche Einkleidung überhaupt erst sichtbar werden läßt, sondern vielmehr "komplexe" Tatbestände in Vereinfachungen übersetzte, wodurch sie scheinbar verständlicher wurden. Ich sage: scheinbar, weil uns diese großen und einfallsreichen Vereinfachungen,

Folgeerscheinungen ebenfalls großer und einfallsreicher Vereinfachungen, die Irrationalität, in der wir und unsere Mitmenschen objektiv gefangen sind, nicht restlos zu erklären vermögen. Dieser überwältigenden Irrationalität erwehren sich vielfältig colorierte Rationalisten durch Tragen einer Brille, deren Glas durch Pappscheiben ersetzt worden ist. Wirklich beunruhigt sind wir erst von solcher Verkleidung, welche in jener nicht aufgeht: Parabel, Allegorie, Symbol—wo wir sie hundertprozentig erschließen, stellt sich sogleich Zufriedenheit über die Leistung unseres Intellektes ein, so daß wir darüber vergessen, was wir entschlüsselt haben. Der gänzlich bekanntgewordene Gegenstand verschwindet in uns auf Nimmerwiederdenken. Wo etwas vom Rätsel anhält, das, weil es eben eines ist, sich nicht definieren läßt, aber in osmotischer Verbindung zur erwähnten Irrationalität steht, da hält auch unser Interesse an, unsere Neugier, unser Aufgestörtsein. Da bleiben die Fragen offen, auf die es zwar nie Antworten gibt, wobei jedoch die ergebnislose Suche nach ihnen zu ganz anderen Antworten und zugleich auch zu anderen neuen Fragen führt.

Anmerkung

1. Siehe Peter Szondi, "Antike und Moderne in der Ästhetik der Goethezeit," in *Poetik und Geschichtsphilosophie,* I (Frankfurt: Suhrkamp, 1974).

Kasimierz Braun, Modern Acting Theory and Practice

Theoretical statements about the art of acting can be traced back to classical writing, but only the 20th century has generated a plurality of elaborated
methods and theories of acting. In the background of several new ideas concerning
the psychic, physical and social aspects of acting, Kasimierz Braun describes the
contributions made by Stanislawski, Brecht and Grotowski in this area. Stanislavski's method is conceived to enable the actor to impersonate a character as perfectly as possible; Brecht's didactic motives require an alienation of the actor—
being aware of his social position—from the character; Grotowski's "poor theatre"
demands that the actors first of all examine their own personalities in the theatre.
The effects of these theories are partly paradoxical: the "bourgeois" Stanislavski's
method was petrified as the doctrine of Socialist Realism in the theatre, while
Brecht is only hesitatingly accepted in the Communist countries. Polish directors
staged Brecht between 1956 and 1966 to escape the Stalinist doctrines in the arts.
Apart from this, Brecht remains insignificant in Poland, because his "Prussian"
theatre does not appeal to Polish mentality.

Kasimierz Braun. Theorie und Praxis des Schauspielens in der Moderne

Theoretische Äußerungen über die Kunst des Schauspielens können bis in
die Antike zurück verfolgt werden, aber erst das 20. Jahrhundert brachte eine
Vielfalt von vollentwickelten Methoden und Theorien des Schauspielens hervor.
Vor dem Hintergrund zahlreicher Neuerungen, die psychische, physische und
soziale Aspekte des Schauspielens betreffen, beschreibt Kasimierz Braun die
Beiträge von Stanislavski, Brecht und Grotowski auf diesem Gebiet. Stanislavskis
Methode soll dem Schauspieler ermöglichen, eine Rolle so perfekt wie möglich zu
verkörpern; Brechts pädagogische Motive erfordern die Verfremdung der Rolle
durch den Schauspieler, der sich seiner sozialen Position bewußt ist; Grotowskis
"armes Theater" verlangt, daß der Schauspieler in erster Linie seine eigene Person
im Theater ergründet. Die Wirkungen dieser Theorien zeigen paradoxe Züge: die
Methode des "bürgerlichen" Stanislavski wird zur Doktrin des Sozialistischen
Realismus versteinert, während Brecht in den sozialistischen Staaten nur zögernd
aufgenommen wird. Polnische Regisseure benutzten Brecht zwischen 1956 und
1966, um dem stalinistischen Kunstdogma zu entkommen. Abgesehen von dieser
Zeit bleibt die Brecht-Rezeption in Polen unbedeutend, weil das "preußische"
Theater Brechts der polnischen Mentalität nicht zusagt.

Kasimierz Braun. Des méthodes et théories sur l'art dramatique de la moderne

On peut remonter jusqu'aux textes classiques pour trouver des énoncés
théoriques sur l'art dramatique, mais c'est le XXe siècle qui a engendré une
multiplicité de méthodes élaborées et de théories variées sur l'art de l'acteur. Se
situant dans le cadre de différentes idées nouvelles sur les aspects psychiques,
physiques et sociaux du jeu de l'acteur, Kasimierz Braun décrit les contributions
de Stanislavski, de Brecht et de Grotowski dans ce domaine. La méthode de
Stanislavski vise à rendre l'acteur capable d'incarner un personnage le plus par-
faitement possible. L'intention didatique de Brecht exige que l'acteur, en pre-
nant conscience de sa situation sociale, prenne ses distances par rapport à son
personnage; le "théâtre pauvre" de Grotowski requiert de l'acteur qu'il
réfléchisse d'abord sur sa propre personnalité. En fait, les conséquences de ces
théories sont assez paradoxales: la méthode "bourgeoise" de Stanislavski est
devenue la doctrine du réalisme socialiste au théâtre, alors que Brecht n'est

accepté qu'avec beaucoup de réserve dans les pays communistes. Des metteurs en scène polonais montèrent des pièces de Brecht de 1956 à 1966 pour échapper aux doctrines artistiques staliniennes. A cette exception près, Brecht est resté un auteur de peu d'importance en Pologne, parce que son théâtre "prussien" offre peu d'attraits pour la mentalité polonaise.

Modern Acting Theory and Practice

Kasimierz Braun

1

Reflection on the actor's art as a part of performance theory has been with us from the very beginning of theatre history. Spectators have responded to actors or not, liked their "play," faces, gestures, bodies, or disliked these. Remarks on acting—often if only incidental and superficial, without deep analysis—can be found in many literary works, letters, memoirs throughout history. Such remarks are scattered in *The Golden Ass* by Apuleius, in letters of Cicero, in Samuel Pepys's *Diary,* and so on.

The first full-scale theoretical essay on the art of acting is usually thought to be that of Denis Diderot. In his *Paradoxe sur le comédien* (1830), Diderot introduced a fundamental typology which divided the actor's art into two species of actors. The first is an actor who is affective, spontaneous, who follows his reflexes, who acts as his heart tells him; he is violent, unreliable; he expresses sentiments and appeals to sentiments. The second actor is intellectual; his actions are calculated, he controls himself; he is cool; he conveys thoughts and appeals to the intellect. This typology remains a very useful descriptive device even until today.

By the end of the eighteenth and the beginning of the nineteenth centuries a few practical books for actors had been written. Among the earliest we have the *Prescriptions for Actors* by Johann Wolfgang von Goethe and *The Mimic Art* by Wojciech Boguslawski.

Goethe was a great poet, but at the same time he was for many years the director of the court theatre in Weimar, an actor, and the Minister of Internal Affairs (in which position he was the administrator of the police). With a typical clerk's pedantry he compiled several rules for

111

actors, teaching them how to behave on stage and in the city. For example, he describes how an actor must never turn his back to the audience, because the prince sits in the audience!

Less known, I believe, is the book by Boguslawski, the great Polish actor, director of the National Theatre in Warsaw at the end of the eighteenth century, playwright and patriot. *The Mimic Art* is a large handbook for actors. Boguslawski teaches the techniques of expressing "the interior states of the soul" by using all parts of the face and the whole body. He tells how to move eyes, lips, cheeks, brows; which position the whole body should assume; what to do with the hands; how to walk. Chapters of the book have titles such as "Anger," "Fear," "Horror," "Love," and are developed in conjunction with sketches and fragments of plays.

In the nineteenth century, and especially as theatrical criticism developed, the art of the actor became the subject of many studies. It will be enough to note here only the names of French commentator Sarcey or the Pole Wladyslaw Boguslawski, the grandson of Wojciech. Other deep observations about the actor's art are contained in letters and works by Cyprial Norwid, (such as his plays *The Actor* and *In the Wings*). Very popular, too, has been the handbook by the famous French actor Constant Coquelin.

2

I mention these to show that analytic considerations of acting did not just suddenly appear in the twentieth century. In our century, however, there have evolved many different approaches to the work of the actor, principally the methods of Stanislavski, Brecht and Grotowski, which are not only the most distinguished and concise, but are based on actual practice, though they have been articulated at a theoretical level. To see the real dimensions of the thought and practice of Stanislavski, Brecht and Grotowski we must analyze, however briefly, the context of their work. Common to all three innovators are (1) the research on the psychic aspect of acting, the analysis of the mechanism of the actors' ways of creating sentiments, sensations, feelings, thoughts, emotions; the research of the interior of the actor; (2) the research of the physical aspect of acting; the exploration of the body and its capacity of movement, its physical expression; the research of the exterior; and (3) research of the human being in the actor; the interest in the actor as a person, as an individual, as a member of a society and a nation, a subject of history, an artist independent and responsible for his actions.

The first level is connected with the general pursuit of realism in the theatre. "Truth" was the goal, not only the truth of make-up, costumes, props, but of the "genuine" image of the soul. Rehearsals in the theatre became longer and served to let the actor build the complex internal shape of a character, to condition him or her with the variety of circumstances which conditioned the character's behavior. The actor was expected to live the "real" life of the character. Many actors looked for this instinctively, but the method was provided with a theoretical and practical foundation by Stanislavski.

At the second level, at the end of the nineteenth century acting was confronted with a very large movement dedicated to liberating the human body, to redefining the body in both social and artistic terms. As early as the middle of the century (more or less), many societies were organized having social, political and aesthetic goals, which practiced group gymnastics in the open air. In Czechoslovakia such an organization, Sokol, was established in 1862, the Polish Sokol in 1867. About 1880 gymnastics, as a subject, was introduced in all schools in England. In 1896 the first modern Olympic Games were held in Athens. In Geneva, in 1892, Emile-Jacques Dalcroze organized his Institute in which he joined gymnastics with music and dance. Dalcroze's work fascinated and influenced Adolphe Appia and Jacques Copeau, two leaders of the great reform of the theatre. In 1902 the American dancer Isadora Duncan came to Europe introducing the new dance, barefoot on the stage.

Vsevolod Meyerhold believed that the body was the main factor in the theatre. He maintained that the human body reacts primarily by movement, not by thought; that it reacts biologically, mechanically. So Meyerhold invented and practiced exercises which served the actor to develop the capacity to perform using mainly movement and physical actions as the base of performance. Meyerhold called his style and method "biomechanics."

But the belief that the actor's art is first of all visual led farther to experiments in which the actor became only a big puppet, a moving prop, a live rack for costumes. Gordon Craig searched for the ideal actor—and he found the "super-marionette." Alexander Tairow saw the actor more as a dancer. In another important tendency of modern theatre—the theatre of painters—the actor was either completely swept away from the stage, or was used only as a piece of sculpture, the slave of objects, lights, lines. Such theatre was created by the Italian futurists and the German expressionists. Oskar Schlemmer led a theatre of this kind in the Bauhaus in the twenties.

In contrast to these methods of work, on the third level, the actor was regarded especially as a human being, as an individual, as an autonomous and fascinating creature. In 1905 Stanislaw Wyspianski, Polish

113

playwright, poet and printer wrote a beautiful essay/poem/drama, *The Study of Hamlet.* He consecrated it "to the Polish Actors." In that work he envisioned the actor as the bearer of great historical and national traditions, as the proper creator of performance. Wyspianski was interested both in the artistic activity and the ordinary life of the actor; he stressed that the quality of the personality of the actor is a decisive factor in the actor's art.

But the real revolution in asserting the quality of the actor as a person was made by the great Polish actor Juliusz Osterwa. In 1919 he founded a theatre called Reduta. It was at the same time a theatre, a school, a community, a secular monastery. For Osterwa, the most important factor was the individual, personal and moral development of the actor. In Reduta the whole process of life and creating of a group of actors were developed together. These actors lived together; they shared a kitchen and their money; they studied, rehearsed and did research together. They analyzed and discussed their deficiencies and successes as a group. They did not want to be theatrical stars (the posters did not contain their names); they wanted to be servants of art and society.

From the live object, on the one hand, to the humble and poor actor-servant, on the other—many different currents and views on the actor's art and personality were disseminated and practiced in the theatre of the twentieth century even before Brecht and later Grotowski came on the scene.

3

Stanislavski, Brecht, Grotowski were not alone. They appeared sequentially and sometimes acknowledged the achievements of their predecessors. We have to remember that they acted in chronological order: Stanislavski's long activity began just before the turn of the century and extended to the late nineteen-thirties. Brecht wrote his best plays just after Stanislavski's death and became director of the Berliner Ensemble after the Second World War. He had died before Grotowski created the Laboratory Theatre. The line of change and development is obvious in their programs and theories. But using the synchronic method for an overview of the whole problem of acting in the modern theatre, we can distinguish more clearly the differences and similarities of the principal artists and theoreticians.

Let's then discuss the main points of the practice and theory of Stanislavski, Brecht and Grotowski chapter by chapter, confining our discussion to their work as related to acting only.

Predecessors

Stanislavski was associated with the search for realism in the theatre of the nineteenth century. He admired the work of the theatre of the Duke of Saxe-Meiningen, who, in 1871, first introduced realism on a large scale.

Brecht was educated both by modern European art (especially Futurism and Expressionism) and by history, that is the First World War. He loved the "mass theatre" of Max Reinhardt, the political theatre of Erwin Piscator and the political cabarets then common in Germany. He admired also the opera and operetta and later the American "musical." The musical theatre in Germany always had had a very strong tradition, particularly after the 1870s, following Richard Wagner's activity.

Grotowski admitted that he had two masters—Stanislawski and Osterwa. The first gave him tools for exploring the actor's technique; the second helped him to discover the human being in the actor. When studying the capacity of the human body Grotowski based his work on Far Eastern Theatre Kathakali, on No and Kabuki, on Meyerhold's biomechanics, and on Artaud's call to the actor as shaman.

Connections outside the theatre

Stanislavski, we know, was closely associated with Russian psychological, realistic and social playwrights. The most important single collaborator with the Art Theatre was Anton Chekhov; *The Seagull,* the title and the symbol taken from a play by Chekhov, became the sign of the Moscow Art Theatre and was painted on the curtain. Stanislavski also collaborated with Maxim Gorki, who afterwards helped him survive Stalin's terror in the thirties. The director of the Art Theatre surrounded himself with literary people, musicians, high bourgeoisie; in the main he was rather distant from any of the movements in modern art in Russia, whether in poetry of painting or, most importantly, in politics.

Brecht, on the other hand, became in the twenties a participant in political actions, demonstrations, and struggles. He was closely connected with the whole modern artistic movement in Germany, Austria, and Switzerland and knew of experiments of the radical avant-garde in the newly established Soviet Union. His friends were the painters, poets, musicians of the international avant-garde. He simultaneously believed that art had to be a tool to foster and sustain social revolution, while remaining extremely experimental in form and content. After 1933 and Hitler's coming to power, Brecht emigrated and eventually settled in the USA (1941) where we know he was rather isolated. Obviously Americans did not recognize him as a genius. Not until the German Democratic

Republic was established and he went there to eventually become the director of the Berliner Ensemble Theatre did he again become world-famous. In Berlin he developed his practice, surviving strong criticism by the government of the GDR.

Grotowski started as a militant of the Communist youth organization in Poland. In his theatrical work he has been, and is still, very much alone in the Polish theatrical milieu. Only a few supported him in the beginning. He looked for scholars, doctors, psychologists, specialists of psychodrama; he surrounded himself with youth. He became the leader and the hero of world avant-garde theatre. He sought believers and pupils rather than collaborators. After his youth he never participated either in direct political activity or in the work of any traditional, professional theatre.

Main points of the methods and theories

Stanislavski ordered the actor to experience, to embody the character. His method had to enable the actor to become the character. So Stanislavski's method was based on the integration of the actor and the character. The whole work process of the actor had to lead to his identification with the role. Stanislavski stressed that this incarnation had to be both interior and exterior, but he considered the interior incarnation as the first, basic most important element. In terms of psychology he referred to the "empathy" (the identification) of the actor with the character. The Stanislavski method included many exercises, steps and procedures which would permit the actor to bridge the long distance between himself and the character. The most important of these are "circumstances"—psychological, social, personal factors of a character's life. The actor was supposed to describe, to imagine, to articulate, to discover as much as possible the various conditions, factors and "circumstances" of the character's life, to "enter into them" and to live somebody else's life. For this Stanislavski loved and used illusion. He submerged the actor in a flood of props, decors, colored lights—all designed to imitate "the real." The actor was fully integrated in this "real" environment.

Brecht emphasized the process of thinking. He described the actor as a social and political militant who uses the theatre only as a tool in his struggle. He attempted to radically disconnect the actor and the character—not to play or to act it, and not even to show it in its entirety, but rather to perform only the main aspects of a character, condensing them by using certain techniques. That is, in the staging: white, bright light, white curtains, slogans and inscriptions on streamers. In the acting: songs distinct from dialogue, dance, expressions coming from the circus, real objects as props, all on a clean, empty stage. The main discovery and the main point of Brecht's theory was the so-called *Verfremdungseffekt*. In terms of acting it meant the alienation of the actor from the character, their separation.

Grotowski called his method "the poor theatre." In it he sought the "poor actor." What does this mean? Grotowski demanded that the actor play himself, that he reject the character. He wanted the actor to explore his own subconscious, the deepest levels of his existence, and to develop the attitudes, the images, the sounds found there. Afterwards, during a process of constant improvisation, to maintain this, to be able to repeat this, not as an external structure (like character) which has to be reproduced every evening, but as a living process every day the same and every day as new as before. To achieve this the actor would need to become "empty" and "poor." He could only follow his internal stirrings. For this, the actor should not develop several performance techniques, should not be "rich" in terms of available techniques; he would rather reject all "blocks," obstacles, hindrances which would prevent him from delivering himself to the utmost process of discovery, completely and totally. The old methods of trance were obviously useful for this. Improvisation was the major form of work. Spontaneous movements and sounds, hysterical reactions and uncontrolled behavior subsumed the most precious discoveries. In short the actor explored his own biography, his own life. He should not perform, he should be.

The morality of the actor

In terms of ethics the Stanislavski method was the method of the perfect lie. The actor hid himself behind the character and claimed to the public that he was somebody else. He directed the public to believe that he was not Mr. Stanislavski, a very well known person, but that he was Dr. Stockman. The public had to forget that this was in fact Mr. Stanislavski (Mr. Moskvin, Mrs. Lilianana, etc.) and had to take him for Dr. Stockman. Stanislavski called for the high integrity of the actor, but his method was based on the fundamental contradiction between the truth of the actor's real life and the imaginary truth of the character's life.

In Brecht's work this contradiction was overcome. Separating actor and character, Brecht did not want to hide the actor behind the character. Conversely, he stressed with ostentation that *this* is an actor, with a name, personal life, political opinions, a member of a specific society, and *that* is a character, a creature of literature and imagination. The actor was not subordinated to the character. He looked at the character from a distance. The actor or actress accepted the character or criticized it and remained independent.

Grotowski wanted the actor to be himself, to perform nothing and no one apart from himself. In terms of morality Grotowski called for the pure, absolute, complete truth of the actor's behavior, words and actions. The actor was supposed to discover himself, to reveal his intimacy, to sacrifice himself for, and to the spectator. This was an extremely personal approach to the actor's work. The actor should perform himself. Therefore, he should improve himself, work on his own, personal morality. Grotowski used—literally—the term "saint-actor," "actor-saint."

Influences of Stanislavski, Brecht, Grotowski

Stanislavski's work has been very highly esteemed in Russia and in the Soviet Union. But in the thirties it became frozen as the official doctrine of "Socialist Realism" in the theatre, and since then its history has been paradoxical. Stanislavski's method is the only one officially permitted and taught in the Soviet Union, but as an official doctrine it is simultaneously hated by many artists and avoided by all possible means. Stanislavski's method has also been introduced and officially imposed after World War II in all Eastern Bloc countries. The result has been somewhat similar. Actually it has remained the official method in Rumania and Bulgaria, but in other countries, including Poland, it is rather forgotten. I personally see Stanislavski's method as a very useful, primary, way of teaching acting, and I use it when working with my students, at the basic level.

Stanislavski is not popular in his country but at the same time has become a sort of father of the American modern theatre and film. As is well known, in the twenties The Moscow Art Theatre toured the United States and a few of its actors remained here. They became teachers, and thus introduced the Stanislavski method. Among them was a Pole, Richard Boleslawski. The method—only "The Method", not "Stanislavski's Method"—has been until now the principal vehicle for the teaching of acting in America. The teachers—actors from Moscow—had pupils who became teachers. I was once present at a lesson of Lee Strasberg at his Actor's Studio; he used the identical vocabulary as Stanislavski used in his works.

The Brechtian method was no more fortunate. In his own home Brecht has been criticized; in fact his acting method has not had much influence in East Germany and in other Eastern European countries. In Poland this was not because of political reasons. The cool, calculated, artificial, expressionistic acting is against our traditions and spirit. Grotowski, rather than Brecht, succeeded Stanislavski. But I should explain that it is not because Brecht is not very well known in Poland. In fact, the situation is just the converse. Before the war Leon Schiller produced *The Threepenny Opera* just after its Berlin premiere. After the war, the Berliner Ensemble visited Poland. Several great directors such as Erwin Axer and Ludwik Rene staged Brecht's plays. Konrad Swinarski had been Brecht's pupil. I personally staged three plays by Brecht: *The Caucasian Chalk Circle, The Good Person of Sezuan,* and *Mother Courage and her Children.* But in all these productions we searched for the humanistic aspect of the dramas, concentrating on people involved in history and in their own passions, rather than on the rules of the *Verfremdungseffekt.*

The real "new country" for Brecht was situated in the many groups of guerilla, revolutionary street theatre all over the world, especially in South and North America. The Brechtian method of acting—acting regarded as a social or political action—is of obvious use to them.

What about Grotowski? I have seen in my life many performances all over the world based on his method, but never have I seen a performance that could convince me. They were artificial, shallow; they took only the skin of this method, not its heart.

The real and deep influence of Grotowski is, for me, connected with a new attitude in theatrical work, an attitude which is now characteristic of many people and groups: the responsibility for the work, for the word, for the public, for the human act. After Grotowski's activity it is no longer possible for an actor or director to be unaware of his responsibility for his work, not to assume the responsibility for the others also—the collaborators and the spectators. New relations have also been created in the theatre, between audience and theatre, between actors and spectators.

But despite the importance of Grotowski, Brecht's influence and presence in my country remains as an important historical fact. The first thing to note is that Brecht made an important contribution to the Polish theatre in a relatively short time. Before the Second World War (as I have just mentioned) there was only one production. Of course, nothing was produced during the War. And also nothing during the imposed "socialist-realistic" period. Only after October 1956 did a wave of Brecht's plays come in, but this activity lasted only up till about 1966. Later Brecht was performed only from time to time; in fact rarely. Recently he is almost never performed.

Historians and theoreticians of culture discuss whether there exists such a phenomenon as "national character," or does a nation have "character?" Of course not, at least not in precise terms of psychology. Of course yes, if we consider "national character" as a metaphor. Being conscious of this distinction we can say that from a historic distance Brecht's theories and plays appear very "German," and even (which is a surprise) very "Prussian." They express the advantage of "mind" over "heart;" they stress such values as purity, innocence, order; they present the firm belief that history is logic and has its logical development (Hegel!), that the world can be described and has a coherent structure, that society *should* be organized and have a permanent and righteous set of laws, just rulers (Azdak!)—and so on.

Those contentions, obvious in German culture, historically were aimed in Brecht's work against the chaos, anarchy and frustration following the First World War; later against fascist madness. Paradoxically, it is possible to say that Brecht opposed Hitlerism because it was an anti-German movement, anti-German with its deep mysticism, fanaticism, non-objectivity, superpower, ideology, disdain for facts and reasoning, disregard of reality.

And here we are able to connect those rather self-evident statements with a sense of Brecht's influence in Poland. Generally speaking, Brecht's work was absolutely foreign to the "Polish character," which can be roughly described as spiritual, non-realistic, sentimental; stressing such human values as freedom, independence and self-determination of the individual; disregarding organization, order, even law, and so on. Actually, Brechtian theatre could not be widely accepted by the Polish public, especially in its "orthodox" version. It could not be close to Polish directors and actors. It was not by chance that two best Polish "Brechtian" directors were strongly connected with German culture: the late Konrad Swinarski had spent two years in the Berliner Ensemble as a pupil and assistant of Brecht himself and Erwin Axer, bilingual, born in Vienna, lover of Goethe and Thomas Mann. And the best "Brechtian" actor, Tadeusz Lomnicki (Arturo Ui), an actor using and loving the most sophisticated techniques among Polish actors, a "formalist" actor.

But Brecht was manifest in Poland and had a great impact especially, as I have said, between 1956 and 1966. In the same measure as it opposed Hitlerism Brecht's work was also against Stalinism. So it was important, useful and "at hand" in Poland when the reaction against Stalinism was both strong and common. Brecht was in fact a tool with which we tried to exorcise, to expel Stalin's madness and illness out of the Polish culture.

At the same time, in that period Brecht was one of the previously prohibited authors; Polish theatre people would thus consider him first of all as a new playwright, offering new plays, excellent parts for actors, imaginative visions for directors and humanistic messages for the public.

But Brecht never became widely familiar in the Polish theatre and did not remain permanently in the repertory. Now he is only occasionally included as a great world classic.

A question for discussion might be whether Brecht did have an impact on Polish acting. Probably, but not to a high degree. His influence was primarily as an advocate of his technique, as someone who stressed the formal aspect of acting, an aspect which in recent Polish theatre is rather disregarded. Brecht's call for an "actor-activist," and what was worse, an activist colored red, was absolutely unacceptable to Polish actors who preferred to be "artists," "prophets," and "saints." Generally, Brecht's contribution to the treasury of Polish acting seems to be very limited.

4

The above paragraph about "Brecht in Poland" was essential to the author of this study, who is himself a Pole and a director. But in our main subject it was rather a digression. Let's come back to our topic by way of a summary: Brecht in the context of the main acting methods in the 20th Century theatre.

Even as brief a look at the acting in the 20th Century as we have undertaken enables us to come to some final conclusions. We have seen that the evolution proceeded from actor-artist through actor-militant to actor-saint. The spectator evolved at the same pace as the actor: he was a spectator; he became a participant, even a brother. From Stanislavski to Grotowski, and further, to several groups which are currently working, there is the constant line of re-evaluation of human presence and the human morality in the theatre. From aesthetics to ethics; from an actor to a full person. These three methods—and we should add also the Meyerhold biomechanics, the Osterwa community, and the Artaud trance—show us the theatre as a wide field in which, using different instruments, we can work and receive a rich harvest.

Luigi Squarzina. "Brecht and Breughel: Mannerism and the Avant-garde."

Luigi Squarzina investigates the influence on Brecht of the Flemish painter, Peter Breughel. He shows the sources that Brecht used and cites Brecht's various published comments on Breughel. An examination of various Breughel interpretations demonstrates why the 20th century avant-garde could feel an affinity with the Mannerism of the 16th century.

Breughel's influence on Brecht is shown to be particularly evident in two major plays. The construction and thematic drive of *Fear and Misery of the Third Reich* clearly shows Breughel's influence. In *The Caucasian Chalk Circle* Breughel's influence is best seen in the composition of various scenes in Brecht's stage production. In addition, the character of Grusche in *The Caucasian Chalk Circle* derives much of her meaning from Breughel's painting "Dulle Griet" and this painting can be shown to have influenced in the Berliner Ensemble production of the play.

Luigi Squarzina. "Brecht und Breughel: Manierismus und die Avantgarde."

Luigi Squarzina untersucht den Einfluß des flämischen Malers Peter Breughel auf Bertolt Brecht. Er stellt die Quellen von Brechts Breughelrezeption vor und zitiert dessen Äußerungen über Breughel. Eine Betrachtung verschiedener Breughel-Interpretationen zeigt, warum sich die Avantgarde des 20. Jahrhunderts dem Manierismus des 16. Jahrhunderts verwandt fühlen konnte.

Der Einfluß Breughels auf Brecht wird besonders in zwei Stücken sichtbar. Der Aufbau und die Thematik von *Furcht und Elend des Dritten Reiches* zeigen deutlich Breughelsche Züge, ebenso *Der kaukasische Kreidekreis*, in dem der Einfluß Breughels bis in die Komposition einzelner Szenen reicht. Darüber hinaus hat Brecht die Figur der Grusche bewußt an seine Deutung von Breughels Gemälde *Dulle Griet* angelehnt und dieses Gemälde auch in Bühnenbildern seiner Inszenierung im Berliner Ensemble benutzt.

Luigi Squarzina. "Brecht et Breughel : Maniérisme et Avant-garde."

L'article de Luigi Squarzina recherche l'influence du peintre flamand Peter Breughel sur Brecht. Il met en évidence les sources utilisées par celui-ci et cite ses différents commentaires publiés sur Breughel. Un premier examen des diverses interprétations de Breughel démontre pourquoi l'avant-garde du XXème siècle pouvait se sentir des affinités avec le maniérisme du XVIème siècle.

L'influence de Breughel sur Brecht est particulièrement évidente dans deux de ses pièces les plus importantes : la construction et le thème de *Grandeur et misère du Troisième Reich* démontrent clairement l'influence de Breughel ; dans *Le Cercle de craie caucasien* l'influence de Breughel est particulièrement évidente dans la composition et dans l'ordre des scènes de la production originale de ce travail de Brecht. De plus, le personnage de Grusche tire beaucoup de sa signification de "Dulle Griet" de Breughel. On peut d'ailleurs vérifier que cette peinture a influencé la mise en scène du Berliner Ensemble.

Brecht and Breughel: Mannerism and the Avant-garde

Luigi Squarzina

The theme cannot be treated exhaustively here. I have proposed it, however not only because I consider it intrinsic to both *Fear and Misery of the Third Reich,* perhaps a minor but certainly a very particular Brechtian play which I staged in 1973 in Rome, and to an undisputed masterpiece like *The Caucasian Chalk Circle,* which I staged in 1971 in Genova, but also and moreover because the theme deals with the entire Brechtian system of visualization, a field too rarely inquired upon. Furthermore the present essay is the first of two studies probing the relationships between visual arts and twentieth century dramaturgy, the second one referring to "Shaw's *Heartbreak House* and late Pre-Raphaelitism" on the occasion of my staging of Shaw's play, Rome 1980.

I suggest starting from the note "On the Formalistic Character of the Theory of Realism" dated around 1937, the same time when Brecht, in exile, was working on *Fear and Misery* and an argument against him was going on by Georg Lukács and other Marxist writers, the "theorists of realism" as Brecht calls them. He does not defend himself, he counterattacks, denouncing, paradoxically, "the formalistic character" of such a theory and makes a case out of the two works he has at hand, a historical novel and a play. They are *The Business Deals of Julius Caesar* and *Fear and Misery.* He says that he is writing both of them "merely for realistic reasons" and yet the theory of realism, he adds, is of no use to him, in spite of the fact that, in the first work cited, "the novel [as a genre] is the very domain of our theorists," and, in the second example, "some scenes can be

123

fitted into the 'realistic' scheme, though from rather afar." He specifies that in shaping his novel and drama by means of the montage-technique considered "formalistic" by his opponents, he obeyed the necessity "to firmly grasp reality": a reality which, in the case of the drama, is "life under the Nazi dictatorship." Furthermore, in composing *Fear and Misery of the Third Reich* he claims to have been helped and influenced "more by Breughel's paintings than from any dissertation on realism." (*GW*, XIX, 299–300.) The mention of Peter Breughel—whom he calls "the Breughel of the peasants"—will surprise only those who have not grasped the deeply Breughelian sense of many of Brecht's works: a sense which, as I will try to show, goes far beyond a certain kind of folk-life, pauperism, distress, plasticity of assemblage, and Flemish taste: all legitimate though obvious aspects often exploited in staging some of his plays. But the question, in my opinion, is not at all that simple. In fact, if my own *Theaterarbeit* can be of any use, I must say that I did not try to speculate on these aspects in staging either *Fear and Misery* or *The Caucasian Chalk Circle*, a play which is, as we will see, so intrinsically Breughelian.

In 1939, in a brief essay on *Experimental Theatre*, Brecht states that "the Chinese theatre, for instance, the classic Spanish theatre, the popular theatre of Breughel's time and the Elizabethan theatre have obtained artistic results through *Verfremdungseffekte*." (*GW*, XV, 305.) Practically speaking, it is easy to understand what he means by "the popular theatre of Breughel's time," though the definition cannot be said to fit into the *Theaterwissenschafts* criteria. We find much more about Breughel in a page of Brecht's *Arbeitsjournal* dated December 8 of the same year, 1939, where a short list of objects belonging to him during his exile is written almost in verse-form. The list begins as follows:

> I own a Chinese roll *The man who doubts*
> three Japanese masks
> two small Chinese carpets
> two Bavarian knives . . .

and it continues at line 28—five lines from the end—with: "two volumes of Breughel's paintings." (*AJ*, 73.) From another page of his *Arbeitsjournal*, dated November 19, 1942, we learn that the volumes referred to were the great study "by the art-historian Glück whose edition of Breughel has toured the world with me." (*AJ*, 545.)

After *Fear and Misery*'s years, the late thirties, further references to Breughel as a source of inspiration appear towards the end of World War II when in his American exile he is writing *The Caucasian Chalk Circle*, starting off from a proposal aimed at a Broadway production by Luise Rainer—the actress who had also worked with Erwin Piscator. Though the Broadway project was soon abandoned (luckily we should add, judging from the fiasco of Brecht's previous Broadway experiment: the adaption, in collaboration with Auden, of Webster's *Duchess of Malfi*) it must have influenced and conditioned his writing of the *Chalk Circle*. He admits to have found many difficulties in composing the play; and he states twice in his *Arbeitsjournal*—I will fully quote it further on—that the "impasse" in which he found himself while working on the character and the actions of the female protagonist—the poor servant who saves and brings up the son of a governor—was finally overcome thanks to two things: Lion Feuchtwanger's advice, and the image of one of Breughel's greatest paintings, *De Dulle Griet*, Margot the Mad. "Dulle Griet" in Flemish, "Die tolle Grete" in German; from Grete to Gretchen and then to the Georgian Grusche—even the name of the character of the tentative Katia of the first draft was finally changed in a Breughelian way.

The iconic ambiguity of the *Dulle Griet*—one of Breughel's most "mysterious" masterpieces (the adjective "mysterious" referring to the Flemish master can be traced back to Baudelaire—as we shall see—and it appears also in an intriguing page by Antonin Artaud, which I will quote later on)—was a quality Brecht exploited cleverly in his work.

We have to remember that in the twenties Max Dvorak, the art-historian and theoretician, wanted to free Breughel's mysterious world from the current and simplistic labels, and confirmed the inclusion of the painter in Mannerism, as the crisis-ridden period between late Renaissance and Baroque was called. Max Dvorak was suggesting a fascinating comparison between the artistic crisis-and-revolution of the late sixteenth century and twentieth century avant-garde movements. Brecht too, in the thirties, considered Breughel to be the creator of a system of signification and communication by no means so simple as it was thought to be by those who insisted on classifying him as the last of the Primitives. Brecht was well aware of Breughel's complexity; and it is this complexity which is often eluded by the scenographers and the directors who adopt Breughelian images in staging Brecht literally, even though correctly and at times (as in Strehler's *Galileo*) very successfully indeed.

Without losing myself in such fields as history of art or iconology, I will quote the very first of Breughel's biographers, Carel Von Mander (1604). Listing some of the things Breughel painted he writes: "He made a Dulle Griet, who is stealing something to take to Hell, and who wears a vacant stare. . . ."[1] Baudelaire, who speaks about the "carphanaüm diabolique et drôlatique de Breughel," says that much of Breughel's art "contient, ce me semble, une espèce de *mystère*" and that his oddities, if they may be called so, "donnent le vertige." "Mystère" and "vertige" are, according to Baudelaire, the privileges of the "comique absolu" and not

125

the "significatif" one.[2] The art-historian Grossman notes that at the beginning of the twentieth century

> one began to look [in Breughel] for political allusions, which in contrast to Baudelaire's opinion, one hoped to be able to decipher. . . . Breughel's works seem to contain more than meets the eye, and this fact has also tempted students . . . to search for a hidden message in Breughel's compositions.[3]

Nowadays Michel Foucault, pointing out the differences between the madness in Breughel and in Goya, says that in the latter "madness has become man's possibility of abolishing both man and the world," while in the former "the landscape that Dulle Griet moved through was marked by a whole human language."[4]

What is it, then, the fantastic and dismal cosmos that surrounds Griet? Is it the wreck of a subconscious violence exercised by herself against herself? Or is it the image of a spiritual plunder of which, like the symbol of Avarice (one of the Medieval vices), she carries on herself the spoils (pots, cups, coins, gold chains, etc.)? Or is it an episode of real violence, of social unrest, of war, of which Griet and the other possessed women in the painting, loaded with sacks, run away so as not to perish as victims, seizing what is at hand? I think that Brecht's interpretation is primarily this last one. The similarity is strikingly evident between the destruction, burning and plunder in Breughel's painting and the scene in the *Chalk Circle,* where the servants, in the residence of the Governor, run away taking with them what they can.

The photos come from the *Chalk Circle* staged by Brecht himself in the fifties with the Berliner Ensemble. I am including these not because of their rarity—they are rather common, in fact—but because I don't think they have ever been analyzed in a Breughelian sense. Well, as you know, during the pillage of the Governor's house, Grusche, not so much the best-hearted as the "dullest" of the female servants, finds herself looking after the Governor's baby heir, abandoned by his mother in a basket. "The temptation of pity is terrible," says the folksinger who narrates the play (*GW,* V, 2025.): Grusche does not have the heart to abandon the new born baby to the rioting princes—they would slaughter him—and she escapes carrying her dangerous hostage in swaddling clothes. You can see how faithfully the two buildings in the mise-en-scene of the Berliner Ensemble correspond to the "mouth of hell" on the left and to the pillaged houses on the right side of Breughel's composition; furthermore, Griet's foolish empty stare corresponds to the *Ersatz* of motherly love that Grusche feels, almost monomaniacally, for the baby which is not hers. (See illustrations on page 139.)

At this point, and before going further, a statement must be made, or repeated. In the workshop of Brecht the playwright and metteur-en-scene there is no place for literal mimetic complacencies. We have to be aware of his strong anti-Aristotelian, anti-Wagnerian posture against the idea of the theatre as the unity of all arts. For him, painting, music and dance cannot be reduced to the role of servants to drama. So, his recourse to Breughel is not to be restricted to a cultural exercise. Brecht's taste is of the highest quality, but the *category* of taste is foreign to him. His urge to explore a variety of media, to cross the boundaries of all the arts, has, in a sense, a shocking similarity with the multi-media, multi-experience attempts of the artistic generation of the seventies: a "manneristic" generation indeed.

Going back to our subject, in the description of Grusche's wandering up and down in the mountains, defying abysses and crossing hanging bridges, meeting brutal peasants and having to escape soldiers (but also to strike them: in the painting Griet carries a sword, and in the play Grusche hits a cuirassier hard on the head), the *Chalk Circle* is a clear example—the clearest among Brecht's plays, with the exception of *Fear and Misery*—of a twentieth century neo-Manneristic "losing of the centre." The same can be said of the second part of the *Chalk Circle,* showing the adventures and misadvantures of Azdak. This "losing of the centre" is in few Manneristic artists more evident than in Breughel—perhaps not particularly in the *Dulle Griet,* where Griet can be said to dominate the landscape. It is a well-known fact that in Breughel's canvasses the protagonists, or the eponymous episodes, are often hidden at first sight in the multiformity, in the scattering, in the dislocation, in the synchronic assemblage of dia-chronic gestures. Now, what we must ask ourselves is if late sixteenth century Mannerism, especially in Breughel's imagery and style, spoke for Brecht, the playwright, the language of the twentieth century avant-garde, as it did for Dvorak, the art-historian. I do think so. In defending—against Lukács—the avant-garde techniques necessary to him to express the state of the disrupted capitalistic world, Brecht must have felt close to the myths, the personalities, the language, the cult of ambiguity of the so-called Mannerists. If it is so, the question whether Griet is a melancholic or a frantic character is, at least in part, a useless one. Breughelian ambiguity, with its irony and fury, is welcome to Brecht. Ambiguity, iconoclasty, irony and fury are the very same anti-values proposed by the anti-literature, anti-art, anti-organistic movements of our century, the spirit and tech-niques of which Brecht nurtured in himself up till his *Schweik,* a play still to be analyzed in the Dada perspective which I think to be apt.

As for *Fear and Misery of the Third Reich,* it recalls Breughel's Manner-ism in many of its characteristics. It is a play with no focal point, no centre, no unity, no structure, frankly aleatory (why choose those episodes and not

127

others?) and apparently casual; it was written in fact on the request of Slatan Dudow, who had worked with Brecht for the film *Kuhle Wampe,* and of a small group of actors in exile, Helene Weigel among them. The play is conducted on a double narrative level, the enumerative one of the "parade" ("here they come . . .": the SS, the SA, the doctors, the physicists, the judges, the professors, the proletarians . . .), and the level of each separate episode with small but well-enunciated characters. It is the same double level to be found in Breughel's disquieting technique of storytelling: a technique extremely close to reality but impossible to fit—as Brecht puts it about his play—"within the realistic scheme . . . if for nothing else at least for the simple fact that the scenes are too short" (*GW,* XIX, 299–300.), as provocatively diminuitive as so many Breughelian episodes. Breughel's faithful, scientific observation of everyday life corresponds to *Fear and Misery* being "based on eye-witnesses and newspapers reports," as Brecht states (*GW,* III, 1187.); nevertheless, on stage the play results in "a dance of ghosts of damned reality," as it was pointed out in review of the Paris performance of May 1938,[5] and as it can be said of so many of Breughel's paintings.

Among the audience of the Paris première-in-exile there was an exceptional spectator, Walter Benjamin, who highly praised the play for its unity of the artistic with the political. I think that the compliment made Brecht happy, coming from a critic he esteemed profoundly. The contrary can be said of a compliment he had received in the same year 1938 from a very different source.

Among the episodes of *Fear and Misery of the Third Reich,* one of the best is surely "The Informer," in which a professor and his wife are terrorized by the fear of being denounced to the police by their ten year old boy for some phrases mildly critical of Hitlerism. The episode, published in *Das Wort,* the Moscow review for banished intellectuals, was polemically appreciated by Georg Lukács in an article which appeared in the same publication three months later:

> And Brecht has published a short scene in one act ("The Informer") where he already fights against the fascist brutality in a realistic way which is new for him. . . . Telling various *people's stories,* he offers a living image of the fascist terror in Germany, and shows how this terror uproots the human basis of any kind of social life—the relationship of man, wife and child—and how the fascist brutality destroys to the very roots what it pretends to protect: the family.[6]

Brecht's refusal of this kind of approval by the chief of the "theorists of realism" was clear and sharp, even if not openly expressed. For him, no scene in *Fear and Misery* could be understood without grasping the stylistic quality of the montage as a whole, and he jotted down cogent, even if hypothetical instructions for the production:

> In *Fear and Misery of the Third Reich,* more than in other works, there is a great temptation to use an Aristotelian type of acting. In order that the play can be immediately staged in spite of the difficult conditions of exile, it is structured in such a way that it can be performed by small companies (like workers' troupes) already existing, and in extracts with a free choice from the 24 scenes. The workers' troupes are neither able nor willing to force the audience to participate emotionally; the few professional artists are very well acquainted with the epic style of acting they had acquired in theatrical experiments in the decade preceding Fascism. The styles of these actors and of the workers' troupes match perfectly. The theoreticians who recently discussed the "mon--tage technique" as if it were a purely formal principle, are here faced by the "montage" as a practical device, which ought to bring their speculations back down to reality. (*GW,* XVII, 1099.)

Another crucial point which brings us back to the visual aspects of the play is the "comic" treatment of most of the material. *Fear and Misery* is Breughelian in its being catastrophic *and* hilarious, disquieting *and* grotesquely funny, as it resulted to be at the Parisian première of May 1938. The audience laughed often and heartily, to Brecht's satisfaction.

Certainly, the comic element in *Fear and Misery* is of the kind Baudelaire calls "comique significatif," related to social satire and criticism of manner. It is not the "comique absolu," metaphysical and unrestricted, that the French poet, who ascribed the former to his countrymen, attributed, above all, to the Germans, but also to the English. And it was almost, we could say, to let Baudelaire discover the whole essence of the comic element, that the English had sent to Paris the very famous clown (famous nowadays, after Baudelaire's influential pages, but ignored in Paris at that time) who created a sanguine and anti-Debureau Pierrot. If we limit ourselves to Brecht's references, the comic in *Fear and Misery* is undoubtedly similar to Grosz's grotesque (or to Beckmann's exasperation). Grosz-like seems to have been the back-stage canvas in the Paris performance of 1938. Among Brecht's contemporaries I shall also refer to Heartfield with his photomontages. Heartfield, one of the self-declared German dadaists, together with Grosz, is one of the "five artists" (Grosz, Heartfield, Piscator, Eisler, and Brecht himself) who, as Brecht says in a short essay of the thirties, "took sides with the people" during the years of the Weimar Republic (*GW,* XIX, 336.). It is a montage technique we are dealing with in *Fear and Misery,* because its dramaturgy is segmented and centrifugal and because its episodes are to be selected and arranged by different directors into different sequences in different stagings. This is a characteristic Brecht repeatedly stresses about his play. Therefore, each

129

producer can organize and superimpose various scenes in such a way that they become mutually related as to form, just as in Heartfield's photographic and graphic fragments, pluri-eloquent images of one aspect or another of the "social monster" under analysis. The thematic similarity with Heartfield is evident, as in the episode with the judge.

In my production I tried to make the play speak a "montage language." A composite scene about science resulted from the combination and the *enchevêtrement* of two episodes, "Physics" and "Professional Illness." In a sequence about the "Proletarians," the same five actors and the same set were used to bind together four different episodes of proletarian life under the Nazis.

Leaving Brecht's contemporaries aside, we will continue checking the "help" which, according to his own statement, Brecht received from his spiritual contemporary of the late sixteenth century.

In *Fear and Misery,* apart from the schematic street scene of the two SS men which opens the "German Parade," and apart from a glimpse of the concentration camp (where the still great division and hatred among the leftist parties, a split which had favored Hitler's rise to power, is painted with tragic irony) or of forced labor (object: the class division), the focus is on a succession of interiors. For Brecht the play was a demonstration of the capability of the epic theatre of offering a series of interiors. The Breughelian originality of *Fear and Misery* consists in its showing the worst mass-horror in history through flashes from private life. The American title given to the play by Eric Bentley, during the war, was *The Private Life of the Master Race.* The life of upper middle class, low middle class and proletarian families is revealed in the kitchens of the very rich and in their elegant bedrooms, in the middle-class diningrooms, in the poor houses of the working class. The living and working conditions of a whole nation are observed in the workshop of a textile industry or in the office of a judge, etc. And we will not draw from the text the permanent meaning of "keeping on guard" that Brecht promises, if we are not able to make the text live on stage in its peculiar theatrality; if we don't transform its stylistically composite valences into serious and comic genre-demonstrations: into a *love drama* for "The Jewish Wife," into a *judicial thriller* for "The Search of Night," into a family *tragicomedy* for "The Informer," into a *Lehrstück* of the conspiration practice for "The Man Released From Prison," into a *parodistic palinode* of the inter-party struggles for "The Soldiers of the Mud," into the demonstration, in "The Chalk Cross," that through *theatre within the theatre* truth, dialectic truth, can always be told.

In a dialogue written in 1938, Brecht makes somebody describe a performance of *Fear and Misery* he has seen:

These plays show how the people behave under [Hitler's] rod of steel. One saw people of almost every class and the ways of their suppressions and revolts. One saw the fear of the oppressed and the fear of the oppressors. It was like a collection of gestures, artistically realized; the persecuted looking over their shoulders (or the persecutor doing so); falling suddenly silent; taking one's hand to a mouth that has already spoken too much; laying a hand on the shoulder of a person caught red-handed; lying when blackmailed; telling the truth through whispers; mistrust between lovers—and many other things. But the extraordinary was that the actors did not at all present these horrible incidences in a way that the spectators were tempted to shout, "Stop!" The spectators seemingly did not share the terror of those on stage at all, and this is why there was a continuous laughter among the audience without the profound seriousness of the presentation being disturbed by that. For the laughter seemed to concern the stupidity, which saw itself as being forced to be violent, and to address the helplessness, which showed up as brutality. (*GW*, XVI, 602–603.)

This shows the Breughelian qualities of *Fear and Misery*, though the "collection of gestures" does not fully do justice to the variated and even bizarre corporality of the play: if we could scatter the 24 situations high and wide over a big two-dimensional surface, using the different depths suggested by the artifices of Manneristic perspective, or anti-perspective, the result would be one of Breughel's multifocal paintings, like *Path to Calvary*.

Now we have to consider that, while *Fear and Misery* is rather imperfect regarding epic theories, having been conceived in 1935 to 1938 as a tool to be used in the political struggle waged with minimal and inconsistent theatrical means against the then all-powerful Nazism, the epic treatment of *The Caucasian Chalk Circle*, on the other hand, is satisfying and coherent. This epic quality was reached by Brecht in 1944, jumping out from the compromises inherent in the Broadway project. In summer 1944 the victory against Hitler was well in sight, and Brecht could then have in mind a future production to be acted by a company of German actors trained in his new techniques.

As you know, in the *Chalk Circle* we admire the succession, the parallelism and then the masterly fusion of two stories, the stories of Grusche and of Azdak; *Fear and Misery* is, on the contrary, a mosaic of related stories to be chosen by the director and the actors among the 24 episodes of the text. So, the common Breughelianism so clearly felt in both plays (as well as in the carnival scene of *Life of Galileo*, conceived in the same time-span of that crucial decade of world history), is an inspiration which produces, in Brecht's words, very different "artistic results obtained through the use of the *Verfremdungseffekt*" like the ones of the "popular theatre of Breughel's time."

131

Fear and Misery is related to the presentation technique of the agit-prop, and it can be acted by a dozen actors, politically engaged but not all of them professionals—and this is indeed a kind of "popular" stagecraft in Brecht's sense of the word. In a different way, what is "popular" in the extremely sophisticated *Chalk Circle,* full of Chinese theatre assumptions, is the story-telling technique of the singer-narrator and the almost Propp-like structure of the fabula, to be sustained by interpretors like Angelika Hurwicz and Ernst Busch, the unforgettable Grusche and Azdak of the Berliner Ensemble in the fifties, politically engaged and professionally skilled actors; Busch even doubled as the singer-narrator.

Though I do not want to go too deeply into the too superficially accepted polarity between Artaud and Brecht, I think it worthwhile, and not a digression from my subject, to dwell a little on the particular interest that they both had in Breughel's art, and specifically in the *Dulle Griet.* Brecht's attitude towards Griet results from two pages of his *Arbeitsjournal,* as follows:

June 15, 1944
All of a sudden the Grusche of the *Chalk Circle* does not satisfy me any longer. She should be more naive, more similar to Breughel's "Dulle Griet," a beast of burden. She should be stubborn, and not rebellious; willing, and not good; firm, and not incorruptible, etc. Her naivité should not be equivalent to wisdom (as the usual cliché), nevertheless it should be compatible with some practical talents, with the shrewdness and the capability of judging human qualities. Since Grusche represents the backwardness of her social class, she should allow for less identification, and she should objectively present herself, in a sense, as a tragic character (the salt of the earth). (*AJ,* 662.)

August 8, 1944
It took me three weeks to rewrite the character of Grusche, and it has been a hard and detailed job. In fact for the here and now [i.e. for Broadway] the more pleasant Katia of my first draft is undoubtedly more effective. But I came to realize the inadequacy of Katia in her confrontation with Azdak in the fifth act; what I had to refer to was the "Dulle Griet" of Breughel's painting. (*AJ,* 671.)

As for Artaud, we have to go back more than ten years from Brecht's statements in the *Arbeitsjournal,* to the last of the four *Lettres sur le language,* dated 1931 to 1933 and published by Artaud in 1938 in *Le théatre et son double.* In this letter Artaud—in one of his most passionate claims to the creative rights of the metteur-en-scène—gives his interpretation of the *Dulle Griet* and other paintings by Breughel, Bosch, Lucas van den Leyden, Goya. The low profile of Brecht's phrases about the

132

Dulle Griet contrasts, as we can expect, with the intensity displayed by Artaud in throwing himself, we can say, into the paintings he examines:

> Even if the *mise en scène* did not have to its credit the language of gestures which equals and surpasses that of words, any mute *mise en scène*, with its movement, its many characters, lighting, and set, should rival all that is most profound in paintings such as van den Leyden's "Daughters of Lot," certain "Sabbaths" of Goya, certain "Resurrections" and "Transfigurations" of Greco, the "Temptation of Saint Anthony" by Hieronymus Bosch, and the disquieting and mysterious "Dulle Griet" by the elder Breughel, in which a torrential red light, though localized in certain parts of the canvas, seems to surge up from all sides and, through some unknown technical process, glue the spectator's staring eyes while still yards away from the canvas: the theatre swarms in all directions. The turmoil of life, confined by a ring of white light, runs suddenly aground on nameless shallows. A screeching, livid noise rises from this bacchanal of grubs of which even the bruises of human skin can never approach the color. Real life is moving and white; the hidden life is livid and fixed, possessing every possible attitude of incalculable immobility. This is mute theatre, but one that tells more than if it had received a language in which to express itself. Each of these paintings has a double sense, and beyond its purely pictorial qualities discloses a message and reveals mysterious or terrible aspects of nature and mind alike.[7]

In this programmatic openness toward the "mysterious" and the "double sense"—already recognized in Breughel by Baudelaire—, in such semantic oscillation between the "purely pictorial qualities" and the message, there lies the possibility of contrasting interpretations—contrasting and yet not cancelling out one another—that Artaud and Brecht give of the seemingly inexhaustible Griet. For Artaud, the theatrical nature of paintings of such a power lies and lives in the swarming and tumultous mass, the "bacchanal of grubs," the contrast between the white light of "real life" and the "livid light of the background where the "hidden life" is. What Brecht finds and cherishes in the *Dulle Griet* is something else. In epic terms, what he aims at is to make the spectator's and the actress's identification with Grusche more difficult, as he declares in his *Arbeitsjournal*. No contrast could be stronger between him and Artaud, who spoke rapturously of "the spectator's staring eyes" glued to the picture. What is a virtue to Artaud the shaman, is of course a mortal sin to Brecht the didactic writer, who links impersonation and identification to the fascination exerted by Fascist and Nazi rulers in what he calls "fascism's bad theatre." So, let's try to ascertain the type of attention the theoretician of the *Verfremdungseffekt* paid to the *Dulle Griet*.

Brecht had probably become acquainted with Breughel's painting through Glück's color reproduction or through some other illustrated books on the Flemish artist, since the *Dulle Griet* is not in Germany but in Antwerp, at the Maier van der Berg Museum; at least this is my opinion, even if Glück mentions a copy in Germany, "a good water-color copy, perhaps by Peter Breughel the younger in the Art Academy in Düsseldorf."[8] I don't have the slightest intention of doubting Brecht's ability to give his own autonomous interpretation of the ambiguous painting; anyway, considering the place of honor given by Brecht to Glück's book, as mentioned above, I looked through Glück's paragraph about the *Dulle Griet*.

Concerning the subject of the painting, and the possible intentions of the painter, Glück writes:

> The expression "Dulle Griet" (Mad Margareth) means Xantippe or a hag, a kind of woman-like infernal ember. It is significant that nowadays one of the guns of Phillippe's time found at Gent market is still called by that name just like the Scottish or Irish guns are called "Mad Meg" or "Roaring Meg." In some old German inventories the expression "Fury" can be found too, since the hag was one of the Erinyes. It is the same evil hag, able "to tie a devil to a cushion," a scene which appears in a corner of Breughel's *Sprichwörterbild* and also in the *Dulle Griet* close to the central figure. The painting at the Maier van der Berg Museum shows Griet standing by Hell, staring numbly with her mouth open ready to shout. She is dressed in war-like attire, wearing a helmet, a cuirass, a sword and a kitchen knife [an attire both parodistic and frightful] and she is carrying her prize under her arms and in her apron. On the ground there is a chest full of money. She looks like the leader of a group of women who are ready to face even the devil in hell, in a brief and bloody fight. Max J. Friedlanders rightly refers to folk-sentences as: "A raid, made at the gates of Hell," or as "Going to hell with a sword in one's hand." A French Catholic critic perceives in the painting a hint to great chaos of the war.[9]

The fact that the painting deals with Hell, on its left-hand side, results from the previous iconography of the "mouth of Hell" which goes back not only to Hieronymus Bosch but to the Hell mansions of Medieval mystery plays all over Europe. Such an iconological genealogy is important in my opinion because, in relating it to the "Gothic taste" of the Mannerists, we can point to the *theatrical* origin of the icon of Hell. Clearly, Brecht's Grusche is not the leader of a group of women, who in the *Chalk Circle,* like on the right side of the painting, flee from the fire burning far away, and from the house which they have plundered: Grusche is defined "the dullest one" by one of the women. Furthermore, Griet's *negative* features (a fury, according to Glück, a hag, a woman-like hell ember, one of the Erinyes) are the features Brecht has relied upon in order to avoid the danger of giving benefit and rhetorically *positive* attitudes to his Grusche, whose name is so transparently Breughelian and, perhaps, was intended by Brecht to remind us of his beloved Margarete (Grete) Steffin, dead in Moscow in exile.

"Terrible is the temptation of goodness" for Grusche, who finds herself alone in the court-yard of the Governor's palace, in the blazing of fire, staring at the sleeping baby. The Governor has been killed. The frail, dangerous heir has been abandoned by his frivolous and cruel mother and is now being sought by the princes' soldiers who want to kill him. It is a real "temptation," because it is a voice opposing the sound principles of egotism and self-preservation; and in fleeing with the baby in her arms Grusche acts against Brecht's celebrated dictum, "first the stomach and then morality." (*GW,* II, 457.) As in Glück's reading of Griet, so in the function assigned to Grusche in Brecht's play, "morality" is an element beyond discussion. What matters are the facts, the images, the gestures, the epic narrative. The scattering of images in the painting suggests to Brecht, much more than metaphysical questions—though they were certainly present in Breughel's mind—an artistic language fit to express a twentieth century equivalent to the sixteenth century religious wars. Grusche's solitary "flight into Egypt" takes place in a pseudo-Caucasian world peopled by country men, mountaineers, soldiers, in a landscape covered by snow and rich in every kind of other Breughelian motif. The Breughelian imagery appears in the play from the start, with the reunion of the two Soviet kolkhozes whose socialist dispute about a valley gives occasion to the story-telling, and goes on and on, with children playing, wedding feasts, etc., till the final folkdance. In the photo from Brecht's own staging of his play in the Berliner Ensemble in the fifties, we can see how deeply but freely Breughelian the style of Grusche's wedding feast is, an episode which I assume to be the absolute master-work of Bertolt Brecht as a director, together perhaps with the battle scenes in *Coriolanus.* And Brecht's almost obsessive care about a full photographic documentation of his work with the Berliner Ensemble, together with his careful assemblage of pictorial and graphic material for his *Arbeitsjournal* and *Kriegsfibel,* should be made the object of a particular study in order to reach a better understanding of what I call his "system of visualization," perhaps a psychological even more than a theoretical need for iconic evidence.

However, though the *Chalk Circle* is obviously full of what Artaud calls the Breughelian "turmoil of life," we shall not forget that the metaphor of a "bacchanal of grubs" coined by the same Artaud is even more pertinent to the ex-Weimar society now ruled with *Fear and Misery* by Nazi demons. That's why I thought it meaningful to quote the Parisian review of 1938 which compares *Fear and Misery* to a "dance of ghosts." As for the *Chalk Circle,* even if we did not know about the *Dulle*

Griet, we could easily refer to a lot of other Breughelian paintings of folk-situations, real people in real moments of the year and of countrylife. That's why I said that we needed a subtle approach to understand the process which led Brecht from Katia to Griet to Grusche and to the play as a coherent, original epic structure. What struck Brecht, and influenced him in characterizing his Grusche, was the outward appearance of Breughel's female protagonist, her antiheroic gestus, her stubbornness and ignorance, her state of pre-consciousness; so, as an epic writer, he could pass from the "dramatic" shape of the more agreeable but for him unsuccessful Katia of the first draft (influenced by such a sweet actress as Luise Rainer) to the "epic" shape of the almost bestial Grusche, "not rebellious . . . not good . . . not incorruptible": Grusche—Griet, "a beast of burden."

Not incidentally, we can verify how undogmatic a Marxist Brecht is, with his almost bestial Grusche, who is far away from the square "positive hero" dogma of socialist realism. The same can be said for the male protagonist of the *Chalk Circle,* the cowardly prudent Azdak, the Hegelian philosopher in rags. Azdak's carnivalesque system of making justice and mock-utopian way of changing very small aspects of society looks like an elegant intellectual revenge against the rhetoric of "soul engineering," another main point of Soviet "state optimism" in the arts, with whose blindness Brecht was destined to fight later in his East-Berlin years, and whose stultifying power is still at work in the Soviet Union and in East-European socialist republics—and more or less, let me say, even if certainly in much less dangerous way, in the Broadway system which Brecht happily eluded.

I referred to Azdak because, in order to reach my conclusion, I have to state that the *Chalk Circle* is not only Grusche's play; it is also, and perhaps even more, the play of Azdak, the drunken hobo philosopher, the poor scribe of the court house who is appointed judge by the rioting pretorians and who will have to sentence in the case of the wife of the Governor against Grusche, who is accused of having stolen the child. At the end, the "travelogue-technique" applied in Grusche's half of the play, and the "open-air trial technique" of Azdak's half bring the two characters to a tragicomic confrontation. And it was exactly when he worked on this confrontation, at this "scène-à-faire," that Brecht came to realize the inadequacy of Katia, of the agreeable servant of his first draft of the play, and shifted the character to the *Dulle Griet.* It is clear that only the maieutic Azdak is able to awaken to consciousness Grusche-Griet, the "beast of burden," before declaring that she is the true mother of the child; but it is also clear that only Grusche, "the salt of the earth," the "objectively tragic" Grusche who does not hesitate in defying Hell itself in order to assert her *historical* maternity against the *natural* maternity of the Governor's wife; only Grusche with her hands and nerves, with her deeds and needs, Grusche with her unconscious revolutionary struggle against the undisputed social order, only Grusche-Griet is able to give Azdak, Azdak the failed intellectual, Azdak the glutton and the lecher, the opportunity of his lifetime, the occasion to fully realize himself and his hidden potentialities through what amounts to a dialectics between the masses and the party. This dialectics, as it is metaphorized in the *Chalk Circle,* does not aim to demonstrate the superiority of any of the two forces; but the clear priority of Grusche's action, of the masses with their deeds and needs, brings to light and life something hidden in Brecht as in Azdak, something never forgotten nor repudiated by Brecht—even if historically set aside for years (the years of the Lehrstücke!)—: the latent "Luxemburgian" intonation of his early years, the debt to "rote Rosa's" mortal struggle. In assuming the *Caucasian Chalk Circle* to be Brecht's most "Luxemburgian" work, which is my opinion, we have to take into consideration Brecht's enthusiasm in the forties for the victory of *both* the Russian people *and* the Soviet apparatus against Nazism: the masses *and* the party. In the atmosphere of 1944, the anguishing worries about Stalin's degenerations expressed in some pages of his *Arbeitsjournal* in the late thirties, as in some of his poetic works, are remote. In the play, the debate about socialist agriculture is idealized and no more reminiscent of the terrible years of forced collectivization. The dialogue between Grusche and Azdak shows that the rights of the masses *and* the leadership of the party appeared reconciled to Brecht, even if he was absolutely not reconciled with the "socialist realism" aesthetics of the party; and it is relevant that the role of the party was to be taken by somebody like Azdak, not a bureaucratic cadre at all but a man expressed by the social struggle in a kind of Luxemburgian way, and in the same way destined to disappear as soon as his task, as the task of the workers' councils in Luxemburg's theory, is fulfilled. Was it only by chance that on September 10, 1944, just a month after the re-elaboration of his Grusche, he wrote in his *Arbeitsjournal:* "Recently I have been thinking about another project: 'The Life and Death of Rosa Luxemburg' "? (*AJ,* 685.) In the *Chalk Circle,* "Rosa Luxemburg" is also the name of the partisan kolkhos whose technician—a young woman!—offers the best plan to raise the crops in the valley.

But, undoubtedly relevant as they are, the ideological and political implications I have tried to elucidate do not explain the powerful emotional and rational impact of the last scene, one of the most original and powerful trial scenes in theatre history. The image that gives name to the play—the circle of chalk with the child inside, the two mothers grasping him, and the Solomon-like Azdak perched above the action—is a human knot which explodes in a galaxy of tensions, between tradition and change, nature and history, law and justice, rule and love, mere existence and true life, destiny and human will, identity and contradiction, Aristotelian "A-equal-A" and Hegelian "A equal non-A." Thanks to Brecht's visualizing power, the grotesque of the play rises itself from the level of "comique significatif" to the level of "comique absolu," and is able to satisfy and intrigue the spectator just as does Breughel's *Dulle Griet* with its double level, realistic and metaphoric.

As for *Mother Courage,* which is of course among Brecht's plays the historically closest one to Breughel's period, it presents a battered yet strong woman in a ravaged landscape (I am indebted to John Fuegi for this suggestion), with kitchen objects around herself, coupled with another woman, a young one, Kate, with psychophysical problems and in the last part of the story with an obsessed face. *Mother Courage* happens to be another Brecht that I staged, in Genova, in 1970. And my fourth Brechtian mise-en-scène (the first in chronological order) has been *The Seven Deadly Sins* (Rome, Filarmonica Romana, 1961) in which another "Breughelian" theme (from the famous "vices" series) is assumed, with a female protagonist. Anyhow my reflections have remained pointed, here, towards *Fear and Misery* and *The Caucasian Chalk Circle* not only because in these cases we have explicit relationships established by Brecht himself between his two plays and the styles and world of the painter, but also because in them the basic concept of the "lack of center" is much more easy to be discerned and discussed.

Notes

1. Carel von Mander, *Dutch and Flemish Painters* (1936, rpt. New York: Arno Press, 1969), p. 155.
2. Charles Baudelaire, "Quelques caricaturistes etrangers" (1857), *Ouvres completes* (Paris: Gallimard, 1961), pp. 1014–1024.
3. Fritz Grossman, *Breughel: The Paintings: Complete Edition* (London: Phaidon Press, 1955), pp. 34–35.
4. Michel Foucault, *Madness and Civilization: A History of Insanity in the Age of Reason* (New York: Pantheon Books, 1965), pp. 280–281 (translation of *Histoire de la folie,* 1961).
5. The editors were not able to provide documentation for this review.
6. Georg Lukács, "Es geht um den Realismus," *Das Wort,* 3, No.6 (1938), 138.
7. Antonin Artaud, *The Theatre and Its Double,* translated from the French by Mary Caroline Richards (New York: Grove Press, 1958), p. 120.
8. Gustav Glück, *Das Große Breughel-Werk* (Wien: Verlag von Anton Scholl & Co., 1952), p. 58.
9. Ibid., this text was reprinted in this edition from Glück's 1932 Breughel edition of which Brecht owned a copy.

Photo from a production of *The Caucasian Chalk Circle* staged by Brecht with the Berliner Ensemble.

De Dulle Briet (Margot the Mad). 1592 or 1594. Peter Breughel. Musée Mayer van den Bergh, Antwerp.

David Pike. "Brecht and Stalin's Russia: The Victim as Apologist (1931–1945)."

David Pike describes how, in the Soviet Union, the reception of Brecht was determined by two antagonistic forces, first the critique that his theatre was not realistic, and second by attempts to win it over to Socialism as defined in the USSR. Pike introduces new material from a debate about Brecht's theatre which lasted, in spite of the final failure of Brecht's art in the Soviet Union, until the early forties. Brecht was attacked—sometimes covertly—by Julius Hay, Georg Lukács and Johannes R. Becher, and in turn defended by Bernhard Reich and Timofej Rokotov.

Part II examines Brecht's reaction to the reality of the Soviet state. Using Brecht's remarks about André Gide's attack on Stalin, about the collectivization, about the hegemonial claims of the Russian Communist Party, and about the purge trials, the author demonstrates how Brecht's thinking—usually referred to as "dialectical thinking"—distorts his perception of reality in such a way that his public statements about these subjects repeatedly result in justifications of Stalin's despotism. Since Brecht never really questioned the historic role of the Soviet Union as long as Germany was suppressed by Fascism, he could never bring himself to criticize the Soviet dictatorship publicly, although he knew about Stalin's bloody deeds. The victim became an apologist.

David Pike. "Brecht und Stalins Rußland: Das Opfer als Apologet (1931–1945)."

David Pike beschreibt, wie die Rezeption Brechts in der Sowjetunion von zwei widerstrebenden Kräften bestimmt wurde: der Kritik, sein Theater sei nicht realistisch, und dem Versuch, es dennoch für den Sozialismus sowjetischer Prägung zu gewinnen. Pike stellt bislang unberücksichtigtes Material einer teilweise verdeckt geführten Brecht-Debatte vor, an der als Ankläger u. a. Julius Hay, Georg Lukács und Johannes R. Becher, als Verteidiger Bernhard Reich und Timofej Rokotov teilnahmen und die trotz des letztendlichen Scheiterns von Brechts Kunst in der Sowjetunion bis in die vierziger Jahre reicht.

Teil II untersucht Brechts Reaktion auf die sowjetische Realität. Anhand von Äußerungen zum Angriff André Gides auf Stalin, zur Kollektivierungspolitik, zum Vorherrschaftsanspruch der KPdSU und zu den Säuberungsprozessen zeichnet der Autor nach, wie Brechts gemeinhin als "dialektisch" bezeichnetes Denken seine Realitätswahrnehmung in einer Weise verzerrt, die seine öffentlichen Äußerungen zu diesen Themen immer wieder zu einer Legitimierung der Stalinschen Terrorherrschaft verkommen läßt. Weil Brecht die historische Rolle der Sowjetunion niemals grundsätzlich in Frage stellt, solange Deutschland vom Faschismus unterdrückt wird, kann er sich trotz seines Wissens um die Bluttaten Stalins nicht dazu durchringen, die sowjetische Diktatur beim Namen zu nennen. Das Opfer wird zum Apologeten.

David Pike. "Brecht et la Russie de Staline : la victime comme apologiste."

Selon David Pike la réception de l'oeuvre de Brecht en URSS fut déterminée par deux forces antagonistes : en premier lieu la critique de manque de réalisme faite à son théâtre, et puis les tentatives de le gagner au socialisme (version russe). Pike introduit du nouveau dans le débat sur le théâtre de Brecht, débat qui a duré jusqu'au début des années '40, malgré l'échec de son art en URSS. Brecht fut attaqué parfois de façon dissimulée par Julius Hay, Georg Lukàcs et Johannes R. Brecher, et fut défendu par Bernard Reich et Timofej Rokotov.

Dans la deuxième partie Pike examine la réaction de Brecht à la réalité de l'état soviétique. Il se sert des remarques de Brecht sur la critique de Staline par André Gide, où l'écrivain français dénounce la collectivisation, les exigences hégémoniques du parti communiste russe, et les purges staliniennes. L'auteur montre que la pensée de Brecht, d'ordinaire qualifiée de dialectique, déforme sa perception de la réalité à tel point que ses prises de positions publiques sur ces sujets n'aboutissent qu'à des justifications du despotisme de Staline. Puisque Brecht n'a jamais contesté le rôle historique de l'URSS tant que l'Allemagne fut étouffée par le fascisme, il ne put jamais critiquer publiquement la dictature soviétique, quoiqu'il fût au courant des crimes de Staline. C'est ainsi que la victime devint apologiste.

Brecht and Stalin's Russia:
The Victim as Apologist (1931–1945)

David Pike

For Sidney Hook

> Zunächst ist aber wohl nur zu sagen, daß
> die bolschewiki es eben nicht verstanden,
> eine literatur zu entwickeln. . . . die li-
> teratur wurde von der machtübernahme
> des proletariats überrascht.[1]

I

By the late thirties Brecht's attitude toward Soviet cultural policy
had lapsed into a state of despair. The "theoretical line" thwarted everything he had struggled for over the past twenty years, he told Benjamin
in 1938;[2] "literatur und kunst scheinen beschissen," he added in his
journal,[3] and five years later his disenchantment slumped to a new low.
"[E]igentliche untersuchungen werden nicht veranstaltet, oder sie haben
prozeßcharakter," he said of Soviet literary criticism; "der ton ist er-
schreckend unproduktiv, gehässig, persönlich, autoritär und servil zugleich. offensichtlich ist das keine atmosphäre, in der eine lebendige,
kämpferische, üppige literatur gedeihen könnte."[4] Something was glar-
ingly wrong, but the unembellished fact that Soviet literature had been
Stalinized escaped Brecht. Because he missed the point of Stalinism,[5] the
havoc it was bound to wreak on literature and art took him by surprise.
Although the situation in the Soviet Union had been building to a climax
since the early thirties, Brecht failed to read the warning signs and was
caught off guard by the impact of Stalinism upon all facets of Soviet art as
well as by the natural consequences for the reception of his own work in
the USSR.

143

Was the picture all bleak? Brecht also had friends in the Soviet Union who stood up for him and his work with surprising success, producing an odd state of affairs. The German and Russian Stalinists were fond of confrontation with Brecht because of their allegation that his theory of epic theatre was a byproduct of the general decadence that infused bourgeois art and ran directly counter to socialist realism. So how did Brecht manage to get his writings into print in the USSR at all? How can the various favorable reviews and articles be explained? Brecht's modest successes were made possible by conflicting official policies whose shifting configuration in the thirties and early forties allowed the natural affinities between Brecht and the Soviet avant-garde to produce occasional results. Specifically, his fortunes in the USSR were tied directly to the clash between two political strategies that jostled for position throughout much of the thirties: the popular front, which acted as a tranquilizer upon the Stalinists in their dealings with Western writers who (unlike their Soviet counterparts) could not be shackled by socialist realism; and the Stalinization of Soviet cultural life that eclipsed brilliant theatrical experimentation and literary innovation in Soviet art and blotted out Brecht's work in the process. Although the policies were never evenly matched and the eventual outcome probably inevitable, the contest waxed and waned enough for Brecht to slip into periodic breaches in the Stalinist line with a handful of his plays, a sampling of his poetry, an occasional essay, a *Lehrstück* or two, and the *Dreigroschenroman*.

The attacks upon Brecht began well before 1933, those published in *Die Linkskurve* in 1931 and 1932 by Johannes R. Becher, Andor Gábor, Georg Lukács, and others coming at a time when the absence of a popular front policy left Brecht defenseless. Although this initial Stalinist foray into literature augured ill for the future, the early criticism was motivated by slightly different theoretical considerations. The shoddy treatment accorded not just Brecht but Ernst Ottwalt and Willi Bredel as well by leading voices in the "Bund proletarisch-revolutionärer Schriftsteller" was a reflection of Soviet literary theoretical disputes raging at the time in the Soviet Union. The objections to Brecht's work were distinctly "official" because Becher, Gábor, and Lukács largely mimicked the opinions on aesthetics and cultural politics held by the BPRS' Soviet relative, the Russian Association of Proletarian Writers (RAPP), and the Soviet Central Committee happened to back RAPP at this specific time. Granted, Soviet cultural policy soon developed a warp; the Central Committee began to distrust RAPP and disbanded it in April 1932, abolishing its dialectical materialist creative method in favor of a new style of writing (socialist realism) that would be defined in the coming years under the supervision of an "amalgamated" Soviet Writers' Union. But until RAPP was thrown on the Soviet rubbish pile of ideas that had exhausted their political usefulness, the party gave the organization a free rein to harass other writers and literary associations, including those whose interest in innovation and experimentation was as unwelcome and inopportune to the party almost as much before April 1932 as afterwards, under socialist realism. Becher's supercilious remarks about Sergej Tretjakov and Lukács' blacklisting of both Ottwalt's montage method and Brecht's theory of epic theater are relatively undistorted reflections of these Soviet disputes.

But there was always a fine line separating Lukács from those, like Becher, around him. In the USSR Becher never really bucked the tide and habitually backed whatever literary theory boasted an official Soviet stamp of approval at any given time. Tactical considerations notwithstanding, Lukács had a mind of his own, even though his brand of independent thought was often glazed with Stalinism. In 1931 and 1932 Lukács echoed many themes that read like passages from RAPP's periodical *On Literary Guard,* passages that espoused literary theoretical views then in favor with the party. But Lukács ought not to be regarded in these years as a mirror image, say, of Averbakh. RAPP no doubt exerted a considerable influence upon Lukács, and his essays in *Die Linkskurve* bore unmistakable traces of RAPP terminology. But Lukács was at work developing his own literary aesthetic, and at least some of the similarities between RAPP's ideas and Lukács' resulted from his need to dress them up as products of whatever literary style the party backed at a specific time, RAPP's in this instance, socialist realism later. The two "creative methods," after all, shared a deep-seated animosity toward avant-gardist theories of art, and that animosity served Lukács' purposes perfectly. When "left-wing radical nonsense" was officially added to the socialist realist index in mid 1936, it provided Lukács and the Stalinists who glommed on to him with all the arguments they needed to complicate matters for Brecht in his dealings with the Soviet Union.

The early antagonism toward Brecht caused chiefly by RAPP's domination of the BPRS let up after Hitler's accession to power during the lull preceding the introduction of a more exact definition of socialist realism and as a Communist-backed united front of writers gradually took shape. Brecht, it seems, was high on the list of writers whose backing of a united front the Communists considered imperative, but, ironically, he broached the subject with them first. It evidently occurred to Brecht to convene a writers' conference significantly before the thought ever crossed Becher's mind. As early as June 1933 he proposed the organization of "eine autorisierte Konferenz zwischen einigen Kollegen . . . auf der Ziel und Methode unserer zukünftigen Arbeit

endgültig festgelegt werden."[6] Even though Brecht may have envisaged
a slightly different kind of meeting than the one that took place two
years later, this proposal might have prompted Communist plans for a
"Weltkonferenz aller antifaschistischer Schriftsteller" that Becher first
sketched in a letter to Moscow in October 1933.[7] But regardless of
possible tactical differences, both Brecht and Becher had at least one
identical overriding concern. The intellectuals needed to be steered into
acceptance of a "correct" Marxist-Leninist-Stalinist view of fascism that
called as much for support of the Soviet Union as opposition to Germany. The time to begin was right now, Brecht thought, for the
left-wing bourgeois writers had no set platform or viewpoint for the
struggle against fascism: "Man verleiht ihnen keinen solchen, indem
man sich ab und zu für irgendwas ihre Namen ausborgt. Dabei gäbe
gerade der Umstand, daß sie ihre Standpunktlosigkeit und Wehrlosig-
keit jetzt z.T. empfinden, uns bei ihnen eine wirkliche Chance, deren
Zeit allerdings bemessen sein dürfte. . . . Wenn überhaupt jemals,
dann würden sie jetzt für eine wirkliche politische Schulung zu haben
sein."[8]

The only difference between Brecht and Becher was that Brecht made
no secret of his opinion, whereas the more orthodox party writers and
cultural functionaries tended toward dissemblance. As the Communist
plans for a congress evolved, it was Becher's turn to approach Brecht. He
was apparently still concerned about too tactical a strategy. "Ich habe ein
kleines Grauen vor Zusammenkünften zum Zwecke des Zusammenseins,"
he told Becher; "man zählt die Häupter seiner Lieben und versichert sich,
daß man einer Meinung ist usw."[9] When the congress eventually met in
June 1935 in Paris, Brecht's speech expressed his anxiety that, to avoid
disunifying debates, there might be a predisposition to slough over the
most vital aspect of fascism. So Brecht made one point emphatically:
"Kameraden, sprechen wir von den Eigentumsverhältnissen. Das wollte
ich zum Kampfe gegen die überhandnehmende Barbarei sagen, damit es
auch hier gesagt sei oder daß auch ich es gesagt habe."[10] In spite of Brecht's
bluntness, there is no real indication that his speech put him at particular
odds with the Communists, who appear to have attached continued importance to his involvement in any united front.[11]

The full extent of the role now played by the literary united front
in forestalling a reoccurrence of attacks upon Brecht like those in *Die
Linkskurve* cannot be properly assessed. But it surely combined with the
respite in Soviet literary politics between the dissolution of RAPP and the
real onset of Stalinism in mid 1936 to create an atmosphere more congenial to Brecht's work in the Soviet Union than would exist again for years
to come. Responsibility for Brecht's good fortunes from 1933 to 1936

rests with a close-knit group of friends and supporters in Moscow: Margarete Steffin, Sergej Tretjakov, Bernhard Reich, Asja Lazis, and Mikhail Koltsov. Steffin proved to be Brecht's greatest asset, and her first trip to the Soviet Union coincided with Brecht's. She was, after all, his helpmate in more than literary affairs. With the assistance of the KPD[12] Brecht saw to it that Steffin spent several weeks in a Crimean sanatorium during his and Dudov's visit to Moscow to attend the premiere of *Kuhle Wampe* in May 1932.[13] Just over two years passed before Steffin again left for the Soviet Union;[14] this time she stayed for several months in Leningrad, Moscow, and Georgia,[15] and apparently returned to the West with Brecht after his visit to Moscow in March, April, and May 1935.

Der Dreigroschenroman (in German and Russian) and *Die Rundköpfe und die Spitzköpfe* may not have been published in the Soviet Union had Steffin not been on the spot to push them through. Shortly after her arrival in Moscow in mid September 1934,[16] Brecht sent her these instructions: "*Der Dreigroschenroman* ought to be the easiest to sell. You should be able simply to walk right into the State Publishing House [Goslitizdat], where they speak German. They ought to pay more for a manuscript, but it would be good to have a portion of the page proofs to show them that it is being printed. That's what Wieland Herzfelde says, who is here at the moment. A Russian signature ought to bring at least 350 rubles, but they should make their own offer."[17] A month later Brecht provided Steffin with the latest information: "The novel is supposed to be out today in Amsterdam; I still don't have a single copy—I'll send you the first. What is the situation in Moscow? Tell me more about the atmosphere there! . . . Who else did you speak with?" It would be good, he said, if Goslitizdat would publish something of his.[18]

By December Steffin had a signed contract for the *Dreigroschenroman*.[19] Whether this applied just to the German edition to be brought out by the Verlagsgenossenschaft ausländischer Arbeiter (VE GAAR) or also to Goslitizdat's Russian version is unclear, but the two editions were originally supposed to appear simultaneously.[20] The translation itself was evidently also arranged for in late fall or winter 1934; it was to be done by Valentin O. Stenich, whom Steffin had met in the offices of VEGAAR. A talented man who, among other things, had rewritten the libretto for Meyerhold's Leningrad production of Tchaikovsky's *Pique Dame*, Stenich had also made a name for himself with excellent translations of Dos Passos, Joyce, Faulkner, Kipling, Malraux, and others.[21] He died in 1939 at the age of forty-one.

Prospects for Brecht's work seemed promising elsewhere. Nikolaj Okhlopkov, a former actor and student of Meyerhold and since 1930 director of the Realistic Theater, took an interest in staging *Die heilige*

Johanna der Schlachthöfe. Whether Brecht first met Okhlopkov in 1932, or not until 1935, is unclear, but a production of the play was already under discussion in mid 1933. In July Brecht told Tretjakov that—"nach wie vor"—he would like to work in Russia in the fall, asking specifically, "Wie geht es der 'Heiligen Johanna'? Haben Sie übrigens jemals etwas gehört von der Schauspielerin Carola Neher, die seit über einem halben Jahr nicht mehr in Deutschland ist und in Rußland sein soll? Wie ich hörte, sei sie zunächst nach Odessa gereist. Sie hat Russisch gelernt und war auch in die deutsche Partei eingetreten. Vielleicht könnten Sie sich bei Deutschen nach ihr erkundigen (vielleicht bei Piscator)? Sie wäre eine wunderbare Johanna. Wenn die Rolle schon besetzt ist, könnte sie doch eventuell die Rolle nachspielen?"[22] After Tairov's staging of *Die Dreigroschenoper* in 1930 for his Kamernyj teatr, *Die heilige Johanna* would have been just the second of Brecht's plays to be performed on a Soviet stage. But this particular production never materialized. Rehearsals were scheduled to begin in September, Tretjakov told Brecht in July, though he had evidently not yet finished his translation of the play.[23] Tretjakov told Brecht that he would soon talk with Okhlopkov, Neher, and Piscator "um die Theaterfragen, und insbesondere die Johanna Perspektive, zu besprechen."[24] A production never resulted, but—in spite of what Reich implies—there is no information to conclude that political pressures were brought to bear upon Okhlopkov and blocked his plans.[25] (Incidentally, Tretjakov now began planning his edition of *Die heilige Johanna, Die Maßnahme,* and *Die Mutter.* The volume, *Epicheskie dramy,* which Tretjakov also supplied with an introduction, came out the next year.)[26]

Hasty conclusions from the situation in which Sergej Tretjakov now found himself should also be avoided. He certainly sensed that trouble was brewing for his kind of literature. Tretjakov spoke at the First All-Union Congress of Soviet Writers in August 1934 (Brecht, by the way, was initially supposed to be invited)[27], and he was definitely uneasy about the atmosphere. "Momentan sind wir an einem wendepunkt," Tretjakov wrote Brecht; "[d]er einseitige intellektualismus (technizismus) wird vom emotionellen prinzip schärfst angegriffen. Emotionelle kompliziertheit wird gefordert." He added: "[E]s gibt eine reihe principiell neuen Lagen die man besprechen und studieren muß. Und gerade mit Ihnen möchte ich besonders das tun."[28] Tretjakov's uneasiness does not mean, though, that he sensed the severity of what was coming; neither he nor Brecht (nor very many others) ever dreamt that Soviet art under Stalin would become so utterly vassalized, and Tretjakov's involvement in past vituperative literary theoretical polemics that led neither to accusations of ideological delinquency nor, worse, to bloodshed, may have given him a false sense of security. But if there ever had been a particularly favorable constellation for Tretjakov's work since the late twenties, it was rapidly changing. A hint of cynicism seems apparent in a letter that Tretjakov wrote Brecht about the upcoming writers' congress in Paris, which Tretjakov did not attend: "Du bist ein alter Komiker, wenn du dich wunderst wie so habe ich nicht 3 Wochen für den Kongreß. Das ist ja gar nicht meine private Angelegenheit."[29] But the temptation should be resisted to look for signs of Tretjakov's arrest either in his difficulties now or even later in 1936 and the first half of 1937. Tretjakov disappeared (like most of the six hundred other arrested Soviet men and women of letters) suddenly; he was not attacked beforehand for his "decadent" views on literature anywhere in the Soviet press that I am aware of, and there is no indication that he feared for his life any more than other Soviet writers after mid 1936.[30]

But Tretjakov and Brecht were, of course, mindful of their shaky standing within a certain sector of Soviet and Soviet-influenced literary criticism. When Alfred Kantorowicz reviewed the Amsterdam edition of *Der Dreigroschenroman* in Münzenberg's Parisian journal *Unsere Zeit*, Brecht, upon hearing that Kantorowicz was Becher's "secretary,"[31] immediately complained to Becher that the article took on "eine sehr offizielle Note." Kantorowicz' review had a strange air of cordiality about it. "Brecht will nicht *erbauen*, sondern *erziehen*; seine Schriften sind nicht Genuß—sondern *Lehrmittel*. Er will zum Nachdenken anregen. Er versetzt seine Leser, wie seine Zuschauer nicht in die handelnden Figuren hinein, er stellt sie ihnen als Betrachter *gegenüber*," Kantorowicz explained; and those who regarded Brecht as a cynic would now understand that he was a moralist, albeit one "mit revolutionären Konsequenzen."[32] Brecht was unimpressed and told Becher: "[D]ie schleimige Freundschaft drum rum ist ganz uninteressant angesichts des zentralen Vorwurfs, der Roman sei nicht realistisch und er sei idealistisch."[33] What was Kantorowicz' specific reproach? "Den (auch sehr weit gefaßten) Forderungen des *Realismus* entspricht der Roman von Brecht nicht. Man darf, ohne zu schematisieren sagen, dass es ein *idealistisches* Buch ist. Es ist ein Buch, das Diskussionen sehr fruchtbarer Art anregen wird."[34]

Now Brecht was probably incorrect to assume that the article had been commissioned by Becher (who was not naturally ill-disposed toward Brecht).[35] But Brecht felt it necessary to defend himself:

> Vorausgesetzt wird, daß alle Romane, die nicht realistisch sind, damit idealistisch sind; darüber ließe sich vielleicht reden, wenn nicht dann als realistisch nur Romane gelten sollten, die ohne Erfindung sind. . . . Und ich dachte, idealistisch sei dann ein Werk, wenn das Bewußtsein als bestimmender Faktor für die jeweilige Realität der gesellschaftlichen Einrichtungen hingestellt wird. Da ich in meinem Roman den bestimmenden Einfluß der

ökonomischen Lage und Klassenzugehörigkeit auf das Bewußtsein der Personen darstellte, glaubte ich, einen materialistischen Roman geschrieben zu haben. Da ich, da es keinen Sinn hat, die Welt zu interpretieren, sondern man sie verändern muß, die Realität so dargestellt habe, daß man Ursachen und Wirkungen deutlich sieht, also eingreifen kann, glaubte ich einen Roman für Realisten geschrieben zu haben, nicht nur einen Roman, in dem Realität vorkommt. Nun, Ihr belehrt mich. Ich wünschte nur, es geschähe auf eine weniger oberflächliche und hochmütige Rappweise.[36]

Becher concurred and promised to set the record straight by publishing a piece of countercriticism in the near future.[37] Then the matter took a curious turn. Kantorowicz' comments definitely irritated some of the Communist writers. Otto Biha (Peter Merin) had either decided on his own to write an article about Brecht (one that objected to gratuitous criticism of Brecht) or one was now commissioned from him. For one reason or another, Kantorowicz also offered to send an article to Willi Bredel (who was then working in the editorial offices of *Internationale Literatur* in Moscow). Bredel responded: "Nun zu Brecht. Gerade eben erhalte ich von Peter die Nachricht, daß er einen Artikel über Brecht fertig hat, sehr umfangreich. Ich schreibe ihm gleichzeitig, daß er ihn uns schicken soll. Falls er dies tut, so möchte ich Dich bitten, Dich nicht zu ärgern, daß ich ihn um den Artikel gebeten habe: wir haben von Peter unendlich lange Zeit nichts veröffentlicht. Willst Du Dich mit ihm dessethalben in Kontakt setzen? Schickt er den Brechtartikel aber nicht, so bitte ich Dich um einen Brechtaufsatz."[38]

Merin's article came out later in the year; meanwhile, *Unsere Zeit* published not one but two short articles on Brecht's *Der Dreigroschenroman*. Bodo Uhse wrote the first, a certain Paul Haland the second. Uhse wrote favorably. Why Brecht, the brunt of vitriolic attacks in Germany, should be subjected to criticism "aus dem befreundeten Lager" perplexed Uhse. *Der Dreigroschenroman*, after all, took its place among the great classical prose accomplishments of German literature, and Brecht's language was on a par with Luther's, Kleist's, and Büchner's. Uhse went on to say: "Nicht ob Brechts lehrhafte Aussagen bis aufs i-Tüpfelchen richtig sind—sie sind es nicht (und nicht nur das i-Tüpfelchen steht falsch)—ist die Frage, die wir uns vor seinem Buche vorlegen, sondern wem das Buch nützt und wem es schadet, wessen Schande es singt und wessen Ruhm, wen sein Spott vernichtet und wen er mit Ruten vorwärts treiben möchte."[39]

Uhse shied away from highlighting theoretical differences that only obscured the underlying political significance of Brecht's writing. But Haland (by coincidence?) had the last word, and his opening remarks smacked of the same sort of "schleimige Freundschaft" that had characterized Kantorowicz' article. No one denied that Brecht was a talented playwright. "Seine Theorie ist bestreitbar, seine dichterische Begabung und die Bühnenwirkung seiner Dramen sind es nicht. . . . Bert Brecht gehört zu uns und zur Zukunft der proletarischen Revolution."[40] Then Haland turned on Brecht. He had changed, said Haland, "in einem Sinne, den wir bejahen." Unfortunately, though, Brecht's transformation was less apparent in the *Dreigroschenroman.* "Die Undeutlichkeit beginnt mit der Themenwahl. Diese hat andere Undeutlichkeiten zur Folge. Der Roman konfrontiert die bürgerliche Praxis mit der bürgerlichen Ideologie, die der Bürger verbreitet. Die Konfrontation wird zu einer erbarmungslosen Kritik. Indes: diese Kritik beweist nur, daß diese Welt die schlechteste aller Welten ist. Das Proletariat als die Vollbringerin der historischen Kritik an der bürgerlichen Gesellschaftsordnung ist in Brechts Roman nicht vorhanden."[41] Only one brand of anticapitalism deserved to be taken seriously—the socialist anticapitalism of the proletariat. "Alle andere Kritik läuft Gefahr, mißbraucht zu werden und ist oft selber Mißbrauch." Not that he (or "wir," as Haland put it) was out to assign topics to writers; but: "Die Lehren, die er erteilt, sind wie gesagt nicht eindeutig genug. Und daß er sie überdies in der verzwickten Art seiner Themenstellung illustriert, droht, ihren Wert zu vermindern."[42] Haland concluded by saying that the writers who aligned themselves with "us" would be expected to choose their topics "in unmittelbarstem Zusammenhang mit der drängenden Wirklichkeit und mit den Forderungen, die sich aus ihr ergeben."[43]

The more naturally vocal and contentious Stalinist wing of the party had spoken out against Brecht for the first time since Hitler's accession to power.[44] But publication of *Der Dreigroschenroman* was proceeding at a normal pace in the Soviet Union, and it appeared likely that *Die Rundköpfe und die Spitzköpfe* would be both staged and published as a book. Steffin was back in Moscow, and Brecht asked her to be sure to sing his praises "in Mecca."[45] By then the date of his own departure for Moscow was nearing, and in early March he told Steffin that he expected his visa within a week or so; he would then depart immediately.[46] "What is the name of the organization that issued the invitation," he asked, "Morp or Mort? I can't figure any of this out."[47] He also wondered whether his *Versuche* were going to be published and whether he would be received in the Soviet Writers' Union.[48] He apparently arrived in Moscow to find that a tentative agreement to produce *Die Rundköpfe und die Spitzköpfe* in both Moscow and Leningrad had been reached, even though the play had yet to be translated into Russian.[49]

Brecht was treated well in Moscow. Gustav von Wangenheim behaved "saumäßig und unvergeßlich," but then his relations with Brecht had been strained for some time.[50] Otherwise, a reception was arranged for Brecht and attended by the German cultural and political elite in Moscow at the time, for instance, Wilhelm Pieck, Arthur Pieck, Fritz Heckert, Margarethe Lode, Erwin Piscator, J.R. Becher, Reich and Lazis, Friedrich Wolf, and others.[51] Bela Kun and Valdemar Knorin (both disappeared within a few years) were there from the Comintern, Sergej Tretjakov and Semjon Kirsanov represented the Soviet writers. At least some of the talk during Brecht's visit revolved around Piscator's vision of a resident German theater in the USSR, which never materialized; on this score, Brecht had few illusions. He wrote Weigel: "Mit deutschem Theater steht es faul. Wenige Schauspieler, nur schlechte, außer der Neher, die aber nicht besonders geschätzt wird."[52] He also tried to land an acting role of some sort for Weigel, but found nothing, a minor part in a film about Dimitroff being rejected because Wangenheim wrote the script.[53] There were simply no opportunities, not even for Neher, though plans for a German theatre continued to be discussed. Tentative talks were also underway to start a theatre in Engels, the capital of the Volga German Republic. Nothing ever came of this project either, which Brecht dismissed as "kaum eine drittklassige Sache."[54] But evidently Brecht still left Moscow happy with his reception there. He wrote Koltsov (who had asked Brecht to attend the writers' congress in Paris): "Meine UdSSR-Fahrt war eine grosse Erfrischung in jeder Hinsicht, ich merke es bei der Arbeit. Einige Tage war ich noch in Leningrad, wo ich ebenfalls ungemein freundlich aufgenommen wurde. Auch die Heimreise, alles ist gut gegangen."[55]

Upon his return to Skovsbostrand, Brecht began pressuring Tretjakov for information about Okhlopkov's plan to produce *Die Rundköpfe und die Spitzköpfe*. Okhlopkov was not moving ahead very quickly, perhaps because he was preoccupied with his search for a new building to house his company, and Tretjakov had trouble locating him to discuss his intentions.[56] In mid July Okhlopkov was still out of town; "darum kriegen die Rundköpfe keine bewegung," wrote Tretjakov,[57] who then also left town, postponing a discussion between him and Okhlopkov until mid September, when he wrote Brecht: "Okhlopkov ist gekommen. Er hat mit Stenitsch einen Vertrag geschlossen für die Übersetzung von Tschuchen [*Die Rundköpfe*] und bittet mich ich möchte nach dem übersetzen es auszuredaktieren. Gut."[58]

In summer and fall 1935 two articles dealing with Brecht's work appeared in Soviet periodicals. Peter Merin's was the first, and a Russian, A. Brustov, published the second. Both made honest attempts to treat Brecht fairly; the result was a significant amount of honest praise combined with a reticence to accept Brecht's theory. Merin divided Brecht's writing into two phases, classifying works written prior to 1930 as his "Dichtung der Negation." About these Merin explained: "Die klassenmäßig wirkenden Kräfte sind in dieser Schaffensperiode Brechts nebelhaft. . . . Alle Elemente der Negation sind gezeichnet. Aber die Gegenpole fehlen. Es fehlte die andere Seite in ihrer Kraft."[59] Merin then took up some later works, *Die Mutter, Die heilige Johanna der Schlachthöfe, Die Rundköpfe und die Spitzköpfe,* and the *Versuche.* These represented a transition—"den Übergang von der Schaffensperiode der Gesellschaftskritik, der Negation des Gegebenen zu dem Werk der Bejahung der kommenden Ordnung."[60] *Der Dreigroschenroman,* however, came in for criticism that was slightly redolent of Haland's. Why had Brecht decided not to portray the type of capitalism characteristic of the present? Where was the working class? Not that Brecht had ignored modern capitalism altogether, nor was he oblivious to its "zukünftigen Bezwinger." But he had opted to focus upon a sick, putrefying, and expiring order without bringing in "die Exekutoren dieses Todes." Notwithstanding this particular shortcoming, Merin still emphasized the positive: "So bleibt die Grundidee dieses Buches, wie auch des wesentlichen Teils des Werkes von Brecht die pamphletische Entlarvung der bürgerlichen Welt in ihrem Überbau. . . . So entsteht eine große Zeitsatire der kapitalistischen Ethik, der faschistischen Ideologie."[61]

Brecht's theory was a different matter. Although Merin tried to be conciliatory, his comments came across as slightly condescending: sooner or later Brecht was bound to abandon his experimentation and adopt a reasonable attitude. This was especially important because all artistic creation mired in formal experimentation ended in art that distorted reality. "Gerade die Entwicklung Brechts beweist, wie wichtig es ist, sich um jene im Irrgarten des Formalen suchenden Talente der Gegenwart zu kümmern, um ihre Kräfte in den Dienst des Fortschritts zu ziehen." Brecht's artistic theory was incapable of achieving the desired result, Merin said, but it was hard to fathom why anyone would wish to reject summarily such a fruitful artistic praxis, which transcended the theory.[62] The revolutionary and artistic significance of Brecht's work, after all, was unimpeachable, he concluded: "Nicht an ihren Theorien—an ihren Werken solltet ihr die Dichter erkennen."[63]

Brustov followed a similar line of reasoning. Brecht's early works failed to depict "the proletariat—the only force capable of leading the world out of the blind alley. . . . He sees the world falling apart, but regards its condition as immutable and enduring."[64] But Brecht was still the "most significant playwright and poet of postwar Germany"; no German writer since Heine had managed to combine anecdotes, irony, satire, and content as brilliantly as Brecht. "There is nothing in contemporary German literature to compare with the stridency of his criticism, his sarcasm, and his aggressiveness."[65] Brustov raised the question of Brecht's theory in a section entitled "Catharsis or Cigar." The theory fell apart under close scrutiny, he argued, but Brecht essentially went beyond it in his writing anyway. "Brecht poses a question that precludes a third answer: catharsis or cigar? He choses (or thinks he does) the latter. But as definitely as the viewer of Brecht's plays falls into a state of catharsis, he just as definitely forgets about his cigar and lets it burn a hole in his pants! . . . This points toward catharsis plus a 'smoking observer.' "[66]

Brustov alternated praise of *Der Dreigroschenroman* with familiar objections. However dazzling the satirical form used to cloak Brecht's criticism of bourgeois society, the executor of the death sentence imposed upon this society, the proletariat, was inexcusably absent. Brecht had experienced the proletariat at the height of its strength and vitality, after all; moreover, he believed in the proletariat as the eventual victor, the builder of socialism, but "no trace of this knowledge" was to be found in the novel. If Brecht had overcome this deficiency, *Der Dreigroschenroman* would have become the "epochal book of our era" that Brecht intended it to be. Instead, the idea remained only half-realized, outstanding within certain bounds, but a torso nonetheless. Brustov was confident, however, that Brecht would fill in the gaps; his "exceptional talent," his "genius," virtually guaranteed it. "The struggle for liberation of the German proletariat from fascist dictatorship, the fight for the Soviet power of German workers and peasants, has acquired a resounding voice.[67] He will continue to supply the antifascist united front with an even greater number of powerful works."[68]

In late 1935 or early 1936 Steffin arrived back in Moscow, and many of the projects begun the year before were finished. In February Steffin told Brecht that *Die Horatier und die Kuratier* was in print and scheduled to appear in two weeks.[69] *Der Dreigroschenroman* was about to go on sale in German,[70] Steffin wrote Brecht, and Stenich would be bringing her the Russian translation the next day. The publisher had it a few days later, and Steffin wrote that it would be out "soon."[71] Prospects for a licensed VEGAAR edition of Herzfelde's planned four-volume edition of Brecht's plays to be published by the Malik Verlag (and of a poetry volume) also appeared promising.[72] Although the first warning signs now became apparent (Steffin told Brecht about the "formalism discussion" filling the pages of the Soviet daily press), Okhlopkov was still interested in staging *Die Rundköpfe und die Spitzköpfe* both in Moscow and in Leningrad's Music Hall. Moreover, Lenfilm had suggested that Brecht write the script for a film version of *Schweik*,[73] and Goslitizdat hoped to publish *Die Rundköpfe und die Spitzköpfe*. Brecht wanted the edition to include two additional plays, but Steffin told him on 5 March, with no further explanation, that *Die Rundköpfe und die Spitzköpfe* would come out alone. She also reported that Semjon Kirsanov had earlier agreed to translate the play and had been advanced 5,000 rubles. Because he failed to deliver a single line, Stenich had now been approached instead, and Kirsanov agreed to work off his advance by doing twelve songs for the play. As far as Brecht's royalties were concerned, both Steffin and Stenich thought that Okhlopkov should assume the responsibility because he was staging the play. Brecht was anxious to go to Moscow himself at the time, but Steffin told him that, according to Stenich's "privately" expressed view, there was no point in it.[74] Still, by the end of 1936 Brecht had no reason to be dissatisfied. *Die Rundköpfe und die Spitzköpfe* appeared that year in translation,[75] and Tretjakov's book of portraits (including one of Brecht), *Ljudi odnogo kostra,* also came out.[76] Okhlopkov's hope of producing *Die Rundköpfe und die Spitzköpfe,* on the other hand, fizzled. Although his theatre was shut down just a year later, there is no hard evidence that a worsening political and artistic climate caused Okhlopkov to drop his plans.

Considering the hostile atmosphere toward Brecht in the German Section of the Soviet Writers' Union, it seems extraordinary that he was asked to edit the new monthly *Das Wort* (which was originally planned as the official organ of the German Section). But those men who disliked Brecht the most were least involved in the early stages of planning for the journal.[77] Key roles were played by Mikhail Koltsov and his mistress Maria Osten. Brecht had probably met Koltsov for the first time in 1932, and Koltsov, in fact, had his hand in the showing of *Kuhle Wampe.*[78] The relations between him and Brecht grew closer in 1934 and 1935, presumably as a result of Koltsov's position as head of the Foreign Commission within the Writers' Union, and the selection of Sergej Tretjakov to be Koltsov's deputy points to still further associations between the three men.[79] These appear perfectly understandable in light of certain literary affinities. Koltsov was a journalist with a solid reputation as an *ocherkist* long before he wrote his *Spanish Diary.* His opinion of socialist realism is unknown, but it seems unlikely that he would have disdained Tretjakov's kind of artistic publicism—"bio-interviews," literature of fact, and the like—as long as his, Koltsov's, work fit into the same general category. These connections make it appear likely that Koltsov was directly responsible for placing Brecht on the editorial board of *Das Wort* along side the more natural choices of Feuchtwanger and Bredel; and, most importantly, the Jourgaz publishing operation that Koltsov headed was in charge of bringing out *Das Wort.* In addition, Maria Osten (who had become friends with Steffin) was actively involved with Wieland Herzfelde[80] in getting the journal off the ground in early 1936. By 1 April Osten had received Brecht's agreement to serve as an editor,[81] and she continued to correspond with him and Feuchtwanger until Willi Bredel arrived from Paris in May and Osten left for the West.[82] There she continued to work on the journal. By 24 June she was with Brecht, evidently in Paris,[83] and met Benjamin also to discuss his collaboration. She stayed with Brecht for a few weeks before joining Koltsov in Spain.

Brecht's initial collaboration was problematical; he seems to have been unimpressed with *Das Wort* at first, asking Piscator in October 1936, for instance, to write something for the journal—"daß es ein wenig besser wird[.] Es ist zum Kotzen."[84] On the other hand, Brecht displayed little tact in his efforts to improve the journal; his advice in the early months regarding the publication of specific manuscripts evidently fell into one of only two categories: acceptance or rejection, with few reasons given. Bredel wrote Herzfelde in December 1936, for instance: "Die Einwände, die B.B. gegen die 'Tochter des Bombenkönig' von Winder hat, kenne ich nicht; er verlangte nur kategorisch, daß sie nicht erscheinen. Vielleicht 'kennen' sich die beiden." Herzfelde, for his part, considered it unpardonable to reject a manuscript because the editor disliked the author. He told Bredel to demand a concrete explanation.[85] Although this may have been characteristic of Brecht's posture at the beginning, by early 1937 Bredel's complaints had tapered off; all that stood in the way of the journal's excellence was the regrettable circumstance that the editors lived in three different cities, he wrote Osten in March.[86]

But just as Brecht's interest in the journal picked up and things were proceeding somewhat smoothly, trouble began. Brecht's first brush with the German Stalinists came in the form of a quarrel with an hysterical Julius Hay (who certainly acted with the backing of others in the German Section).[87] Bernhard Reich published an article ("Zur Methodik der deutschen antifaschistischen Dramatik") in the January 1937 issue of *Das Wort* that included too much praise of Brecht's *Die Rundköpfe und die Spitzköpfe* and too little of Hay's *Der Damm an der Theiss* and *Haben* to suit the latter's taste. Now Reich's critical remarks, unlike the kind regularly expressed by Hay himself,[88] had no denunciatory undertone; he voiced his opinion politely and unabrasively, pointing out that Hay tended to prefer widely diverse topics that reflected an element of political circumspection caused by his uncertainty in the question of artistic tactics during the period of the popular front. As a result, Hay "camouflaged" his work. Reich explained: "Mit Rücksicht auf die natürlichen Bundesgenossen des Proletariats, welche sich im Banne von verschiedenen Illusionen und Traditionen befinden, müßte man die Terminologie und die Inhalte 'tarnen'. Man müßte sozusagen neutrale peripherische Themen finden, nicht direkte revolutionäre Stoffe zum Ausgangspunkt nehmen, die Darstellung abschwächen, für das 'Menschliche' interessieren. . . . Meiner Meinung nach ist das ein grobes Mißverständnis. Not tut eine wirkliche Massenkunst."[89]

Hay promptly lost his temper and fired off a letter to Brecht, demanding that an article he enclosed be published. The essay (Brecht described it in a letter to Piscator as "einen netten kleinen dreckigen Aufsatz . . . mit klotzigen Attacken auf Reich, mich und, getarnt, Dich"[90]) produced letters to Reich, Hay, and Becher. Brecht told Reich that he had just received copies of the Russian version of *Rundköpfe,* and he hoped that "the Russian comrades" would read it with more understanding than "unser Hayhaufen." He explained Hay's reaction: "Es wird Dich interessieren, daß der Hay (der mit seiner Meinung ebenso unmöglich allein stehen kann wie irgendein Philister mit irgendeiner Meinung) hauptsächlich 2 listige Einwände erhebt: *Erstens)* Das Stück gießt dadurch Wasser auf die Mühle der Faschisten, daß in ihm die faschistische Behauptung, die Rassenmerkmale der Arier seien von denen der Juden deutlich (auch anatomisch) feststellbar unterschieden, aufgenommen sei. . . . *Zweitens)* habe ich nicht den Faschismus dargestellt, denn der könne in einem agrarischen Lande nicht vorkommen." Brecht realized immediately that Hay had not acted on his own, and he feared that Reich may have made things difficult for himself in Moscow. He added: "In meinen Augen sind diese Leute, die in solcher Lage nichts als die Form zu diskutieren wünschen und die größten Streitigkeiten deswegen vom Zaun zu brechen bereit sind, eine sehr unangenehme Sorte von Formalisten."[91]

Hay was told firmly that it had never entered Brecht's mind to repress criticism of his own work and theory; if Hay could manage an informative essay minus the invective, however much it took issue with Brecht, *Das Wort* would publish it. But Brecht would not stand for polemics that were bound to precipitate a divisive debate. "Ich rate Ihnen ab, gerade diesen Artikel zu veröffentlichen, er nützt unserer gemeinsamen Sache nicht, und Sie machen besser keine Renommeesache daraus."[92] Brecht explained his reasoning to Becher: because Hay's attack had been directed at Brecht, he would have been compelled to answer—"und ich fürchtete von der Wucht meines Gegenangriffs entschieden mehr als von der des Angriffs." Brecht went on: "Diese Leute wie Hay haben über ihren formalistischen Interessen alles Praktische des wirklichen Kampfes einfach vergessen. Du kannst Dir denken, daß es mir nicht ganz leicht fiel, hier nur den Redakteur zu spielen und mit allerhand gemurmelten Redensarten wie 'haben sich wohl im Ton ein wenig vergriffen' und 'können uns doch nicht vor allen Leuten raufen' eine so schöne Gelegenheit, daß alles zu *schreiben,* zu beerdigen, indem ich das Aufsätzlein einfach nicht abdrückte und antwortete." A public debate on literary forms was not in their interest, Brecht said, and he asked Becher to explain his standpoint to "the comrades" in Moscow. "Kurz, wir können keinen Hayschnupfen brauchen."[93]

Hay thereafter bore a continual grudge against Brecht, and this particular skirmish—behind it stood Georg Lukács[94]—might have made the coming events inevitable. Now Brecht was an editor of *Das Wort,* and this produced an awkward situation that made it difficult for the men around Lukács to carry out any sort of vendetta against Brecht. But Willi Bredel left for Spain in early 1937, and his place in the journal was taken (de facto, if not de jure) by a pair of Lukács' acolytes, Fritz Erpenbeck and Alfred Kurella. Thereupon the situation deteriorated rapidly. A measure of the changed circumstances in the Moscow office of *Das Wort* was the treatment accorded Walter Benjamin, whose difficulties with the journal mounted. Bredel had told Benjamin in late March 1937 that he wished to wait for the time being with publication of "Das Kunstwerk im Zeitalter seiner Reproduzierbarkeit." It was too long.[95] With Bredel gone, however, the new acting editor reached a quick decision. The article was being returned to him at Bredel's request, he said, adding: "Abgesehen davon, daß es für unsere Zeitschrift zu lang ist, haben wir kurz vorher einen Essay bekommen, der sich zum grossen Teil mit dem gleichen Problem beschäftigt."[96] More rejections followed. Benjamin's review of *Der Dreigroschenroman* was returned—"da es doch nicht angeht, daß wir nach so langer Zeit des Erscheinens des Brecht-Buches in unserer Zeitschrift Deinen Beitrag bringen. Ich selbst kann Ihnen leider nicht den Grund angeben, warum dieses Manuskript so lange bei uns lag."[97] When Benjamin inquired about his second "Pariser Brief," "Fotografie und Malerei," which the editorial board had commissioned and whose acceptance Bredel had expressly confirmed ten weeks earlier,[98] Erpenbeck replied that a decision had to await Bredel's return from Spain.[99] The article never appeared. In late 1937 Brecht prodded Erpenbeck into commissioning Benjamin to review the first two volumes of Brecht's plays in the Malik edition,[100] but this review never showed up in the pages of *Das Wort* either.

Then the attacks upon Brecht started. The first, and harshest, appeared in the monthly *Literaturnyj kritik,* where most of Lukács' works appeared in Russian translation. Written by Lukács' friend, V. Aleksandrov, the censure of Brecht's *Die Mutter* had the unmistakable ring of Lukács to it. Comparing Brecht's adaptation with Gorky's novel, Aleksandrov bandied about words like "mathematical formulas" to describe the dialogue. "This is how you can adapt for the stage the 'logic' of Sigwart or a textbook on geometry, but not Gorky's novel." Such arithmetic was occasionally "quite witty," but arithmetic it remained, "as if the play were supposed to strike the spectator as a logical equation."[101] Ehrenburg had once employed geometry like this to create Nikolaj Kurbov, an approach to writing characteristic of someone who, said Aleksandrov, "overate and poisoned himself with the foul emotionalism of decadent bourgeois art and who has no desire to look for a different form of healthy emotionalism." But Aleksandrov was not finished with Brecht. He might have the best of intentions; he might despise the bourgeoisie. But this intentional flaunting of didacticism should be regarded "above all else as a *formal,* innovative technique." No wonder Brecht's didactics were directly linked to formalistic art, Aleksandrov went on; "they spring not from the new relations that exist between human beings but from the quest for newness (*novizma*). Brecht failed to grasp and embrace Gorky's humanism and realism, and yet this is exactly the humanism and realism that must be learned. For they are the true instruments required in the struggle against, among other things, the bourgeois decadence that Brecht opposes even as he bases himself upon the 'achievements' of this very same decadence. But decadence is not an achievement at all but a sickness, one that must be overcome forthwith."[102]

The expressionism debate began in *Das Wort* three months later, one of the prime purposes of which was to provoke Brecht into an open defense of his ideas on theatre. Although he held back at first, Lukács' article "Es geht um den Realismus," which insulted Hanns Eisler, goaded Brecht into writing.[103] He had seen the article in manuscript form and immediately protested to Erpenbeck. Kurella received the letter and passed it on to Erpenbeck with these accompanying remarks:

> Schnell ein neues Intermezzo: Soeben traf der beiliegende Brief von Brecht ein. Tahü-tata! Jetzt steckt die Katze den Kopf aus dem Sack. Besonders in der Nachschrift. (Nebenbei: du hattest doch den richtigen Riecher als du Lukács um Abschwächung der Eislerstelle batst) (Ein anderes Nebenbei: die von Br. besonders beanstandete Stelle ist gerade die, die auf Bitte von Lukács selbst geändert worden ist. Ich habe ihm das in meinem sofort geschriebenen Antwortbrief sofort leicht ironisch gesteckt.) Zur Sache: wie ich schon telegrafierte, bin ich der Meinung, daß wir aus formalen Gründen nachgeben müssen. Er hat formal recht, daß in der Zeitschrift im Namen der Redaktion nur Artikel erscheinen können, gegen die keiner der Redakteure etwas einzuwenden hat. . . . Ich hoffe, du bist auch der Meinung. Eine Kopie des Briefes gebe ich Walter und werde auch mit ihm sprechen, wie wir uns verhalten sollen. Zum Fond der Sache: jetzt ist er jedenfalls so 'angeregt,' daß er bestimmt schreiben wird. Und das ist auf jeden Fall ein Gewinn. Schön

enthüllt sich jetzt auch der von uns längst vermutete Zusammenhang in jener Kulisse. Natürlich ist Bloch-Eislers Kampagne (denn eine solche war es ja) nicht aus deren hohlem Bauch entsprungen. Gespannt bin ich ja auf die 'allerweitherzigste' Interpretation des Realismus, die wir nun aus dieser Ecke zu erwarten haben. [104]

Lukács' article came out, apparently with "Walter's," Ulbricht's, blessing and in spite of Brecht's protestations. A few weeks later, Brecht promised Kurella that he would send the essay "Volkstümlichkeit und Realismus" soon, [105] but it never showed up in *Das Wort,* nor did another essay, "Weite und Vielfalt der realistischen Schreibweise," that had clearly been written for publication in the journal. Whether the articles were ever sent off in the first place is an open question; Brecht may have suspected that they would merely serve Lukács as negative illustrations followed by an essay in which he would utter the final word on the subject. Brecht had been outmaneuvered. Although he warned Bredel in summer 1938 that his patience was wearing thin, he remained as editor until the journal folded in March 1939 following Koltsov's arrest four months earlier. [106]

Several months later Lukács' influence among Soviet literary critics began to wane, [107] and his dwindling ability to make his points with little danger of contradiction or dissent caused Brecht's fortunes in the Soviet Union to take a modest upward swing. In early 1939, some of Brecht's friends ventured to criticize (however cautiously) one of Lukács' hidebound followers, Julius Hay. They appear to have gone about it by using the same type of tactics employed in the past by the Lukács circle: they published an essay by Hay—"The Road to Realism"—in the periodical *Teatr* and followed it up with lengthy articles of their own. These were written by Timofej Rokotov (chief editor of *International Literature*) and Bernhard Reich. Hay's essay must have been a revised edition of the article whose publication Brecht blocked in 1937. He began with unmistakable criticism of "political" theatre in Weimar Germany, the salient points being that this "topical" (*zlobodnevnyj*) theatre had restricted the number of available themes, confined the front of the revolutionary struggle by overlooking the general humanistic appeal of communism, and "ignored" the classical heritage. Revolutionary writers and artists had hoped to create art for the broad proletarian masses; "instead, they failed to take advantage of all the possibilities available to them and persisted in following a sectarian path in their work." [108] But it would be "unjust" to forget about certain "very positive developments" that paralleled the general incorrect trend in art, said Hay. For there were also writers disinclined to delimit the sphere of their activity. These artists (Hay counted himself among them) went about the task of exploring different possibilities vigorously and with great resourcefulness, discovering a sort of Aesopian language, a form of "camouflage," and achieving "interesting and valuable results." A prime example was Gustav Wangenheim, whose plays were performed time and again even after Hitler's accession to power and up to the burning of the Reichstag. They managed, argued Hay, to attract far greater numbers of spectators than plays with a "distinct political tendency." After February 1933 the new situation demanded new techniques, and Wangenheim broke free of the now outdated approaches. Bertolt Brecht, on the other hand, "who displays an uncommon degree of talent," went on in the wrong direction and tried to turn "a passing, transitory phenomenon into a principle." Life had shown this to be a hopeless undertaking; *Die Rundköpfe,* for instance, failed to attain its political purpose, the exposure of fascism's racist demagogy. But in recent years, Brecht, whose "talent not even his own false theory can stifle," moved forward on the road to realism. *Die Gewehre der Frau Carrar,* for example, or *Der Spitzel* and *Die Rechtsfindung* served as proof that Brecht had "successfully liberated himself from the formalistic 'epic doctrine' " and that he was well on the way to writing realistic plays.[109]

Rokotov's and Reich's articles followed. Neither piece was polemical, neither mentioned Hay by name, and the recent works by Brecht that came in for praise were the ones Hay had mentioned.[110] Perhaps no more could be risked at the time, but within a year Lukács' standing had eroded almost entirely, and critics of him and his followers came out into the open. The swift deterioration of Lukács' authority was accompanied by overtures to Brecht. Rokotov wrote him in August 1939:

> Wie Ihnen bekannt sein dürfte, weilt gegenwärtig unser gemeinsamer Freund, Martin Andersen Nexö, zu Besuch in Moskau. Vor kurzem hatte ich mit ihm ein ausführliches Gespräch über literarische Fragen, wobei Martin Andersen Nexö, unter anderem, sich wunderte, daß Sie mit unserer Redaktion keinerlei Verbindung aufrecht erhalten. Martin Andersen Nexö sagte mir, daß das seiner Ansicht nach ein Versäumnis meinerseits wäre und bat mich Ihnen zu schreiben. Er gab mir dann auch Ihre Adresse. Mit umso grösserer Freude erfülle ich seine Bitte, als wir in der Redaktion aufmerksam Ihr Schaffen verfolgen und mit grösstem Interesse Ihre in der "Kommune" veröffentlichten Einakter aus dem Dritten Reich gelesen haben. Diese Stücke haben uns derart gefesselt, dass ich mich speziell an den Sekretär des Pariser Verbands der Deutschen Schriftsteller mit der Bitte wandte, mir die Manuskripte dieser Stücke im Original zuzusenden. Es handelt sich nämlich darum, dass wir hier in allernächster Zeit einen Sammelband antifaschistischer Einakter herauszugeben beabsichtigen. Ihre Stücke werden meiner Ansicht nach (ich bin der Redakteur dieses Buches) eine Zierde für diesen Band bedeuten.[111]

Perhaps trying to impress upon Brecht that the other editions of *International Literature* were not controlled by the same persons who ran the German version, he added that the entire editorial board, himself naturally included, would be pleased if permanent and cordial ties could be established between the journal and Brecht: "Sie wissen wahrscheinlich, daß unsere französische und englische Ausgaben ganz verschieden von der deutschen Ausgabe der 'IL' sind. Falls dieselben Sie interessieren sollten, wäre es mir eine Freude, sie Ihnen schicken zu können. . . . In unserer russischen Presse war schon lange nichts über Ihr gegenwärtiges Schaffen veröffentlicht. Wir würden uns freuen von Ihnen einen Brief zu erhalten, den wir in der 'IL' veröffentlichen könnten und auf diese Weise unsere Leser mit Ihren schöpferischen Plänen bekanntzumachen. Ich glaube, daß wir ausser im Sammmelband noch ein oder zwei Ihrer Einakter auch in der russischen Ausgabe der 'IL' veröffentlichen konnen."[112]

Rokotov's timing was bad (Hitler and Stalin reached their agreement a week later, stopping the publication of all antifascist books), but his sentiments were genuine. Although the various editions of Brecht's *Furcht und Elend des Dritten Reiches* published in the Soviet Union had to await the outbreak of war,[113] the pact did not prevent some stridently polemical articles directed at Hay and Lukács from appearing in print. In early 1940, a certain N. Kozjura published a blistering denunciation of Hay's *Haben,* which had just appeared in Russian. The play was supposed to illustrate Marx' notion of the dehumanization caused by the ownership of private property. The artistic realization of this profound idea, however, had "regrettably" been undertaken in a vulgar-sociological fashion. The attempt to portray the intractibilities of an economic social system as it affected individual human beings was carried "to the point of absurdity" in Hay's play, the result being a caricature. At the heart of it all was the "venerable history" of Hay's literary techniques, Kozjura said sarcastically. "They spring purely and simply from the arsenal of decadent dramaturgy." The play was devoid of human beings; there was no evolution in their mental processes, no interiorized or individualized tragedy that made the crimes later committed by them plausible. "The distorted, hysterical, unnatural caricatures offend an elementary sense of artistic good taste," and it was unpardonable for a Soviet publisher to bring out this book, "archaic in its errors, tasteless, and boring."[114]

Reich's turn came next, and he vented the pent-up frustrations of several years. In June 1940 he accused Lukács, among other things, of attempting to "revise and distort Marxist-Leninist views on art."[115] Then, in early 1941, he leveled a devastating attack ("Distorted Reality") upon the leading figures of the German Section, beginning with Becher, proceeding to Hay, and finishing with Lukács. Becher had recently written a review of Hay's play *Der Putenhirt,* which *Internationale Literatur* had published. His review, as Reich surely spotted immediately, was probably meant more as a refutation of Brecht's work than as an appreciation of Hay's, and underlying it all was Lukács' notion of decadence. "Gerade in der linksgerichteten Literatur des Westens gab es zahlreiche Anhänger des 'epischen' oder des revuehaft ausgestatteten dokumentarischen Dramas, die unter einem revolutionären Vorzeichen auf diese Weise sich den Auflösungstendenzen des Kapitalismus anpaßten," said Becher. Hay, on the other hand, resisted the attempts to "enrich"—that is, to "dissolve"—the drama lyrically, epically, novelistically, or with the methods of reportage. The need for "Menschengestaltung," "Neuigkeitsreiz," "willkürliche, lose aneinandergereihte Bilderfolge," " 'neuzeitliche,' weitschweifige, langweilende Belehrung"—the various pejoratives were aimed at Brecht, the diction was vintage Lukács. Becher concluded with words that likewise harked back to Lukács' essays: "Der Kapitalismus muß nicht nur in Worten bekämpft werden, sondern auch in der Tat. Die Tat aber im Künstlerischen ist die Gestaltung. Gegen die barbarische Entmenschlichung, wie sie der heutige Kapitalismus auf seinen Schlachtfeldern erzeugt, wirkt nur eine tiefe allumfassende Menschengestaltung, worin uns die künstlerische Vollendung an das menschlich Vollkommene, an eine andere und bessere Welt glauben läßt. Literarische 'Schattenspiele' jeder Art müssen gegenüber der barbarischen Brutalität des Imperialismus versagen."[116]

Reich used Becher's complimentary remarks about Hay to fulminate against his, Reich's, and Brecht's longtime detractors. Hay's "demagogic" distinction in *Putenhirt* between the various social strata that existed in a capitalist system made him guilty of grievous errors. Becher, who understood the nature of these errors, had nonetheless expressed his "solidarity" with Hay.[117] Reich's line of reasoning then plummeted to the same low level of his opponents, taking on the identical sort of denunciatory tone typical of Lukács and his followers. Hay neglected to portray the intensity of the class struggle, and the idealistic impression that the play left in the reader's mind was inexcusable given the current state of world affairs. How was it, in fact, that Hay (a political emigre who had found a "second homeland" in the Soviet Union) lost his ability to empathize with daily life abroad? Reich then brought up various plays that Hay had written previously, including his trashy account of spies and class vigilance in the USSR, *Tanjka macht die Augen auf,* which Reich said demonstrated Hay's inability to deal with such matters on a serious level; in other words, "he has not yet found his bearings in Soviet reality."[118] Reich went on and on, before he finally brought Lukács into the picture: "We can scarcely go wrong by ascribing Hay's efforts to picture contemporary conflicts in an indirect, weakened form, and his predilection for depicting life that gives off only a faint and indistinct echo of the sound of revolutionary struggles, to the influence of Lukács' 'theory.' " Whereas Hay, in *Haben,* had still managed to hold his own against this "baleful" influence, in *Der Putenhirt* he had capitulated to it, sending "Lukács and his sidekicks" into raptures in their praise of an obviously unsuccessful play. Becher had spoken of the programmatic quality of *Putenhirt.* "In a certain sense, this is correct," said Reich; "but what kind of a program leads inevitably to a politically pernicious falsification of contemporary life? This program ignores the ideological content of sharp conflicts that characterize the reality of today's world. Lukács and his sidekicks extol *Der Putenhirt,* in which they see—justifiably so—the creative realization of their aesthetic theories."[119]

Thus ended this latest episode in Brecht's running battle with the Stalinists. War broke out several months later, and the various issues that he and his detractors had debated throughout the thirties and early forties would not come up again until after Brecht's return to the Soviet Zone of Occupation.

Brecht treated the Soviet Union like a puzzle. During the Hitler years he managed to put parts of it together perfectly, but forced other pieces into places where they did not belong. Brecht then thought that the emerging image represented an unvarnished and authentic Soviet reality, whereas the picture was actually badly disjointed. As a result, he misinterpreted some basic verities about daily life in the Soviet Union. Brecht knew that the major source of his personal difficulties lay with men like Lukács, Gábor, Kurella, Erpenbeck, Hay. "Mit diesen Leuten," said Benjamin, "ist eben kein Staat zu machen," to which Brecht replied sarcastically, "Oder *nur* ein Staat, aber kein Gemeinwesen. Es sind eben Feinde der Produktion. Die Produktion ist ihnen nicht geheuer. Man kann ihr nicht trauen. Sie ist das Unvorhersehbare. Man weiß nie, was bei ihr herauskommt. Und sie selber wollen nicht produzieren. Sie wollen den Apparatschik spielen und die Kontrolle der andern haben. Jede ihrer Kritiken enthält eine Drohung."[120]

Much of this particular characterization is sound, but it contains faulty reasoning; and because Brecht was unable to spot the underlying flaw, he could not bring the larger picture of Stalin's Russia into focus. Brecht evidently believed that mindless apparachiki of the kind he had just described, with their insatiable urge to exert control over things, had functions of some kind to fulfil in the state and party apparatus. Just let them keep their distance from literature. But Brecht seemed heedless of the fact that precisely this cast of party bureaucrat was responsible for what he thought were great revolutionary changes in the country and that men of this ilk would scarcely be inclined to keep their hands off literature. A prominent part of the puzzle was missing, but Brecht, apparently, failed to realize that the piece was even lost. "[M]an muß nicht einmal behaupten, daß [die methoden der bolschewiki] auf diesem feld versagten," he said in reference to Soviet literary politics; "es genügt vielleicht zu sagen, daß die methoden, die sie auf diesem feld anwendeten, versagten."[121] Did they? Viewed from whose perspective? Brecht draws a fine distinction between "Bolshevist methods" in general, which he commended, and the methods that these selfsame Bolsheviks applied to literature, which, Brecht implies, were in some way not Bolshevist. The faceless bureaucrats who managed the affairs of government set out to regiment Soviet literature. In so doing they resorted to the same methods that they employed to bolshevize the Soviet Communist party, dekulakize the kulaks, break the will of oppositionists, and transform the ordinary Russian into the new Soviet man. Now could Brecht reasonably expect the same functionaries to make an exception of literary life? Their methods did not fail them at all; rather, these Bolsheviks—Stalinists, to be more precise—utilized tactics in their dealings with cultural matters that produced as a natural result the very conditions to which Brecht objected.

II

> Aber man wird nicht sagen: Die Zeiten waren finster
> Sondern: Warum haben ihre Dichter geschwiegen?[122]

> Ist also schweigen das beste?[123]

Writing about the "the most frightful instruments of oppression and the most frightful police force which the world has ever known," Brecht inveighed against Hitler in 1943 for having "ravaged his own country" before ravaging others. "Whole armies" were in concentration camps; in 1939 the number of prisoners added up to the astonishing figure of two-hundred thousand.[124] For the sake of comparison, figures reputedly compiled in 1956 for an official Politburo investigation of Stalin's crimes place the prison and camp population in the USSR in 1938 at sixteen million. From 1935 to 1940 some 18,840,000 persons— one quarter of the adult population of the Soviet Union—are said to have "passed through the Lubjanka and other affiliated institutions." Seven million of these were executed in prison, the overwhelming majority of the rest died in the camps. Before 1935, twenty-two million persons perished in the collectivization of agriculture through famine and more overt forms of repression; after 1940 and until Stalin's death in 1953, some nine million more died in other assorted campaigns of terror and repression.[125] Why did these "dark times" fail to elicit a response from Brecht? Why was he silent? Why did he scream at the top of his lungs about Hitler's brutality and turn a deaf ear to the cries of anguish coming out of Russia?

Calling his reasoning dialectics, Brecht accounted for Stalin's various infamies by contriving every imaginable extenuating circumstance and christening it dialectics. He began by toying with the concept of freedom. The urge to be free, Brecht explained, meant different things at different times, always depending upon the class in active pursuit of liberty. The bourgeoisie, for instance, which maintained its hold on power by controlling the economy, set clear economic boundaries to freedom of speech by manipulating the means by which opinions could be turned into factors in the struggle for power. So it was no coincidence that information was disseminated differently in the USSR: "Nicht umsonst wiederholen die Redner des Sowjetkongresses, der über die Stalinsche Verfassung beriet, immer wieder die Anerkennung des Anspruchs der proletarischen Klasse auf sämtliche Druckereien, Papiervorräte, Versammlungsräume und Radiostationen."[126] Did Brecht really credit the pronouncements of Stalinists in 1936 at a Soviet Communist party congress about the need for worker access to the mass media? According to every indication, he did, even though he had earlier cautioned Tretjakov: "Den Marxisten interessiert nicht das, was die Staatsmänner über ihre Politik sagen, sondern das, was sie tun."[127]

The "proletarian Soviets," Brecht argued, had their own way of "organizing opinions," and it was entirely unlike the bourgeois tack.[128] Now this new approach to molding and influencing public opinion had nothing in common with crass propaganda or demagogy; rather, it involved clear methods of enlightenment, persuasion, conversion. After all: "Kann man sich vorstellen, daß das Riesenwerk eines kollektiven Industrieaufbaus (ohne Privatinitiative) und der Kollektivisierung und Mechanisierung der Landwirtschaft eines Sechstels der Erde, die Leistung zweier Fünfjahrespläne, eine Pionierarbeit auf unbeschrittenen Pfaden, zustande gebracht in einem der rückschrittlichsten Länder, von einer Bevölkerung, der jahrhundertelang jede Bildung entzogen wurde, durch alle ihre gefährlichsten Phasen im Angesicht einer feindlichen Welt von einigen Leuten am grünen Tisch diktatorisch und unter Ablehnung aller Kritik verfügt werden könnte?"[129] How indeed could the gargantuan feat of collectivization and industrialization have been carried out just because a few men at the top ordered it? Brecht deduced that the revolutionary transformation of town and countryside must have enjoyed the wholehearted, if occasionally critical, support of the people. How could it have been otherwise? Of course, Brecht was not blind to the role played by

repression; the "criticism" of some farmers, because it was not constructive, was answered with a rifle butt or muzzle. This violence, though, fit
into the category of historical necessity: "Ohne die Unterdrückung jener
Bauernmassen, welche den Aufbau einer mächtigen Industrie in Russland
nicht unterstützen wollen, kann nicht ein Zustand eintreten, das heißt
geschaffen werden, in dem Diktaturen überflüssig sind."[130]

Did images of a bloody civil war waged by the state against the
largely defenseless rural population, women and children included, form
in Brecht's mind when he used the word "repression"? Did vivid scenes of
mass deportation by cattle car, starvation, murder flash by? Some twenty-
two million persons presumably died in the campaign of forced collectivization, and Brecht rationalized: "Sie [die Bolschewiken] müssen die
Landwirtschaft selbst in eine Industrie umwälzen. Das ist eine gewalttätige Sache."[131] The end justifies the means. Now Brecht, one may
object, was ignorant about the extent of the terror; he had no idea that it
was so pervasive. Perhaps so, but all Brecht had to do was take Stalin at
his word, and he must surely have read some of Stalin's important writings, particularly those collected in *Problems of Leninism* and republished
time and again as Marxist-Leninist-Stalinist classics. Consider the speech
"Questions of Agrarian Policy in the Soviet Union." Railing at the Zino-
vievist-Trotskyist opposition for advocating a policy of harmlessly
"scratching the kulaks," Stalin lectured on the subject of real bolshevism:
"To attack the kulaks means to smash the kulaks, to liquidate them as a
class. Without these aims, attack is a mere declamation, mere scratching,
empty noise, anything but a real Bolshevist attack. To attack the kulaks
means to make proper preparations and then deliver the blow, a blow
from which they could not recover." What did Brecht think that Stalin
meant by "liquidate?" Was the harsh measure of "dekulakization"—
expropriation (and deportation) of the kulaks—to be permitted, asked
Stalin with a rhetorical flourish. "A ridiculous question," he answered
himself; "don't lament the loss of the hair of one who has been
beheaded."[132]

Now all appearances to the contrary, Brecht had not foresworn
skepticism altogether; but it all came down to the country involved. So
Brecht assailed a man like André Gide, for instance (who had written two
books critical of the USSR), for his one-sided skepticism: it was not
broadly enough applied—"nicht nach allen Seiten gerichtet."[133] And
Brecht's? True, he later began to question some parts of the Soviet
puzzle. "Sehr skeptische Antworten erfolgen, sooft ich russische
Verhältnisse berühre," wrote Benjamin;[134] but the skepticism invariably
touched only upon "details." According to Sternberg, Brecht thought
that it was not his responsibility to take up minor matters such as certain

"schauerliche Dinge" associated with the trials; "worum es ihm ging, war die grosse Linie".[135] Brecht's cardinal failing—the dominant flaw in his "dialectic"—was his inability to relate "details" back to the overall line. Brecht used collectivization to make the point that governmental policy was subject to criticism, albeit a sui generis form: "Tatsächlich wird die Generallinie der Partei nicht in Zeitungsartikeln kritisiert und nicht von plaudernden Gruppen an Kaminen festgelegt oder umgeworfen. Es erscheint kein Buch gegen sie. Allerdings kritisiert das Leben selber sie. Als die Kolchosierung vor einigen Jahren durch ihr allzu stürmisches Tempo das Land in grosse Gefahr brachte, erschienen keine Zeitungsartikel dagegen. Aber wurde das Tempo beibehalten? Es wurde nicht beibehalten. Man muss annehmen, daß Kritik stattgefunden hatte; das, was das Tempo herabgemindert hatte, könnte man nicht das vielleicht Kritik nennen? Es wäre dann eine ungewohnte Kritik, eine neue Spezies, aber was spricht dagegen?"[136]

Brecht was probably much impressed by Stalin's seminal article "Dizzy with Success"; his logic in the above passage was certainly redolent of Stalin's. Brecht added by way of explanation: "Wenn ich Auto fahre, selbst am Steuer, kritisiere ich den Lauf meines Wagens, indem ich steure."[137] The comparison is peculiarly apt. Just picture Stalin at the wheel of a car careening wildly down the road. First, after running over the "left opposition," Stalin swerves to the right; he then veers back to the left, hitting the right wingers. Finally, because he was speeding, he loses control of the car altogether and almost runs it off the left side of the road, "repressing" a few million peasants who got in the way. So he slams on the brakes, jumps out, and, gesticulating wildly about irresponsible people, accuses them of being intoxicated by success and making "reckless attempts . . . to settle all the problems of Socialist construction 'in a trice.' "[138]

In the thirties Brecht never understood the role of brute force in Stalin's leadership. He believed that dictatorships of all kinds were part of a natural historical process. "Diktaturen sind Werkzeuge der Unterdrückung," Brecht wrote. "Zu jeder Unterdrückung sind diese Werkzeuge nötig. Sind die Kämpfe der unterdrückenden Klasse mit den unterdrückten Klassen sehr schwer, dann führen sie meist sogar zu der Diktatur einzelner Personen innerhalb der unterdrückenden Klasse. Dies kommt daher, daß die unterdrückende Klasse starke Disziplin benötigt und den eigenen verschiedenartigen Interessen nicht angesichts eines starken Feindes mächtigen Ausdruck verleihen darf."[139] But, according to the Bolsheviks, there was one critical difference in the case of their dictatorship: "Für die Bolschewiken entscheidet über Ablehnung oder Forcierung der Diktatur (in der einzigen bisher aufgetretenen Form, nämlich derjeni-

gen, die in einem einzigen Mann gipfelt) nur die Erwägung, ob eine solche
die Produktivkräfte hemmt oder entfaltet."[140] Because Brecht sided with
this reasoning, his capacity to inquire critically into major features of
Soviet policy underwent serious erosion. Brecht believed in historical exigencies that placed one man at the top of a power pyramid. But he
overlooked the fact that the base thereupon thinned out quickly and that,
as Stalin's genuine and imagined political opponents grew rapidly scarcer,
the number of persons able to influence policy shriveled to one. Just which
luckless "Bolshevik" was supposed to scratch obsequiously at Stalin's office
door, inform him politely but firmly of the Politburo decision that he was
now hampering the *Produktivkräfte,* and request diffidently that the general
secretary step down? By late 1936, 1937, and 1938, after all, "Bolsheviks"
(especially those in the Central Committee and Politburo) were in very real
danger of becoming a vanishing breed.[141]

Now Brecht certainly had reservations about Stalin; the praise lav-
ished upon the greatest of the great, for example, discomfitted Brecht,[142]
who wrote in *Me-ti:* "Ni-ens Ruf ist durch schlechtes Lob verdunkelt. So
viel Weihrauch, daß man das Bild nicht mehr sieht und man sagt: Hier
soll etwas verborgen werden. Dieses Lob schmeckt nach Bestechung."[143]
Something was definitely awry, but the correct inferences were again just
beyond Brecht's grasp, and he allowed his skewed dialectic to determine
his thinking. The adulation, justified or not, served a useful purpose and
furthered the historical cause: "Freilich, wenn Lob nötig ist, dann muß es
wo immer beschafft werden. Damit sie eine gute Sache loben, müssen
schlechte Leute bestochen werden. Und damals war viel Lob nötig; denn
der Weg war dunkel, und der führte, hatte keine Beweise."[144] What
mattered to Brecht was not the incredible image of an earthly divinity, of
superhuman greatness, but Stalin's "usefulness." He described this particular distinction in a poem[145] and incorporated similar passages into
Me-ti: "Me-ti schlug vor, den Ni-en nicht immer den Grossen, sondern
den Nützlichen zu nennen."[146] But Brecht then seems to have lost his
way in another of the dialectical word games that so often misled him.
The time was not right to employ "usefulness" as a term of praise: "Die
Nützlichen waren zu lange ohne jeden Ruhm geblieben, so daß jetzt die
Aussage, er sei nützlich, keinem mehr das Vertrauen verschaffte, er könne
führen. Immer hatte man die Führer daran erkannt, daß sie sich selber zu
nützen verstanden. Me-ti sah bald die Untauglichkeit seines Vorschlags
ein. Er sagte selber: Was ich eigentlich wollte, war, daß die Nützlichen
als gross anerkannt werden. Aber gerade das geschieht jetzt mit Ni-en.
Der Haufen Unterdrücker, der früher die Macht hatte, hat immer den
Unterdrückten zu beweisen versucht, der größte der Unterdrücker sei
eigentlich sehr nützlich. Jetzt nennt man den Nützlichen groß."[147]

Brecht backed himself into approval of the personality cult, shunting all substantive criticism of Stalin off to the side to make way for an historically adequate appreciation of his "immense Verdienste."[148] Brecht's various arguments in the thirties sound like recordings of the sophistry that filled the pages of the Soviet press: because criticism of Stalin undercut the struggle against fascism and paved the way for war against the USSR, all genuine antifascists were obliged to defend unpleasant but necessary developments in Russia. Brecht wrote: "Der Kampf gegen die Sowjetunion wird von vielen Intellektuellen unter der Parole *Für die Freiheit!* geführt. Man weist anklagend auf eine große Unfreiheit hin, in der sowohl der einzelne Mensch als auch die Masse der Arbeiter und Bauern in der Union leben sollen. Die Knechtung geht angeblich [sic!] von einer Anzahl mächtiger und gewalttätiger Leute aus, an deren Spitze ein einziger Mensch steht, Josef Stalin." Not only fascists, bourgeois democrats, and Social Democrats, but Marxist theoreticians too shared this attitude, said Brecht. The Marxist thinkers would naturally deny that they opposed the Soviet Union itself, even when fascists and democrats of one form or another claimed them as allies: "[S]ie würden sagen," Brecht characterized Marxists who disagreed with Stalin, "sie seien nur gegen den 'Zustand, in dem sich die Sowjetunion gegenwärtig befindet', gegen eine Anzahl mächtiger und gewalttätiger Leute dort, gegen einen einzelnen Menschen, Josef Stalin."[149] But this was dangerously defective thinking, according to Brecht: if the USSR were embroiled in a war, the "Marxist theoreticians" would find their position intensely problematical and untenable. By drawing a dividing line between the Soviet Union and Stalin, they rendered themselves incapable of defending the country unreservedly unless the Soviet Union broke with Stalin; a Soviet victory in war would be undesirable if it came under Stalin's leadership, if it were Stalin's victory. Therefore, the Marxists found themselves hard-pressed to escape the charge that their argument "nur gegen Stalin" smoothed the way for a military buildup against the USSR.[150] As usual with Brecht's reasoning in such matters (it was quintessentially Stalinist), once one accepted the premise, the rest of the argument followed logically.

The biggest Stalinist lie linked the danger of war with Trotsky and the show trials. Brecht was unmindful of the fact that Soviet politicians, Stalin especially, had been screaming about the imminent threat of "imperialist" war against the USSR ever since the revolution.[151] Brecht failed to recognize that, particularly after Stalin began tightening the noose around the country's neck after 1927–28, this war hysteria was meant for domestic consumption and believed by Stalin least of all. Talk of foreign enemies created a siege mentality that made it easier for internal criticism to be discredited by pointing to the need to rally around the *vozhd*. After the mid thirties, of course, the danger was no longer just imaginary, but Stalin still used it as a screen to mask his blows at former and purely imaginary oppositionists within the party. The show trials were a prophylaxis, a preventative defense of the *rodina* against fascism and Trotskyism, said the Stalinists. Brecht believed every word of it, even if he chose not to come out publicly in favor of the courtroom spectacles.

His utterances on the trials, which in terms of his specific points could have fit into any of Vyshinskij's speeches, fall neatly into place within this general explanation. "Die Prozesse sind ein Akt der Kriegsvorbereitung,"[152] wrote Brecht, who then became so enmeshed in the snarled logic used by the Stalinists to account for the trials that he overlooked the simple truth: Stalin had launched the NKVD upon a program of mass terror. Brecht, who conceded that the Soviet Union was a one-man dictatorship, somehow missed the point of it all. Why? Perhaps his gaze was fixed too intently upon Germany. Hitler was a dictator, yet Brecht certainly thought he knew who pulled his strings; he was a marionette of big business, nothing more. Brecht must have convinced himself that, in a somewhat similar fashion, Stalin too was answerable to others in the party who wielded real power in the country. Consequently, Brecht never concluded that Stalin called all the shots, set all policies, designed his actions with the primary goal of holding onto power, and murdered Bolsheviks young and old as the mood struck him. Brecht's notion of dictatorships "welche ihre eigene Wurzel ausreißen"[153] makes no allowances for a dictator who had acquired absolute power.

If in the thirties Brecht had appreciated Stalin's true nature, he might have grown at least slightly suspicious about the trials and the confessions. As it was, he resorted to the same dialectic that had deluded him on earlier occasions. The lack of evidence at the trials was apparently little more than a *Schönheitsfehler*. He wrote in *Me-ti:* "Me-ti tadelte den Ni-en, weil er in seinen Prozessen gegen seine Feinde im Verein vom Volk zu viel Vertrauen verlangte. Er sagte: Wenn man von mir verlangt, daß ich etwas Beweisbares glaube (ohne den Beweis), so ist das, wie wenn man von mir verlangt, daß ich etwas Unbeweisbares glaube. Ich tue es nicht. Ni-en mag dem Volk genützt haben durch die Entfernung seiner Feinde im Verein, er hat es jedoch nicht bewiesen. Durch den beweislosen Prozess hat er dem Volk geschadet."[154] The mistake lay, therefore, in the failure to produce evidence, but Brecht apparently never doubted the truth of the accusations[155] and criticized Stalin only for an error in judgment: "Er hätte [das Volk] lehren müssen, Beweise zu verlangen und das besonders von ihm, dem im allgemeinen so Nützlichen."[156] Just picture Stalin insisting that the people demand proof from him when the general rule in the secret police was, "Give us the man and we'll make the case"! For Brecht, however, proof or not, nothing that had thus far transpired in Stalin's Russia could possibly serve as justification for a genuine antifascist to *question* the USSR. Why? "Was die Prozesse betrifft, so wäre es ganz und gar unrichtig, bei ihrer Besprechung eine Haltung gegen die sie veranstaltende Regierung der Union einzunehmen, schon da diese ganz automatisch in kürzester Zeit sich in eine Haltung gegen das heute vom Weltfaschismus mit Krieg bedrohte russische Proletariat und seinen im Aufbau begriffenen Sozialismus verwandeln müßte."[157]

Brecht's capacity for critical thought proved just as wanting when he took up the question of the "conspirators' " political objectives. The defendants' goals were based on "defeatism," Brecht imagined, identifying their major miscalculation as the conviction that no possibility existed for the construction of socialism in one country and that fascism would prove to be durable in other lands. For that reason, argued Brecht, they secretly conspired to *restore* capitalism in the USSR. Now this was no less than the logic of Stalin's prosecutor Vyshinskij. But there was more, for Brecht had yet to account for the confessions, whose believability, he said, hinged only on the articulation and understanding of a political program that culminated naturally in the defendants' "remorse" once they realized the depth of their own depravity. Brecht's (and, again, Vyshinskij's) dialectic: the men now in the dock had come to believe that an unbridgeable chasm yawned between the Soviet regime and the masses, and between workers and peasants, a gap that was endangering worker control of the means of production and of the army. The defendants were therefore understandably anxious to make compromises or concessions with foreign powers as a means of saving what they could and staving off a total national collapse. Their cooperation "mit kapitalistischen [that is, fascist] Generalstäben"—"gewisse Verhandlungen mit faschistischen Diplomaten"—may well have been "mere" contact with individual persons in the pay of these foreign powers,[158] but this point was relatively immaterial: "Sie sehen sich eben umringt von jedem Gesindel, das an solchen defaitistischen Konzeptionen Interesse hat."[159] Brecht concluded:

> Was wir zu tun haben, ist: [die Anklage] begreiflich zu machen. Wenn die in den Prozessen angeklagten Politiker zu gemeinen Verbrechern herabgesunken sind, so muß für Westeuropa diese Karriere als eine politische erklärt werden; das heißt diese Politik als zu gemeinen Verbrechen führend. Hinter den Taten der Angeklagten muß eine für sie denkbare politische Konzeption sichtbar gemacht werden, die sie in den Sumpf gemeiner Verbrechen führte. Solch eine Konzeption ist natürlich leicht schildbar. Sie ist durch und durch defaitistisch, es ist, bildlich gesprochen, Selbstmord aus

Furcht vor dem Tod. Aber es ist einleuchtend, wie sie in den Köpfen dieser Leute entstanden sein mag. Die ungeheuren natürlichen Schwierigkeiten des Aufbaus der sozialistischen Wirtschaft bei rapider und immenser Verschlechterung der Lage des Proletariats in einigen großen europäischen Staaten lösten Panik aus.[160]

This panic led the accused to search for compromise along the lines of Lenin's partial restoration of capitalism during the New Economic Policy (1924–1928). Of course, said Brecht, NEP had been correct and called for within the context of the times, but today any such program was "anachronistisch, konterrevolutionär, verbrecherisch."[161] As for the confessions in particular, the riddle was easily solved: "Schon in den paar Jahren, die seit dem Entstehen dieser Konzeption vergangen sind, hat sich das Anachronistische der Konzeption selbst für ihre Konzipienten herausgestellt. Sie können selber ihre Meinungen nicht mehr aufrechterhalten, empfinden sie als verbrecherische Schwäche, unverzeihlichen Verrat. Die falsche politische Konzeption hat sie tief in die Isolation und tief in das gemeine Verbrechen geführt. Alles Geschmeiß des In- und Auslandes, alles Parasitentum, Berufsverbrechertum, Spitzeltum hat sich bei ihnen eingenistet: Mit all diesem Gesindel hatten sie die gleichen Ziele." Brecht added: "Ich bin überzeugt, daß dies die Wahrheit ist, und ich bin überzeugt, daß diese Wahrheit durchaus wahrscheinlich klingen muß auch in Westeuropa, vor feindlichen Lesern."[162]

"[I]m faschismus erblickt der sozialismus sein verzerrtes spiegelbild. mit keiner seiner tugenden, aber allen seinen lastern," reads Brecht's journal entry for 19 July 1943.[163] The existence of vices and virtues along side each other in Soviet Russia—this point crops up frequently in Brecht's writing, especially in *Me-ti,* always with the implication that, in any sort of historical context, the vices that plagued the system were outweighed by its virtues and would eventually be overridden by them.[164] The developments that Brecht placed in the category of virtues is clear enough; what, on the other hand, was he prepared to subsume under the other rubric? Violence and terror? Did he understand what was happening or did the same mental block that kept him from seeing the simple truth of the trials cloud his vision here too? His dialectical approach to the problem of collectivization funneled his thinking in a direction that ended with Brecht condoning the repression of any "rich" Russian peasant who owned more than a pig and three chickens. Whether Brecht was actually aware of the senselessness of it all is beside the point; as long as he accepted the necessity of "repressing" a dozen peasants who belonged to "gewisse besitzende Schichten der Bauern,"[165] the murder of many times that number could scarcely be objected to unless Brecht was willing to impugn the validity of the original premise.[166]

173

Brecht's writing is dotted with words like "Zwang" and "Gewalt" when he speaks of the Soviet Union, and passages containing them uniformly underscore the need for coercion and force—as long as the right side resorts to such practices. He explained the dialectic in *Me-ti,* addressing the question of "Unfreiheit unter Mi-en-leh [Lenin] und Ni-en" and comparing the accomplishments of the Bolsheviks with the actions of the old rulers: "[D]as Land haben sie ebenfalls von allen hemmenden Gewalten befreit. Sie wissen natürlich, daß sie, anders als die Schmiedeherren und Landherren, nicht als Einzelne wirtschaftlich frei sein können sondern nur insgesamt. Ihre Befreiung nun haben sie organisiert, und so ist Zwang entstanden; gegen alle Strömungen, welche die grosse Produktion der Güter für alle bedrohen, wird Zwang angewendet."[167] The necessary repression of "well-to-do" peasants for the betterment of the country? "Das ist eine gewalttätige Sache."[168] The abolition of classes? "[Das] bedarf eines gewaltsamen Anstosses."[169] Even killing was acceptable if it occurred as part of a regulated revolutionary process; after all, the "classics"—Marx and Engels—had given their stamp of approval because killing would take place in order to make killing needless: "Die Klassiker stellten keine Satzungen auf, welche das Töten verboten. Sie waren die mitleidigsten aller Menschen, aber sie sahen Feinde der Menschheit vor sich, die durch Überredung nicht zu besiegen waren. Das ganze Sinnen der Klassiker war darauf gerichtet, solche Verhältnisse zu schaffen, daß das Töten niemandem mehr Nutzen bringen konnte. Sie kämpften gegen die Gewalt, die zuschlägt, und gegen die Gewalt, die die Bewegungen hindert. Sie zögerten nicht, der Gewalt die Gewalt entgegenzustellen."[170] As Brecht put it in *Die heilige Johanna der Schlachthöfe:* "Es hilft nur Gewalt, wo Gewalt herrscht." Or even more crassly in *Die Maßnahme:*

> Welche Niedrigkeit begingest du nicht, um
> Die Niedrigkeit auszutilgen?
> Könntest du die Welt endlich verändern, wofür
> Wärst du dir zu gut?
> Wer bist du?
> Versinke in Schmutz
> Umarme den Schlächter, aber
> Ändere die Welt: sie braucht es![171]

In line with revolutionary necessity the plowshares were to be beaten into swords for use against enemies of the people. But assume for a moment (along with Brecht) that those ordering the repression were genuinely committed to what they perceived to be historically necessary, revolutionary action. What about innocent people who got in the way? Or was innocence even a consideration? What constituted guilt? What brought the revolutionary sword down upon the necks of luckless wretches whose misfortune it was to be in the wrong place at the wrong time? Brecht's version of "when wood is chopped, chips fly" sounded like this: "Das Brot wird mit solcher Wucht ins Volk geworfen, daß es viele erschlägt."[172] But who "hurled" the bread anyway, why, and at whose behest? "Die segenreichsten Einrichtungen werden von Schurken geschaffen," he said, "und nicht wenige tugendhafte Leute stehen dem Fortschritt im Wege."[173] How so? By accepting the underlying rationale of "socialist construction," the need for some sort of special treatment of persons unintentionally but objectively inhibiting progress is clear. But where does Brecht allow for the early-morning NKVD knock at the door because someone's neighbor wanted a bigger apartment and denounced him to the police as the head of the Moscow Central of the Gestapo (or because the NKVD was behind in its weekly quota of arrests)? Where does Brecht betray an awareness that millions of those arrested stood in the way of the "revolution"—Stalin's revolution—neither subjectively nor objectively?

How indeed can "die segenreichsten Einrichtungen" be created by scoundrels? Perhaps such men were active in lower-level positions and kept in check by decent superiors, who called upon the scoundrels to fulfil unpleasant but necessary tasks in pursuit of some greater good. If so, who were the good men at the top directing it all, say, in 1937? Ezhov, Mekhlis, Molotov, Stalin? Notwithstanding the presence of honest and forthright superiors, were the scoundrels—say in the police force—not certain to get out of hand anyway? Brecht recognized that the type of police work necessary in a revolutionary situation was not for the tender-hearted. Being a policeman was not an occupation; "es kann eine kurze Mission sein," Brecht said, adding that certain "jobs" were sure to undermine a policeman's humanity: "Es gibt Arbeiten, die nur kurz ausgeführt werden können. Dazu gehört die Polizeiarbeit."[174] The state had no right, he elaborated elsewhere, to expect a man to perform police duties permanently.[175] Brecht had the Soviet Union in mind; he knew about the Cheka-NKVD and perceived certain dangers inherent in its very existence. "Was aus der Tscheka werden kann, sieht man an der Gestapo," he said as early as 1934.[176] But he viewed the danger as a potentiality, not as an overriding fact of daily life in the Soviet Union. On the other hand, he had a curious confidence in the power of "good posts" to exert a sort of magical control over scoundrels: "Verlangt nicht gute Leute, sondern schafft gute Posten! Ein guter Posten ist ein Posten, der keinen guten Menschen benötigt."[177] Did such positions already exist? Evidently not, according to Brecht, who remarked to Benjamin in 1938: "Daß auf der einen Seite, in Rußland selbst, gewisse verbrecherische Cliquen am Werke sind, darin ist kein Zweifel. Man ersieht es von Zeit zu Zeit aus ihren Untaten."[178]

In what areas were these "criminal cliques" active? In the police? In the courts?[179] Were scoundrels to be found in the upper echelons of the government as well? Brecht seemed to believe that—should they exist— mediocre and even disreputable men at the top were similarly held in check by sound institutions administered "by the people." He wrote: "Ein Land, in dem das Volk sich selbst verwalten kann, hat keine besonders glänzende Führung nötig. . . . Sind die Institutionen gut, muß der Mensch nicht besonders gut sein."[180] But how could such a system function, one infested by scoundrels at various levels of the governmental apparatus who, despite their best efforts to subvert it for their own benefit, found themselves pressed by their "posts" willy-nilly into formation of "die segensreichsten Einrichtungen"? Perhaps such men formed a part of the power that constantly wills evil but always creates good. But who designed sound posts in the first place, jobs that caused the Soviet Mephistos trying to derail the locomotive of history to shunt it inadvertantly onto tracks actually leading in the proper progressive direction? And if the posts were yet to be created, how could Brecht sustain the hope that they ever would be, given the dark designs of all the imps and ogres active within the party and secret police apparatus? What messiah would eventually drive the heathen from the temple? Did he speak Russian with a Georgian accent? Maybe the *vozhd* ("[der] im allgemeinen so Nützliche") had indeed been betrayed by scoundrels in the police and the judiciary who, unbeknownst to him, had been arresting countless innocent millions on the sly?[181] Of course it was no coincidence that Stalin, after Ezhov and Jagoda had murdered for him, turned on his tagtails and, to cover his own tracks, blamed various "excesses" upon them before sending the two former NKVD chiefs down the same road traveled by millions of their victims. Was this not graphic evidence of the emperor's own goodness? Had Stalin not acted resolutely in the interests of the people once dogs like Jagoda and Ezhov were shown to be devils? What one misses in Brecht is the slightest glimmer of understanding such as the kind that, put into a poem, led to the arrest of Osip Mandelshtam:

> His cockroach whiskers leer
> And his boots gleam.
> Around him a rabble of thin-necked
> leaders—
> Fawning half-men for him to play
> with.
> They whinny, purr or whine
> As he prates and points a finger,

One by one forging his laws, to be
  Flung
Like horseshoes at the head, the eye
  or the groin.
And every killing is a treat
For the broad-chested Ossete.[182]

Brecht never protested publicly about the arrest of his friends in the USSR, nor was he particularly quick to place these incidents in the category of "Untaten." Brecht was exceedingly well informed about the fate of German and foreign Communists in the Soviet Union. He had drawn up this balance sheet in 1938: "auch kolzow verhaftet in moskau. meine letzte russische verbindung mit drüben. niemand weiß etwas von tretjakow, der 'japanischer spion' sein soll. niemand etwas von der neher, die in prag im auftrag ihres mannes trotzkistische geschäfte abgewickelt haben soll. reich und lacis schreiben mir nie mehr, grete bekommt keine antwort von ihren bekannten im kaukasus und in leningrad. auch bela kun ist verhaftet, der einzige, den ich von den politikern gesehen habe. meyerhold hat sein theater verloren, soll aber opernregie machen dürfen."[183] The news reached him quickly, too. Rumors about the fate of Carola Neher were circulating in the West shortly after she and Erich Mühsam's widow Zensi were taken in by the NKVD, and—within certain limits—Brecht tried to help her. He asked Lion Feuchtwanger (who had visted Moscow in December 1936 and January 1937) to find out what he could about her whereabouts.[184] Ottwalt's arrest was brought to Brecht's attention at about the same time. He had been picked up in November 1936, and in February 1937 Brecht received a peculiar letter from Bernard von Brentano, who told him that "bourgeois newspapers" had accused him, Brentano, of denouncing Ottwalt to the Soviet government for writing him letters "friendly to Hitler." The news about Ottwalt's arrest had also reached him, Brecht replied to Brentano, but he otherwise knew nothing about the case.[185] As for some of the others, Tretjakov disappeared in July 1937, and Brecht had information about his arrest at least by summer 1938;[186] by then he already assumed that his friend was dead. Finally, Brecht got news of Koltsov's disappearance directly from Maria Osten. He had been picked up in December 1938.

Now were Brecht's friends innocent or were they "tugendhafte Leute" who, alas, accidentally stepped in the way of the revolutionary locomotive? Brecht was reluctant to believe the news about Ottwalt. The information, he told Brentano, "stammt anscheinend nur aus bürgerlichen Blättern." He personally had been out of touch with Ottwalt for years, and in any case: "Ich selber halte immer noch die bolschewistische Partei für in dem russischen Proletariat tief verankert und die russische

Wirtschaft in einem großen revolutionären Prozeß begriffen."[187] So even if Ottwalt had been arrested, for whatever reason, Brecht's faith in the essential desirability of the Soviet system remained unshaken. In the meantime, he advised Brentano to await some sort of "authentic" news. Brecht would then inform the editorial office of *Das Wort* that Brentano had neither received letters from Ottwalt sympathetic to Hitler nor passed any such information on to the Russians.[188] Several months later Brecht's attitude toward the Ottwalt case had turned into cynicism. When Benjamin asked him if Ottwalt was still in jail, "sitting," Brecht replied: "Wenn der noch sitzen kann, sitzt er."[189] By this time Brecht obviously accepted the authenticity of the rumors about Ottwalt's arrest, but it is entirely possible that he also believed the charges.

He certainly had difficulty understanding that the NKVD was busy arresting innocent people, as his reaction to Neher's disappearance indicates. Neher, he wrote Feuchtwanger, was said to be in jail in Moscow— "ich weiß allerdings nicht weswegen."[190] If Brecht had even suspected the truth of what was going on in Russia, how could he have ever asked "why"? But Brecht pressed on in his search of explanations: "Vielleicht ist sie (Neher) durch irgend eine Frauenaffäre in was hineingeschliddert. . . . Wenn Sie nach ihr fragten, würde ihr das schon nützen. Ich selber habe von niemand auf eine Frage eine Antwort erhalten, was ich nicht schätze. Aber vielleicht haben Sie drüben von ihr erfahren, dann wäre ich Ihnen dankbar für einige Zeilen darüber. Ich werde immerfort ihretwegen um Auskunft angegangen."[191]

Why was Brecht so reluctant to identify senseless terror as the explanation? Perhaps his experience with Hitler's Germany again narrowed his vision; Hitler did not go around arresting innocent people, "only" Jews and Communists; so if significant numbers of persons in the USSR were vanishing, Brecht may have told himself, there must be an explanation somewhere. For him it lay (in Neher's case) in one of two possibilities: either she had indeed implicated herself in "hochverräterische Umtriebe" (the notion did not strike Brecht as preposterous); or she had fallen victim to an NKVD mistake committed in the act of otherwise necessary spy sweeps: "Bei den sehr berechtigten Aktionen, die man den Goebbelschen Organisationen in der UdSSR entgegensetzt, kann natürlich auch ein Fehlgriff passieren."[192] Brecht's "große Linie" still took precedence over "details," for he urged Feuchtwanger to be discreet about his inquiries: "[E]ine einfache (nicht publike) Erkundigung würde ihre künstlerische Bedeutung schon unterstreichen, ohne die Arbeit der Justizbehördern zu erschweren. Es wäre mir allerdings recht, wenn Sie diese meine Bitte ganz vertraulich behandelten, da ich weder ein Mißtrauen gegen die Praxis der Union säen, noch irgendwelchen Leuten

Gelegenheit geben will, solches zu behaupten."[193] Feuchtwanger later told Brecht (Feuchtwanger appears to have believed it): "carola neher war, während ich in m war, eingesperrt. sie soll in ein verräterisches komplott ihres mannes mit verwickelt sein." He added: "details weiß ich nicht."[194]

Brecht's reaction to Koltsov's arrest exhibits the same helplessness in the face of the simple truth. He wrote Maria Osten (she too later perished): "Ihre Zeilen über Kolzow haben mich sehr erschreckt. Ich hatte gar nichts gehört. Jetzt sagt man mir, daß auch in Kopenhagener Zeitungen Gerüchte, er sei verhaftet, wiedergeben worden sind. Ich hoffe so sehr, daß sich die Gerüchte nicht bestätigen. Bitte teilen Sie mir gleich mit, wenn Sie Genaueres erfahren oder überhaupt etwas." As late as 1939 Brecht was still looking for nonexistent "reasons": "Ich kann mir einfach nicht denken, was er getan haben könnte, ich habe ihn wirklich nur immer unermüdlich für die Sowjetunion arbeiten sehen. Haben Sie irgendeine Ahnung, was ihm zur Last gelegt wird?"[195] What if Brecht had known that Koltsov, at least according to one account, was charged with being an agent of Lord Beaverbrook?[196] Would this explanation (it made as much sense as most others) have satisfied him?

The fate of Sergej Tretjakov (charged, of all things, with being a Japanese spy) inspired a poem that discloses none of the astonishment or outrage befitting such an absurdity. Certainly Brecht's repetition of the line "Gesetzt, er ist unschuldig?" betrays an element of doubt; but where in the entire poem "Ist das Volk unfehlbar?" is there any sense of utter incredulity? Brecht struggled to understand:

> Was 5 000 gebaut haben, kann einer zerstören.
> Unter 50, die verurteilt werden
> Kann einer unschuldig sein.[197]

Brecht believed the stories of rampant "wrecking" activity, that is sabotage, throughout the land; here he suggests merely that one person out of fifty might be innocent. But what about the forty-nine others? Did Brecht ever suspect that even the opposite—forty-nine innocent and one guilty—went too far? Was Tretjakov's arrest, like Neher's, an instance of judicial error? Or was there another explanation? Perhaps his demise was the handiwork of demons in high places (say, in the courts) whose misdeeds had not been restricted by good posts. Brecht wrote:

> Über die Feinde reden, die in den Gerichten des Volkes
> sitzen können
> Ist gefährlich, denn die Gerichte brauchen ihr Ansehen.[198]

But Brecht undercut the power of his argument by turning it into a suggestion (sitzen *können*), besides which his conclusion reverted back to his old dialectic: even if occasional enemies of the people were sitting on the courts, condemning guiltless Soviet citizens like Tretjakov, it was dangerous to speak about them. Why? Not because you would be picked up yourself before the day was out, but because loose talk undermined the authority of the courts, and "die Gerichte brauchen ihr Ansehen." These were, after all, trying times; was the Soviet Union not on the threshold of a great war? Did the crisis not call for draconic measures that could not always satisfy the norms of judicial practices appropriate to less unsettled times? The Communist party felt that enemies (spies and saboteurs) were busy hatching conspiracies within the land, and, Brecht implies, extraordinary circumstances demanded that extraordinary steps be taken to preserve the Union. Yes, errors were made and innocent people suffered; the medicine tasted bitter, but the patient had, after all, been in grave danger:

> Zahlreiche Verhaftungen waren durchgeführt worden. . . . Me-ti hob lobend hervor, daß beinahe niemand Leute schon deshalb für schuldig hielt, weil sie verhaftet worden waren. Dagegen billigten es viele, daß man auch nur Verdächtige verhaftet hatte. Daß die Behörden nicht imstande waren, die Schuldigen herauszufinden, wurde als Fehler betrachtet; jedoch billigte man es, daß sie, außerstande zu prüfen, doch wenigstens im plumpen gegen das Übel vorgingen. Die guten Chirurgen lösen den Krebs vom gesunden Fleisch, die schlechten schneiden gesundes Fleisch mit heraus, wurde gesagt. Me-ti fand die Haltung des Volkes bewundernswert und sagte: Sie behandeln ihre Polizei als schlechten, plumpen, dummen Diener, das ist schon etwas.[199]

How well it spoke of ordinary Soviet citizens that they refused to regard a person as guilty just because he had been arrested! How politically mature of them, on the other hand, to applaud the courage of the NKVD in arresting those merely suspected of having committed crimes. Granted, the authorities' inability to determine guilt with some measure of precision was a "mistake," but squeamishness at the thought of picking up innocent persons had fortunately not caused the NKVD to shy away from acting against the evil—"wenigstens im plumpen." True, the secret police had not acquitted itself well from a surgical standpoint; healthy flesh, alas, had been destroyed, but at least the patient was free of cancer. Brecht failed to see, however, that the patient was also dead.

In August 1938 Brecht asked if there would also be singing "in the dark times" and replied, "Da wird auch gesungen werden / Von den finsteren Zeiten."[200] But confronted with Tretjakov's arrest, he asked a different question: "Ist also schweigen das beste?"[201] He responded by filing his poem away among his unpublished papers. "Keine Stimme hat sich für ihn erhoben,"[202] he wrote with a tinge of remorse, and Brecht may indeed have suffered from the pangs of a guilty conscience. In

October 1938 he had been taken to task in the Trotskyist journal *Unser Wort* by a furious Walter Held: "Sie, Herr Brecht, haben Karola Neher gekannt. Sie wissen, daß sie weder eine Terroristin noch eine Spionin, sondern ein. tapferer Mensch und eine grosse Künstlerin war. Weshalb schweigen Sie? Weil Stalin Ihre Publikation 'Das Wort', diese verlogenste und verkommenste Zeitschrift, die jemals von deutschen Intellektuellen herausgegeben worden ist, bezahlt? Woher nehmen Sie noch den Mut, gegen Hitlers Mord an Liese Hermann, an Edgar André und Hans Litten zu protestieren?"[203]

Can Brecht be accused of doing nothing? He tried time and again, wherever he was, to obtain information about Neher's whereabouts.[204] On one particular occasion Brecht and Ruth Berlau visited the Soviet ambassador to Denmark, and Brecht's first question concerned Neher.[205] All to no avail. This must have produced in Brecht an agonizing feeling of helplessness. His poem "Das Waschen" (for "C.N.") reads:

> Jetzt höre ich, du sollst im Gefängnis sein.
> Die Briefe, die ich für dich schrieb
> Blieben unbeantwortet. Die Freunde, die ich für dich anging
> Schweigen. Ich kann nichts für dich tun. . . . [206]

The same emotions may also have prompted similar lines in "An die Nachgeborenen," which Brecht probably wrote in late 1938:

> Der dort auf der Straße geht
> Ist wohl nicht mehr erreichbar für seine Freunde
> Die in Not sind?[207]

But if Brecht was beyond his friends' reach, unable to take action on their behalf, then he bears sole responsibility for the limited possibilities at his disposal. He did what he could for Neher, but only within narrowly prescribed bounds; he wrote letters, asked questions in private, and the results were understandably nil. His own words, uttered in 1935 at the writers' congress in Paris, came back to haunt him: "Wenn die Verbrechen sich häufen, werden sie unsichtbar. Wenn die Leiden unerträglich werden, hört man die Schreie nicht mehr. Ein Mensch wird geschlagen und der zusieht, wird ohnmächtig. Das ist nur natürlich. Wenn die Untat kommt, wie der Regen fällt, dann ruft niemand mehr halt!"[208] What might have saved Neher and others was a public protest—if the Feuchtwangers, Heinrich Manns, and other genuine antifascists had joined with Brecht to insist that a halt be put to the carnage. But this was the one step that, in the interests of antifascism, Brecht was unwilling to take, and his dialectic presumably caused him to regard his vanished friends as casualties of fascism rather than victims of Stalinism.

To change the world Brecht embraced the butcher. Listen, once again, to the words of Walter Held:

> Wenn Felix Halle, Ernst Ottwald, Karola Neher, Rudolf Haus etc. in Hitlers Kerkern säßen und in Todesgefahr schwebten, wie würdet ihr schreien, schreiben, das arme 'Weltgewissen' maltraitieren. Doch wenn Stalin die gleichen Leute umbringt, so rührt euch das nicht im geringsten. . . . Und ihr wundert euch noch, dass ihr Schritt für Schritt an Boden verliert, der Faschismus stets größere Kreise zieht? Dem Faschismus wird der Vormarsch ja nur deshalb so leicht gemacht, weil ihr im voraus geschlagen seid, weil ihr selbst die mageren Prinzipien, die ihr gegen den Faschismus zu verteidigen vorgebt, schon hundert und tausendmal in den Kot getreten habt, weil ihr keine überzeugten Kämpfer und Charaktere seid, sondern von Stalin geistig und moralisch völlig ausgehöhlte Paradefiguren. Stalin kaufte eure moralische Autorität, um das Weltgewissen einzuschläfern, ihr gabt euch dazu her und wundert euch noch, wenn euch danach das Weltgewissen den Hintern zukehrt? Eure Tätigkeit erschöpft sich in dem einen Wort: Verrat. Verrat an euren Büchern und eurer Moral, Verrat an den Opfern Hitlers und an den Opfern Stalins, Verrat an den Massen und Verrat an euch selbst. Wahrhaftig, bessere Alliierte könnte der Faschismus nicht finden, als solche Gegner. Wenn es euch nicht gäbe, Göbbels müßte euch erfinden.[209]

Held, by the way, attempted to reach the United States in 1940 following the same route later used by Brecht and, along with his wife and child, was pulled from the Trans-Siberian Express, never to be seen again.[210] Two years earlier Brecht had given Held a response of sorts when he explained his public silence about the unpleasantries occurring in Russia to Benjamin, who wrote in his diary: "Der russischen Entwicklung folge er; und den Schriften von Trotzki ebenso. Sie beweisen, daß ein Verdacht besteht; ein gerechtfertigter Verdacht, der eine skeptische Behandlung der russischen Dinge fordert. Solcher Skeptizismus sei im Sinne der Klassiker. Sollte er eines Tages erwiesen werden, so müsste man das Regime bekämpfen—und zwar *öffentlich*. Aber 'leider oder Gottseidank, wie Sie wollen,' sei dieser Verdacht heute noch nicht Gewißheit."[211] Brecht never concluded that the Soviet apple was rotten to the core.[212] For him the various *Kinderkrankheiten* of the Stalinist system were just tantamount to an occasional worm hole that, viewed from an historical perspective, disfigured but never spoiled the fruit.

Notes

1. Bertolt Brecht, *Arbeitsjournal* (Frankfurt am Main: Suhrkamp Verlag, 1973), p. 636.
2. *Brecht-Chronik. Daten zu Leben und Werk.* Zusammengestellt von Klaus Völker (Munich: Carl Hanser Verlag, 1971), pp. 72–73.
3. *Arbeitsjournal.* p. 36.

4. Ibid., p. 636.

5. See part two of this article.

6. Brecht to Becher, 28 June 1933, in Brecht, *Briefe* (Frankfurt am Main: Suhrkamp Verlag, 1981), pp. 166–67. According to Brecht, "autoritative Freunde" such as Karl Radek, Mikhail Koltsov, Sergej Tretjakov, and Sergej Dinamov needed to be invited to such a conference, calls for which, he said, had been made independently of him by Kurt Kläber, Ernst Ottwalt, Trude [Richter?], and Peter Merin (Otto Biha).

7. Becher's proposal was made in his "Bericht über die Tätigkeit während meiner Reise vom 5. Juli bis 17. September 1933." In: *Zur Tradition der sozialistischen Literatur in Deutschland. Eine Auswahl von Dokumenten* (Berlin-Weimar: Aufbau-Verlag, 1967), p. 585.

8. Brecht to Becher, 28 June 1933, *Briefe*, pp. 166–67. Brecht's comments about the "borrowing" of names was intended as criticism of Willi Münzenberg's organizational tactics.

9. Brecht to Becher, December 1934, ibid., pp. 227–28.

10. "Eine notwendige Feststellung im Kampf gegen die Barbarei," *Gesammelte Werke* (hereafter *GW*), XVIII, p. 246.

11. Becher continued to seek Brecht's advice in matters relating to cooperation with non-Communist writers and various joint literary-political projects. (Cf., e.g., Brecht to Becher, July 1935, *Briefe*, pp. 259–60). Brecht's pronouncements at the congress, incidentally, were later included (unabridged) in the Russian volume containing the various speeches.

12. See Jurij Okljanskij, *Povest o malenkom soldate* (Moscow: Izdatelstvo "Sovetskaja Rossija," 1978), p. 78.

13. Ibid., pp. 52–94. Brecht's papers, incidentally, were confiscated by Soviet border guards when he left for the West. (Ibid., p. 87).

14. Béla Illes (head of the Internationale Vereinigung revolutionärer Schriftsteller) had offered Brecht his help in obtaining another entry visa for Steffin as early as summer 1933. (Ibid., p. 146).

15. See ibid., p. 145.

16. Steffin apparently went from Denmark to Leningrad first. She had not yet reached Moscow by early September (see Sergej Tretjakov to Brecht, 8 September 1934, Bertolt-Brecht-Archiv [hereafter BBA]: 477/139), but must have arrived there soon after.

17. Brecht to Steffin, 20–23 September 1934, quoted from Okljanskij, *O malenkom soldate*, pp. 48–49. Brecht refers here to the page proofs of the first edition published in 1934 by Allert de Lange in Amsterdam. The imprecise dating of letters cited from Okljanskij was done by him.

18. Brecht to Steffin, 21 October–4 November, ibid.

19. Ibid.

20. Cf. ibid., p. 158.

21. Cf. ibid., pp. 153–58.

22. Brecht to Tretjakov, 11 July 1933, *Briefe*, pp. 172–73.

23. Tretjakov to Brecht, 15 July, BBA: 477/147.

24. Tretjakov to Brecht, 16 July 1933, BBA: 477/144.

25. See Bernhard Reich, *Im Wettlauf mit der Zeit. Erinnerungen aus fünf Jahrzehnten deutscher Theatergeschichte* (Berlin: Henschelverlag, 1970), p. 371.

26. Bertolt Brekht, *Epicheskie dramy*. Perevod s nemetskogo i vvodnyj etjud S.M. Tretjakova (Moscow-Leningrad: Gosudarstvennoe izdatelstvo khudozhestvennoj literatury, 1934). In a Russian review "F. Ivanov" referred to the "schematism" of Brecht's plays and expressed his hope that Brecht would one day break free of his " 'edifying' asceticism" and write plays in which his characters would not be burdened with the "command to 'instruct.' " Although he also called Brecht "one of the most significant revolutionary writers [*literati*] of contemporary Germany," Ivanov contrasted Brecht's *Mother* with Gorky's novel and noted: "This most talented writer of the German revolution must depart from rhetoric (however gifted and accomplished it may be) to Shakes-

peareanism, to a theatre of great passions, a theatre of living, full-blooded personalities who make history." (*Izvestija*, 23 July 1934).

27. Béla Illes had extended the invitation in August 1933; at the time, the congress was scheduled to convene in September 1933. Whether the invitation was reissued a year later is unknown. (Okljanskij, *O malenkom soldate*, p. 146).

28. Tretjakov to Brecht, 8 September 1934, BBA: 477/139–40.

29. Tretjakov to Brecht, 24 June 1935, BBA: 477/131.

30. Tretjakov was ill often in 1936 and early 1937; his last letter to Brecht, dated 3 May 1937 (BBA: 477/120), ought not to be read as if it bears traces of changes in Tretjakov's frame of mind that indicate fear of imminent arrest. Cf. also in this vein Herzfelde to Graf (16 April and 5 May): "Tretjakow sah ich nur einmal. Er scheint eine grosse Krise durchzumachen" and "Tretjakow habe ich nur zweimal und ziemlich kurz gesehen. Er leidet an einer Krise, auch geht es ihm wohl gesundheitlich nicht gut—kurz gesagt, er kümmert sich nicht um uns. Aber vielleicht hat er wirklich zu viel anderes im Kopf." (Tsentralnyj gosudarstvennyj arkhiv literatury i iskusstv [TsGALI]: 631/12/141/323 and 320). Tretjakov's correspondence with Graf (Oskar Maria Graf, *Reise in die Sowjetunion 1934* [Neuwied: Luchterhand, 1974], pp. 163–90) reveals more about Tretjakov's general attitude toward events in the USSR in 1936 and 1937 than his less frequent letters to Brecht. "Ich bin voll mit diesem Lande," he wrote, for example, on 22 May 1936. (p. 182).

31. Brecht to Becher, early 1935, *Briefe*, pp. 231–32.

32. Kantorowicz, "Brechts 'Der Dreigroschenroman,' " *Unsere Zeit* VII (12 December 1934), pp. 61–62.

33. Brecht to Becher, early 1935, *Briefe*, pp. 231–32.

34. Kantorowicz, "Brechts 'Der Dreigroschenroman,' " p. 62.

35. See Becher's reply to Brecht of 16 January 1935, in Brecht, *Briefe. Anmerkungen* (Frankfurt am Main: Suhrkamp Verlag, 1981), p. 958. The article in *Unsere Zeit*, said Becher, represented Kantorowicz' personal opinion and not any sort of official party attitude toward Brecht's novel. Michael Tschesno also wrote Brecht on behalf of the SDS, telling him that the criticism was—"gelinde gesagt"—absurd; it represented Kantorowicz' "Privatvergnügen" and was shared by none of the other members of the SDS.

36. Brecht to Becher, early 1935, *Briefe*, pp. 231–32.

37. Becher to Brecht, *Briefe. Anmerkungen*, p. 958.

38. Bredel to Kantorowicz, 2 February 1935, TsGALI: 631/13/63/3.

39. Uhse, "Zu Brechts 'Dreigroschenroman,' " *Unsere Zeit* VIII (2–3 April 1935), pp. 65–66.

40. Haland, "Zu Brechts 'Dreigroschenroman,' " ibid., pp. 66–7.

41. Ibid.

42. Ibid.

43. Ibid.

44. The East Germans handle the above episode elliptically. Dieter Schiller mentions the controversy that broke out over Kantorowicz' article and quotes from Uhse's reply. But his conclusion is intentionally misleading: "Es kann angenommen werden, daß Uhses Gegenrezension nicht ohne Absprachen im Kreis der sozialistischen Schriftsteller in Paris entstanden ist. Jedenfalls lassen Bechers Briefe an Brecht darauf schliessen, daß sie die Funktion hatten, in der Vorbereitungsphase des Pariser Kongresses sinnlose Konfrontationen zu vermeiden, über schematische Wertungen der Literatur hinauszugelangen und den Besonderheiten des literarischen Schaffens gerecht zu werden. Das entsprach auch Bechers Bestrebungen in der Pariser Zeit." (Dieter Schiller, Karlheinz Pech, Regine Herrmann, Manfred Hahn, *Exil in Frankreich* [Leipzig: Verlag Philipp Reclam jun., 1981], p. 543). Why (apart from a brief reference to its existence) does Schiller ignore Haland's attack? Were Haland's pronouncements also intended to avoid "sinnlose Konfrontationen" in the preparatory period leading up to the Paris Congress?

45. Brecht to Steffin, 10–15 February 1935, Okljanskij, *O malenkom soldate*, p. 44.

46. Brecht to Steffin, 2–6 March 1935, ibid., p. 50. By 20 March Brecht was in Moscow (see Brecht, *Briefe. Anmerkungen,* p. 962). Brecht stayed in the same hotel, the Novaja Moskovskaja, in which Ernst Ottwalt and his wife had been living since their arrival in the USSR. Brecht found his behavior somewhat strange. He wrote Weigel: "Ottwalt ist wieder Dampf in allen Gassen, verliert viel und hat nichts." (Brecht to Weigel, March—April 1935, *Briefe,* p. 247). See also Okljanskij, *O malenkom soldate,* p. 49. Ottwalt was a heavy drinker who had not let up in the least after taking up residence in Moscow.

47. Brecht to Steffin, 2–6 March 1935, Okljanskij, *O malenkom soldate,* p. 50. He had been invited by MORT (in German, IRTB), which stood for Internationaler Revolutionärer Theaterbund, headed by Piscator. Reich also played a leading role in the organization until its dissolution in 1936.

48. Brecht to Steffin, 26 February–1 March 1935, ibid., p. 47.

49. Cf. ibid., p. 44.

50. Brecht to Weigel, April 1935, *Briefe,* pp. 248–50.

51. The reception held on 21 April was organized by the Soviet Writers' Union. Kirsanov read his translation of Brecht's "Ballade vom toten Soldaten," various members of Tairov's Kamernyj teatr performed segments from the *Dreigroschenoper,* and Carola Neher gave her rendition of ballads and songs from the opera. Wieland Herzfelde discussed Brecht's position within German poetry, and Asja Lazis dealt with the subject of Brecht as a producer. ("Bert Brekht v Moskve," *Pravda,* 23 April 1935. See also the report on a "Brecht-Abend" published in the *Deutsche Zentral-Zeitung,* 10 May 1935).

52. Brecht to Weigel, April 1935, *Briefe,* pp. 247–48.

53. Brecht to Weigel, March—April, ibid., pp. 247–49.

54. Brecht to Weigel, April 1935, ibid., p. 248.

55. Brecht to Koltsov, late May/early June 1935, ibid., p. 251. Asked later why he had not stayed in Moscow, Brecht replied, "Ich konnte nicht genug Zucker für meinen Tee und Kaffee bekommen." Quoted in Martin Esslin, *Brecht. Das Paradox des politischen Dichters* (Frankfurt am Main: Athenäum Verlag, 1962), p. 229.

56. Tretjakov to Brecht, 2 July 1935, BBA: 477/129–130.

57. Tretjakov to Brecht, 19 July 1935, BBA: 477/127–128.

58. Tretjakov to Brecht, 17 September 1935, BBA: 477/121–122.

59. Peter Merin, "Das Werk des Bert Brecht," *Internationale Literatur* 7 (1935), p. 83.

60. Ibid.

61. Ibid., p. 91.

62. Ibid., p. 96. Incidentally, Lukács denied this possibility. A "triumph of realism," as Lukács called literature in which a particular writer overcame his own class affiliation to depict the truth, only occurred when a writer employed an objective art form. Lukács made the point that a Zola (or a Brecht) could not achieve a triumph of realism because he utilized a subjective art form, one engendered, moreover, by the declining bourgeoisie.

63. Ibid., p. 97. Karl Schmückle, one of the editors of *Internationale Literatur,* wrote Merin on 16 May 1935: "[D]ein großer Aufsatz über Bert Brecht ist in Satz, er soll in zwei Hälften in Nr. 6 und 7 erscheinen. Ich finde den Aufsatz gut und schön, richtig in der ganzen Grundlinie der Behandlung. In einer Anzahl von Fragen habe ich jedoch Einwände, z.B.: ich glaube, das spezifische Verhalten Brechts zu einigen großen Vorbildern des Erbes, sage z.B.: zu Swift, um nur einen einzigen Namen zu nennen, hätte mit mehr Nachdruck und etwas tiefer behandelt werden können. Was Swift angeht, so behandelt Dein Aufsatz allerdings noch nicht die 'Spitzköpfe und Rundköpfe'. Auch Deine Darstellung der 'Epik' und 'Pädagogik' scheint mir nicht ganz zwingend genug. . . . Ich glaube, dieser Aufsatz ist besonders nützlich und sehr ergiebig für die Diskussion über Methoden und Bedeutung Brechts. Du wirst wissen: Er ist gegenwärtig hier. Ich habe eine Menge Diskussionen mit ihm gehabt." (TsGALI: 631/13/69/67).

64. A Brustov, "Bertolt Brekht," *Zvezda* 9 (1935), p. 145.

65. Ibid., p. 146.

66. Ibid., pp. 153–54.
67. Brustov was slightly out of touch with the times in his reference to the "fight for the Soviet power of German workers and peasants," a slogan that the party had scrapped just a month or so earlier.
68. Brustov, "Brekht," p. 162.
69. Steffin to Brecht, 20 February 1936, Okljanskij, *O malenkom soldate*, p. 159. Steffin must have been referring to the version that came out in (the chronically late) *Internationale Literatur* 1 (1936), pp. 25–60.
70. Steffin to Brecht, 4 March 1936, Okljanskij, *O malenkom soldate*, p. 158. The novel carried a 1935 publication date, but many Soviet publications appeared after their official release date. The novel was favorably reviewed in a well-written article by Hugo Huppert in the Soviet German-language daily *Deutsche Zentral-Zeitung* (29 June 1936). Brecht heard about the review and asked Otto Bork (head of the German section of VEGAAR) to send him a copy (Brecht to Bork, 20 July 1936, *Briefe*, p. 293). He also told Bork: "Der Roman ist wunderschön gedruckt, weit besser als beim holländischen Verlag." (Brecht to Bork, 30 November, ibid., p. 299).
71. Steffin to Brecht, 5 March 1936, Okljanskij, *O malenkom soldate*, p. 159. Steffin put "soon" into quotation marks. The novel, in fact (published by Goslitizdat), was not out until 1937. V. Admoni ("Roman Bertolta Brekhta," *Literaturnyj sovremmenik* 3 [1937], pp. 244–50) reviewed it well, but raised all the familiar points made in the previous articles by Kantorowicz, Uhse, Haland, Merin, and Brustov.
72. See Brecht's correspondence with Otto Bork (Brecht to Bork, 20 July and 30 November 1936, *Briefe*, pp. 293–94 and 298–99).
73. See also Brecht's exchange of letters with Piscator about the latter's plans for a film adaptation of "Schweik" (Brecht to Piscator, 4 and 21 April, and June 1937, ibid., pp. 321–24). The relationship between Piscator's and Lenfilm's plans is unclear.
74. Steffin to Brecht, 5 March 1936, Okljanskij, *O malenkom soldate*, p. 159.
75. Brekht, *Chiki i chuki* (Moscow: Gosudarstvennoe izdatelstvo khudozhestvennoj literatury, 1936).
76. S. M. Tretjakov, *Ljudi odnogo kostra. Literaturnye portrety* (Moscow: Gosudarstvennoe izdatelstvo "Khudozhestvennaja literatura," 1936). There was apparently some talk of bringing out Tretjakov's book in a German translation (Tretjakov to Graf, 25 February 1936, Graf, *Reise in die Sowjetunion*, p. 179). Most of the individual portraits, by the way, had already appeared in various German-language monthlies in one version or another.
77. Brecht's name may have come to mind as editor of *Das Wort* because Herzfelde had earlier tried to persuade him to help edit *Die neuen deutschen Blätter*. (See Brecht to Becher, July–August 1933, *Briefe*, pp. 176–77). Following the writers' conference in Paris, Brecht wrote Becher: "*Wichtig ist, daß die gegründete Vereinigung* [that is, the Writers' Association for the Defense of Culture, formed at the congress in Paris] *ein Sprachrohr erhält und als literarische Gesellschaft zu funktionieren anfängt. d.h. literarische Arbeiten herstellt und ediert.* . . . In den ernsten Zeiten, die bevorstehen, muß die publizistische Basis schon geschaffen sein. . . . Eine Zeitschrift halte ich für weniger wirksam, weil da doch immer nur die mittleren Leute ständig mitarbeiten, Es muß ein Prozeß der *Selbstverständigung der Schriftsteller* eingeleitet werden. Der Kongreß ist da immerhin ein Anfang. Aber eben nur ein Anfang." (Brecht to Becher, July 1935, *Briefe*, pp. 259).
78. See Okljanskij, *O malenkom soldate*, p. 153.
79. See ibid., p. 151, and Tretjakov to Graf, 3 February 1936, Graf, *Reise in die Sowjetunion*, p. 177. Mikhail Apletin (who later befriended Brecht) was the "shtatnyj zamestitel"—evidently the official state and party representative acting, together with Trejakov, as Koltsov's deputy.
80. Becher's involvement apparently ended in late February or early March 1936, when Herzfelde and Osten assumed responsibility for preparing the first issue of the journal.
81. Osten to Feuchtwanger, 1 April 1936, TsGALI: 631/13/65/10.

David Pike

82. Cf. Osten (in Moscow) to Feuchtwanger, 23 May 1936: "Ich reise am 9. oder 15. Juni von hier ab." (TsGALI: 631/13/65/26).

83. Osten to Ljudmilla Scheinina (in Moscow), 24 July 1936: "Wie gehts denn, ich wohne bei Brecht. Die Stadt ist fast nicht zum aushalten. . . . Hier kann man fast nicht atmen. Brecht, der mich dauernd nach Dänemark entführen möchte, sagt, unten bei Feuchtwanger würde ich vor Hitze 8 Tage nicht schlafen können." (TsGALI: 631/12/143/432).

84. Brecht to Piscator, 12 October 1936, *Briefe*, p. 295.

85. Bredel to Herzfelde, 21 December 1936; Herzfelde to Bredel, 28 December 1936, TsGALI: 631/12/143/57 and 55.

86. Bredel to Osten, 17 March 1937, TsGALI: 631/12/143/415.

87. In Soviet exile Hay had been advanced early on by the Lukács circle as a sort of antipode to Brecht. Although Hay was not particularly successful as a playwright during his years in the USSR (which no doubt intensified his hostility toward Brecht and Friedrich Wolf), he was continually suggested by Lukács' backers as a dramatist of international stature. In unpublished *Gutachten* written by Lukács' lieutenant, Andor Gábor, Hay's *Haben* was called "das bedeutendste Werk der mitteleuropäischen linksgerichteten Bühnenliteratur der letzten Jahrfünft," "ein bleibendes Repertoire-Stück von hohem Wert." Upon his return to East Berlin in 1948, Brecht was taken to a performance of *Haben*. Gábor later called the play *Kamerad Mimi* "das beste Erzeugnis des Genossen Hay" and praised *Der Putenhirt* in similar terms. (See Gabor's *Gutachten*, the one of *Haben* dated 23 July 1937, the others undated, in Gabor's literary estate. Magyar Tudomanyos Akadémia [Budapest]: 4481/79 and 80; and 4482/87).

88. Cf., e.g., Hay's evaluation of a book submitted to *Das Wort* for review: "Spießbürgerlicher Dilettantismus ohne eine Spur von einer Begabung oder nicht ohne boshafte Sowjetfeindlichkeit. Es besteht keine Veranlassung, das Buch zu besprechen oder überhaupt zu erwähnen." (Dated 28 January 1939, TsGALI: 631/12/154/272).

89. Reich, "Zur Methodik der antifaschistischen Dramatik," *Das Wort* 1 (1937), p. 71.

90. Brecht to Piscator, March 1937, *Briefe*, p. 316.

91. Brecht to Reich, 11 March 1937, ibid., pp. 312–13.

92. Brecht to Hay, March 1937, ibid., pp. 313–14.

93. Brecht to Becher, 11 March 1937, ibid., pp. 314–15.

94. Cf. Hay's letter to Brecht (7 March 1937, *Briefe. Anmerkungen*, pp. 986–87). Hay's argumentation contained one of Lukács' pet phrases ("Trotz Ihrer guten Absicht . . .").

95. Bredel to Benjamin, 28 March 1937, TsGALI: 631/12/141/81.

96. Redaktion "Das Wort" to Benjamin, 27 May 1937, TsGALI: 631/12/141/80. There are reasons to doubt that the rejection resulted from a decision taken by Bredel. Nor is it clear what essay had been received that covered the same territory, and why, after all, was Benjamin never asked to shorten his essay?

97. Erpenbeck to Benjamin, 3 July 1937, TsGALI: 631/12/141/79. *Das Wort* regularly published reviews (some by Erpenbeck) of books that had appeared two or three years earlier.

98. Benjamin to Bredel, 20 December 1936; Bredel to Benjamin, 11 March 1937; Benjamin to "Werte Genossen," 14 July 1937, TsGALI: 631/12/141/86, 83, and 77.

99. Erpenbeck to Benjamin, undated, TsGALI: 631/12/141/76.

100. Erpenbeck to Benjamin, 9 December 1937, TsGALI: 631/12/141/70.

101. V. Aleksandrov, "Obraz materi," *Literaturnyj kritik* 6 (1937), p. 44.

102. Ibid., p. 47.

103. For details see Pike, *Deutsche Schriftsteller im sowjetischen Exil 1933–1945* (Frankfurt am Main: Suhrkamp Verlag, 1981), pp. 386–401.

104. Kurella to Erpenbeck, 8 June 1938, TsGALI: 631/12/152/80.

105. Brecht to Kurella, 17 June 1938, *Briefe*, pp. 372–373.

106. Brecht to Bredel, July/August, ibid., pp. 373–74.

107. See *Deutsche Schriftsteller im sowjetischen Exil 1933–1945*, pp. 401–410.

187

108. Julius Hay, "Put k realizmu," *Teatr* 2–3 (1939), p. 34.

109. Ibid., p. 35.

110. T. Rokotov, "Po puti demokratii," ibid., pp. 51–56; and B. Rejkh, "Novinki antifashistskoj dramaturgii," pp. 57–62.

111. Rokotov to Brecht, 14 August 1939, TsGALI: 631/13/69/171.

112. Ibid.

113. *Furcht und Elend des Dritten Reichs* (Moscow: Mezhdunarodnaja kniga, 1941); *Der Spitzel*. *Winterhilfe* (Moscow: Izdatelstvo literatury na inostrannykh jazykakh, 1944); *Strakh i otchajanie v III. imperii* (Moscow: "Khudozhestvennaja literatura," 1941); *Ts . . . tishe! ili opasnyj malchik*. Pesa v l d. (Moscow: Iskusstvo, 1941). Some of the one-act plays also appeared in Soviet periodicals.

114. N. Kozjura, "Imet," *Literaturnoe obozrenie* 16 (1940), p. 38.

115. B. Rejkh, "Uroki literaturnoj diskussii," *Teatr* 6 (1940), p. 136.

116. Becher, "Kenntnis und Aufrichtigkeit," in Becher, *Publizistik II 1939–1945* (Berlin-Weimar: Aufbau-Verlag, 1978), pp. 19 and 23. The article first appeared in *Literaturnja gazeta* (26 May 1940).

117. B. Rejkh, "Iskazhennaja dejstvitelnost," *Teatr* 2 (1941), p. 150.

118. Ibid., p. 152.

119. Ibid., p. 153.

120. Walter Benjamin, *Versuche über Brecht* (Frankfurt am Main: Suhrkamp Verlag, 1971), p. 132.

121. *Arbeitsjournal*, p. 636.

122. "In finsteren Zeiten," *GW*, IX, p. 587.

123. "Ist das Volk unfehlbar?" Ibid., pp. 741–43.

124. "The Other Germany," *GW*, XX, pp. 283–84.

125. Anton Antonov-Ovseyenko, *The Time of Stalin: Portrait of a Tyranny* (New York: Harper & Row Publishers, 1981), pp. 210–13, 307.

126. "Kraft und Schwäche der Utopie," *GW XIX*, p. 435.

127. Fritz Sternberg, *Der Dichter und die Ratio. Erinnerungen an Bertolt Brecht* (Göttingen: Sachse & Pohl Verlag, 1963), p. 24.

128. "Kraft und Schwäche der Utopie," pp. 435–36.

129. Ibid. These passages strike me as a more reliable and certainly more elaborate indication of Brecht's attitude toward collectivization than Sternberg's rendition of a 1931 conversation between Brecht, Tretjakov, and members of the Communist opposition party (the KPO). (See Sternberg, *Der Dichter und die Ratio*, p. 23).

130. "Über die Diktaturen einzelner Menschen," *GW* XX, p. 103.

131. Antonov-Ovseyenko, *The Time of Stalin*, p. 307; "Über die Diktaturen einzelner Menschen," *GW*, XX, p. 103.

132. Joseph Stalin, "Questions of Agrarian Policy in the Soviet Union," Stalin, *Leninism*. Vol. 2 (New York: International Publishers, 1933), pp. 272–73; and Isaac Deutscher, *Stalin. A Political Biography* (New York: Vintage Books, 1960), p. 320.

133. "Kraft und Schwäche der Utopie," p. 437.

134. Benjamin, *Versuche über Brecht*, p. 130.

135. Sternberg, *Der Dichter und die Ratio*, p. 42.

136. "Kraft und Schwäche der Utopie," p. 438.

137. Ibid.

138. Stalin, "Dizzy with Success," *Leninism*, p. 281.

139. "Über die Dikaturen einzelner Menschen," pp. 101–2.

140. Ibid. Later on in the thirties Brecht grew more critical of the party, without, however, attributing its failures or shortcomings to Stalin. He told Benjamin in 1938: "In Rußland herrscht eine Diktatur *über* das Proletariat. Es ist so lange zu vermeiden, sich von ihr loszusagen, als diese Diktatur noch praktische Arbeit für das Proletariat leistet." (Benjamin, *Versuche über Brecht*, p. 135). The devastatingly critical remark that Brecht made in his *Arbeitsjournal* (January 1939, p. 36) about the general state of affairs in Soviet intellectual life is in a similar vein: Brecht's attitude toward the situation, which

he never tied in with the existence of Stalin's dictatorship, remained "positiv kritisch." See also note 187.

141. According to Antonov-Ovseyenko, of the 1,961 voting delegates to the Seventeenth Party Congress in 1934, perhaps two dozen survived Stalin's terror (Antonov-Ovseyenko, *The Time of Stalin,* p. 126). Brecht had at least some idea of what was happening to the party; he wrote in *Me-ti* ("Theorie des To-tsi [Trotsky]"): "Zwanzig Jahre nach der Machtübernahme durch den Verein waren die Gefängnisse noch immer überfüllt, und es gab allenthalben Todesurteile und Prozesse, in die selbst alte Mitglieder des Vereins verwickelt waren. Große Kriege mit bürgerlichen Ländern standen bevor." (Brecht, *Me-ti, GW,* XII, p. 524). The passage is worth considering carefully and indicates how difficult it sometimes is to pin Brecht down on issues pertaining to the USSR. The comments contain, however, no hint that Brecht regarded the inhabitants of the cells or defendants in the docks as, in the main, entirely innocent.

142. Brecht's perceptions must have coincided with Feuchtwanger's. In *Moscow 1937* Feuchtwanger had been quite critical of the personality cult, but, upon closer examination, his criticism deteriorates into meaninglessness. For, calling Stalin a "modest" man, Feuchtwanger supported virtually all of Stalin's policies. (Brecht, by the way, found *Moscow 1937* "sehr interessant" [Brecht to Dudow, July 1937, *Briefe,* p. 331], telling Feuchtwanger: "Ihr 'De Russia' finde ich das Beste, was von Seiten der europäischen Literatur bisher in dieser Sache erschienen ist. Es ist ein so entscheidender Schritt, die Vernunft als etwas so Praktisches, Menschliches zu sehen, etwas, was seine eigene Sittlichkeit und Unsittlichkeit hat; dabei kommt erst ihr experimenteller Charakter heraus, an dem die Menschheit doch interessiert ist und der verschwindet, wenn man eine starre Moralität über sie setzt, da ja das Experimentieren selber schon etwas von sittlich zweifelhafter Natur ist. Ich bin sehr froh, dass Sie das geschrieben haben." [Brecht to Feuchtwanger, August 1937, *Briefe,* p. 334].) By mid 1943, however, Brecht's willingness to believe bad things about Stalin had increased, helped along by, among other things, Souvarine's "niederdrückendes buch über stalin." (*Arbeitsjournal,* p. 589).

143. "Ni-ens Ruf," *Me-ti,* p. 467.

144. Ibid. One finds the same kind of thinking concerning the absence of proof in Brecht's poem "Ist das Volk unfehlbar?" "Papiere verlangen, auf denen schwarz auf weiß die Beweise / der Schuld stehen / Ist unsinnig, denn es muß keine solchen Papiere geben. / Die Verbrecher halten Beweise ihrer Unschuld in Händen. / Die Unschuldigen haben oft keine Beweise." ("Ist das Volk unfehlbar?", p. 743). In other words, the availability or lack of "documentary evidence" proved nothing. In the case of Stalin, Brecht says in *Me-ti,* a dark path was being traveled for the first time in history; therefore, proof that the path led in the proper direction did not exist, and the people would be more inclined to follow their leader blindly if he were enveloped in an aura of greatness and infallibility.

145. "Ansprache des Bauern an seinen Ochsen," *GW,* IX, pp. 683–84.

146. "Ni-ens Ruf," p. 467.

147. "Vorschlag Me-tis, Ni-ens Beinamen betreffend," *Me-ti,* p. 467. See also "Die Verehrung des Ni-en (2)," ibid., p. 536: "Me-ti sagte: Einige wissen, daß Ni-en in manchem ein nützlicher Mensch ist. Das bedeutet viel bei ihnen. Einige wissen, daß er ein genialer Mensch ist, der größte der Menschen, eine Art Gott. Das bedeutet bei ihnen vielleicht nicht soviel, wie das andere bei den anderen."

148. Benjamin, *Versuche über Brecht,* p. 131.

149. "Über Freiheit in der Sowjetunion," *GW,* XX, pp. 104–5.

150. Ibid.

151. If the fears were understandable (if exaggerated) in the years immediately following the revolution, they were utterly groundless after the civil war.

152. "Über die Moskauer Prozesse," *GW,* XX, p. 115.

153. "Über die Diktaturen einzelner Menschen," p. 102.

154. "Die Prozesse des Ni-en," *Me-ti,* p. 538.

155. Brecht wrote also: "Demgegenüber ist folgende Darstellung unwahrscheinlich: daß sich, schon während der Revolution, vom Kapitalismus bezahlte Agenten in die Regierung der Sowjets eingeschlichen haben mit dem Vorsatz, in Rußland den Kapitalismus mit allen Mitteln wieder einzuführen. Diese Darstellung klingt unwahrscheinlich, weil sie das Moment der Entwicklung außer acht lässt, mechanisch, undialektisch, starr ist." ("Über die Moskauer Prozesse," p. 115). But this was a major point of the accusations raised against the defendants. If Brecht found it "improbable" (though not utterly absurd), why was he unable to discern any sort of pattern of improbability in the other charges?
156. "Die Prozesse des Ni-en," p. 538.
157. "Über die Moskauer Prozesse," p. 111.
158. Ibid., pp. 111 and 113.
159. Ibid., p. 113.
160. Ibid., p. 114.
161. Ibid.
162. Ibid., pp. 114–15.
163. *Arbeitsjournal*, p. 589.
164. See, for more details, Iring Fetscher, "Brecht und der Kommunismus," *Merkur,* 9 (1973), pp. 878–79. Cf. also, Brecht's remarks after Stalin's death: "Die Revolution entfesselt wunderbare Tugenden und anachronistische Laster zugleich." ("Über die Kritik an Stalin," *GW, XX,* p. 325).
165. "Über die Unfreiheit unter Ni-en-leh und Ni-en," *Me-ti,* p. 438.
166. Not that Brecht directly advocated cruelty or even torture. But he objected staunchly to a placid form of humanism, explaining that Lenin, when he called for the use of terror, had spoken strongly against a kind of "konterrevolutionären Humanismus" that was out of touch with the social state of affairs. On the other hand: "Damit wird nicht der physischen Folterung das Wort geredet, eine solche kann unmöglich angenommen werden und braucht auch nicht angenommen zu werden." (Über die Moskauer Prozesse, p. 113). But how about the separation of families and mass deportation of "rich peasants" to uninhabitable regions of arctic Siberia, where they quickly froze or starved to death, during the forced collectivization of Soviet agriculture? Was that not a form of torture? And did Brecht never hear of the NKVD's standard application of torture to extract confessions from innocent prisoners? Such stories circulated widely in the West, but perhaps Brecht chose to ignore the unpleasant "rumors." Given his propensity for shutting his eyes to the truth or dismissing various Soviet "Laster" as historically transitory phenomena, are there really grounds for Bormans to believe "firmly" that Brecht would never have countenanced the invasion of Czechoslovakia in 1968 or the use of weapons against striking Polish workers in 1970 (or in 1981 and 1982)? (See Peter Bormans, "Brecht und der Stalinismus," *Brecht-Jahrbuch* [Frankfurt: Suhrkamp Verlag, 1974], p. 73). Perhaps yes, perhaps no; but the dialectic that Brecht resorted to as a means of accounting for Stalin's "mistakes" could surely have been put into service again (and was) after 1953.
167. "Über die Unfreiheit unter Mi-en-leh und Ni-en," *Me-ti,* pp. 438–39.
168. "Über die Diktaturen einzelner Menschen," p. 103. Cf. also "Theorie des To-tsi [Trotsky]," *Me-ti,* pp. 523–24.
169. "Über die Diktaturen einzelner Menschen," p. 101.
170. "Über das Töten," *Me-ti,* p. 553.
171. *Die heilige Johanna der Schlachthöfe, GW,* II, p. 783; *Die Massnahme,* ibid., p. 652. See also the comments in "Über die Unfreiheit der Schriftsteller in der Sowjetunion," *GW,* XIX, p. 439: "Die Wahrheit ist, daß die bürgerliche Herrschaft verschiedene Formen der Gewaltanwendung benutzt, in den Demokratien stille und in den faschistischen Staaten laute Formen. Und die Wahrheit ist, daß jede Gewalt nur durch eine andere Gewalt gebrochen werden kann. Wie ist es nun, wenn man sich zu keiner dieser beiden Gewalten, um die es sich hier handelt, stellt? Dann unterstützt man jene der beiden Gewalten, die herrscht."

172. "Die Widersprüche in Su," *Me-ti*, p. 524.
173. Ibid.
174. "Die Polizei von Su," *Me-ti*, p. 547.
175. "Über Polizei," ibid., p. 568.
176. Benjamin, *Versuche über Brecht*, p. 124.
177. "Die Polizei von Su," p. 547. Cf. also "Über Länder, die besondere Tugenden hervorbringen," *Me-ti*, p. 518, and, in the same vein, in *Galileo*, the comment "unhappy the land that needs a hero."
178. Benjamin, *Versuche über Brecht*, p. 132. My understanding of these lines is that Brecht perceived the existence of Soviet criminal elements at work in the USSR, not—as could be plausibly argued, that he imagined these "criminal elements" to be working in the pay of the Gestapo. This latter interpretation—the mass terror as an insidious Gestapo plot to infiltrate the secret police and judiciary and deprive the party of its best cadres through denunciation and false arrest—was widespread in the USSR at the time.
179. Cf. "Die Verfassung des Ni-en," *Me-ti*, p. 535: "Da [das neue System] von geringen Einheiten von Menschen erzwungen wird, gibt es überall Zwang und keine richtige Volksherrschaft. Die Meinungsunfreiheit, Koalitionsunfreiheit, Lippendienerei, *die Gewalttaten der Magistrate* [my italics] beweisen, dass noch lange nicht alle Grundelemente der *Großen Ordnung* verwirklicht sind und entwickelt werden."
180. "Das Land, das keine besonderen Tugenden nötig hat," *Me-ti*, p. 520.
181. Pasternak told Ehrenburg one snowy night, "If only someone would tell Stalin about it!" Similarly, Meyerhold's remarks: "[T]hey conceal it from Stalin." (Robert Conquest, *The Great Terror: Stalin's Purge of the Thirties* [New York: Collier Books, 1973], p. 113).
182. Quoted by Nadezhda Mandelshtam, *Hope against Hope. A Memoir* (New York: Atheneum, 1976), p. 13.
183. *Arbeitsjournal*, p. 36.
184. One of Brecht's two letters to Feuchtwanger, asking him to press for information about Neher, was, however, probably never sent. (Brecht, *Briefe. Anmerkungen*, pp. 992–93).
185. Brentano to Brecht, 23 January 1937, ibid., p. 983.
186. Benjamin, *Versuche über Brecht*, p. 130.
187. Brecht to Brentano, early February 1937, *Briefe*, pp. 302–3. There is no denying, on the other hand, that in the late thirties Brecht developed serious doubts about the Soviet Communist party, even if he never came close to breaking with it. He wrote in September 1939: "das gerede, das man überall hört, die bolschewistische partei habe sich von grund auf verändert, ist gewiß nicht richtig. es ist eben das unglück, daß sie sich nicht verändert hat. . . . immer noch nicht entscheidet das volk, die masse, das proletariat. sondern die regierung entscheidet für das volk, die masse, das proletariat, so und so weit hat [Stalin] das volk nicht, das und das interesse hat das volk 'noch' nicht oder erkennt es 'noch' nicht." *Arbeitsjournal*, p. 67.
188. Brecht to Brentano, early February 1937, *Briefe*, pp. 302–3.
189. Benjamin, *Versuche über Brecht*, p. 130.
190. Brecht to Feuchtwanger, May 1937, *Briefe*, p. 326.
191. Ibid.
192. Brecht to Feuchtwanger, June 1937, ibid., pp. 326–7.
193. Ibid.
194. Feuchtwanger to Brecht, 30 May 1937, BBA: 478/68.
195. Brecht to Osten, undated (late 1938 or early 1939), *Briefe*, pp. 382–83.
196. Conquest, *The Great Terror*, p. 441.
197. "Ist das Volk unfehlbar?" *GW*, IX, p. 743.
198. Ibid., pp. 741–43.
199. "Besser Fehler zu billigen als Fehler zu rechtfertigen," *Me-ti*, p. 546. Brecht's dialectical explanations ought to be compared with the common perceptions of many Soviet citizens passed on to us by Nadezhda Mandelshtam: "We never asked, on hearing about the latest arrest, 'What was he arrested for?' but we were exceptional. Most people,

crazed by fear, asked this question just to give themselves a little hope: if others were arrested for some reason, then they wouldn't be arrested, because they hadn't done anything wrong. They vied with each other in thinking up ingenious reasons to justify each arrest. . . . Both public opinion and the police kept inventing new and more graphic ones, adding fuel to the fire without which there is no smoke. This was why we had outlawed the question 'What was he arrested for?' *'What for?'* Akhmatova would cry indignantly whenever, infected by the prevailing climate, anyone of our circle asked this question. 'What do you mean, *what for?* It's time you understood that people are arrested *for nothing!*' " (Mandelshtam, *Hope against Hope,* p. 11).

200. "Motto," *GW,* IX, p. 641.
201. "Ist das Volk unfehlbar?" p. 743.
202. Ibid.
203. Walter Held, "Stalins deutsche Opfer und die Volksfront," *Unser Wort* 4–5 (October 1938), p. 8.
204. According to what Ruth Berlau told Hans Bunge, she regarded Brecht's concern for Neher as "großartig," for Neher "hat ihm wirklich direkt geschadet."
205. "[D]as war sehr peinlich für mich," Berlau told Bunge.
206. "Das Waschen," *GW,* IX, p. 607.
207. "An die Nachgeborenen," ibid., pp. 722–25.
208. "Eine notwendige Feststellung im Kampf gegen die Barbarei," p. 242. See also, "Wenn die Untat kommt, wie der Regen fällt," ibid., p. 552.
209. Held, "Stalins deutsche Opfer und die Volksfront," p. 8.
210. See Victor Serge and Natalia Sedova Trotsky, *The Life and Death of Leon Trotsky* (New York: Basic Books, Inc., 1975), p. 255. I put little stock, by the way, in the rumors of Brecht's own near arrest in Moscow in 1941, in spite of Reich's ambiguous remarks (*Im Wettlauf mit der Zeit,* p. 378) that seem to support the story, which ostensibly comes from a reliable source. But nor can it be discounted entirely. Certainly 1941 was not 1937 or 1938, but anyone in the USSR with as many arrested friends as Brecht would have had a bulging NKVD file. It is also entirely conceivable that factions existed in the NKVD, one, say, influenced by highlevel party officials who wished to avoid the embarrassment of having to explain Brecht's arrest (after, like Held, he had been given an entry and transit visa) by the faction that hoped to act on the accumulated denunciations of Brecht and "proof" of his past association with enemies of the people. Brecht, on the other hand, seemed oblivious to the general danger he was in, whether or not he narrowly escaped arrest in 1941. He had planned trips to Moscow not only on two occasions in mid and late 1936, but also for late 1937. (See, e.g., his letter to Herzfelde, 24 August 1937, *Briefe,* p. 337). But then the arrest of his various friends had not caused the volume of his plays brought out by Tretjakov in 1934 to be withdrawn from the library, indicating, perhaps, that he was not in imminent danger. Only the introduction by Tretjakov to *Epicheskie dramy* was ripped out of the book and the phrase "Translated and with an introductory study by S.M. Tretjakov" obliterated from the title page (this is the way one of two copies in the Lenin Library exists today). Otherwise, presumably, the three plays remained available to readers.
211. Benjamin, *Versuche über Brecht,* p. 131. According to Henry Pachter, Brecht admitted to him about the trials, "it's terrible, but do we have anything besides the Soviet Union?" Upon Pachter's urging that he say something publicly, Brecht allegedly remarked: "In 50 Jahren wird man von Stalin nichts mehr hören, aber ich will, dass man dann noch Brecht liest, und darum kann ich mich nicht von der Partei trennen." (See Pachter's letter to *The New Leader,* 28 April 1969; the original German text of Brecht's remarks is in a private letter from Pachter to Sidney Hook, which the latter made available to me).
212. These conclusions have to be modified somewhat if they are to retain their validity for the years from 1945 to 1956, for, after the XXth Party Congress of the Soviet Communist party, Brecht finally came to realize some basic truths about Stalin. More needs to be said about the subject than can be mentioned here. But the belatedness of Brecht's private

conversion to an anti-Stalinist cheapens its moral-political significance in my mind. Had Brecht inveighed publicly in 1937 or 1938 about the "verdienter Mörder des Volkes" [BBA: 95/03], as he did in one of his unpublished Stalin poems written after Khrushchov's so-called secret speech, his anti-Stalinism would have gained a far greater measure of credibility. His three anti-Stalin poems notwithstanding, did Brecht grasp the nature of Stalinism even after 1953? Granted, one line in another of his Stalin poems indicates a level of comprehension missing earlier, a line to the effect that the one, Stalin, issuing all the orders did not personally carry them all out (BBA: 95/06). So there had been those aiding and abetting Stalin in his "mistakes" after all. But consider the following analysis: "Ohne Kenntnis der Dialektik sind solche Übergänge wie die von Stalin als Motor zu Stalin als Bremse nicht verstehbar." ("Über die Kritik an Stalin", *GW*, XX, p. 326). Now what has Brecht really divulged to us about his understanding of Stalin? More verbiage about the dialectic was a poor substitute for a sober analysis of what had gone wrong under Stalin, when, and why Brecht and others had fallen for it. Nor did it augur well for Brecht's capacity to protest against inchoate forms of Stalinism elsewhere. After all, with Russian tanks rolling through the streets of Berlin in 1953, he telegraphed "Genosse Semjonov" (Soviet High Commissioner), "darf ich Ihnen in diesem Augenblick meine unverbrüchliche Freundschaft zur Sowjetunion ausdrücken." (BBA: 07/08). Brecht probably believed that Stalinism had died with Stalin and that the revolutionary locomotive was back on the right track. He certainly sensed no need for serious soul-searching (or, rather, self-criticism) about his part in it all, though the following remark might apply equally well to Brecht: "Eine der schlimmen Folgen des Stalinismus ist die Verkümmerung der Dialektik." ("Über die Kritik an Stalin," p. 326).

Patty Lee Parmalee, "Brecht's Americanism and His Politics."

Brecht's vision of America (closely connected as it is with his political Weltanschauung and his artistic creations) develops in the 1920s in three phases. At first, even though Brecht is already concerned about the drawbacks of the capitalist system, he is fascinated by the energetic progressiveness of America. Brecht's first phase is manifested in the play *In the Jungle of Cities*. This fascination drives him to the study of American literature, to the attempt to understand the social and economic realities of America and to capture all this in his plays. When he fails in his intellectual and artistic efforts, Brecht turns to Marx. His study of Marx allows him to denounce capitalist "progressiveness." This stage of Brecht's development is represented in the play *Rise and Fall of the City of Mahagonny*. Brecht saw the collapse of the American Stock Market in 1929 as a confirmation of the Marxist position. From now on, Brecht saw America from the viewpoint of a committed Socialist. Brecht describes the development of his own point of view vis à vis America in the poem "Vanished Glory of the Giant City New York." The now more mature author shows his fear at the way America had coined the world with its complete absence of human values. This final stage of Brecht's view of America is represented in his play *St. Joan of the Stockyards*.

Patty Lee Parmalee. "Brechts Amerikanismus und seine politische Entwicklung."

Das Amerikabild Brechts, das eng mit seiner politischen Weltanschauung und seinem künstlerischen Schaffen verknüpft ist, entwickelt sich in den zwanziger Jahren in drei Stufen. Zunächst ist Brecht, obwohl schon jetzt um die Benachteiligten des kapitalistischen Systems besorgt, von der Energie und dem Fortschritt Amerikas fasziniert, was sich im frühen *Im Dickicht* manifestiert. Die Faszination treibt ihn zum Studium amerikanischer Literatur, zum Versuch, die soziale und wirtschaftliche Realität Amerikas zu verstehen und dramatisch festzuhalten. Als die intellektuellen und künstlerischen Anstrengungen scheitern, wendet sich Brecht Marx zu. Die Beschäftigung mit Marx erlaubt ihm, den kapitalistischen Fortschritt zu verurteilen, was er künstlerisch mit *Aufstieg und Fall der Stadt Mahagonny* erreicht. Als 1929 die New Yorker Börse zusammenbricht, sieht Brecht die marxistische Philosophie bestätigt. Von nun an betrachtet er Amerika aus der Sicht eines überzeugten Sozialisten. Die Entwicklung der eigenen Haltung zu Amerika beschreibt Brecht in dem Gedicht "Verschollener Ruhm der Riesenstadt New York"; der gereifte Dichter erschrickt über die Wertfreiheit, mit der der junge Amerika bestaunt hat. Die Versuche, Amerika dramatisch zu erfassen, nehmen jetzt Gestalt an in *Die Heilige Johanna der Schlachthöfe*.

Patty Lee Parmalee. "L'"américanisme" de Brecht et ses positions politiques."

Cet article présente la vision brechtienne de l'Amérique (en étroite relation avec la "Weltanschauung" de l'auteur et ses créations artistiques) dans les trois phases qu'elle a traversée au cours des années 1920. Tout d'abord, bien qu'il soit conscient des défauts du système capitaliste, Brecht est fasciné par le progressisme et la vitalité des Etats-Unis. On peut voir un reflet de cette première phase dans la pièce *Dans la jungle des villes*. Ensuite cette fascination l'amène à étudier la littérature américaine pour essayer de comprendre la réalité économique et sociale des Etats-Unis et la traduire dans ses pièces. Quand il échoue dans ses efforts artistiques et intellectuels, Brecht se tourne vers Marx. Son étude de Marx lui permet de dénoncer le "progressisme" capitaliste. Cette étape de la pensée de Brecht est représentée dans la pièce *Mahagonny*. Brecht vit l'effondrement de la

Bourse américaine en 1929 comme la confirmation de la position marxiste. A partir de ce moment, sa vision de l'Amérique fut celle d'un socialiste engagé. Il décrit l'évolution de son point de vue vis-à-vis de l'Amérique dans le poème "La gloire évanouie du géant New-York." L'auteur, en sa maturité exprime ses craintes devant le triomphe mondial de l'Amérique, fondé sur une complète absence de valeurs humaines. La pièce *Sainte Jeanne des Abattoirs* est l'expression de cette dernière phase de la vision brechtienne de l'Amérique.

Brecht's Americanism and His Politics

Patty Lee Parmalee

This paper makes two claims: first, that Brecht's political development can be seen in the changing interpretations he gives to his image of America (i.e., the United States); and second, that American events and literature actually *caused* his turn to Marxism, at least as much as any other identifiable factor. We all know his literary device of setting plays that are really comments about his own society in faraway lands so that the audience could more easily accept the polemical message and understand the structure of events. But that was not only a technique for the audience: it was also the way Brecht himself perceived. Distance helped him to make judgments, to see the larger picture, to simplify and so understand relationships in society. When Brecht spoke of Chicago, even among friends, he meant Berlin.

Discounting his earliest schoolboy writings, there are three identifiable phases in Brecht's early political development (and the rest of his life is a deepening, humanizing, and refining of the third stage). First there is the fashionable Weimar avant-garde cynicism (coupled with pacifism and identification with the underclasses); second, the turn from this cynical kind of hedonism to serious study of economics and Marxist writings; and third, the beginning of a lifelong commitment to active participation in the struggle for working-class socialism. Each of these phases is prepared by events in America and by American literature that Brecht read avidly, and each is announced as a break from the past with works by Brecht set in America.

Events in Germany—World War I, inflation, Weimar culture, the rise of fascism, the depression—must of course have made the stongest emotional impact on him, but we find him making them intelligible to himself (he was always extremely intellectual) by his own internal *Verfrem-dungseffekt*. Thus, when by the end of World War I he is utterly disgusted with the Germany he had once (as a schoolboy) praised, he writes in 1920, addressing "Germany, You Blond, Pale . . .":

> . . . O carrion land, anxiety hole!
> Shame strangles the memory
> And in the youth that you
> Haven't corrupted
> Awakes America! (*GW*, VIII, 69.)

Whenever he later looks back on his development, he always seems to start with this early Americanism as if that were when he came into the world. He is harsh in his assessment of his early harshness, himself originating the now widespread notion that he was totally enamored of America's virility and ruthless, tasteless energy, and that he later made a complete about-face to hating America. James Lyon's researches into Brecht's years in exile here show that he was certainly not so unambiguously against it later on, and a careful reading of the early works shows he was certainly not so unambiguously for it earlier on. Rather, he was absolutely ambiguous.

Brecht's first play set in America, *In the Jungle* (1920–22), takes place in the cold Chicago that Brecht discovered in Sinclair's *Jungle* and Jensen's *Wheel* and used publicly and privately to mean the cold Berlin he moved to during that time, and also to mean cities in general. (He thought of many of his works during his first ten years of writing as belonging to a series he called "The Migration of Mankind to the Big Cities," and the America theme is inseparable from the urban theme.) This supposedly abstract play is supposedly about a completely individual, "existential" struggle between two men. But look closely: it is also a play about what Brecht would later have called class relations under capitalism.

The very first time Brecht tells the public about reading an American book (in his 1920 review of Schiller's *Don Carlos*), he makes it clear that he was moved by the class reality of Sinclair's *Jungle*, and that that glimpse at real oppression by real material forces had closed forever his ability to take the more metaphysical kinds of oppression seriously. And we can see his understanding of issues of class, sexual prejudice, and race prejudice in the ways he transforms source material from Jensen's *Wheel*, a fascinating but offensively romantic/conservative/Aryan/misogynist book.

If we have the impression that Brecht's early image of America was a positive one, it comes largely from the *language* of *In the Jungle*. Although the American urban system is degrading and murderous to poor immigrants, so that they can only survive by learning to be ruthless, we cannot really locate a moral judgment by the author in the play, because it is also lush, fascinating, vigorous, a kind of *Fleurs du Mal*. In the 1927 version (*In the Jungle of the Cities*), Brecht demands more clarity of himself, but in the early version, he is ambivalent. What he wants from America is not moral values but energy—a wild, creative energy that was, in fact, historically generated for mankind by capitalism. Perhaps the sacrifice is worth it, or necessary; perhaps for the young poet-playwright in an old society, creative energy is the highest good.

For America represented the extreme of civilization, or over-mechanized experience that one wants to escape, but it was simultaneously primitive; the two are brought together in the word "barbarous." Hence it was a new beginning, the chance to feel the elemental emotions again: love, hate, fear. The experience of vicarious emotion has always been the function of "escape" entertainment in a decadent society. But Brecht was not just in search of experience; for him the myth of America meant much more. Being a creative talent, he saw America as just a beginning. He saw the mammoth technical development achieved there not only as the furthest extension of Europe's own tendency toward progress, but also as a qualitatively new stage, the beginning of a new era. Although the Americans had carried civilization even farther then the Europeans, they had done it with such a confidence, naiveté, and ruthlessness that they were now in the early, barbarous stage of a new culture. The brilliant incarnation of this paradox is the city of Chicago as jungle; the (in Brecht's symbology) most unnatural city becomes a new kind of nature.

For Brecht the dawning of a new age (a theme treated again thoroughly in *Galileo*) is grounds for hope, because new experiments can be made, human nature can be changed, new social orders can be attempted. This is where the next stage in Brecht's development actually took him. But right now the positive feeling only came from the newness itself, from the feeling of being young and having a young world to experiment with, rather than being old before one's time in a world afraid to try any more experiments.

But how quickly that changes. Already at the end of *In the Jungle* he mourns the passing of "chaos." And indeed, from then on his stylistic aim was to make things clear, not thick rich and muddy. Judgments and understanding to make those judgments became necessary.

In the next few years Brecht read American works voraciously: Whitman, London, Harte, Sandburg, Edgar Lee Masters, more Sinclair, Ida Tarbell's *Live of Gary*, Frank Norris's *Octopus* and *The Pit*, a pseudo-autobiography of Dan Drew, Frank Harris, Sherwood Anderson's *Poor White*,

Gustavus Myers' *History of the Great American Fortunes*—to say nothing of the many American newspaper articles that Elisabeth Hauptmann collected for him and the works written in Germany about America.

It is possible to trace influences and impressions from nearly all those books in Brecht's work, but there are two that led to major attempts at adaptation: *The Book of Daniel Drew* by Bourck White, and Norris's *The Pit*. Both these books are directly about economics, especially market manipulation, written from the point of view of the speculator; both treat the heroic period of the growth of capitalism; and both led to fragments that Brecht never finished. His interests had already moved clearly in the direction of trying to portray the economic interests underlying social life, and he used America as the setting because virtually all the relevant works he read were from and about America, and because of the clarity about capitalism that distance gave him. Of his "economic" works only the fragment *The Bread Store* is set in Germany, and even there the depression is described as a made-in-America disaster.

The Dan Drew project seems to have been abandoned fairly quickly, but *Joe Fleischhacker,* based on *The Pit* and begun in 1924, haunted Brecht for decades. In the pieces of this interesting play, written in sparse, lapidary free verse language unlike any of the published plays, Brecht tries to interweave two plots that sum up many of his themes of the period. One is the story of a naive farmer family that emigrates to Chicago, believing in the American upward mobility dream and learning too late how to be ruthless. The other is the story of Joe Fleischhacker, a tycoon in wheat whose market manipulations ultimately ruin what is left of the family. When the catastrophe hits them it seems like a natural disaster, and the language in *St. Joan of the Stockyards* about the impossibility of little people understanding the laws of economics originates here. In the Archive there are many times more pages of notes than text to this play, and the comparison of a "money catastrophe" to a "physical catastrophe" accounts for quite a few of them.

By now the story of Brecht's inability to finish this play is well known. Less well known perhaps is the enormous amount of research and calculation he did trying to understand the economics of the wheat market. As he informs us in two poems that he wrote about the experience, "This Babylonian Confusion" (*GW,* VIII, 149–51.) and "When I Years Ago" (*GW,* IX, 547–68.), he was trying to make sense of something which doesn't make sense. In the first one, written in 1926, he imagines himself explaining and explaining seven years long, and none of his unborn audience understanding, till he finally realizes that what he is describing is incomprehensible for a reason:

> Then I recognized that I
> Was relating something that
> A person cannot understand. (*GW*, VIII, 15.)

His listeners ask him why he could not see through such an obviously false system, and when he tries to explain they simply give up on him, "With the casual regret/Of happy people." It was like a revelation to him: the flaw lay not in his meager understanding, but in the illogic of an irrational system itself.

By now he was persuaded that the subjects he wanted to write about were the great social and economic themes.

> As for material, I have enough . . . For a heroic landscape I have the city, for a point of view relativity, for a situation the human migration to the big cities at the beginning of the third millenium, for content the appetites (too big or too little), for training of the audience the social battle of the giants. (The American histories alone yield a minimum of eight plays, the World War just as many . . .) (*GW*, XV, 70.)

(This paper doesn't mention the ways in which this interest in American economics also affected his *style*. Not only his politics, but also epic theatre were born out of his attempts to put the aforementioned subjects on the stage.) But he was not sure he could take writing seriously as a career. Virtually all his writing from 1924–26 consists of false starts, abandoned as he lost control over their direction. He drove himself deeper and deeper into confusion with this almost manic study of the details of the commodity market system, and finally he just gave up, took a vacation, and started reading *Capital*.

It was clearly the attempt to understand the economics of the U.S. that brought Brecht to his creative crisis and to Marx. But if we look closely at *Joe Fleischhacker* and other fragments of 1924–26 (and *A Man's a Man* as well, the only play finished in that time), we see another crisis growing that also stopped him and sent him to Marx. It is the question of progress.

On the one hand:

> Many say the age is old
> But I have always known it is a new age
> I tell you: not by themselves
> Have houses grown for twenty years like mountains from ore
> Many move each year to the cities as if they expected something
> And on the laughing continents
> The word is getting around that the great dreaded ocean
> Is a little water.

> I will die today, but I am convinced
> The big cities now await the third millenium
> It begins, it cannot be stopped; already today
> It only requires one citizen, and a single man
> Or woman is enough.
>
> Of course many will die in the upheavals
> But what is it for one person to be crushed by a slab
> If the cities are consolidating:
> This new age may only last four years
> It is the highest that will be given to humanity
> On all continents one sees people who are foreign
> The unhappy ones are not longer tolerated, for
> To be human is a great affair.
> Life will be considered too short. (*GW,* VIII, 143–44.)

This poem is spoken by Calvin Mitchell, the hard, ambitious son of the poor family in *Joe Fleischhacker.* The blind belief in progress is rendered ironic by the speaker's position, namely, in the electric chair. But nevertheless it is recognizable as Brecht's own early attitude, that caused him to be fascinated by America to begin with.

Brecht never really stopped believing in progress, as we will see; but there are other suggestions that he was disturbed by it. The fragment variously called *The Flood* and *Decline of the Paradise City Miami* (1926) portrays the end of an heroic age, with the cities themselves as characters in a drama of destruction:

> conversation of the rebuilt cities   they are indestructible
>
> in the years of the flood human types change
> that is the greatest age humanity has experienced
> (the types get stronger bigger darker   they laugh . . .)
>
> in the final years epidemics of monstrous inventions
> proliferate   flying people appear   they achieve greater fame
> than people ever have
>   they fall in the water   laughter
> atheism increases
>
> in the third month the nameless waters storm
> the mainland of Europe and a great fear spreads (BBA, 214/6, 17, 18.)

And in an earlier fragment (which also has a Biblical title and an American title: *Sodom und Gomorrah* or *The Man from Manhattan,* 1924), a man is fascinated by the growth of the American cities so that he betrays the man who is his substitute in a plot out of Schiller's poem "Die Bürgschaft":

> the man is gripped by the fever of construction   of the con- quest of
> america and the founding of cities so much that he
> can't think of the suffering of one single honest man (BBA, 214/76.)

In the *Man from Manhattan* version, the man is held back by a woman who recites to him the story of America's growth, in a splendid (unpublished) poem, "anne smith tells the story of the conquest of america." Both the cruelty and the fascination of America's development find clearer and deeper expression here than anywhere else in Brecht's work, for instance in the final lines:

> but the states that were there called:
> arkansas   connecticut   ohio
> new york   new jersey and massachusetts
> and today still
> there are oil and men and it is said
> it is the greatest race on earth
> that lives now and they all
> build houses and say
> mine is longer and are there when there is oil
> ride in iron trains to the ends of the world
> grow wheat and sell it across the sea
> and die no longer unknown but are
> an eternal race in the earth's
> greatest age

Anne Smith's poem has a long section on the genocide against the Indians, which Brecht had already mentioned with anger in *In the Jungle*. She begins with the idyllic scene: grazing lands from Atlantic to Pacific, nothing but red men, bears and buffalo. But:

> one day a man with white skin came
> he roared and spewed out chunks of iron
> when he was hungry and he was
> always hungry

Three hundred years long the red man died, but the white man split open the earth and brought forth oil, and the rivers produced gold

> . . . and all around
> the wooden huts grew out of rotting grass and
> out of the wooden huts grew mountains of stone   they were
> called cities   into them went
> the white people and said on the earth
> a new age had broken out that is called: the iron . . .
> and with music and shrieking the white people sat
> in the eternal prairies of stone . . . (BBA, 214/75.)

Here we see clearly growing in Brecht a real conflict over progress. He was drawn to it, caught up in the postwar mood, thrilled with all the signs of the beginning of a new age—but he also saw its human cost, especially to the lower classes. He may even have picked up a little nostalgia from his reading of *Poor White.*

The opera *Mahagonny,* written while Brecht was reading Marx, and set in a mythical America that is part Florida and part Las Vegas, shows the emptiness of the pleasures that capitalism allows. Four workers who have earned their money the hard way in Alaska come to the pleasure city to buy the best capitalism can offer. But precisely because food, drink, boxing, and love are all money transactions, rather than ends in themselves, they are hollow. *Mahagonny* condemns capitalism by showing not its punishments but its rewards. Here, briefly, "progress" is only regress, and there is no hope for the future. Real human values have become impossible.

The provisional solution to this conflict over progress came with Brecht's reading of Marx, which taught him to see *capitalist* progress as regressive. Capitalism was no longer "the new" for him, and therefore neither was America. It was only disguised in new clothes.[1]

The next big jolt to Brecht's world view occurred in 1929. Although he had been reading Marx and developing a critical view of capitalism since 1926, he held himself aloof from commitment to an alternative (and from most serious writing) until the stock market crash. Now he was convinced that Marx's predictions were true, capitalism was in decline, and the working class would win the struggle for socialism to replace it. Socialism was now "the new," always one of Brecht's highest terms of praise. And he would commit himself actively to fighting for it. And he did, for the rest of his life.

The *content* of Brecht's images of America hardly changes at all. But the value given to each image changes drastically. Brecht himself shows he is very aware of that in the remarkable poem, "Vanished Glory of the Giant City New York." We will look at the poem in detail, because Brecht is nowhere more explicit about his attitudes toward America. He is also explicit that this is a turning point in his life, at least as important as the other turning point described in the poem about trying to write *Fleischhacker.*

The first half of "Vanished Glory of the Giant City New York" is a summing-up of Brecht's own previous positions on America. But he speaks not in the first person singular, but rather first completely impersonally, and then in the first person plural. This is his own story but it is also the story of his generation, and of Europeans in general. The poem contrasts confidence and conspicuous consumption during the decade of economic expansion after the war (which was also Brecht's first decade of dramatic production), with sudden revelation of the unsound structural base. Flamboyant waste turns out to have been overproduction of commodities which are produced not to fill human needs but to gather profit.

Brecht had already used the trick of turning all the supposed pleasures and riches into their opposite, in *Mahagonny*. There, eating, boxing, loving, drinking, and being free (anarchy) were shown to be fatal if indulged in to excess—and the entire first half of "Vanished Glory" is about excesses. The excesses climax in the eleventh section, where the poet dissolves in superlatives.

But not only this dialectic comes from earlier works like *Mahagonny*. The images are, in fact, a compilation of the kinds of images and human types that filled Brecht's own plays, poems and stories until 1929. For example, the third section talks of the U. S. as a country which assimilates all races beyond recognition; this recalls the poor French family and Shlink in *Jungle,* and all the literature we know Brecht read about immigrant Americans.

In the seventh section he writes, with what appears to be admiration, "Poverty was considered a disgrace there."[2] That was certainly the case in *Jungle, Fleischhacker, Threepenny Opera, Mahagonny* . . . and it reminds us of an early note about the postwar generation's interest in America: it seemed to them that "the new age had come greater than any previous one," and that it was "of a great hardness and extraordinary boldness. In the image of this creature of our imagination neither injustice nor cruelty bothered us." (BBA, 460/63.) Americans considered it a sign of pride to be hard and cruel, as Brecht describes it in section 6 of "Vanished Glory": they openly, in front of the whole world, got everything they could from their workers and then shot them.

> . . . and threw their worn-out bones and
> Used-up muscles on the streets with
> Good-natured laughter.

Cramming the mouth full of Beechnut chewing gum (in section 8) may be an allusion to an unpublished song for *Mahagonny* called "The Chewing-Gum Song," which is sung by two men and two women standing by Beechnut posters and chewing in time to the music. It is a song about the hardest, handsomest, meanest, and in fact only man in *Mahagonny*, whose "whole philosophy was that he chewed gum." (BBA, 460/60.) And there are many other images from the early works here, from boxing to the evening waters of Miami. In short, the entire imagery and diction of "Vanished Glory" are a kind of autobiography of Brecht's American plays. But we also know that America served him as an allegorical model, that Chicago represents Berlin; and in the eighth section the poet confesses that he himself admired and imitated the American mannerisms.

There are few "Ach's" in Brecht's poetry; this poem contains two. "Ach, the voices of their women . . ." in section 4 is a parody (he is speaking ironically of his past) of stupefied admiration; it is how he *used* to feel. But the tone in section 8 is completely different: first the frenzied explanation, "What glory! What a century!" and then a new voice, subdued, thoughtful, perhaps after a long pause: "Ach, we too demanded those impressive suits . . ." This "Ach" is spoken in the present. It says: those *were* golden days when our pleasures were so simple. At the beginning of the poem Brecht suggested America had been "our childhood friend, known to everyone, unmistakable!" and now he describes the influence of that friend. We are reminded too of the early poem in which he declared:

> And the best thing about America is:
> That we understand it. (*GW*, VIII, 286.)

But this explicit statement of fascination with America is a description of a time long past. "Vanished Glory of the Giant City New York" eradicates that early statement and many others with its first three lethal lines:

> Who still remembers
> The glory of the giant city New York
> In the decade after the great war?

Six years earlier Brecht had written a similar sentence: "Almost every one of us remembers the fall of the Roman cities Herculaneum, Pompeii and Stabiae, which took place 2000 years ago." (BBA, 214/23.) There he stated his intention to write a history of Miami so that after its destruction it should not be forgotten, and he proceeded to describe the structure of Miami, making clear where the irrationality lay that would lead to its destruction (symbolized by him at that time by the Flood). The story of the vanished glory of New York is very similar. By using the cadences of the introduction to the Miami story, Brecht can create the impression that New York existed around 2000 years ago and is known only through archaeology. That stylistic trick is important, because what Brecht is really saying in this poem is that for him and his generation the depression divided history into two. The postwar decade of enthusiasm is ancient history; 1929 is the end of an epoch in Brecht's life. And so there is a tremendous distance, the images are pulled up out of another eon— although they were actually still current and believable immediately before the poem was written.

The perversion of social relations into their opposites is introduced through a mere rumor ("For one day a rumor of strange collapses ran through the world"). The myths of American capitalism depended on confidence for their success. The moment doubt began to infect people—Americans and Europeans—the system began to fall apart. That is a fairly accurate representation of stock-market psychology, but also of Europeans' quick loss of admiration for America: suddenly now they could throw off their inferiority complexes. Why, America's superiority had been all bluff! The last lines of the poem are:

> . . . What a discovery:
> That their system of living together showed
> The same lamentable flaw as that of
> More modest people!

Although the turning point is indicated by nothing more than a rumor, the language used in reaction to the discovery of a new perspective is violent and vituperative. Brecht is not merely disillusioned, he is angry. The second half, a dialectical tour-de-force, uses exactly the same examples of America's culture as the first half, but it reveals now the hollowness, decadence, and bankruptcy at the core, often quite rudely:

> Records are still sold, admittedly few
> But what are these goats telling us, really, who never
> Learned to sing? What
> Is the point of these songs? What have they
> Really been singing to us all these years?

But—and this is central to an understanding of Brecht's entire concept of America—if we reread the first half after knowing the second half, we wonder just how positive those images at the beginning really were. And we realize that many of them are quite horrible, that they are only made to seem positive by the tone. The tone forces acceptance of the assumption that if America does something that seems cruel, it is because she cannot be bothered by weakness, she has a great destiny to fulfill. "They erected their gigantic edifices with incomparable waste/Of the best human material." It can be seen as either glorious or inhuman that the Americans used their human beings so.

Brecht is shocked not only by the crash but also by his own earlier value-free stance. That is why the economic crisis marks the great hiatus in his life: never again will he be an uncommitted or value-free writer. The first half of the poem now sounds very ambivalent. "Poverty was considered a disgrace there!" Does that mean there were no poor, or they were cursed and rejected? "Truly, their whole system of living together

207

was incomparable." Incomparably good or bad, kind or cruel, progressive or irrational?

So, the striking structure of this poem is an accurate representation of the form taken by Brecht's own changing attitude toward America. We have been able to say both that this attitude changed and that it did not, because he kept the same images and impressions but changed his assessment of their virtue. He always associated America with opulent waste, contrast of rich and poor, sport, virility, gambling, jazz, skyscrapers, automobiles, toughness and unsentimentality, get-rich-quick schemes and swindles, gangsters, and anarchy. At first he saw some positive value in these qualities, namely progress. But by 1929 America had already begun to lose the excuse of newness and when the crash happened it became one big ghost town for Brecht.

The fatalistic prophecy of destruction of the cities in the famous poem "Of Poor B.B." (1922) is fulfilled in "Vanished Glory," complete with the same imagery of useless skyscrapers. But in the earlier poem Brecht identified himself with the dying culture; now he is observing its death and liberating himself from its influence. The difference between the resigned tone in "Of Poor B.B." and the fighting, angry tone in "Vanished Glory" tells a whole story in itself. In 1922, Brecht could only hope he would not let his cigar go out in the earthquakes to come; in 1930, he knows what he is going to fight *for* and so has a transcendent, not nihilistic reason to say earthquakes be damned.

But he does not say that; he does not even mention earthquakes. It is in fact remarkable that among all the other imagery of America from his early works, natural catastrophes are completely ignored in "Vanished Glory." There is no hint of the Flood, or hurricanes, earthquakes, or Sodom and Gomorrah, though all these would seem to fit in well. The disaster of the depression is completely secular and man-made, and Brecht has no intention of mystifying it. In *Fleischhacker* he still spoke of financial crises as hurricanes, but the people of *Mahagonny* showed that man is more destructive than hurricane or God (whose moral wrath the hurricanes represented). After that, causation in Brecht's work is secular; it is in fact economic, and traceable to particular men. The Wall Street crash was caused by the irrationality of a system built by men and serving particular men, and by the time of the depression Brecht wanted to use no more literary devices that might obscure that crucial recognition.

But the years of study of the American system did not go to waste; all those fragmentary works and themes found their final embodiment in Brecht's great America play, *St. Joan of the Stockyards*. The commodities market in *Joe Fleischhacker*, the depression in *The Bread Store* and "Vanished Glory of the Giant City New York," the Salvation Army in *Happy*

End (Written by Elisabeth Hauptmann with some help from Brecht), the imagery of natural vs. man-made catastrophe from *Miami/The Flood/Mahagonny,* the new emphasis on the positive revolutionary role of the working class, and even more themes from his American reading all come together in this play, Brecht's farewell to Americanism and welcome to revolutionary engagement.

Notes

1. This paper is intended to be a quick summary of some of the themes of my book, *Brecht's America* (Columbus, Ohio, 1981). The book does not, however, explicitly raise the question of Brecht's attitude to *progress.* If I were to carry that question up through his later works, especially his poetry, I would say that he never really solved it; "capitalist progress bad, socialist progress good" is too simple a formula to withstand the hindsight of the latter half of the century. I believe now that a thorough study of Brecht's complete work would show that beneath his apparent sureness from 1929 on that "the new" was always preferable to "the old," a subversive streak of regret for the passing of many aspects of "the old" persists. His particular position in history made it impossible for him to see all the ramifications of unbridled progress that we can see today, but the questions are there, and they are never really answered.
2. All quotations from "Vanished Glory of the Giant City New York" are from *GW*. IX, 475–83.

James K. Lyon. "The FBI as Literary Historian: The File of Bertolt Brecht."

James Lyon describes the creation of and the literary historical value of one of the most unusual sources for a literary historian: the FBI file on Brecht. Between 1943 and 1948 FBI agents shadowed the "subject Brecht," they read his poems and plays as well as his private letters, they collected documents and newspaper articles about him (even up to 1956), listened in on his telephone conversations, bought information on Brecht's privately expressed opinions, and finally launched a "listening attack" with bugs. Their interest lay in the political viewpoints in his plays and poems, his attitude towards the United States and his political activities and contacts which more than once brought him close to the world of international espionage.

In this manner, a certain amount of biographical and literary historical material was assembled. The file is particularly useful in illuminating Brecht's relationship with Ruth Berlau. Heretofore unknown contacts, unpublished political statements and, above all, details on Brecht's important artistic projects of the America period (1941–1947), and finally a wealth of details that are in direct contradiction of the carefully guarded official picture of Bertolt Brecht.

James K. Lyon. "Das FBI als Literaturhistoriker: Die Akte Bertolt Brecht."

James Lyon beschreibt die Entstehung und die literaturgeschichtliche Bedeutung einer der ungewöhnlichsten Quellen für einen Literaturhistoriker: die Akte Brecht des FBI. Zwischen 1943 und 1948 beschatteten FBI-Agenten das "Subjekt Brecht", lasen Gedichte und Stücke, aber auch Privatbriefe, sammelten Dokumente und Zeitungsartikel, sogar bis 1956, hörten sein Telefon ab, kauften Informationen über private Äußerungen Brechts und wagten schließlich gar einen "Lauschangriff" mit Wanzen. Das Interesse galt politischen Aussagen seiner Stücke und Gedichte, seiner Haltung zu den Vereinigten Staaten und seinen politischen Aktivitäten und Kontakten, die der Spionageszene mehr als einmal nahe kamen.

Auf diese Weise wurde wertvolles biographisches und literaturhistorisches Material zusammengetragen, besonders über die Beziehung Brechts zu Ruth Berlau. Bislang unbekannte Kontakte, nicht veröffentlichte politische Aussagen und vor allem Einzelheiten aus Brechts künstlerischer Arbeit, die fast alle wichtigen Projekte der fraglichen Zeit betreffen, ergänzen das Bild von Brechts amerikanischer Zeit, zumal sie dem sorgsam gehüteten offiziellen Bild meist zuwiderlaufen.

James K. Lyon. "Le F.B.I. historien littéraire: le dossier Brecht."

James Lyon évoque, dans cet article, la création et la valeur historico-littéraire d'une des sources les plus insolites qui puisse s' offrir à l'attention d'un historien de la littérature: le dossier établi sur Brecht par le F.B.I. De 1943 à 1948, les agents du F.B.I. filent le "suspect", lisent ses poèmes, ses pièces et ses lettres personnelles, recueillent documents, articles de journaux sur lui (jusqu'en 1956), épient ses conversations téléphoniques sur table d'écoute, achètent des informations sur les opinions exprimées en privé par l'écrivain et finalement déclenchent une opération de grande envergure avec micros espions, installés partout.

Les agents s'intéressaient aux opinions politiques exprimées dans ses pièces et dans ses poèmes, à son attitude envers les Etats-Unis; ils voulaient connaître ses activités politiques et ses contacts qui, plus d'une fois, le mirent en rapport avec les cercles de l'espionnage international.

Le dossier se révèle particulièrement éclairant sur les rapports de Brecht avec Ruth Berlau. James Lyon met au jour des contacts ignorés jusqu'ici, révèle des prises de position politiques inédites, et surtout des détails sur les projets artistiques de Brecht durant sa période américaine (1941-1947). Finalement, il livre une foule de notations qui sont en complète contradiction avec l'image officielle, si soigneusement gardée, de Bertold Brecht.

The FBI as Literary Historian: The File of Bertolt Brecht

James K. Lyon

Until recently, the period Bertolt Brecht spent in American exile counted as one of the most obscure in his life. That began to change a few years ago, thanks in part to the release of a peculiar historiographic source generally unknown to literary historians who have written on Euripides, Ovid, Po Chu-yi, Dante, or other banished poets of the past with whom Brecht identified himself in his poems.[1] That source is the file which the FBI kept on him in America from 1943 to 1956. Yet these are not the earliest confidential records on a German writer living in exile. Accounts of the exiled Heinrich Heine's life in Paris are known from reports by secret agents of the Prussian and Austrian governments, which have since been published.[2] But we know nothing of the records which French internal security organs of the time kept on Heine. Hence this FBI file from our recent past represents a unique biographical source. It is not the purpose of this study to discuss moral questions involved in gathering such information or in the FBI's *modus operandi*, which by now is hardly a secret. Instead it will describe these documents, analyze their accuracy as they relate to Brecht's life and works, and assess their usefulness for those who consult them.

In 1974 Clarence Kelley the then head of the FBI, wrote to this author that the FBI held a file of approximately one thousand pages on Brecht.[3] With the permission of that writer's heirs, four scholars since then have obtained selected documents from that file. To date, the FBI has released a total of four hundred and twenty-seven pages, which they now claim is the complete file. Among the sources cited in the file are documents from the Immigration and Naturalization Service; newspaper and magazine clippings; ship manifestos; information provided by unpaid and by paid informants; agent reports describing surveillance of Brecht's house and his activities away from home; copies of letters and telegrams acquired through informants and through Western Union; material taken from telephone wire taps; and letters and telegrams from J. Edgar Hoover.

Yet the file seems incomplete, especially since individual names as well as complete sentences or paragraphs have been blotted out. In some cases, these gaps can be filled by a knowledgeable reader; in others, one is left to surmise what the FBI has not yet declassified, but clearly alludes to. Presumably what has not been released would add some new information about Brecht. Whether it would change appreciably what is known is another matter, for surrounding all these documents is a major reliability problem. Factual information often cannot be distinguished from hearsay. Masses of uncorroborated data, based on rumor and in many cases error, are indiscriminately interwoven into allegedly factual reports.

Some of these fictional accounts provide delightful reading. One source reports: "Brecht had been imprisoned by the Nazis at one time and apparently had been severely treated by them," a statement with no basis in fact. By confusing the manner in which Brecht's friend Lion Feuchtwanger escaped from a French concentration camp in 1940, another informant advises "that from the conversations overheard, Brecht is supposed to have escaped from a concentration camp in Germany disguised as a woman." Though Brecht first saw Los Angeles in 1941, another source identifies him as having been there in 1936 as a member of a group "that formed the German Communist Modern Music Group under the direction of Professor Eli Jacobson, Soviet Agent." And when a Los Angeles newspaper reported on the first postwar production of *The Threepenny Opera* in Berlin in 1945 and identified Brecht as "one of the most famous Jews in Germany," the FBI not only recorded that remark—one of their sources also reported Brecht's response: "A Jew did you say? They have murdered so many Jews over there that they need a new crop and so they enlist me among them." Discrepancies on the dates of Brecht's activities, errors which are repeated from one report to the next, and poor or erroneous translations compound the reliability problem. Yet because the file does contain data that can be corroborated as well as documents which qualify as sound primary sources, it possesses a moderately high usefulness quotient in regard to Brecht's political and literary activities in American exile.

How the FBI became aware of him is, at this point, still uncertain.

The first document in the released portions of the file bears the date March 6, 1943, though others summarize his activities since his arrival in July, 1941. A synopsis of facts preceding the March 6th report states that: "Subject alleged to have been a Communist in Europe, where he engaged in underground activities." It continues: "Subject's writings, some published as late as 1939, advocate overthrow of capitalism, establishment of Communist state, the use of sabotage by labor to obtain its ends." Basing these assertions on the testimony of two German émigré informants, the report continues with translated excerpts from a number of poems published by Brecht in 1939. They include "Song against the War," "Song of the United Front," "Revolution," "Speed of Socialist Construction," "Great October," "Cantata to the Day of Lenin's Death," and other Marxist/revolutionary poems. Though highly literal, these generally accurate translations relay Brecht's revolutionary message more clearly than do later "literary" translations of the same poems. In an FBI report of March 30, 1943, the agent who translated *Die Maßnahme* for the file under the title *The Disciplinary Measure* provides a detailed, accurate plot synopsis of this play, which he assesses as one that "not only advocates overthrow of the government by force of arms with the intent of founding a Communist state, but advocates the use of sabotage by labor as a means of accomplishing its ends." In addition to accounts of these works, of his film *Kuhle Wampe*, "a picture of Communist tendencies," and of the film *Hangmen Also Die*, the FBI quotes an informant who alleges that "Brecht is looked upon by German communists as their poet laureate" and cites a report from the United States attorney at Los Angeles who advises that Brecht "appeared to be a proletarian, bordering on an anarchist."

Brecht's self-advertised role as an "exile" in the United States did little to deflect attention from him in a country where assimilation of emigrants was the norm, and where Germans who insisted on retaining their national identity at a time when America was at war with Germany were viewed with suspicion.

Among the poems in Brecht's file, the FBI has included one entitled "On the Designation Emigrant." The beginning of their prose translation reads:

> Emigrant: I always found this name given us is wrong because it means one who leaves his country behind. But we didn't emigrate, did we, of our own free will, choosing another country? Instead we fled. We were driven out, and the country that accepted us is no home, but a place of exile. We sit restlessly, as near the border as possible, waiting for the day of our return.

Though Brecht wrote this poem while living in Denmark, the FBI correctly construed it to represent his attitude toward America, and it did

215

nothing to mitigate his reputation as a subversive. On three separate occasions the file cites this poem. Reporting on a 1943 presentation where Brecht's works were read and performed before emigrants in New York City, the FBI notes how Peter Lorre, from whom they obtained a copy of the printed program for the evening, read a number of Brecht's poems, including this one. The FBI's comment on this poem reads: "It was noted therein that the word 'emigration' has been changed to 'exile.' This poem was set out in full in a prior report, and the above is being mentioned simply to indicate that persons connected with subject, that is, Brecht, do not consider themselves emigrants here, but look upon themselves rather as exiles who wait to return to Europe."

Reporting on a telephone conversation in 1945, the FBI again notes that the unknown man with whom Brecht was speaking "had heard a rumor that Thomas Mann might be sent to Germany as an American, to which Brecht replied, 'Yes, and I am going with him as a German.' " Clearly he was scoring no points for his patriotism. From rumors circulating in the German exile colony, Brecht, according to another FBI report, had heard from the nephew of Eduard Beneš, leader of the Czech government-in-exile, "that refugees now in the United States had already been listed by the government for purposes of custodial detention after the war." The report continues: "Brecht is alleged to have stated that in view of this, he would escape from the United States with a Czechoslovakian passport which he could secure through Beneš." This was in November, 1943. On June 6th, 1944, Brecht and Hanns Eisler met with Beneš, the Czech consul in San Francisco, and inquired about obtaining passports. The FBI notes: "They apparently believed that possession of Czech passports will facilitate their travel, particularly their departure from this country." The subsequent paragraph illustrates how devious the FBI perceived them to be. Referring to their conversation with Beneš, it reads: "Brecht and Eisler, in response to a suggestion that possibly they would have to get exit visas from the United States government, indicated astonishment at this and then remarked, 'Well, the border is close by'."

After his testimony before the House un-American Activities Committee on October 30, 1947, Brecht's journal claims that in contrast to the Hollywood Ten who preceded him and were indicted for contempt of Congress, "It was in my favor that I had had almost nothing to do with Hollywood, had not been involved in American politics, and that those who preceded me on the witness stand had refused to answer the congressman." While generally accurate, the phrase about his non-involvement in politics demands re-examination. Though not active in American politics, the FBI file reveals that he involved himself freely in exile political activities during the six years of his American exile. Of the fifteen exile years Brecht spent outside Germany between 1933 and 1948, the period in America was probably his most politically active. To the FBI his association with Gregori Kheifetz and other suspected Soviet spies was most damning. According to the FBI, Kheifetz, Vice-Consul in the Soviet Consulate at San Francisco, was "alleged to have engaged in military and political investigation on the West Coast as the close assistant to a high NKVD officer heading the Soviet secret police in the United States. It has been ascertained that Kheifetz was engaged in espionage in Los Angeles." A later report states unequivocally that he was "in charge of Soviet espionage activities on the West Coast before 1946." On at least four different occasions between April, 1943 and June, 1944, Kheifetz visited Brecht's home, usually for periods of one and one-half to two hours. Following one of the 1943 meetings, the FBI file states: "It is also known that Kheifetz has described Bert Brecht as a good friend." FBI men surveilled Kheifetz's visits to Brecht's house, but when Brecht testified before the House un-American Activities Committee in 1947, he claimed to have had no recollection of ever meeting Kheifetz, though he did state that somebody visited him, "some of the cultural attaches." This latter statement was true, for after Kheifetz left the United States, his replacement, Gregory Kasparov, as well as a representative from the Soviet Consulate in Los Angeles, Andrei Vassiliev, continued to meet with him. The FBI file also notes visits by two other Soviet Vice-Consuls from the Los Angeles Consulate in August and October, 1945. In addition, Brecht frequently attended cultural and social functions sponsored by the Los Angeles Soviet Consulate. On one occasion, he is reported to have met an unnamed woman journalist from Russia. On another, he attended a farewell party at the Consulate for the Russian film maker, Mikhail Kalatazov.

The FBI received information that on January 17, 1944, while Brecht was in New York, "Gerhart Eisler, an alleged Comintern agent and brother of Hanns Eisler, visited the apartment occupied by Brecht and remained for approximately one hour and a quarter." Again the implications were overwhelming. Gerhart Eisler was suspected not only of being a Comintern agent; within three years he would be arrested as the leader of a large Soviet espionage network in the United States.

This was by no means the limit of Brecht's suspicious political contacts. FBI reports vainly tried to link him to the Communist-backed "Free German" movement in Mexico and South America. A detailed account of a meeting at the home of Berthold Viertel in August, 1943, connected him to the "National Committee for Free Germany" in Moscow, an organization of German prisoners of war who had been "reeducated" in Moscow and who now called on the German people to rise against Hitler. Brecht met with Thomas Mann and other German writers at the Viertel home, but FBI reports reveal nothing more of this abortive attempt to issue a proclamation (Thomas Mann withdrew, and no proclamation was issued) than what is known from available sources.[4]

FBI records of Brecht's participation in the Council for a Democratic Germany, an organization founded in 1944 that hoped to influence the government and social structure of postwar Germany, are considerably more detailed and less given to name-calling than other reports which repeatedly characterize him as a "Communist sympathizer," "a radical," and, in one passage "a suspected agent of the Soviet government." In monitoring the activities of the Council, which was thought to be a Communist front organization, the FBI specifically inquired of the theologian Paul Tillich, the chairman of that Council, about Brecht's politics. Tillich's answer, though exasperating to them, is perhaps the most valid description in the file. One reads that "Tillich regards Brecht as one of the almost Communist representatives. Tillich said literally 'We have two and one-half Communist representatives on the Council; the half is Bertolt Brecht'." The real extent of Brecht's involvement in Council work, while partially recorded by the FBI, is known today only from unpublished documents in the Brecht Archives.

In his associations with American leftists, Brecht must have frustrated the FBI. Though the file reports on telephone conversations and visits with a number of known members of the American Communist party, Brecht clearly was not close to them. Those with whom he associated regularly were either suspected Communists or fellow travelers such as Don Ogden Stewart, Clifford Odets, George Sklar, Mordecai Gorelik, and Archibald MacLeish. One relationship that puzzled them was Brecht's "Hindu-connection" to Christopher Isherwood. A Marxist during the 30's, Isherwood had since retreated into a Vedanta Monastery on Ivar Street in Hollywood. Not only did Brecht visit him and receive mail from him there; the file indicates that the Soviet Vice-Consuls in Los Angeles and San Francisco also called on Isherwood. A friend had heard Brecht say that Isherwood had betrayed the cause of world revolution and was dissipating a great talent by withdrawing into this private world.[5] The FBI knew none of this, but only that Brecht was consorting with other dubious types who scarcely adhered to the pattern of patriotism prevalent in America during World War II.

In its zeal to establish guilt by association, a theme which pervades this file, the FBI appears both comic and ominous. Responding to a request from the Los Angeles Field Office for the re-installation of "technical surveillance" on Brecht's home (i.e., a telephone wire tap), J. Edgar Hoover reproved his agents on March 9, 1945, with the remark that "the

Bureau has no record of any authority previously granted to install and operate a technical surveillance on Brecht." Hoover instructed them to provide full details of the earlier, apparently unauthorized wiretap. In a reply dated March 16th, the Los Angeles Field Office noted that its request on this subject "inadvertently states that a technical surveillance was previously made on Brecht. Brecht was confused with Heinrich Mann." This was untrue, since a record in the file shows that a telephone wire tap on Brecht was indeed conducted between February and May, 1943. A letter from J. Edgar Hoover to the Los Angeles Field Office dated August 8, 1945, also scolded them for making it evident in their reports that information had been gained from a wire tap. He ordered them to conceal this fact in future correspondence. Friends from those years tell us today that the Brechts knew their telephone was being tapped, and that in order to confuse the FBI, Helene Weigel-Brecht on at least one occasion read recipes from a Polish cookbook over the telephone to another friend who also knew no Polish.[6] While this incident did not find its way into the file, one wonders what such precautionary measures had to do with the FBI's discontinuing this telephone surveillance on November 5, 1945, on the grounds that it was "no longer productive."

The FBI was not alone in trying to decipher Brecht's ideological position. From recent information we know that an uneasy relationship existed between him and American Marxists, both in the party and outside it. As early as 1937 he had been attacked in American Marxist journals as "an individualist in collective's clothing" whose theories were decidedly "un-Marxist."[7] American leftists in the 40's viewed him as a "superior Marxist" whose arrogance and superciliousness toward his comrades in the U.S.A. did not endear him to them.[8] Though one FBI source speaks of him as the "poet laureate of German Communism," American Marxists viewed him as an unregenerated Stalinist, a hard-liner whose defense of the Moscow purge trials and everything negative connected with the Soviet Union and the Communist international movement made him uncomfortable in their presence and unacceptable in their ranks. Clearly he was a Marxist, but what kind of a Marxist was an issue which left them just as uncertain in their own way as the FBI was in trying to determine how dangerous Brecht's activities were. Throughout its file the FBI stops short of calling him a Communist. Terms such as "Communist sympathizer," "advocate of the overthrow of Capitalism," and the numerous other appellations carefully qualify his connection to Communism. Even a statement as strong as "a suspected agent of the Soviet government" testifies that the FBI was still trying to fathom this inscrutable man.

Two times before 1947—once on July 10, 1943, and again on May

29, 1946—the FBI closed his case for lack of evidence. Almost a year lapsed before they opened it a third time on May 13, 1947, and this time it was not Brecht's interim activity, but a request from the House un-American Activities Committee which had been investigating Gerhart and Hanns Eisler that again brought him to their attention. The FBI's report of May 13, 1947, opened the third phase of his file; it lasted only seven months and was closed on January 8, 1948.

This period in the file might be entitled "A Comedy of Errors." Had the FBI been less cautious, there is a good chance they might have obtained an historic interview with Brecht. When it discovered that he was planning to leave the United States for what they thought would be an eighteen-month trip to Europe, the Los Angeles field office of the FBI requested permission "to interview Brecht concerning his contacts with Gregori Kheifets, former Soviet Vice-Consul in San Francisco and alleged NKVD agent." J. Edgar Hoover granted permission on October 20, 1947 to interview him in New York, where he was staying. When it was learned that he was under subpoena to appear before the House un-American Activities Committee a few days later, Hoover sent a telegram on October 23rd instructing his agents to "postpone plans to interview subject until after his appearance before the House Committee on un-American Activities." Though the FBI was surely aware that he testified before this committee on October 30th, they did not realize that he left for Europe the next day. The day he departed a German émigré in Philadelphia who had read of Brecht's testimony in the national newspapers called the local FBI office to say "that he knows the subject was a leading European Communist and that he can prove this." On November 5th, this same informant wrote a lengthy letter to the FBI denouncing Brecht. In it he stated:

> I have followed Brecht's career from that time [1919] on. Brecht was an unswerving advocate of Soviet policy in Germany; he wrote several outright Communistic plays . . . I happened to be in contact with friends of Brecht and therefore I know that he has not deviated a bit from the official Russian party line. Several weeks ago he said something like "he and his like are now obliged to palm themselves off as 'Democrats'.[11]

On the basis of this denunciation, Hoover on November 12th sent a telegram to his New York Field Office instructing them "to interview subject without undue delay." But it was too late; Brecht had already gone.

A few days earlier (November 5th), the FBI had begun an investigation to determine if deportation proceedings could be initiated against him. After learning that he had departed for Europe, they did the next best thing on November 20, 1947—put out a so-called "customs stop" on him, which meant he would be detained while passing through customs if and when he returned. Not knowing Brecht, the FBI naively assumed that he intended to use the re-entry permit and come back to the United States. He never did, of course. On December 2, 1947, Hoover wrote to the CIA asking them to furnish "any information you receive or develop on the subject's activities in Europe of a Soviet intelligence nature, and any indications of his return to the United States." Nothing was forthcoming, and the FBI closed his file again on January 8, 1948.

While the case lay dormant between 1948 and 1956, various documents were added to the file, among them an article in *New Leader* magazine of March 3, 1949, denouncing Brecht as a "GPU songbird." Records also describe a protracted, Keystone Cops-like escapade in which the FBI was summoned by Warner Brothers Studios to help locate a missing copy of the German original of his *Threepenny Opera* film which they owned and which, according to inferences by one source, had been used in some sort of international espionage situation many years ago.

The FBI re-opened the file in 1956 when a telegram of March 20th from the Los Angeles Field Office notified Hoover "that according to a recent column by Walter Winchell, subject is to appear at the Open Stage Theatre, New York City, on March 21st next to review his play, *Private Life of the Master Race*. The INS [Immigration and Naturalization Service] has no positive information that subject is in country, but desires to interview him if he appears at Theatre." The telegram touched off a minor flurry of activity. Permission was granted the same day to interview Brecht should he appear. The following day, the FBI wrote an internal memo recommending that its New York office collaborate with the INS in surveillance of Brecht. FBI agents tried in vain to get a copy of the play *The Private Life of the Master Race* from Samuel French, the dramatic publisher who held rights to Brecht's works in America, and from New Directions, which originally published it. According to the file they also planned to interview Eric Bentley, the translator of the play who was alleged to be in contact with the playwright. Walter Winchell had stated that Brecht would be present for this production of his play in a small loft in Greenwich Village, but his report was erroneous. The FBI arranged for physical surveillance of the area around the Open Stage Theatre on the night of March 21st, and two inspectors from the INS attended a performance at which approximately 75 persons were present. An FBI telegram summarizing the evening noted that the

audience during intermission demanded author, stating Walter Winchell indicated in a recent column that subject would be there. One person stated "we

221

expected to see hordes of FBI men here." Eric Bentley, who wrote English version of play, told audience the subject was not there, advising he last saw subject in 1950 in Munich, Germany. An unidentified person exclaimed "We certainly fooled the FBI this time," which was greeted with laughter from audience.

Judging by the way they cite this statement in subsequent reports, the FBI clearly felt stung by what looked like a hoax perpetrated at their expense. Another denunciation by a citizen; an attack on Brecht from a magazine entitled *Top Secret;* and a final letter to the CIA in 1962 dealing with "possible U.S. citizens involved in West German propaganda broadcasts against U.S. Forces" concludes the released portions of the file.

Sifting through considerable trivia and error, one finds some new material, such as the information relating to Brecht's contacts with Soviet consular officials, and elaboration on much more that is already known. A "bugged" telephone conversation of August 2, 1945, for example, between Brecht and Lion Feuchtwanger, records his reaction to plans for the division of postwar Germany into occupational zones. Brecht labelled it "very bad news," in part because Germany would not retain its unity as a cultural state. Noting that the Allies had allowed until 1948 to bring Germany back into the democratic fold, Brecht stated that uppermost in his mind was how willing Germany would be to get rid of capitalist exploitation and the military powers that had ruled it." The unusually detailed account of this conversation confirms what Fritz Sternberg has reported[9] and illuminates Brecht's persistent interest in future European politics throughout his American exile.

Quite aside from political matters, these documents also furnish literary historians with a wealth of biographical data on Brecht's life and works of this period. On an elementary level, one is able to reconstruct a more precise chronicle of his movements and activities than has hitherto been possible. The file also makes it possible to document his contact with Hollywood figures whose names previously have not figured in his biography. A report on a telephone conversation of November 2, 1945, for example, states that "Freddy Bartholomew, the movie actor, inquired of Brecht about the possibility of getting some recordings, and Brecht advised Bartholomew that he would have to contact Mr. [Paul] Henreid about the matter." To date it was not known that Brecht had ever met, much less spoken with Bartholomew, a prominent child actor of the 30's. Other Hollywood notables with whom the file reports he had contact not otherwise evident from his letters or journals include Bud Schulberg, Jed Harris, Norman Corwin, Max Ophuls, Billy Wilder, and Robert Riskin.

From the file one is able to date more precisely his work on a number of writing projects. Previously it had been difficult to establish when he had collaborated with Salka Viertel and Vladimir Pozner on the film story for *Silent Witness*. But the FBI file records that he met and discussed this film story with the two on October 16 and 17, 1944. A precise date when he commenced writing *All Our Yesterdays,* a modernized film story version of the *Macbeth* tragedy set in the Chicago stockyards, which he began to write with the actor Peter Lorre and with Ferdinand Reyher, is also given as September 5, 1945. One learns that Reyher, who helped complete the story, met with him to work on it eight or nine times between the middle of September and October 15th of that year. The file also treats of an abortive project conceived in 1943 which apparently continued through 1944—collaboration on a film story using the classical Lysistrata material. Sometime in July, 1943, Brecht had discussed with the film producer Isador Goldschmidt plans for a modernized version of this material portraying a marriage strike in a Danish town where a suffragette teacher had been fired from her job for being secretly married. Like many projects Brecht began, this one is believed to have died a premature death. The FBI file, however, contains a letter written to Brecht by Helene Weigel, dated November 19, 1943, stating: "I haven't heard anything new about the film from Goldschmidt who will begin in January, and your cooperation belongs in this." FBI mail coverage showing that Brecht received an airmail letter from Goldschmidt dated October 27, 1944, indicates that the project apparently was still alive at that date.

The file reveals information on Brecht's plans for two incomplete projects. The first relates to a character who interested him all his life— Rosa Luxemburg. Through an unidentified source, the FBI was able to acquire a number of notes made by Ruth Berlau during her collaboration with Brecht. One of Berlau's notes dated October 23, 1944, states (in Berlau's flawed English) that Brecht

> is collecting material for an article about Rosa Luxemburg. He is going to tell her story in a biblical style, only the big happenings. He plans to make the first scene at the time she fled to Finland after the abortive Russian revolution attempt of 1905. On the running band [*Fliessband*] she is going with the other fleeing revolutionaries toward the Finnish borders. Her comrades are complaining; they are desperate. The revolution has failed and has cost a lot of blood, but she proves to them that it has been a victory in that at the moment that the exploiters of the workers think to have beaten down the revolution for good, we will arise still stronger. So they are approaching the border and the customs officers. The great problem is now—how to get over that border.

From Berlau's brief outline of what was intended as a play, one gains a clearer concept of Brecht's dramatic intentions than from all the disparate fragments on this topic in the Brecht Archives.

Another note by Berlau touches on an unknown facet of Brecht's "Children's Crusade, 1939," a ballad he had written early in 1941. With the recent discovery of an unknown film story he wrote in 1943 based on this poem, it was evident that he had done more work on this subject that has been realized.[10] A note in the FBI files describing material Berlau had in her possession mentions two booklets of photographic material. One is entitled "The Children's Crusade, 1939—Brecht." Just as he had done with his *Primer of War,* Brecht seems to have envisaged the publication of a book of photoepigrams, or "photograms" as he called them, dealing with this ballad. Yet beyond this reference, nothing is known of this project or what became of it. A number of other statements refer to photographic material he was gathering for his *Primer of War,* and one letter describes his difficulties in another well-known project—the attempt to re-cast the *Communist Manifesto* in classical hexameters as part of an epic poem modelled after Lucretius's *On the Nature of Things.*

Some of the most significant information relates to dramatic works he wrote or tried to have produced while in the United States. We know that Brecht clashed with Erwin Piscator when he wrote *Schweyk in the Second World War.*[11] It is not known how he resolved one of the important points in that dispute, viz. the acquisition of rights to the material. Piscator claimed he held them, but the FBI file contains a notation that Brecht "obtained the rights to Schweik through Beneš, nephew of Eduard Beneš, President of Czechoslovakia." It states that Brecht had "consulted with one Gustav Machaty on several occasions relative to life and conditions in Czechoslovakia, since this information was necessary to Brecht in the writing of his play entitled *Schweik.*" Machaty, who was connected with the San Francisco Consulate of the Czech government in exile, apparently acted as the go-between to Beneš.

Information in the FBI file also illuminates some of the difficulties leading to the production of *The Private Life of the Master Race* in New York during June, 1945, and how the threatre wrangled permission to perform this work from a reluctant Brecht. Apparently the combination of Berlau's urging and a telegram from Ernest Roberts, director of the Theatre of All Nations, convinced him to grant production rights (he had been equivocating for at least two months and had assigned rights to someone else). Originally he planned to go to New York and then discuss the matter with Roberts. On April 19, 1945, Roberts cabled "Cannot wait for decision until you arrive. Need your O.K. immediately otherwise Bassermann not available. Hope you can be here latest 26th of April. Your supervision needed. Traveling expenses will be paid." The name Albert Bassermann, a distinguished German actor, was enough to turn the trick for Brecht after he had heard from Berlau that she approved of the production staff.

On the basis of Brecht's own statements, scholars have accepted the view that during their collaboration on the translation/adaptation of *Galileo,* the apolitical Charles Laughton got along with Brecht largely by ignoring his collaborator's ideological views.[12] The FBI file corrects this view. The account of a taped telephone conversation between Laughton and Brecht's wife notes:

> Laughton stated that he had just read two scenes of the play to Mr. Norman Corwin, who immediately stated he would like to direct it. Laughton went on to point out that this was a good thing. Corwin is a tremendous personality in the country and is a number one patriotic American. He inferred that it would be advantageous for such a man to produce this play of Brecht's, who might be called a "Communist." Laughton described Corwin as a "great patriotic writer" and said that having him direct the play would take away "any sort of business of the church, of Brecht in Russia and everything."

Though Laughton was noted for his squeamishness in political matters, it was not known that he actually looked for an all-American type producer to mitigate criticism of Brecht's ideology, which he understood all too well.

Another bit of unknown information pertains to the *Caucasian Chalk Circle,* a drama Brecht wrote in America under contract to a Broadway producer. Luise Rainer, a two-time Academy Award winning actress who had arranged that Brecht write the play with the financial backing of Jules Leventhal, has reported that shortly after Brecht wrote the play, he insulted her so badly that she refused to play in it, whereupon Leventhal dropped the production.[13] From the FBI file it is clear that this was not the case. Nine months after completing the version which Rainer claims she rejected, Brecht received a telegram dated March 9, 1945, from Samuel French Dramatic Publishers. The FBI reports: "this telegram advised that Leventhal was most enthusiastic over the play. Leventhal desired that Brecht send the name of a scenery designer that Brecht had once suggested and also wished that Brecht would proceed with whatever suggestions he might have concerning the musical background of the play." It stated that Leventhal hoped to get Rouben Mamoulian to direct the play and planned to have a production ready to open in the fall of 1945. This contradicts everything known about this play, for consistent with the myth of Brecht's non-success in the United States, it was generally believed that this, too, found no interest among American backers.

While the FBI file contains virtually nothing about Brecht's sexual peccadillos, it does contain important information about his relationship with Ruth Berlau, whom the FBI discreetly calls his "girl friend," as well as some rare documents pertaining to that relationship. The file recounts how Berlau, after registering in a motel on Wilshire Boulevard in Santa Monica during the summer of 1944, left for new lodgings. It continues: "a man brought her belongings to her new living quarters. They described this individual as a little fellow with dark hair who could hardly speak English and who drove a wreck of an automobile. This is undoubtedly Bert Brecht." At this point in the FBI file, large sections of two separate pages have been visibly obliterated. In all probability they touch on Berlau's admission to the Cedars of Lebanon Hospital during the seventh or eighth month of her pregnancy by Brecht. At this time an emergency operation was performed, allegedly to remove a tumor (the child she was expecting, which survived only a few hours, was given the name "Michael."). When the report commences again, it cites a note contained in an envelope of the Cedars of Lebanon Hospital addressed to Berlau in Room 314. It reads: "Love, I am so glad that you are fighting so courageously. Don't think that I do not want to see you when you are ill. You are beautiful then, too. I am coming tomorrow before noon. Yours, Bertolt." The file continues: "In addition, below the signature appear the letters e/p/e/p which frequently appear at the close of the correspondence between Brecht and Berlau, according to source A (Brecht's abbreviation for Latin 'et prope et procul,' i.e. whether near or far)." This rare document, a translation from the German original, has never been published, and, if held by the Brecht Archives, has been withheld from public view. Such intimate expressions of tenderness are not part of the image of Bertolt Brecht which disciples and publishers have cultivated.

On a level above that of an intimate relationship, the FBI viewed Berlau with suspicion because she had taken a formal course in photography in Santa Monica and was doing extensive photographic work for Brecht. She was in fact photographing his manuscripts for archival purposes, but there is the inescapable implication that this work for Brecht somehow might have been connected with espionage. From a source who must have helped Berlau pack when she left for New York on March 31, 1945, the FBI obtained a detailed account of the types of film and photographic equipment she took. A statement in this part of the file closes with the comment: "Source A was unable to determine the nature of the material copied onto this film."

Immediately after her departure, the FBI wrote a report dealing with her future plans. Because three separate sources advised that she intended to return within two or three months, the FBI hoped to make arrangements to use her in extracting information from an unwitting

Brecht. The report reads: "At the present time it is desired to request of the Bureau blanket authorization for the installation of a microphone surveillance in whichever unit of the Chalet Motor Hotel Berlau might reside upon her return. This authority is requested now to safeguard against the possible return on Berlau's part and to enable the installation to be made prior to her occupancy so that evidence obtained therefrom will be admissible in court. . . . It is believed that this surveillance, if authorized, will furnish almost complete information concerning the activities of Brecht." That portion of the FBI file released to date reveals that permission to plant this "bug" was approved, but that Berlau neither returned as anticipated nor, when she finally did two years later, stayed in that motel.

As a consequence of their interest in Berlau, the FBI managed to preserve what count as the rarest documents in this file. Normally a notoriously bad correspondent, Brecht wrote more letters to Berlau during his lifetime than to any single person. She in turn corresponded frequently with him. Yet not a single letter she wrote to him exists today. Probably Brecht destroyed them intentionally. Here, then, thanks to the FBI, is a rarity in Brecht's biography—transcripts of two letters and one telegram from Ruth Berlau to him. One letter dated April 2, 1945, and postmarked Salt Lake City, Utah, was written while Berlau was enroute to New York. Undoubtedly composed in broken German, the FBI's English translation captures the enormous insecurity and dependence in her relationship to Brecht. It reads in part:

> Oh Bertolt, your letter. If you only could know how much good it has done. Again this time you understood everything. Again this time you have been so very kind, and to think that I was afraid that you might have thought it terrible to find that I had a round-trip ticket. Bertolt, my dear Bertolt, many thanks. You understand how it was I thought that you would be thinking, "glad she has finally left, a good riddance;" and then you told me to come back as soon as you can. . . . I do love you. . . . You were right again when you told me that my photos were still dilettante work. What you have are contact prints only. But I really want to make some progress. . . . Write me which ones you think I should take for the interview. It is good thing that you are so strict with me. In such cases it is more valuable if you say that something is good.

The file mentions that another letter postmarked April 2, 1945, at Omaha, Nebraska, contained nothing of interest, but a letter of April 3, postmarked Chicago, Illinois, and written in English, is quoted in part:

> You know we got in New York that good short wave radio set which Jull gave me through a sailor. It will be useful just now to listen in and hear about

Germany. Don't you think so? . . . Tomorrow I will be in Chicago. I think much about Steff. [Brecht's son by Helene Weigel—at that time in a Chicago hospital.] So kind of you to suggest that I should see Steff . . . If you would allow me to say something and if you would not mind, would you? Take care the first time you come there not to make it appear as if it has cleared the air that I have left, and that you can come again there together with your wife now. You understand. I only say this because it comes in my thought and it is better to have told you. Remember to send me the last Kriegsfibel photo, you know the one about the German girl.

The telegram by Berlau written a few days after her arrival in New York apparently was also dictated in English. It reads: "Alexan excited about your *Städtebauer* book. Viertel considered it best contribution. Send original special delivery to me. Austrian newspaper asked permission to publish it in special issue." Berlau here is referring to the *Austro-American Tribune,* an émigré newspaper which published a number of the photograms Brecht was compiling for his *Primer of War.* Though low in informational content, these two letters and this telegram count as rarities in the current state of Brecht's biography.

Nor are these the only letters of significance in the file. In addition to the note written to Berlau while she was hospitalized, the FBI includes part or all of a half dozen unknown Brecht letters and one telegram. Though translations of German originals, they are still valuable for having preserved materials otherwise lost. A letter from Brecht to Karl Korsch written sometime in late 1944 or early 1945 asks for his assistance on his long didactic poem modelled on Lucretius. Besides describing what concerns him about the project, it notifies Korsch that Brecht has already mailed to him a second canto containing the first half of the Communist Manifesto. He solicits Korsch's reactions and asks that he send them as quickly as possible, for he wants to get on with the work. The sole telegram by Brecht found in his files dated April 20, 1945, is addressed to Berlau and was probably written in his own English. It reads: "You are right. Master Race should be played. Please tell Roberts to send contract."

Two letters from Helene Weigel to Brecht belong among other documents in the file which might not have been preserved but for the FBI. Most letters, including the ones Weigel wrote, deal less with Brecht's writings than with mundane affairs. There are several exceptions. One of them, a telegram from the producer Paul Czinner to Brecht dated August 3, 1945, reads: "Enthusiastic about Galileo. It is the greatest and most important thing I have read in years. I am looking forward to producing it with Charles Laughton in the title role. How far are you with the translation? And how far can we go ahead? Best regards to you and to Charles Laughton." This and similar information adjusts ever so slightly the image Brecht cultivated of himself in American exile as a struggling, unrecognized artist. Czinner was a wealthy producer who easily could have provided Brecht the means to stage *Galileo* had Brecht wished. But Brecht declined.

There are other letters. Perhaps the most interesting for literary historians are several relating to Ignazio Silone's attempt to produce one of Brecht's plays in Italy immediately after the war. On March 20, 1945, Paolo Milano wrote Brecht from New York:

> My very good friend, Ignazio Silone, who is back in Rome, has found there some kind of theatre and is very eager to put on your play, *The Man of Szechuan.* (By the way this may not be the correct title, but I have read the play in the German manuscript and enjoyed it deeply.) I do hope that the plan interests you. Have no doubt that Silone would do an excellent job with your play. Would you be kind enough to send me right away a German script which I would forward to Rome? The matter seems to be quite urgent, since I have got in the meantime two more pathetic appeals on the matter of Silone. I think that an Italian audience deserves to hear your voice on the stage after so long an absence.

A few days later on March 29, Berthold Viertel, who knew Brecht's propensity for consigning such letters to the wastebasket, wrote urgently:

> My dear Brecht, I had to tell the go-between who came from Silone to ask for *The Good Woman of Setzuan* that I referred the request to you. It might be useful if you reacted yourself on this request. Silone ought not be able to say that he is one of those whom you consider as not worthy of an answer. If you, for whatever reason, do not think it right that the play come out now on the new Silone stage, please let me know it in a few words. They ought not . . . see the real cause of your unwillingness. All these things are confidential and will remain between ourselves.

If Brecht did reply to Silone, that letter has been lost. In all probability, he did not, for the real cause of his unwillingness, as Viertel knew, was his decision that the production of his plays in Europe would not begin again until he was there to supervise them personally. Consequently, he denied permission to a number of other European directors who sent similar requests to him.

In his book on literary biography, Leon Edel asks rhetorically: "Who would think of writing the life of a modern poet on the record of his bank stubs?"[14] The answer might be "Bertolt Brecht." Information on his checking account in the FBI file reveals a side of the man which Brecht preferred to conceal. From his check stubs, we see almost the only external evidence of his deep concern for Ruth Berlau by the way he assumed responsibility for her through payment of her motel room while she lived in Santa Monica; of medical bills for her following her operation in Cedars of Lebanon Hospital; of bills for her confinement to a psychiatric hospital on Long Island following a nervous breakdown late in 1945; of clothes for her, including a fur coat; of her rent in her New York apartment, and many similar acts. Other coverage of his checking account reveals the great generosity of both Brecht and his wife towards friends in America and those in post-war Europe to whom they were sending packages after 1945.

It is true that the Brechts were obliged to live on $ 125 a month during their first year in America, but it has not been generally known that within a five year period they completely bought and paid for a spacious two-story home in Santa Monica; that they were able to afford hired help (the FBI identifies her as "Cornelia McKinney, a colored woman who does cleaning at the Brecht residence one day a week"); and were in much healthier state of financial affairs than has generally been known. For those aware of the intricacies of Brecht's biography, there is also an illuminating inference to be drawn from his check stubs. In his journal Brecht records having received $ 20,000 from the sale of the rights to the play *Simone Machard,* which he wrote in collaboration with Lion Feuchtwanger, and which Feuchtwanger then rewrote as a novel and sold to Samuel Goldwyn. An unconfirmed report indicates that Brecht received more than the amount listed in his journal, and that his failure to tell his wife about it led to serious differences between Feuchtwanger and Mrs. Brecht, who felt that the money had not been evenly divided.[15] The FBI file seems to confirm that something like this did happen, for it lists the figure received for rights to the novel as $ 57,000, of which Brecht received (by contract) 50 %. In all probability, he used the money he withheld to support Berlau, whom Helene Weigel did not suffer gladly in or near her household.

To the literary historian these and similar inferences are important because much of the biography written by Brecht comes perilously close to hagiography. Many have doggedly insisted on preserving the image of an impoverished writer suffering in American exile and deprived of his basic means of existence, not to say of recognition. On this as well as a number of other counts, the FBI file in its present incomplete form helps us in rewriting the biography of a man whose life is by no means completely known, to say nothing of understood.

While the literary historian can be grateful to the FBI for preserving such documentary material, one must also ask if the enormous amount of time, energy and money spent in report writing, technical surveillance, physical surveillance, interviews with informants, mail watch on letters received by Brecht, and all the efforts expended on this case were justified, the moral and legal implications quite aside. Certainly this file is one of the most expensive, not say unusual sources, a modern literary historian will ever use.

Notes

1. Cf. the poems "Die Auswanderung der Dichter" and "Besuch bei den verbannten Dichtern", *GW*, IX, 495, 663.
2. Cf. Karl Glossy, ed., *Literarische Geheimberichte aus dem Vormärz* (Vienna: 1912), I, pp. 3, 58, 60, 96, 172; II, pp. 145, 190, 253; and Hans-Joachim Schoeps, "Ein unbekannter Agentenbericht über Heinrich Heine," *Heine-Jahrbuch* 1967, pp. 67–80.
3. Letter from Clarence Kelley to J. Lyon, December 11, 1973.
4. *AJ*, 597–599.
5. Interview, J. Lyon with Naomi Replansky, December 27, 1972.
6. Interview, J. Lyon with Rhoda Pecker, June 27, 1972.
7. John Howard Lawson, letter to the editor in *Theatre Workshop* (September 1937), p. 27; Edmund Fuller, "Epic Realism: An Analysis of Bert Brecht," *One Act Play Magazine* (April 1938), p. 1130.
8. Interview, J. Lyon with George Sklar, August 7, 1973.
9. Fritz Sternberg, *Der Dichter und die Ratio: Erinnerungen an Bertolt Brecht* (Göttingen: Sachse & Pohl, 1952), p.52.
10. James K. Lyon, " 'Kinderkreuzzug 1939.' Zu einem unbekannten Filmexposé von Bert Brecht," *Film und Fernsehen* (No. 6 [1978]), pp. 24–29.
11. Herbert Knust, ed., *Materialien zu Bertolt Brechts "Schweyk im Zweiten Weltkrieg"* (Frankfurt/M.: Suhrkamp, 1974), pp. 151–152; and John Willett, "Piscator and Brecht: Closeness Through Distance," *ICarbS* (Spring-Summer 1974), pp. 88–91.
12. Cf. Brecht's own statements in the "Foreword" to "Aufbau einer Rolle," *GW*, XVII, 1119.
13. Interview, Luise Rainer with Leonard Lyons, "The Lyon's Den,"*New York Post* (September 15, 1962).
14. Leon Edel, *Literary Biography* (Bloomington, Indiana: University of Indiana Press, 1973), p. 4.
15. Interview, J. Lyon with Marta Feuchtwanger, May 26, 1971.

BOOK REVIEWS

Bertolt Brecht. Briefe
Hrsg. und kommentiert von Günter Glaeser, Frankfurt/Main: Suhrkamp, 1981, 2 vols., 1175 pp.

This collection of 893 letters written by Brecht over a 43-year period (1913–1956) makes available the last large group of his unpublished writings. Yet like so many of Brecht's published works, there is both more and less here than meets the eye. To understand this, it is necessary to describe what this edition is in negative terms, i.e. what it is *not* and does not purport to do.

1. It is not a complete collection of Brecht's letters, since it contains just over one third of at least 2400 letters, post cards, telegrams, and drafts of letters in the Brecht Archives. In his introduction, the editor insists that he has included all Brecht letters that contain vital information ("aussagekräftige Informationen") of interest to the scholar or general reader. But he qualifies himself by the admission that he has omitted most routine business correspondence (which apparently constitutes the major portion of what does not appear here) as well as letters which reveal intimate matters or which might be legally sensitive because of statements about living persons. But the editor never reveals how he made these determinations, nor does he identify the letters he excluded. At first glance, one is struck by the conspicuous absence of all letters written to Margarete Steffin, Käthe Reichel, and Käthe Rülicke, women who played a significant role at various stages of Brecht's life. Isot Kilian, another such woman, is represented by a single letter, while the 65 letters to Ruth Berlau published here represent only a small fraction of the total number he wrote to her. One wonders how valid a claim to inclusion of all "vital information" about Brecht can be in light of such omissions. Further, the exclusion of Brecht's extensive business correspondence (which, it is true, secretaries often wrote for him) does not make it any less interesting or important. Anyone who knows of Brecht's complex dealings with theatre people, publishers, and intellectuals would have to see these letters to understand the mutual hostilities and unilateral animosity that determined his relationships with many people.

2. This edition makes no attempt to provide extensive, much less comprehensive commentaries on many names and events. Though the dating and location of the letter in manuscript or earlier published form is scrupulously done, a different principle governs names and events. Here the editor claims he identifies them only when "conventional reference works or the texts themselves" are inadequate. Yet dozens of names not readily known to scholars well acquainted with Brecht secondary literature are identified cursorily or not at all. How many, for example, would recognize immediately Ernestine Evans, Princess Bibesco, Max Warburg, The American Guild for German Cultural Freedom, René Schwachhofer, Arnold Ljungdal, Simon Parmet, Jonay Rieger, and many others to whom letters are addressed? A significant amount of detective work remains to be done by scholars before these letters will be useful to anyone wishing to understand them in their full context.

3. Since this collection provides no biographical framework for Brecht's life, its usefulness is limited to those well acquainted with his biography. Nothing, for example, is said about his marriage to Marianne Zoff, about his divorce from her, his marriage to Helene Weigel, the birth of his children by three different women, the beginning of his relationship with Margarete Steffin, and many other biographical facts. Yet knowledge of these facts is essential to understanding many of the letters.

4. In contrast to letters by other significant German writers of this century, most of these were not written for public consumption, nor even for posterity. For the most part these are highly personal expressions. One encounters neither the high degree of stylization nor the self-consciousness of writing for a broader audience found in many letters by Rilke, Hesse, Thomas Mann, *et al.* A notoriously poor letter writer, Brecht often reveals the haste in which he composed many of them. Few letters in this collection exceed one printed page—many tend to be shorter. Filled with abbreviations, vernacularisms, jocular, ironic language, they often reflect his desire to get to the end as quickly as possible. Apodictic statements, elliptical argumentation, or lapidary observations usually take the place of careful discursive reasoning. Just as many of Brecht's poems were occasional poems, the overwhelming number of letters published here were "occasional letters" responding specifically to limited and specific circumstances. With a few exceptions, among them his letters to Karl Korsch, he did not use letters to set forth in detail his views on politics or the theatre. Those he usually saved for essays and longer treatises.

After describing what this collection is not, it must be characterized for what it is—one of the most interesting collections of materials by and on Bertolt Brecht this reviewer has seen published in recent years. One encounters the boiling imagination of a witty, fun-loving young man easily given to boredom who has the remarkable talent to cast one letter in a brilliant parody of the language of the German chancery in the 16th Century (p. 21), another in the form of a Biblical parable (a love letter on pp. 65–66 to Dora Mannheim because she has misunderstood him) and yet another in the form of an impious prayer (p. 78). Most of the earliest letters seem to concentrate on two general topics—the theatre, and his relations to women. Later letters from the mid 1920s on include politics, domestic and extra-marital relations, and literary matters in general, while those from exile expectedly treat personal living circumstances, his anti-fascism, and his reactions to America, ideological quarrels within exile circles, etc.

On page after page one encounters biographical surprises and stylistic delights. There is, for example, an uncharacteristically conciliatory letter to Hanns Johst in which Brecht declares himself willing to delete from his play *Baal* matters that reflect negatively on Johst's play *Der Einsame*, which is known to have provoked Brecht into writing his play in the first place (p.57). Another unexpected discovery comes in a letter to Georg Lukács (there is no information as to whether it was sent) written somewhere toward the end of 1930 (p.156). It raises questions about a literary journal which Lukács, Brecht, and Bernard Brentano had conceived of as a joint enterprise. One is surprised to learn that the so-called "realism debate" with Lukács seems to have begun with an exchange of letters between Brecht and Julius Hay (p.313). Other unexpected discoveries include letters to George Grosz that discuss Brecht's plans to have Grosz illustrate the editions of his plays as well as his *Threepenny Novel* (p.240,953). Repeatedly his letters give testimony of his strong visual imagination. Brecht the *Augenmensch* had to see virtually everything in order to conceptualize it for his writings (he speaks of "visual anecdotes" on p.291). It has not been known to this point that he intended to publish his dramas and prose works with illustrations. Another big surprise comes in a letter Brecht wrote on July 27, 1929, to none other than Gerhart Hauptmann, whom he addresses as "sehr geehrter Herr Doktor Hauptmann" (p.150). In this extraordinarily polite letter he thanks Hauptmann for signing a petition that he had written on behalf of Henri Guilbeaux (whom the editor fails to identify) and invites him to see the performance of his own *Badener Lehrstück* the next evening.

Repeatedly one learns of dealings with figures who were not thought to have played an important role in his personal biography—the Hungarian born playwright Julius Hay (p.313–315) or Lee Strasberg, director of the American Actors Studio and one of the co-founders of the Group Theatre, with whom Brecht discussed an English-language production of his *Measures Taken* (p.284). Brecht also indicates that he watched Strasberg rehearse the Group Theatre in New York in 1935–36. From a footnote to a letter written to Johannes R. Becher, one learns that in 1936 Brecht wants to drop as the title of his published works the designation *Versuche*, which most Brecht scholars have viewed as something of a sacred cow (p.977). Other surprises include two letters to Max Frisch, one to Pablo Picasso, and one to Kurt Hirschfeld in Zürich expressing his interest in Dürrenmatt's play *Romulus der Grosse* and making specific suggestions for how he felt the play (with 5 to 8 pages of revisions) could be strengthened (p.602).

Rilke asserted that fame is based on a series of misunderstandings, but for Brecht, fame was based on a series of manipulations and business dealings. In his letters we see him organizing his fame and promoting himself and his works with breathtaking audacity. When Herbert Jhering proposes that he and Arnolt Bronnen share the Kleist Prize in 1922, he writes Bronnen that he is unwilling to share it, and that Jhering must give them separate prizes in two consecutive years. He then invites Jhering, an established critic in Berlin, to visit the Munich premiere of *Drums in the Night*. Never one to be modest, Brecht's letters constantly badger, cajole, and press others to help him. His tremendous drive for success in the theatre and as a writer makes him emerge as an artistic business entrepreneur, with strong emphasis on the second term. Clearly Brecht drives very hard bargains, and in the letters one sees his unflagging self-confidence and certitude in pushing to get his way. Always on the offensive in promoting his cause, he has no misgivings about asking the very best people to help him.

One also finds another theme almost unique among letter writers known to this reviewer—a near obsession with money that becomes a leitmotif in many letters. In the early years one might attribute this to the near-poverty level at which he subsisted briefly in Munich and Berlin; one might claim that in exile the exigencies of survival demanded that he be concerned with money. But this red thread runs through all his letters, from the earliest to the latest, in times of prosperity or poverty. In a witty letter written to the local Internal Revenue Office (*Finanzamt*) in December of 1927, he explained his refusal to submit an income tax return by claiming he had no tax obligation because as a dramatist, he made an extremely marginal living and was able to subsist only on the advance-on-royalties paid by his publishers. Further, he claimed that since his plays were bringing in no money, he was deeply in debt to his publishers and was living in a small studio in Berlin which he invited them to inspect "if you suspect you will find riches at my place" (p. 131). Someone someday needs to examine more carefully the role that money played in Brecht's personal life as it related to his dramas, which show perhaps more business dealings and money transactions than any 20th century playwright does.

One delights at Brecht's wit in these letters. Few German writers of any age write letters with a greater humor (and, in several cases, self-irony) than he. Word plays, puns, mock indignation, and gross exaggeration for effect are hallmarks of his style. We hear his report that his son Stefan is raising Barbara to be "an orthodox atheist" (p.361). We hear him banter with Ferdinand Reyher in an exchange of letters about a jewel theft in Germany. We hear his witty objection to Friedrich Wolf for misspelling Brecht's given name (p.681), and a mock apology when Wolf reminds him that Wolf's name is misspelled in the book *Theaterarbeit* (Brecht blames it on the publisher).

Another more tender side of Brecht also informs these letters. Besides asking for favors, Brecht is constantly doing them for others. His efforts (pp.305–307) to help get Hans Borchardt released from a concentration camp illuminates a side of his character seldom seen (Borchardt was a political reactionary). A brilliant birthday letter to Alfred Döblin (p.375) states that he is honoring Döblin by the manner in which he borrows from or exploits Döblin works ("Ich kann mich in keiner würdigeren Form als der des Exploiteurs bei Ihnen einstellen"). Just as he asks for favors without the least self-consciousness, he responds in the same matter-of-fact, friendly manner to school children in East Germany following his return there, to Paula Banholzer, the mother of his first child to whom he sends money for support of their son, to unknown writers asking him to read their works, or to actors petitioning for a role in one of his plays. This is the gracious, gentle side of Brecht neglected by his biographers because he himself wanted to downplay it.

Above all one theme dominates these letters—Brecht's life as a man of the theatre. While in London in 1936, he reports to Piscator that he just read Stanislavsky's book *My Life in Art* "mit Neid und Unruhe" (p. 292). One wonders about the sources of envy. His letters are not the place for most of his theatrical theorizing, which he seems to do better in essays, but he cannot resist making observations on the theatre inside and outside Germany. In connection with the theatre, Brecht reveals the contradictions that made him such a complex character. In a number of letters he insists that performances of his plays throughout Germany must be done only on his terms, and yet he allows *The Chalk Circle* to be performed in West Germany without the prologue (something he would not allow in East Germany), for, he claims, the government there would not allow it unless the prologue were deleted (p.752). One also reads his refusal to allow his play *The Measures Taken* to be performed, which he claims was written for those playing it and not for the audience, since it would only evoke a "moral response of a lower order" from the audience (p.778).

After Brecht settles in the GDR, a gradual but distinct transition in the tone and content of the letters confirms that he has become an important public person. Correspondence with his publishers, birthday greetings, condolences to a friend's widow, responses to classes of school children or the Academy of Arts or to government officials inevitably lose the highly personal flavor of most of the earlier letters. And there are now statements intended for publication or clarification of his role as public figure—the full text of the letter of support written to Walter Ulbricht on the occasion of the June 17, 1953 uprisings, or a more detailed account of his position on the uprising stated in a letter a few days later to his publisher Peter Suhrkamp, or letters to Otto Grotewohl critical of the cultural bureaucracy in the DDR.

This fascinating, frustratingly incomplete collection adds new facets and small pieces to the increasingly complex jigsaw puzzle that the life and works of Bertolt Brecht have become, but it does not significantly change the picture. A few matters need attention. The editor is unable to date a letter to Hermann Borchardt (p.329), which clearly dates from 1943 or 1944, but which he places in chronological sequence in 1937. Page 617 credits Brecht with the postscript to a letter which in fact Helene Weigel appended to the letter. The editorial comments need to be expanded by a Brecht scholar in the West who could provide more meaningful commentary on names, dates, and events. Nevertheless this collection shows us another side of the man whose character is still not well understood. Perhaps the most moving document of all, a letter written on May 15, 1955 to the German Academy of Arts, reflects something of the complexity of this fascinating human being who had already become a legend in his own time. Written 15 months before his death, it requests that in case of his death there be no public showing of his body and no graveside speeches. He then formally asks that he be buried in the Huguenot Cemetery next to his apartment. Here for the first time one confronts the great theme that Brecht seemed to have avoided in most of his works after leaving *Baal*—the question of death. For no other reason than the range of emotions and ideas covered in these letters, this collection is an invitation to fascinating study and reading.

James K. Lyon
UC San Diego
LaJolla, California

"Brecht-Studien" — Eine neue Reihe

Das Brecht-Zentrum der DDR, 1978 eröffnet und seither unter der Leitung von Werner Hecht in verschiedenster Weise mit der Brechtpflege befaßt, hat 1980 seinen Tätigkeiten eine neue hinzugefügt. Es veröffentlicht eine Buchreihe unter dem Titel "Brecht-Studien". Bis jetzt liegen vor:

Band 1   Johannes Goldhahn, *Vergnügungen unseres Zeitalters. Bertolt Brecht über Wirkungen künstlerischer Literatur.* 243 Seiten. 1980
Band 2   Gunnar Müller-Waldeck, *Vom "Tui"-Roman zu "Turandot".* 297 Seiten. 1981
Band 3   Inge Häußler, *Denken mit Herrn Keuner. Zur deiktischen Prosa in den Keunergeschichten und Flüchtlingsgesprächen.* 303 Seiten. 1981
Band 4   Monika Hähnel, *Partei und Volk im Verständnis Brechts.* 246 Seiten. 1981
Band 5   Rolf Tauscher, *Brechts Faschismuskritik in Prosaarbeiten und Gedichten der ersten Exiljahre.* 301 Seiten. 1981
Band 8   Christel Hartinger, *Bertolt Brecht - das Gedicht nach Krieg und Wiederkehr. Studien zum lyrischen Werk 1945–1956.* 351 Seiten. 1982 (Diese erste Veröffentlichung des Jahres 1982 erreichte mich zu spät, um in diese Besprechung eingeschlossen zu werden.)

Herausgeber: Brecht-Zentrum der DDR (das wohl auch als Verleger fungiert). Alleinvertriebsrecht: Buchhandlung Brecht, 1040 Berlin, Chausseestraße 125. Preis pro Band: EVP 24.90 Mark.

Eröffnet wird die Reihe mit der Studie eines etablierten Forschers, Johannes Goldhahn (Jahrgang 1926), fortgesetzt wird sie ausschließlich mit Arbeiten einer jüngeren Generation (zwischen 1941 und 1947 geboren). Die Bände 3–5 und 8 sind überarbeitete Dissertationen, Band 2 eine überarbeitete Habilitationsschrift (die in der DDR "Dissertation B" genannt wird). Alle Bücher sind als Manuskript gedruckt, was zumindest potentiell die Veröffentlichung beschleunigen sollte, wenn auch bisher zwischen Fertigstellung der Originalfassung und der Veröffentlichung in dieser Reihe im Schnitt 3–4 Jahre lagen. Das mag an Planungsschwierigkeiten eines neuen Projekts gelegen haben oder an der Überarbeitung. Wie weitgehend diese Überarbeitungen sind, für welche Zielgruppe sie gedacht sind, und wer dafür verantwortlich ist, ist nicht festzustellen. Die wiederkehrende editorische Anmerkung, "Dieser Publikation liegt eine überarbeitete Fassung . . . zugrunde" statt "ist" eine überarbeitete Fassung, läßt die Vermutung zu, daß die Überarbeitungen (der Autoren?) für die Veröffentlichung in dieser Reihe nochmals (vom Herausgeber?) überarbeitet wurden.

Bei aller Uniformität des Äußeren—gleicher schwarz-weißer Einband, auf der Rückseite Kurzbiographie des Autors mit Photo und ein bedeutsames Zitat— sind die Bände alles andere als einheitlich. Der erste Band unterscheidet sich in Stil und Zielrichtung von den nachfolgenden besonders deutlich. Es ist ein langer Essay, der sich an ein allgemeines Publikum wendet, während die weiteren Bände wissenschaftliche Arbeiten sind, die eher andere Brechtwissenschaftler ansprechen. So könnte man auf den ersten Blick vermuten, daß sich im Verlauf des Unternehmens die Konzeption geändert habe. Doch dann fällt auf, daß nicht alle wissenschaftlichen Studien, wie man erwarten würde, eine Bibliographie enthalten. In der Tat, nur die Bände 2 und 5 bringen ein "Literaturverzeichnis", ohne Angabe darüber, ob es ein Verzeichnis der benutzten Literatur ist (vermutlich der Fall in Band 2) oder der wichtigsten, zum Thema gehörigen Literatur (vermutlich der Fall in Band 5). Im letzteren ist das Literaturverzeichnis in gewohnter Weise unterteilt in Primärliteratur, Sekundärliteratur und philosophische, historische und ökonomische Literatur. In Band 2 dagegen sind Primär-, Sekundär-, Sachbuchliteratur, Bibel, Wörterbuch, Texte vom Parteitag, von der Deutschen Wirtschaftskommission und anderes mehr in einer alphabetischen Folge vereint.

Nach diesem Überblick können wir uns den einzelnen Titeln zuwenden, die in der Bandfolge besprochen werden sollen.

Band 1

Goldhahns Studie, *Vergnügungen eines Zeitalters*, trägt alle Merkmale einer Einführung. Wie der Autor in seinem Vorwort darlegt, ging es ihm um eine "Darstellung der Einsichten, Auffassungen und Probleme, die Brecht im Prozeß seiner künstlerischen und kulturpolitischen Praxis—hauptsächlich nach 1945 und in unserem Land—gewann und skizzierte . . . " (S. 13). Für den Nichtfachmann und vielleicht den jungen Leser in der DDR erläutert Goldhahn zunächst den "literarischen Autor" als gesellschaftlichen Menschen, das Zeigen als vorrangiges Merkmal des Brechtschen Stils und den "neuen Leser" als den "tätigen" Leser. Im weiteren ordnet er seine Studie den drei für Brecht charakteristischen Kategorien Produktivität, Naivität und Genuß zu. Interessant dabei die Diskussion von Brechts naiver Darstellungsweise, besonders der Verbindung von Naivität und Gestik.

Der Hauptakzent der Abhandlung liegt auf der Aktualisierung von Brecht. Goldhahn betont, daß die erwähnten Kategorien auch "maßgebende Größen" im Literaturprozeß der DDR sind, "und das vor allem und in allem unter dem Blick *neuartiger Vergnügungen* der freien Menschen unseres sozialistischen und kommunistischen Zeitalters." (S. 17). So dient denn Goldhahns Studie vornehmlich der Festigung der Vorstellung von Brecht als dem Klassiker der DDR, als dem sozialistisch-realistischen Autor *par excellence*—aus der heutigen Sicht. Die Tatsache, daß Brechts ästhetische Ansichten und Praktiken durchaus nicht immer mit der herrschenden Kunstauffassung in der DDR konform gingen, wird mit der sachten Umschreibung von dem "gewiß auch nicht immer unproblematischen" Dichter erledigt.

Westliche Leser brauchen daraus nicht zu schließen, daß das Thema "Brecht und die DDR-Kulturpolitik" in der DDR tabu sei. Müller-Waldeck (Band 2) verschweigt keineswegs, wie schwer sich der Staat in den fünfziger Jahren mit der Einordnung und Wertschätzung Brechts, insbesondere seiner Theaterarbeit, getan hat. Er kann sich dabei auf Werner Mittenzwei berufen, der als erster Brechtforscher in der DDR diese Probleme analysiert hat.

Band 2

Mit seiner umfassenden Behandlung der Tui-Thematik in *Vom "Tui"-Roman zu "Turandot"* hat Gunnar Müller-Waldeck eine verdienstvolle, nützliche und interessante Studie vorgelegt. Kernstück der Arbeit ist die Darstellung und Analyse von Brechts Intellektuellenkritik von den späten zwanziger Jahren über die verschiedenen Schaffensphasen des "Tui"-Romans bis zu dem "Turandot"-Stück und seiner Genesis. Seine erklärte Absicht, von daher "zu zentralen Fragen der ästhetischen Wirkungsstrategie Brechts in ihrem Wandel Stellung [zu] nehmen und ein zentrales Thema des Dichters - seine Intellektuellenkritik - als wichtiges Medium seiner gesellschaftsorientierten Konzeption sichtbar [zu] machen" (S. 15), hat der Verfasser erfolgreich ausgeführt. Dabei zeigt er auch die Flexibilität, mit der der Begriff "Tui" von Brecht gehandhabt worden ist, besonders in dem Teil, in dem er die Betrachtung der Intellektuellenkritik auf andere Werke wie "Der kaukasische Kreidekreis" und "Leben des Galilei" erweitert.

Überraschend, aber einleuchtend, wie Müller-Waldeck das "Turandot"-Stück in einen engen Zeitbezug zu dem Arbeiteraufstand vom 17. Juni 1953 und seinen Hintergründen stellt. Er legt dar, daß in dem Stück die Satire auf Zustände in kapitalistischen Ländern verbunden wird mit einer "Warnung vor Relikten des 'Tuismus' [im eigenen Land], die nicht im Selbstlauf, sondern nur durch Kräftigung der sozialistischen Demokratie zu überwinden sind . . ." (S. 242). Diese Studie ist ein wichtiger Beitrag zur Brechtforschung.

Band 3

Ebenfalls wertvoll für Brechtexperten ist *Denken mit Herrn Keuner* von Inge Häußler. Die Studie untersucht zwei von der Forschung bisher vernachlässigte Werkgruppen, nämlich Problematik und Gestalt der "Geschichten vom Herrn Keuner" und der "Flüchtlingsgespräche".

Am Anfang hätte man sich eine rigorosere Bearbeitung gewünscht. Da finden sich Reste der für Dissertationen (leider) typischen Struktur der kleinsten Schritte: Ankündigung der Absicht, Durchführung der Absicht, Zusammenfassung, und wiederum Ankündigung . . . Doch bald strafft sich der Stil, und die Lektüre wird zum Genuß.

In der genauen Analyse einiger Keunergeschichten kann Häußler beispielhaft für alle die in ihnen enthaltene Dialektik von produktivem Verhalten und eingreifendem Denken herausarbeiten. Durch den Nachweis, daß sich die für Brecht allgemein charakteristischen Stilmerkmale des Zeigens, des Zitierens und der Kombination von Dialektik und Artistik auch in diesen Kleinstformen finden, betont Häußler den Werkcharakter der oft nur als Verlautbarungen von Brechts *alter ego* verstandenen Keunergeschichten.

Ebenso genau und methodisch ist Häußlers Behandlung der "Flüchtlingsgespräche". Anhand einer detaillierten Analyse des ersten Gesprächs bringt sie den Nachweis, daß die Gespräche sowohl inhaltlich als auch in der Gesprächshaltung, also gestisch, dialektisch strukturiert sind. Ihre Analyse macht auf einleuchtende Weise anschaulich, "wie dialektisches Denken auf dialektische Weise vorgeführt wird." (S. 191).

Abschließend werden die methodischen Mittel herausgearbeitet, mit denen Brecht seine Absicht, philosophische Gespräche "auf einer 'niederen' Ebene zu plazieren", ausgeführt hat. Häußlers Abhandlung zeichnet sich aus durch methodische Exaktheit in Verbindung mit einem sehr feinen Gespür für Nuancen in Brechts Stil.

Band 4

In *Partei und Volk im Verständnis Brechts* macht es sich Monika Hähnel zur Aufgabe, am Beispiel Brechts "zu Erkenntnissen über den Zusammenhang von Schaffensprozeß und Wirkungspotenzen unter dem übergreifenden Aspekt ihres Wertes für die sozialistische Persönlichkeitsformung vorzudringen." (S. 11) Die Untersuchung stützt sich - vielleicht sollte man sagen: beschränkt sich - auf die Kriterien "Parteilichkeit" und "Volkstümlichkeit". Da Brecht der Verfasserin als Repräsentant für sozialistischen Realismus gilt, untersucht sie seine Biographie im Hinblick darauf, wann er schon und wann noch nicht Ansätze eines sozialistischen Bewußtseins in Richtung auf Parteilichkeit und Volkstümlichkeit gezeigt hat.

Daß eine Untersuchung dieser Art selber parteilich ist, sollte weder verwundern noch *a priori* gegen sie einnehmen. Hier allerdings ist die Parteilichkeit sehr eng. Brechts Lebens- und Werkgeschichte wird nur auf Äußerungen oder Handlungen durchgekämmt, aus denen hervorgeht, ob und wann Brecht auf

Seiten des Proletariats, der KPD, der Sowjetunion und der KPdSU stand, und dazu wird eine Bewertung gegeben. Die anti-bürgerliche Haltung des jungen Brecht, z.B., wird als Vorstufe zu einem sozialistischen Bewußtsein positiv gewertet. Die Tatsache, daß Brecht niemals der KPD beitrat, wird als mangelnde Parteilichkeit getadelt. Über die frühen Gedichte äußert sich Hähnel so: "Da gibt es 'Balladen', 'Legenden', 'Lieder' - im Sinne von 'Volksliedern', 'Bänkelgesänge', 'Serenaden', 'Choräle', 'Moritaten', 'Songs' - alles im Volk gut bekannte Formen, z.T. seit Jahrhunderten im Gebrauch. Gleichzeitig sind aber die Inhalte neu, gehen somit auch eine neue, sinnvolle, r i c h t i g e Bindung mit den bekannten Formen ein, . . ." (S. 31; Sperrung von mir). Bei der Besprechung der frühen Stücke begründet Hähnel ihre bevorzugte Einschätzung von "Trommeln in der Nacht" folgendermaßen: "So kommt auch das Volk ins Kunstwerk, Amoralismus bietet keine Grundlage für parteiliche und volksverbundene Literatur." (S. 39)

Zur Unterstützung ihrer Thesen geht Hähnel nicht immer historisch-chronologisch vor. Noch macht sie immer deutlich, wo ihre Paraphrasierung von Brechts Gedankengängen aufhört und ihr eigener Kommentar beginnt. Ihre Feststellungen sind verallgemeinernd und in ganz un-Brechtscher Weise idealisierend. So spricht sie z.B., um die Volkstümlichkeit von Grusche und Azdak zu betonen, von deren "hohen menschlichen Eigenschaften" (S. 113), was zumindest Azdak in ein falsches Licht rückt. Im Zusammenhang mit Brechts "Bemühungen um Verständlichkeit" erklärt Hähnel: "Künstlerisches Schaffen bedarf eines tiefen, innerlich empfundenen Anlasses, eines tief verstandenen und empfundenen gesellschaftlichen Auftrags." (S. 146)

Die Arbeit ist auch nicht frei von sachlichen Fehlern; dafür zwei Beispiele. "Brechts Leben während des 1. Weltkrieges ist das eines gewöhnlichen Soldaten." (S. 21). Büchner und Grabbe werden als Dramatiker des Sturm und Drang bezeichnet (S. 30). Schließlich beeinträchtigen auch zahlreiche sprachliche Mängel und orthographische Fehler den Gesamteindruck; ein Beispiel für beides: "Wie erst später formuliert wird, verwirklicht BRECHT hier, daß volkstümliche Kunst gleichzeitig Spielraum für Neues, das bekannte Ergänzende gewähren müsse." (S. 31)

Band 5

Mit der Studie *Brechts Faschismuskritik in Prosaarbeiten und Gedichten der ersten Exiljahre* greift Rolf Tauscher ein wichtiges und umstrittenes Thema auf, nämlich inwieweit Brecht das Wesen des Nationalsozialismus richtig erkannt und dargestellt hat. Die Abhandlung umfaßt drei Teile. Im ersten werden die verschiedenen verstreuten Äußerungen von Brecht zum Faschismus zusammengetragen, sodaß sich eine Art Geschichte der Entstehung von Brechts Antifaschismus und der Aspekte seiner Faschismussicht ergeben soll. Im zweiten Teil werden einige Prosasatiren untersucht, also Beispiele von Brechts praktischer Aufklärungsarbeit gegen den Faschismus besprochen. Dies wird im letzten Teil anhand ausgewählter antifaschistischer Gedichte fortgesetzt.

So interessant und wichtig das Thema ist, die Ausführung der Studie bleibt hinter den Erwartungen zurück. Ist es einerseits der Verdienst des ersten Teils, die verstreut publizierten Äußerungen von Brecht zum Thema Faschismus zusammengetragen zu haben, so wird andrerseits der Begriff 'Faschismuskritik' so weit gefaßt, daß ein großer Teil der zusammengestellten Texte Überlegungen Brechts zur Dialektik, zum Denken, zum Verhalten, zu den Besitzverhältnissen, zur Ausbeutung und anderes mehr sind. Damit wird die Frage, wieweit Brecht über die ökonomische Analyse hinaus das Wesen des Faschismus erkannt hat, zwar angereichert, aber nicht befriedigend beantwortet.

Umso gespannter ist man auf die Teile, in denen Brechts antifaschistische Aufklärungsarbeit anhand von künstlerischen Texten behandelt wird. Tauscher definiert zunächst die Selbstdarstellungen der Faschisten als "Perversion" und betont, daß es Brecht in seiner Aufklärung darum ging, die "Wahrheit wiederherzustellen". Anstatt nun herauszuarbeiten, mit welchen Mitteln, Themen, Gesten Brecht in den einzelnen Texten versuchte, die Wahrheit wiederherzustellen und das Denken des Lesers zu provozieren, überlädt Tauscher seine Untersuchungen mit einem Wust von nebensächlichen Hinweisen, in dem die wichtigen Aussagen untergehen. In seinem Kommentar zu der Satire "Eine Befürchtung", zum Beispiel, bemüht er sich um den Nachweis, daß der "Redner" mit Brecht identisch ist. Die Versicherung des Redners, er habe im ersten Weltkrieg nicht an der allgemeinen Kriegsbegeisterung teilgenommen, bezieht Tauscher auf Brecht, indem er an dessen berühmten Aufsatz zum Thema "Dulce et decorum . . ." erinnert und auf unterstützende Aussagen von Brechts Mitschülern verweist. Dann zitiert er den Redner mit dem Satz "Dabei war mein Ideal auf Grund meiner Erziehung der erste Napoleon . . .," ergänzt dies durch ein Zitat aus *Brecht in Augsburg* über Brechts Begeisterung für Napoleon: "Dessen [d.h. Napoleons] Konterfei und Schlachtpläne . . . hingen an den Wänden des Zimmers." und ergänzt "Gemeint ist Brechts Mansardenzimmer, das er als Schüler bewohnte." (S. 113)

Diese Verankerung im Autobiographischen trägt nicht nur nichts zum Verständnis der Satire oder ihrer Wertschätzung bei, sondern sie zerstört auch den Genuß an der Ironie. Hinzu kommt, daß er sie ernst nimmt, statt sie gegen den Strich zu lesen. Wer zöge es da nicht vor, die Satiren für sich, ohne Tauscher, zu lesen? Ähnlich verfährt der Autor mit den antifaschistischen Gedichten. Wiederum gibt er eine Menge Hinweise, aber die Analyse von Brechts antifaschistischer Aufklärungsarbeit und ihrer möglichen Effektivität bleibt er uns schuldig. So kann diese Studie wohl in erster Linie Antrieb sein für eine konkretere und methodisch sicherere Behandlung von Brechts Faschismuskritik.

Trotz der angemerkten Qualitätsunterschiede in den individuellen Bänden, die uns auf die Frage nach den Bearbeitungsprinzipien und nach der Zielgruppe oder den "Adressaten" der Reihe "Brecht-Studien" zurückführen, ist ihr Erscheinen zu begrüßen. Die Reihe stellt relevante Themen zur Diskussion, macht mit dem Forschernachwuchs bekannt und gibt Aufschluß darüber, wie sich die Brechtforschung in der DDR entwickeln wird. Zur Zeit scheinen dort Fragen der Rezeption und Rezeptionsfähigkeit von Brechts Werken den Vorrang zu haben, sie wurden von mehreren Autoren behandelt. Das könnte den Gedankenaustausch mit westlichen Brechtforschern anregen. Wir sehen den weiteren "Brecht-Studien" des Brecht-Zentrums mit Interesse und Aufmerksamkeit entgegen.

Gisela Bahr
Miami University
Oxford, Ohio

Jan Needle and Peter Thomson. *Brecht.* Chicago: The University of Chicago Press, Oxford: Basil Blackwell, 1981.

Ausgehend von der Wirkungsgeschichte Brechts, die sich zwischen seiner Etablierung als klassisches Vorbild und seiner besonders in England anhaltenden Umstrittenheit widersprüchlich entfaltet, haben sich Jan Needle und Peter Thomson das begrüßenswerte Ziel gesetzt, jenseits aller Verherrlichung oder Verunglimpfung eine Neubewertung der Brechtschen Stücke zu liefern, die besonders seine dramentheoretischen wie aufführungspraktischen Überlegungen berücksichtigt. Leider ist dieser eher von *common sense* als von einem reflektierten Methodenbewußtsein geleitete Versuch nicht, wie die Autoren selber apologetisch eingestehen, frei von Inkonsistenzen (S. xv).

Das erste Kapitel ist eine wohl berechtigte, aber oft übermäßig polemische Abrechnung mit der Rezeption Brechts in England und den USA. Sie ist besonders im erstgenannten Land charakterisiert durch die Ignoranz und Böswilligkeit vornehmlich der Theaterkritiker, die immer noch die von Brecht als kulinarisch und aristotelisch bekämpfte Dramennorm gegen seine Theaterkonzeption ausspielen. Nicht zuletzt scheint es diese britische Brechtmisere zu sein, die die Autoren veranlaßt hat, die vorliegende durchaus kritische Rehabilitierung des Stückeschreibers zu präsentieren. Der wirkungsgeschichtliche Ansatz, der besonders für die theaterpraktische Neubewertung Brechts hätte fruchtbare Anregungen bringen können, indem er etwa konsequent die Struktur der Dramen mit neueren internationalen Musteraufführungen zu korrelieren versuchte, wird allerdings leider nicht durchgehalten. Er weicht in den folgenden Kapiteln vielmehr einer stark inhaltsbezogenen, chronologischen Diskussion der Stücke selbst, die häufig aufschlußreich mit der Zeitgeschichte und den theoretischen Schriften Brechts in Beziehung gesetzt werden. Dabei leidet nicht nur das zweite Kapitel über die frühen Stücke unter allzu flotten Werturteilen, so zum "pretty feeble play" *Trommeln in der Nacht:* "The story is extremely thin, and to spread it over five acts was ridiculously hopeful" (S. 27). Das führt sogar zu recht peinlichen "Verbesserungsvorschlägen" der Autoren: "Had he chosen to write it [*Im Dickicht der Städte*] as a long poem, some of its major areas of failure would probably have been successfully transformed. In the play, the suspicion of pretentiousness is hard to avoid." (S. 31). Fragwürdig ist auch, wenn die Autoren bei der Diskussion von *Trommeln in der Nacht* die eigene Skepsis dem Kommunismus gegenüber als Wertungsfaktor mit einbringen. Brechts nachträgliche Einsicht in das seiner Ansicht nach ideologisch "falsche" Portrait Kraglers stellen sie als "actually 'right' " hin: "Even among people who still believe communism to be a way forward, it is the element of naive Utopianism . . . that sticks in the gills." Brechts zynische Schilderung sei nämlich durchaus "clear-sighted" gewesen (S. 27).

Überhaupt verstehen die Autoren Brecht allzu oft besser, als er sich (angeblich) selber verstanden hat. Ohne die inhärente politische Intention der Lehrstücke zu verneinen, sehen sie deren eigentlichen Wert in der "massive and all-pervading ambiguity," die Brechts Verständnis des Marxismus als Infragestellung verhärteter Denkformen reflektiert, nicht in der direkten ideologischen Aussage, wodurch eine enge Interpretation der Stücke als "tracts, propaganda, or even polemic" vereitelt wurde. Dies sei eine Tatsache, die Brecht selber nicht habe verstehen können (S. 78f.). Später, bei der Besprechung der *Heiligen Johanna der Schlachthöfe,* postulieren die Autoren das "communist dilemma," welches—"stated at its simplest, . . . is the weird idea that the poor are good and the rich evil"—

der Grund sei für die Mischung aus Ambiguität und Verwirrung der Stücke jener Zeit. Brecht habe diese "simplistic equation" zwar ständig wiederholt, aber nicht eigentlich an sie geglaubt. Unterstellt wird, daß "his confusion was between his own awareness of what might be called existential despair, and his belief that Marxism offered a way out" (S. 87). Brechts politische Intentionen aber sind nicht von seiner Einsicht in die existentiellen Problem der *condition humaine* abzutrennen, denn die Struktur seiner Stücke zumindest seit der Lehrstückphase ist gerade dadurch bestimmt, daß ethische und existentielle Fragen für ihn nur dann Berechtigung haben, wenn sie mit der marxistischen Perspektive verbunden sind.

Weitaus fundierter dagegen sind spätere Kapitel wie das über "Brecht's Theory of Theatrical Performance" (6), die ausführliche Analyse des Couragemodells (7) und die Erörterung von "Brecht's Dramaturgy" (9). Auch wenn man (nicht nur hier) eine Auseinandersetzung mit wichtigen Positionen besonders der neueren deutschsprachigen Brechtforschung vermißt, etwa der Kontroverse um Steinwegs Lehrstücktheorie, so bieten doch diese Abschnitte fruchtbare Einsichten weniger für die akademische Forschung als für die angewandte Theaterpraxis. Hierin sehe ich den eigentlichen Wert von Needles und Thomsons engagierter Darstellung: sie trägt vielleicht—hoffentlich!—dazu bei, daß Brechts Stücke besonders in England und den USA authentischere Aufführungen und eine breitere Wirkung erleben, als es ihnen bisher zuteil wurde.

Rolf J. Goebel
University of Alabama
Huntsville

Klaus-Detlef Müller. *Brecht-Kommentar zur erzählenden Prosa.* München: Winkler, 1980.

Die Rezeptionsgeschichte von Brechts Schaffen wurde lange Zeit weitgehend von der Aufnahme seiner Theaterstücke und der Dramentheorie beherrscht. So berechtigt dieses Interesse ist, so vernachlässigte es doch entscheidend neben der lyrischen vor allem die erzählerische Leistung dieses Autors. Denn Brechts Modernität stellt sich nicht zuletzt dadurch unter Beweis, daß er in der kritischen Auseinandersetzung mit tradierten Formen des Erzählens—bürgerlicher Roman, Parabel oder Kalendergeschichte—innovative Prosatechniken entwickelte, die zur Realisierung eines Realismusbegriffes dienen, bei dem es nicht um die einfühlend-psychologische Schilderung individueller Problematik geht, sondern um die distanziert analytische Erhellung historischer und gesellschaftlicher Zusammenhänge. Die einseitige Rezeptionsperspektive auf Brechts Werk auch bei einem breiteren Lesepublikum zu korrigieren, dazu kann Klaus-Detlef Müllers ausgezeichnete, von solider Sachkenntnis und sicherem interpretatorischen Urteil getragene, erstmalige Gesamtdiskussion des Prosawerks entscheidend beitragen. Die Einleitung des Buches verfolgt vor allem die Entwicklung von Brechts erzähltheoretischen Überlegungen und setzt damit den Rahmen für die Einzelkommentierung der Romane, Erzählungen und Kurzprosa. Dabei liegt der Schwerpunkt der Erörterungen verständlicherweise auf der Exilprosa, zwangen doch die veränderten Produktions- und Rezeptionsverhältnisse jener Zeit, die eine kontinuierliche Theaterarbeit unmöglich machten, zu einer intensiveren Beschäftigung mit den Möglichkeiten vor allem des Romans. 'Zuverlässig informiert Müller über Entstehungsdaten und zeichnet die Genese der Prosaarbeiten nach. Dabei finden besonders für die größeren Werke die Verbindungen zu den zahlreichen Quellen und Vorbildern—positiven wie negativen—breiten Raum. So werden die komplexen Akte der produktiven Umbildung und kritischen Auseinandersetzung mit dem Vorgefundenen deutlich, die für Brechts Schaffensprozeß so charakteristisch sind. So schließt das *Me-ti*-Kapitel einen aufschlußreichen Überblick über Mo-tzu ein, um nur ein Beispiel herauszugreifen. Erhellung findet auch der Stellenwert des jeweiligen Textes im Gesamtwerk des Autors, wie etwa die Beziehung der Figur des Herrn Keuner zu dem Komplex der Lehrstücke. Müllers Kommentar beschränkt sich jedoch keineswegs auf solche ungemein hilfreichen Hintergrundinformationen, sondern bietet darüber hinaus präzise argumentierende Interpretationen, die nicht nur den Gehalt zur Sprache kommen lassen, sondern besonderes Schwergewicht auf die vielfältigen Erzähltechniken und die formalen Strukturen legen, in denen sich schließlich Brechts innovative Kunstleistung deutlich manifestiert. Der Leser, der sich etwa an die erste Lektüre des *Dreigroschenromans* macht, wird dankbar Müllers ausführlicher Entwirrung der von Brecht so kunstvoll verschlungenen Fäden der Karriere Macheaths und des Coaxschen und Peachumschen Schiffsgeschäfts folgen. Obwohl das Buch kein eigentlicher Forschungsbericht sein will, setzt sich des Verfasser auch mit einigen wichtigen Positionen der Sekundärliteratur auseinander. Leider konnte die Forschung nur bis zum Jahre 1978 berücksichtigt werden, die zitierte Literatur ist in einer 134 Titel umfassenden Bibliographie zusammengestellt. Es bleibt, die Hoffnung zu wiederholen, daß Müllers Kommentar eine breite Aufnahme auch über die akademische Forschung hinaus findet, vor allem bei Studenten und in der Schule, könnten doch nicht nur der *Dreigroschenroman* und die *Geschichten vom Herrn Keuner,* immerhin schon einem größeren Lesepublikum bekannt, die vielbeklagte Brecht-Müdigkeit wieder vertreiben.

Rolf J. Goebel
University of Alabama
Huntsville

Linda Thomas. *Ordnung und Wert der Unordnung bei Bertolt Brecht.* Bern-Frankfurt am Main-Las Vegas: Peter Lang, 1979. Pp. 141. Cloth. Fr. 28.—

Thomas suggests interpretations worthy of consideration in her discussion of some Brecht plays (especially *Leben des Galilei* and *Der kaukasische Kreidekreis*), but her central hypothesis is unpersuasive. Questioning Brecht's changing attitude toward *Ordnung, Unordnung,* and *Ordnungssysteme,* Thomas maintains that his early works reveal a positive view of *Unordnung* that then yields to an accepting attitude toward *Ordnung* in the *Lehrstücke.* This latter assessment, in turn, switches in the later plays to a final, negative approach to *Ordnung* and *Ordnungssysteme* in general. The trouble is, Thomas is unusually ill-equipped to assess the influence of Brecht's Marxism upon his total outlook after the late twenties, causing her arguments to break down completely. She is at a loss to clarify Brecht's feelings about the Soviet Union or about international communism.

A few specific points: One of her main contentions is that Brecht's disappointment with the German proletariat's failure to rise up against Hitler, rather than the bombing of Hiroshima, compelled him to rewrite *Galilei,* changing the scientist from a positive figure who resisted the prevailing order into a man who, like the German workers, goes along with little resistance. Her point may have some validity, but Thomas overlooks the origin of Brecht's position when she generalizes: "Der von Bertolt Brecht durchlaufene Prozeß ist nicht aus intellektuellen Einflüssen, aus von außen an ihn herangetragenen Weltanschauungen oder Ideologien herzuleiten, sondern spiegelt seine individuelle Bewältigung der Erfahrungen des Zeitalters wider" (p. 13). Thomas is completely unaware that the notion of a "different Germany" comprising millions of disaffected workers and ordinary citizens ready to rise up against Hitler and the fascist hirelings of big capital was a dogma in the KPD throughout the Hitler years. This myth sprang directly from an official Soviet-KPD theory of fascism that equated Nazism with moribund imperialist monopoly capitalism. Because the National Socialists defended only the interests of German capital, the masses were bound eventually to see through the demagogy and throw off the fascist yoke, or so the Communists thought. This party-wide delusion was shared by Brecht and certainly helped produce his disappointment when the workers failed to act as Marxist-Leninist-Stalinist theory had been telling him they would. Brecht, after all, subscribed to the official Communist view of fascism (in a remark that Thomas quotes [p. 48], Brecht wrote: "Der Faschismus ist eine historische Phase, in die der Kapitalismus eingetreten ist. . . . Der Kapitalismus existiert in den faschistischen Ländern nur noch als Faschismus, und der Faschismus kann nur bekämpft werden, als Kapitalismus."). But the politics involved in Brecht's thinking and in his work are a closed book to Thomas.

That Brecht took a negative view of fascist or fascistic *Ordnungssysteme,* then, is hardly a surprising discovery, but Thomas goes on to argue that "after 1939" (how about earlier? What was special about 1939?) Brecht saw in Russia too a suspect *Ordnungssystem*—a country that "in vielen Beziehungen sich wenig von den imperialistischen kapitalistischen Ländern unterschied" (p. 33). Thomas owes us some proof of that startling conclusion, but she fails consistently to provide anything resembling a total picture of Brecht and the USSR, which is necessary if we are to test the validity of her claims against all that is known about Brecht's political stance. How can Thomas write about Brecht and the Soviet Union and ignore *Me-ti?* She appears likewise oblivious to the existence of Brecht's writings on the USSR, the show trials, collectivization, and so on published in volumes XIX and XX of the collected works.

Finally, Thomas takes the position that Brecht's "bad experience" with the *Ordnungssysteme* of his time brought about a "Ratlosigkeit" with regard to the system best suited for mankind. Because Brecht's later plays ostensibly showed *Ordnung* only negatively, Thomas concludes: "Brecht sah sich zu keiner Zeit seiner literarischen Tätigkeit in der Lage, die geforderte neue Welt darzustellen, weil er selbst an eine solche Welt nicht glaubte" (p. 13). Here again Thomas indulges in a sweeping generalization that she cannot prove. How would she deal with the following remark by Brecht, just chosen by me at random: "Die Trennung Deutschlands ist eine Trennung zwischen dem Alten und dem Neuen. Die Grenze zwischen DDR und Bundesrepublik scheidet den Teil, in dem das Neue, der Sozialismus, die Macht ausübt, von dem Teil, in dem das Alte, der Kapitalismus regiert" (*GW,* VIII, 552-53). Thomas' treatment of Brecht's attitude toward East

Germany (she refers frequently to the "DDR" in 1946, 1947, and 1948), explained in a scant two pages, is accordingly highly suspect. Citing some comments that Brecht made in his *Arbeitsjournal*, Thomas tells us "daß Brecht sich in der DDR nicht wohl fühlte und das lang gesuchte Ordnungssystem auch dort nicht fand" (p. 50). That is utter nonsense; of course he had reservations; he had them about Soviet Russia too, but none of these concerns and doubts ever led him seriously to consider breaking with official communism in its Soviet or East German form. Now there may well be a point in looking at the plays to ascertain whether or not they illustrate what we can piece together of Brecht's politics, but this has to be a fruitless undertaking for a scholar so hopelessly lost in the world of Brecht's political thinking.

David Pike
University of North Carolina at Chapel Hill

James K. Lyon. *Bertolt Brecht in America*. Princeton: Princeton University Press, 1980. 408 pages (illustrated), $ 19.75.

In 1924, young Bertolt Brecht, poet and winner of the coveted Kleist Prize, set out to conquer Berlin and—succeeded. When, in 1941, as an accomplished playwright and a seasoned refugee from Hitler's Germany, he took up residence in America determined to take Broadway by storm, he—failed. This noble failure is part of the fascinating tale of *Bertolt Brecht in America* by James K. Lyon.

Lyon's rare sense of construction leads him away from a chronological approach towards thematic structure.

For Professor Lyon, distinguished scholar of literature, Brecht is "not only the most gifted and important German writer in the twentieth century . . . he is one of the greatest writers of our century in any language." When, in perusing the numerous biographies in existence, he detected "how little was known about the years Brecht spent in America," he resolved to close this yawning gap. At his disposal were not only Brecht's literary works, most of the great plays written in exile, hundreds of poems (some of haunting beauty), letters—more than the reluctant correspondent had written at any time of his life—, his workjournals, the faithfully kept diaries, and last not least the FBI's file. Each one of these sources is utilized in painstaking research. I venture to say that no more authoritative work has yet been done on "the Einstein of the new theatre," as the revolutionary dramatist was once called.

It was a daring new theatre concept Brecht had introduced to the Berlin of the twenties, Europe's most fertile cultural soil. However, the new theories, even slow in being adapted on his homeground, were completely unacceptable to what Brecht called the "culinary fare of the Broadway theatres." Moreover, any attempt made by friends to open the door for his "epic theatre," was ruined by his own uncompromising attitude. The insistence on total control over casting and performance of his plays forestalled production.

Brecht was a superbly prepared stage director, perhaps second only to the celebrated Max Reinhardt, from whom he had learned more than he himself realized.

Only once, as an exile in Los Angeles, "the mortuary of easy going," did he get everything his way, in the epoch-making Hollywood production of *Galileo*. With Charles Laughton as the most extraordinary collaborator in writing, translating, acting and co-directing, he worked through three full years of planning and eventually rehearsing the play. Lyon devotes thirty-four pages to this crowning achievement, lending perpetuity to a fleeting theatre event never easy to capture in narration. Lyon's detailed description of the show is a highlight of his book. And it seems that for once Brecht himself was pleased. In a letter to a friend, Ferdinand Reyher, his mentor in experiencing New York and America, he could write about *Galileo* in Hollywood: "The stage and the production were strongly reminiscent of the *Schiffbauerdamm Theater in Berlin,* as was the intellectual part of the audience." Lyon adds that, "in large measure this was a consequence of Brecht's being able for the first time on American soil to stage a production completely on his own terms."

Brecht had always complained of the lack of a stage he needed to write effectively, to help visualize what he wanted to write. In John Houseman's Coronet Theatre he had found it. *Galileo* opened on July 30, 1947, and was promptly slated for Broadway. Ironically it was scheduled for a date when Brecht would have already left the country. While his craving for a Broadway production had become tantalizingly close to fulfilment, the playwright was detained by another assignment, his last in America.

In no other publication has his voluntary appearance before the House Committee on Un-American Activities in Washington been given so much space and intelligent interpretation as by James Lyon. To read in gripping detail how, with great care, Brecht rehearsed and practically wrote the "show" in which he cast himself as the leading actor, and how he then performed according to his own text is reminiscent of other trial scenes in his own work. Like his Galileo he outsmarted the institution that tried hard to control him. Like Galileo, he came out on top in his fight against the establishment. By cunningly admitting what the Committee wanted to hear, he won a commendation, as a "friendly witness."

Now, he was in a hurry to leave an America once the land of his dreams that during his stay too often had turned into a nightmare.

In his baggage he carried the manuscript of his constantly revised masterpieces from *Mother Courage and her Children* to *The Good Person of Setzuan* and *The Caucasian Chalk Circle,* all of which would be given final form in his own theatre. To this task he devoted the last years of his life, thereby creating the soon to be world famous "Berliner Ensemble."

All this, and much more about Brecht, the philosopher, the Marxist, the Antifascist, the sociologist, the zealous teacher, and the complex human being, is contained in James Lyon's magnificent book—a book of survival rather than of exile; verily, a moving requiem for a genius.

William W. Melnitz
University of California
Los Angeles

Pike, David, *German Writers in Soviet Exile, 1933–1945*. Chapel Hill, University of North Carolina Press (1982). 448 pp. $29.50.

The truly astonishing thing about this large and extremely valuable book is the fact that David Pike was even allowed to look at the unpublished materials on which the book is so solidly based. Central to the Pike book are resources generally thought to be inaccessible. Yet Pike (and this is a long and fascinating story in itself), was given access to absolutely extra-ordinary unpublished materials not only in Moscow but in Budapest and the German Democratic Republic also. Then, once he had carefully combed the unpublished materials, he was able to complete his panoramic picture by use of extensive interviews and by the use of published but often inaccessible materials in Moscow's Lenin Library. The result of all this detective work is the very best book we have on German/Soviet relations in an absolutely crucial historical period. If you would understand the shaping of the German Democratic Republic you must read this book. The title of the book leads one to imagine that Pike's concern is exclusively with writers, but in fact as he understands under the heading of "writers" not only people such as Becher, Wolf and Brecht, but Ulbricht, Pieck and Lukács the book delivers far more than the title promises. Not only does the book deal thoroughly with the period 1933–1945, but it also provides a surprisingly thorough analysis of the relationship of the Comintern to German communists in the 1918–1933 period. This contribution is vital if one is to understand the complexities of the 1933–45 period. Then again, so thorough is the analysis of events in the exile period that one can see in embryo events that will only develop fully in the German Democratic Republic in the post 1945 period. It is this exhaustive contextual presentation, this piling up of facts that is essential to the book's whole argument.

Where other books on the German exiles largely speculate on what may or may not have happened and why, Pike provides facts. If one might imagine, for instance, that *Das Wort* collapsed because of difficulties in communication between Moscow and the three Western European editors of the journal, one is speedily disabused of this by Pike who checks the dates on which letters were sent and received and finds that mail moved at least as promptly then as it does now. Once having established that mail delivery did not contribute to the demise of *Das Wort*, Pike is then able to deal responsibly with the role of Mikhail Koltsov who had authorized the publication of *Das Wort* and whose own demise on December 12, 1938, really signalled the end of *Das Wort*. This one example of detective work illustrates a central technique of Pike's book: find the facts and lay out those facts no matter where they may lead. If the files reveal highly unflattering things about Stalin or Ulbricht so be it says Pike and sets forth the facts. The technique is a courageous one and Pike is absolutely unflinching in setting forth details.

Another example of Pike's technique is what is revealed about the relationship of Brecht to Walter Ulbricht, Alfred Kurella and Julius Hay. Though many scholars have known that there was no love lost between Brecht and Hay and Ulbricht, specifics on the set of relationships have been hard to come by. It now becomes clear from Pike's book that Ulbricht was directly involved with Kurella in consciously attempting to trap Brecht into risking his very life by making indiscreet remarks in Soviet journals. From earlier published accounts we know that Julius Hay had sought to goad Brecht into entering the deadly debate on "Realism," but we can now see that Alfred Kurella and Walter Ulbricht were also involved in this. As Pike notes, on June 8, 1938, Alfred Kurella, Fritz Erpenbeck's Moscow stand-in for de facto editor of *Das Wort*, writes to Erpenbeck in Yalta:

Quickly a new intermezzo: the enclosed letter from Brecht just arrived. Tahu-tata! Now the cat sticks his head out of the bag. Especially in the postscriptum. (Incidentally: you had a good nose when you asked Lukács to soften the Eisler passage.) . . . To the point: as I already telegraphed, I think we have to give in out of formal considerations. Formally he is correct that articles can appear in the journal in the name of the editorial board only if none of the editors have any objections . . . I hope you concur. I'll give a copy of the letter to Walter and will also speak with him and see how we should react. The crux of the matter is: at any rate he is now so "stimulated" that he will write for sure. And that is a gain however you look at it.

The "Walter" referred to is Walter Ulbricht, future head of the government of the German Democratic Republic. The trap being set for Brecht is absolutely deadly. After being "stimulated" (shades of Pavlov's research methods!), if Brecht comes out for "Realism" then Erpenbeck and Kurella have coopted him to their narrow position. If he comes out against "Realism" he can be clearly tarred with the same brush as the "Formalists" who have all been either murdered or otherwise silenced at the time Kurella (generally acknowledged to have been an NKVD stoolpigeon) writes the savage letter quoted above. It is Kurella and Erpenbeck and Ulbricht who stick their necks out here. It is clear that they deliberately conspired to achieve Brecht's downfall. How much of this did Brecht know when he returned in 1948 to a state headed by Walter Ulbricht where the two leading newspaper critics were Kurella and Erpenbeck, and where "the leading playwright" (to whose play, *Haben* Brecht was taken immediately after his return from exile!) was deemed to be none other than Julius Hay! If one knows this background it helps enormously in understanding Brecht's own complex position vis-à-vis the GDR and its leaders.

But the trap set for Brecht by jealous rivals is but a tiny part of a vast mosaic put together by Pike. The mosaic as a whole adds an extraordinary chapter to the complex history of the wave of terror associated with the name of Stalin's chief of internal security, Nikolaj Ezhov, the wave called in the USSR, the Ezhovshchina. In Chapter Eleven of his book Pike reconstructs the detailed horror of "Stalin's Purge of Germans." This chapter is such a dense chronicle of horror that it ranks (as Hans Mayer has also observed) with Nadezhda Mandelstam's *Hope Against Hope.* You must have a very strong stomach indeed to read this chapter where detail is piled upon detail as body was piled upon body in the mass graves of the Soviet Union's very own holocaust, the Gulag. Either tumbled into mass graves in the USSR or shipped back across the frontier to the waiting Gestapo, the German communist intelligentsia was virtually wiped out except for those few whose sinuousness or pure luck or guile saved them.

If you survive the reading of Chapter eleven, as a finale Pike offers a chapter on those Germans who survive the thirties and who work hard in the Soviet Union during the war to bring about a Nazi defeat. There are tales of horror here again but tales of heroism also. Once one emerges from this final chapter one has been enlightened in a radically unusual way to historical circumstances that continue to shape our contemporary reality. This is an enormous achievement between the covers of just one book.

John Fuegi
University of Maryland
College Park

Patty Lee Parmalee, *Brecht's America, With a Foreword by John Willett* (Columbus, Ohio: Ohio State University Press for Miami University, 1981), 306 Seiten.

Wie bei kaum einem anderen hat Amerika auf Brecht mythenbildend gewirkt. Die Faszination des Stückeschreibers für Amerika, für ihn seiner Zeit gemäß synonym mit den USA, war so überdeutlich, daß wie bei allem Selbstverständlichen erst relativ spät die genaueren Untersuchungen einsetzten. Die jetzt vorliegenden Ergebnisse geben dem zunächst einfach erscheinenden Sachverhalt eine Komplexität wieder, die jener Widersprüchlichkeit entspricht, die Amerika als Land, Gesellschaft und Lebensform eigen ist, die aber auch Brechts Beziehung dazu charakterisiert.

Parmalees Studie hat ihre Vorgeschichte, die 1968 mit den Arbeiten zu ihrer 1970 abgeschlossenen Dissertation begann. Zugänglich machte sie damals viele Materialien aus dem Brecht-Archiv, Interviewauswertungen der Gespräche mit Prominenten des Brecht-Kreises (vor allem Helene Weigel, Elisabeth Hauptmann, Herta Ramthun, Werner Hecht u.a.) und Forschungsergebnisse zu den amerikanischen Quellen vieler Stücke Brechts. Das fundierte nach dem ersten größeren Ansatz bei Barbara M. Glauert zum Amerikabild Brechts (M.A. These, 1961) eine umfassende, materialreiche Darstellung, deren Ziel die Brechtsche Faszination für Amerika bis zum Jahre 1931 war. Undenkbar erschien Parmalee der Brecht der Zwanziger Jahre ohne die Amerikaauseinandersetzung, so wie Brechts Weiterentwicklung ohne die marxistische Wende von 1926 unbegreifbar ist. Paralleles ergab sich aus der 1972 von Helfried W. Seliger fertiggestellten Dissertation über Brechts Amerikabild, 1974 auch in Buchform erhältlich. (Rez. von B. Glauert, Brecht-Jahrbuch 1976, 205-211) Mißlich war, daß Seliger Parmalees Dissertation entweder nicht kannte oder einzuarbeiten verschmähte. Immerhin legte seine Arbeit den ganzen Weg von Brechts Amerikafaszination bis zu seiner Amerikamüdigkeit und späteren klaren Distanzierung zurück, also auch den Zeitraum des Exils und der Rückkehr bis zu Brechts Tod. Bleibt der Wert von Seligers Arbeit umstritten, so ist Parmalees vorliegende Studie dadurch in ihrem Anspruch beeinträchtigt, als ihre Revision der Dissertation nicht den wünschenswerten neusten Stand der Dinge erreicht hat. Denn weder Seliger findet sich wirklich eingearbeitet, noch ist der neuen Situation, die vor allem seit James K. Lyons Beiträgen existiert (besonders *B. Brecht in America,* 1980; *B. Brecht's American Cicerone,* 1978; *B. Brecht's Hollywood Years,* 1971–72) voll Rechnung getragen.

Parmalees *Brecht's America* ist also etwas Altes und Neues, und die vorliegende Mischung ist deshalb nicht sehr überzeugend. Symptomatisch ist in diesem Zusammenhang, daß die Autorin Breon Mitchells Besprechung ihrer Dissertation (Brecht-Jahrbuch 1975, 180–183) nicht zur Kenntnis genommen hat, was umso bedauerlicher ist, als dort sehr berechtigte kritische Einwände erhoben werden (z.B. gegen die These von der Konstanz des Brechtschen Amerikabildes nach 1931) und einleuchtende Vorschläge sich finden (Plazierung von Brechts Amerikainteresse in den Kontext des deutschen Amerikabildes seit dem 18. Jahrhundert oder doch zumindest die Einbeziehung der zeitgenössischen Amerikavorstellungen in den Zwanziger Jahren).

Die zeitliche Begrenzung ihrer Arbeit bis zum Jahre 1931 versucht Parmalee mit ihrem Hauptinteresse an der Interaktion von Brechts Amerikabild und seinen Marxismusstudien zu rechtfertigen, genauer gesagt, ihre Hauptthese erklärt, daß die Desillusionierung von Brechts Amerikafaszination 1926 seine Marxlektüre verursacht habe. Mit einem bloßen Hinweis auf Seligers und Lyons Darstellungen entledigt sich Parmalee dann der jetzt eigentlich anstehenden Gesamtaufgabe, die umso interessanter hätte ausfallen dürfen, als Seligers Ergebnisse einer Weiterführung bedürfen und Lyons Ziel ohnehin mehr im Biographischen liegt. Nicht zu teilen vermag ich deshalb Parmalees Enthusiamus, wenn sie sagt: "I am delighted that the general English-speaking public will now have the chance to see all the information about Brecht's interest in America in the context of his developing politics and aesthetics." (XViii) Obwohl diese behauptete Totalität einzuschränken ist, besteht kein Zweifel, daß Parmalees Studie dennoch einen entscheidenden Zeitraum einer ausführlichen, insgesamt gesehen richtig argumentierenden Analyse unterzieht.

Parmalees Darstellung, so verschlungen ihr Gegenstand auch ist, geht übersichtlich vor. Einteilung und Akzentuierung der Zäsuren erscheinen überzeugend. Weniger überzeugend ist zunächst die Einleitung, die sich an einem raschen Überblick über die Beziehungen der Generation nach dem Ersten Weltkrieg zu Amerika versucht. Was da auf weniger als 9 Seiten angerissen wird, kann selbst als Wegweiser nicht befriedigen. Hier hätte man umfassendere Perspektiven, präzisere Ansätze und ein höheres Reflexionsniveau erwartet. Auch fehlt die Aufarbeitung der neueren Forschung zu den Zwanziger Jahren, von Lethens Untersuchungen zur neuen Sachlichkeit bis hin zu Hermands und Trommlers Darstellung der Kultur der Weimarer Periode. Was sich hier als Mangel an Überblick geltend macht, gelingt in den fünf nachfolgenden Kapiteln wesentlich besser, weil das unfangreiche Material einer im ganzen doch konsequenten Analyse und Argumentation unterworfen wird. Ich würde zwar nicht so weit gehen wie der im Vorwort mit Vorschußlorbeeren nicht zurückhaltende John Willett, die Lektüre als "Spaß" zu bezeichnen, aber klar und zügig geht es schon ab, trotz der zuweilen aufdringlichen Weitschweifigkeit, die zu Wiederholungen führt, trotz einiger schwach formulierter Denkansätze, die kaum auf das wirklich nachfolgende Material vorbereiten und trotz einer gewissen Undifferenziertheit, die sich stilistisch bemerkbar macht, aber auch dazu führt, daß manche These beharrlich wiederkehrt, daß der Eindruck des Klischeehaften entsteht.

Wie Kapitel Eins zeigt, darf als gesichert gelten, daß Brecht in der Frühphase 1920–1922 (erste Amerikaerwähnung allerdings schon in einem Gedicht von 1916) Amerika als Hebel für seine anti-bürgerliche Rebellion benutzt. Amerika, gesehen von Brecht als primitiv, elementar, traditionslos und deshalb befreiend, abenteuerlich, gigantisch, zermürbend, vorwärtsdrängend. Das fasziniert den Deserteur seiner Klasse, der sich im Affront gegen das Establishment gefällt. Amerika als Schockwert. Brechts erste Berlinerfahrungen, die den Mann aus der Provinz, der sich den unbedingten Erfolg zum Ziel gesetzt hat, durchbeuteln, Hunger, Kälte, Krankheit, Isolation, finden im zurechtstilisierten Chicago von *Im Dickicht* (1922) ihre mythisierte Entsprechung. Parmalee zeigt im einzelnen Brechts Aufnahme, Verwertung, Abhängigkeit und Umdeutung seiner Quellen (vor allem Upton Sinclairs *The Jungle*, 1906, dt.: *Der Sumpf: Roman aus Chicagos Schlachthäusern*, 1906, ein Werk von klassisch zu nennender Bedeutung als Zentralmetapher der Zwanziger Jahre, die bei Döblin dann noch biblisch erweitert und metaphysisch aufgeladen erscheint).

Kapitel Zwei gilt der nächsten Phase von 1924–1926, die Brecht zunächst als einen Allesfresser zeigt, der wahllos Amerikanisches absorbiert, sei es als Rohstoff, der kaum verarbeitet eingebaut wird, sei es als Material und Dokument, das seinen Literaturstrategien radikaler Bourgeoisiekritik dient, oder auch als Inspiration, die im kreativen Prozeß verwandelt der eigenen Stilisierung und Mythisierung Amerikas Vorschub leistet. Vor allem die Geschäftspraktiken, das amerikanische System bestimmen jetzt Brechts Interessen. Es zeigt sich der Registrator gesellschaftlicher Realität, der zu Protokollen des Kapitalismus ansetzt, ohne über die Systematik einer kritischen Analyse zu verfügen. Vielfältig ist jetzt das Material, das Brecht im Sinne seiner Vandalen–und Materialästhetik rigoros ausschlachtet und seinen eigenen Zwecken dienstbar zu machen sucht. Drei Werke dürften besondere Aufmerksamkeit beanspruchen: Frank Norris' allegorischer Wirtschaftsroman über Chicago (*The Pit*, 1903), eindeutig eine der Hauptquellen für Brechts gescheitertes "Weizen"-Projekt, dessen Bedeutung Parmalee nachdrücklich in den Vordergrund rückt; Erich Mendelsohns Amerikabuch, das Bilderbuch eines Architekten, für Brecht unschätzbar wichtiges Anschauungsmaterial bereitstellend (bezeichnenderweise hat er auch Amerika-Postkarten gesammelt); und als drittes Gustavus Myers' gesellschaftskritische Darstellung des wunderbaren Aufstiegs der amerikanischen Finanzaristokratie (dt.: *Geschichte der großen amerikanischen Vermögen*, 1916), ein Werk, das zugleich Größe und Grenzen nicht-marxistischer Kapitalismusanalyse aufzeigt.

Hier legt Parmalees Erörterung der amerikanischen Elemente in Brechts dramatischen Fragmenten und in der Lyrik bis zur Schaffenskrise, die gerade am Scheitern des *Joe Fleischhacker*-Projekts evident wurde, nahe, daß die Amerikabeschäftigung des Stückeschreibers sich konsequent zur kritischen Analyse des Kapitalismus hin entwickelte, aber vorläufig leerlaufen mußte, weil dem intuitiven Erfassen der amerikanischen Wirklichkeit die Stringenz materialistischer Wissenschaftlichkeit abging. Nach Parmalee führt aus dieser Sackgasse die Marxlektüre und die Wende von 1926 heraus. Brecht mußte zunächst scheitern, weil er von den Symptomen kapitalistischer Wirklichkeit am Beispiel Amerikas, vor allem vom Spekulationsgetriebe der Weizenbörse sich so faszinieren ließ, daß er die Ursachen nicht begriff, die ihm erst der Marxismus erschloß. Aufgrund ihrer methodischen Undifferenziertheit muß Parmalee Brechts Amerikaauseinandersetzung als Ursache für die Hinwendung zum Marxismus postulieren, während solch schematisches Einflußdenken doch dahingehend zu qualifizieren wäre, daß Brechts schon vor 1926 vorhandener radikaler Kritik der bürgerlichen Gesellschaft am Prüffeld des amerikanischen Experiments die Unhaltbarkeit einer weiterhin nicht-marxistischen Analyse klar wurde. Das macht auch deutlich, warum Brecht, nach Überwindung seiner unbegründeten Vorbehalte gegen Theorie im allgemeinen und den Marxismus im besonderen, das schnelle Kennenlernen materialistischer Philosophie zu einer dogmatischen Position eigener Art ausbaute.

Folgt man der allerdings wie hier modifizierten These Parmalees, so leuchtet auch ihr drittes Kapitel ein, das sich Brechts politische Entwicklung vornimmt. Es ist in vieler Hinsicht der problematischste Teil der Arbeit. Weil es zunächst eben viel zu eindimensional Brechts konsequente Entwicklung vom "embryonalen Sozialisten" (148) zum Marxisten und Kommunisten ansetzt, also die Wende von 1926 als solche einschränkt. Zudem fehlt eine eingehendere Einbeziehung der Debatten, die von den verschiedenen Brecht-Schulen geführt werden, man denke nur an die Kontroversen um seinen "Lehrer" Karl Korsch. Dem wäre neuerdings auch die allmählich in den Blick kommende Bedeutung Jakob Walchers für Brechts marxistische Wende hinzuzufügen. Wenig überzeugen mich Thesen, die besagen, der Marxismus sei wirklich nur der Name für etwas gewesen, was Brecht schon lange wußte. (156) Fragwürdig auch, ob die proletarische

253

Schlägermütze und die Vorliebe für amerikanische Massenkunst (Jazz, Film, Sport usw.) bei Brecht schon eine Präsenz dessen beweise, was hier dann als "logische Einfachheit des Kommunismus" angepriesen wird. (159, 157) Ebenso unkritisch erscheint mir die Inanspruchnahme Brechts für eine "Position der 'Neuen Linken' " (172), die eher als Konstruktion der Autorin, die gegen rechte und falsche linke Brecht-Interpretation sich wehrt, zu werten ist, als ihr politisches Glaubensbekenntnis von 1968, das den Verdacht einer Brecht-Vaterimago aufkommen läßt. Das ist doch zu problematisch, den von Parmalee in seiner Frühphase als amoralisch bezeichneten Brecht, den sie in vielem der Blasiertheit bezichtigt, der ja selbst später (1939) sein "politisches Wissen" anfang der Zwanziger Jahre als "beschämend gering" (34) bezeichnet hat, nachher zum Vorläufer eines ihm fremden politischen Denkens zu machen. Wie denn Brechts politische Entwicklung und Stellung noch keineswegs zufriedenstellend erforscht und dargestellt worden ist.

　　Die Kapitel Vier und Fünf stellen *Mahagonny* und die Lehrstücke, vor allem *Die heilige Johanna der Schlachthöfe* als Negativbilder Amerikas heraus. Das ist, auch die manchmal mühsame Beschäftigung mit der Lyrik, in der Hauptsache überzeugend am Material entwickelt, obwohl gerade hier Länge und Umständlichkeit der Ausführungen das Lesen erschweren. Das Postskript über Brecht und Amerika nach 1933 und die Schlußüberlegungen zum Alten im Neuen versuchen abzurunden, was sich auf den paar Seiten so nicht leicht abschließen läßt.

　　Hat diese Studie auch nicht alle meine Erwartungen erfüllt, so halte ich sie für die Beschäftigung mit Brechts Amerikabild unerläßlich. Die gemachten Einwände ziehen die Nützlichkeit dieses Buches nicht in Zweifel, denn die auf gewissenhafter Forschungsarbeit fundierte Analyse stellt die zentralen Fragen von Brechts Amerikaauseinandersetzung anschaulich dar. Die von Parmalee explizierte These, daß Brecht über Amerika zum Marxismus und zu sich selber gelangt ist, hat vieles für sich. Wenn allerdings der Problemkreis der produktiven Autorenrezeption gegen die zu flache Einflußthese methodisch überzeugend abgesichert worden wäre, hätte Brechts Weg als einzigartiger Selbstverständigungsprozeß noch deutlicheres Profil gewonnen. Denn eines scheint jetzt nach Parmalees Ausführungen klar: Amerika ist in der Dialektik der Brechtschen Selbstfindung beides, Faszination mit dem Mythos als erregendem Schein und zugleich Aufklärungsimpuls, der alle falschen Mythen entlarvt. Brecht hat sich vom amerikanischen Traum nicht blenden, vom amerikanischen Alptraum nicht einschüchtern lassen, die Wahrheit über sich und die Welt herauszufinden. Bleibt zu hoffen, daß eine zukünftige Studie dieses Thema einmal in seiner Gesamtheit darstellen wird.

Peter Beicken
University of Maryland
College Park

Dieter Thiele, *Bertolt Brecht. Selbstverständnis, Tui-Kritik und politische Ästhetik* (Frankfurt am Main, Bern: Peter Lang, 1981), 476 Seiten.

　　Ohne Unterlaß rollen vom Fließband der Brecht-Industrie die dicken Wälzer. Thieles Brecht-Dissertation, 1980 fertiggestellt, jetzt im Druck, vereinigt zwischen zwei Pappeinbänden, was gut drei selbständige Arbeiten ergeben könnte, die sich dem Untertitel nach auch klar voneinander unterscheiden: Brechts an den "Hollywood"- und "Buckower Elegien" dargestelltes "Selbstverständnis" (gemeint ist das seiner "Künstlerexistenz") ca. 107 Seiten; die "Tui-Kritik" mit den beiden Hauptteilen "Intellektuellenkritik" (basierend auf dem "Tui"-Projekt, Galilei und Läuffer) und "Intellektuellenpflicht" (an den "Flüchtlingsgesprächen" exemplifiziert) ca. 130 Seiten; und zum Schluß die "Politische Ästhetik", die zu recht das "Verhältnis von Kunst und Politik bei Brecht" und damit "letztlich die Frage nach dem Tui Brecht", beides seit jeher "umstritten", einmal mehr in den Mittelpunkt stellt (Basis hier Benjamins Aufsatz "Der Autor als Produzent" und Brechts "Dreigroschenprozeß" und "Messingkauf") ca. 100 Seiten. Dazu ein Anhang "Material zum Tui-Komplex (53 Texte aus dem Brecht-Archiv mit so derb-komischen Entwürfen wie "der bund der furzer", Brechts Anraunzen der "Kopfarbeiter" belegend), sage und schreibe 1076 Anmerkungen auf ca. 80 Seiten und 22 Seiten Bibliographie. Fertig ist der Wälzer. Daß Thiele gewisse Teile seit 1976 an verschiedenen Plätzen schon vorabgedruckt oder vorweggenommen hatte, obwohl es sonstigen Dissertationsgepflogenheiten nicht zu entsprechen scheint, sei nur am Rande vermerkt.

Die besondere Zielrichtung von Thieles Arbeit erhellt sich aus seiner Problemstellung, die das "Bündnisproblem" zwischen "Kopfarbeiter" und Proletariat anhand einer "Rekonstruktion grundlegender Elemente von Brechts revolutionär-literarischer Praxis und seines Verständnisses von den Möglichkeiten und Aufgaben der an der Seite des Proletariats kämpfenden Intellektuellen" (9) aufzurollen verspricht. Welcher Eifer hier vorliegt, zeigt sich daran, daß Thiele eine "Lösung" für dieses Problem der Beziehung von Klassenlage und literarischer Produktion geben will. Missionarisch klingt deshalb die ausdrückliche Zweitintention, "die fällige Antwort auf jene unsterblichen (sic!) Brecht-ist-tot-Gesänge, die in regelmäßigen Abständen entweder auf kleineren Tui-Kongressen . . . ertönen oder periodisch in die kritisch-unkritische Forschungsliteratur eingehen," (10) zu geben. Solchem "Brecht ist tot"-Geschrei wird hier überschwenglich "die durchschlagende Aktualität Brechts entgegengehalten," und zwar "nicht als trivialer Auferweckungs-Gegengesang, sondern im Nachvollzug von Brechts tatsächlicher und kaum bekannter revolutionärer Theorie und Praxis." (11) Diese These vom unbekannten Brecht entpuppt sich beim Weiterlesen jedoch allenfalls als "Korrektur eines gängigen Brecht-Bildes" (24).

Ansatz, Fragestellung und, wie die unschöne Formulierung heißt: "Herangehensweise" (15) lassen von vornherein Berechtigung und auch Gespreiztheit von Thieles Arbeit erkennen, von dem Ausschließlichkeitsgehabe in Sachen 'wahrer Brecht' einmal abgesehen. Was da oft weitschweifig, aber ebenso oft um Differenziertheit bemüht vorgetragen wird, erörtert Brechts Künstlerexistenz anhand der Analyse seiner Stellung als bürgerlicher Intellektueller bis zu seiner Solidarisierung mit dem Proletariat, wobei die Elegien als Modelle der Selbstreflexion im Mittelpunkt stehen. Die Ausklammerung der Hauptmasse der literarischen Texte scheint mir das Vorhaben der Untersuchung von Brechts Selbstverständigung erheblich zu behindern. Die ausführliche Durchforstung der kontroversen Kritikermeinungen zu den Elegien entschädigt dafür nicht, obwohl vieles als ideologisch vorbelastet erwiesen und deshalb zurechtgerückt wird. Die Klärung der Brechtschen Elegievorstellung arbeitet nicht mit letzter Deutlichkeit die dialektische Beziehung heraus, die Brechts Verhältnis zu der seit Schiller theoretisch aufgeladenen Tradition der Gattung kennzeichnet. Obwohl Brecht in seinen Elegien eine Zurückweisung moderner Klagehaltungen erkennen läßt, konstatiert er poetisch ein Utopiedefizit der Realität, die ihm in Hollywood fraglos als ruinöse, in Buckow dann als erst in Ansätzen verwirklichte Hoffnung erschien. Elegie ist bei ihm ein Prüffeld, das die Dialektik der Geschichte auf ihre Gewißheiten hin befragt. Was Thiele seinen Vorläufern ankreidet, unterläuft ihm trotz angestrebter Umsicht bei Kritik and Interpretation selber: den Texten Zwang anzutun. In dem Gedicht "Die Lösung", Brechts Kommentar nicht nur zum 17. Juni, sondern auch zum Fehlverhalten des Sekretärs des Schriftstellerverbandes (der wirkliche war Kuba), entgeht Thiele die Bedeutung des auf die namentlich genannte "Regierung" gemünzten hypothetischen Vorschlags. (70ff.) Krasser noch ist die falsche Lesart des Satzes "Freilich wie wenige/Dauerten länger!" ("Beim Lesen des Horaz", 87ff.), die unverständlicherweise auf Personen bezogen wird, eine klare Überstrapazierung, denn schlechterdings "dauern" die Menschen nicht. Hier ist "wenige Fluten" zu interpolieren, was ohnehin sich Brechts geschichtsphilosophischer Perspektive hier einfügt. Thieles Eifer, Brecht den Elegiker vor der Stilisierung "zum verkappten Regimekritiker", "verzweifelnden Marxisten" und "vom Gewissen geplagten Schriftsteller" zu bewahren (116) verbaut ihm zumeist den Weg, Brechts produktive Spannung zwischen Zuversicht und Skepsis als die Energie seiner Elegik voll zu würdigen.

Thieles Darstellung der Brechtschen Intellektuellenkritik begibt sich in die Löwengrube des Tuismus und erklärt kopfscheu, "daß eine definitorische Eindeutigkeit *nicht* möglich ist." (120) Man muß Thiele über weite Strecken dann gleichsam gegen den Strich lesen, um sich Klarheit zu verschaffen. Brechts Tui-Problem, so komplex und in prozeßhafter Weise es auch vorliegt, hat seine theoretische, durchaus diffizile, und seine historische, durchaus konkrete Seite. Einerseits geht es um die Vermietbarkeit, kurz 'Prostitution' des Intellekts in der Warengesellschaft kapitalistischer Prägung, also um die klassenmäßige Abhängigkeit der Intellektuellen von Produktionsbedingungen, die ihre Ausbeutbarkeit zur Folge haben. Andererseits hat Brecht eine historische Misere im Blick. Sein Überdruß an der Wirkungslosigkeit bzw. Handlangerarbeit der bürgerlichen Intellektuellen (auch vieler Linker) der Weimarer Zeit führt, im Ansatz jedenfalls, zu einer materialistischen Analyse und Kritik ihrer fatalen geschichtlichen Rolle, für die der Faschismus der Epitaph ist. Theoretische und historische Perspektive verquicken sich für Brecht, und Thiele weist das einleuchtend nach, wenn er Modelle von Negativfiguren erarbeitet, an denen Brecht vor allem der Widerspruch von folgenlosem Denken (etwa bei den Franfurtisten) und eingreifendem denken klar wurde. Thiele, der mit manchen Kritikern, die ihm vorgearbeitet haben, etwas rauhbeinig umgeht, entwickelt engmaschig und langatmig seine Analysen, die nachvollziehen und immer wieder nachvollziehen, aber eines m.E. nicht genügend leisten: die Widersprüche in Brechts Denken aufzuzeigen. Bei aller Theorie ist Brecht, wie schon der Begriff vom Mißbrauch des Intellekts andeutet, nicht nur Materialist, der über Verhältnisse und materielle Interessen reflektiert; er ist auch Ethiker, obwohl er diese Perspektive in seinem Denken oft beiseite schiebt. Thiele stellt also die Frage nach Brechts Humanismus (gewiß etwas Vertracktes) nicht. Sie ließe aber das ganze Tui-Problem in einem anderen Licht erscheinen, als der Stückeschreiber selber es wollte.

Brechts Vorstellungen von den positiven Aufgaben und Pflichten des Intellektuellen nur auf die Basis des vorgegebenen Interessenbegriffs Brechtscher Prägung zu stellen, erscheint mir als zu unkritisch. Brecht ist ein vehementer Ethiker, wenn er die negative Realität kritisiert. Sein Selbstverständnis, als

Künstler seinen revolutionären Beitrag zu leisten, also vor allem durch die Veränderung der künstlerischen Produktionsbedingungen, ist, darauf zielt Thiele zu recht hin, ein Rettungsversuch dieser Form der menschlichen 'Arbeit', d.h. Selbstdarstellung und Selbstbegegnung im Zeitalter der Ideologie.

    Thieles Eifer belohnt sich. Zwar verwendet er nicht den Begriff der Rettung, aber sein eigener Versuch, anhand seiner detaillierten Ausführungen zu Brechts politischer Ästhetik, die sich als eine notwendige anthropologische Realität enthüllt, den Kunstbegriff des marxistischen Dichters Brecht als einen mit Zukunft auszuweisen, kommt ebenfalls einer Rettung gleich. Benjamin zeigte die Richtung an, der Brecht folgte, indem er Kunst als Selbstbetätigung und Selbstbestätigung auch über die Periode des Untergangs der kapitalistischen Welt hinaus als Notwendigkeit kommender Gesellschaft bestimmt. Es ist das die Aufhebung der bürgerlichen Autonomiekunst in dem autonomen Kunstmachen der sozialistischen Periode. Thiele weist nachdrücklich darauf hin, daß Brecht nicht daran dachte, der Kunst und dem Künstler ein Ende zu bereiten. Was operativ im revolutionären Sinne wirkte, wird danach zur Befreiung bestätigenden Operation. Also erweist sich die "gegenwärtige Kunst als Vor-Kunst." (359)

    Wer Thiele ausgelesen hat, stellt fest, daß er am Anfang eines neuen Nachdenkens über Brecht steht. Bei allen Einwänden, Abstrichen, kritischen Vorbehalten, Differenzen: Thieles Brecht-Buch ist ein Wälzer, den zu lesen sich lohnt.

Peter Beicken
University of Maryland
College Park

Notes on Contributors

Gisela Bahr was born in Berlin and now lives in Oxford, Ohio. Immediate Past-President of the IBS and founder of the IBS newsletter (*Communications*), Gisela Bahr has published several edited volumes of major Brecht texts with Suhrkamp Verlag in the German Federal Republic.

Rustom Bharucha was born in India and lived in Calcutta until 1977. He now lives in New York City and the University of Hawaii Press will publish his book on *Rehearsals of Revolution: The Political Theatre in Bengal* in Fall 1983.

Kasimierz Braun was born in Poland. He is presently the Artistic Director and General Manager of the Teatr Wspolczesny in Wroclaw and also teaches drama in Wroclaw and Cracow.

Vittorio Felaco was born in Italy and now lives in College Park, Maryland. Professor Felaco's major research interests are in modern Italian theatre and poetry.

John Fuegi was born in England and now lives in the United States. With Reinhold Grimm he established the International Brecht Society in 1971. He has served on the editorial team of the *Yearbook* since its inception. He has published, in addition, *The Essential Brecht* (1974) and is now at work on a volume on Brecht as a Stage Director to be published by Cambridge University Press in 1983.

Heinz-Uwe Haus is a resident of the German Democratic Republic. He has been a stage director in several European countries and is also active in the training of actors in the GDR.

259

Uwe Hartung was born in Germany but spent the 1981–82 academic year in the United States as a Fulbright exchange student to the University of Maryland from the University of Mainz.

Erwin Leiser was born in Germany but was driven into exile in the Hitler years. He now lives in Switzerland where he directs his international work in documentary film.

James K. Lyon lives and teaches in San Diego, California. He is the author of *Brecht in America* and has published books on Brecht and Ferdinand Reyher and on Brecht and Kipling.

Patty Lee Parmalee was born in the United States and lives in New York City. She is a former IBS vice-president and has been active in the Society since its inception in 1971. Professor Parmalee is the author of *Brecht's America*.

David Pike teaches German at the University of North Carolina at Chapel Hill. His book *German Writers in Soviet Exile* (1981) as well as the essay in this volume are based on his research of heretofore unexamined archive materials from Moscow, Berlin and Budapest.

Joel Schechter was born in the United States and now teaches at the School of Drama at Yale University where he also edits *Theater* magazine.

Luigi Squarzina was born in Italy. He has staged several Brecht plays and presently holds the position of Artistic Director of the Teatro di Roma.

John Willett was born in England where he continues to live and work. Author of major studies of Piscator, Expressionism, the Weimar Republic, and Bertolt Brecht and editor (with Ralph Manheim) of Brecht's collected works in English. Past President of the IBS. John Willett recently produced a record sung by Robyn Archer and a TV version of *Baal* with David Bowie.

Hans-Dieter Zimmermann is a professor at Johann Wolfgang Goethe University at Frankfurt. His theses on Brecht were first introduced at the 1978 Brecht Symposium in that city and have not been available to an international audience up to now.